X-MEN WOLVERINE

LYN

JAY FAERBER writer **KARL WALLER** penciler **MARK McKENNA** inker

AN X-MEN MOVIE PREQUEL

CHRIS ELIOPOULOS letterer **ATOMIC PAINTBRUSH** color art **MIKE RAICHT** assistant editor **MIKE MARTS** editor **BOB HARRAS** editor in chief

D1456447

X-MEN® MOVIE PREQUEL: WOLVERINE®, August, 2000. Published by MARVEL COMICS, Bill Jemas, President; Bob Harras, Editor-in-Chief; Stan Lee, Chairman Emeritus. OFFICE OF PUBLICATION: 387 PARK AVENUE SOUTH, NEW YORK, N.Y. 10016. Copyright © 2000 Marvel Characters, Inc. All rights reserved. Price $5.95 per copy in the U.S. and $8.95 in Canada. GST #R127032852. No similarity between any of the names, characters, persons, and/or institutions in this magazine with those of any living or dead person or institution is intended, and any such similarity which may exist is purely coincidental. This periodical may not be sold except by authorized dealers and is sold subject to the condition that it shall not be sold or distributed with any part of its cover or markings removed, nor in a mutilated condition. X-MEN and WOLVERINE (including all prominent characters featured in this issue and the distinctive likenesses thereof) are trademarks of MARVEL CHARACTERS, INC. Printed in the U.S.A. MARVEL COMICS is a division of MARVEL ENTERPRISES, INC. Peter Cuneo, Chief Executive Officer; Avi Arad, Chief Creative Officer.

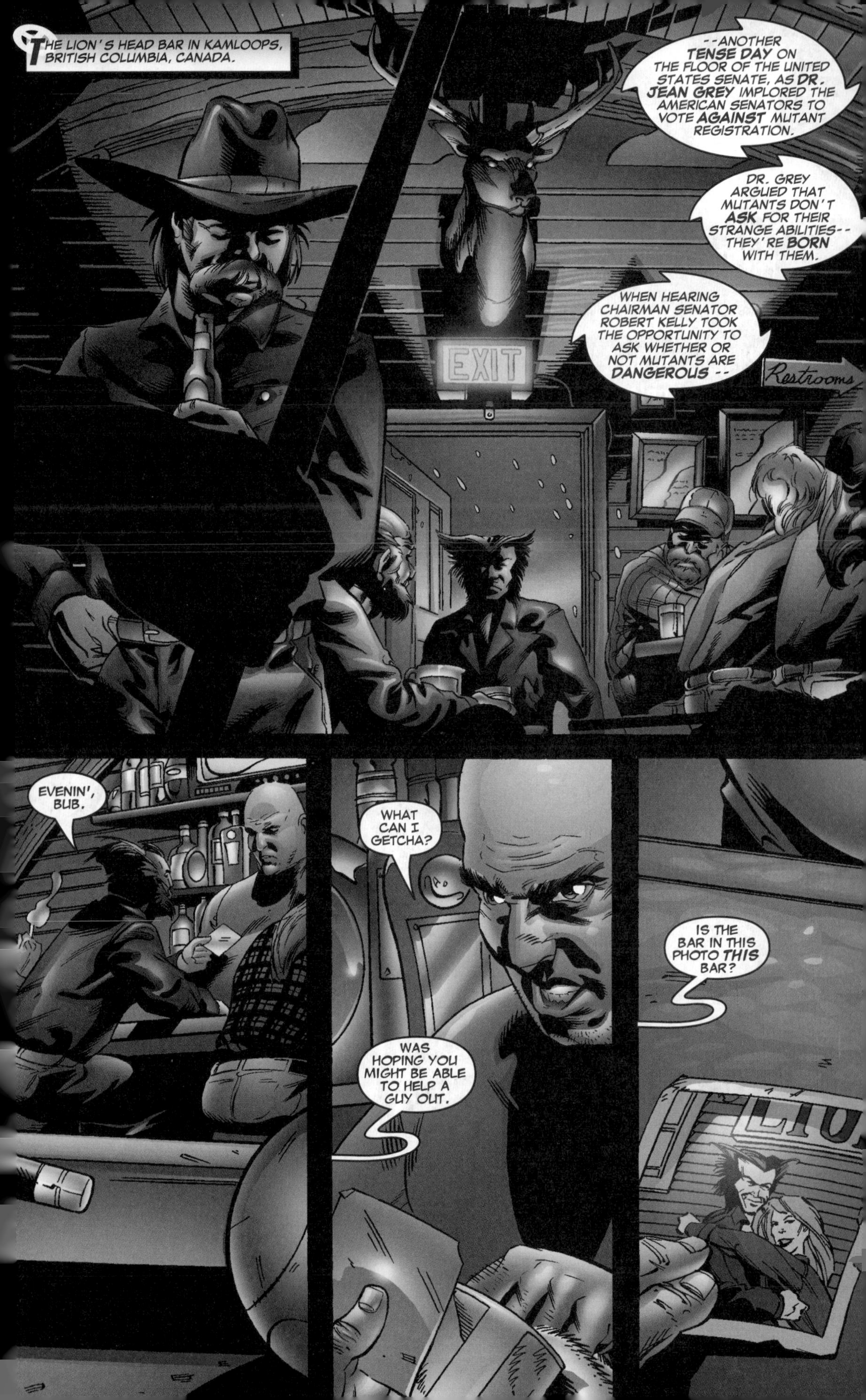
THE LION'S HEAD BAR IN KAMLOOPS, BRITISH COLUMBIA, CANADA.
--ANOTHER TENSE DAY ON THE FLOOR OF THE UNITED STATES SENATE, AS DR. JEAN GREY IMPLORED THE AMERICAN SENATORS TO VOTE AGAINST MUTANT REGISTRATION.
DR. GREY ARGUED THAT MUTANTS DON'T ASK FOR THEIR STRANGE ABILITIES--THEY'RE BORN WITH THEM.
WHEN HEARING CHAIRMAN SENATOR ROBERT KELLY TOOK THE OPPORTUNITY TO ASK WHETHER OR NOT MUTANTS ARE DANGEROUS--
EXIT
Restrooms
EVENIN', BUB.
WHAT CAN I GETCHA?
WAS HOPING YOU MIGHT BE ABLE TO HELP A GUY OUT.
IS THE BAR IN THIS PHOTO THIS BAR?

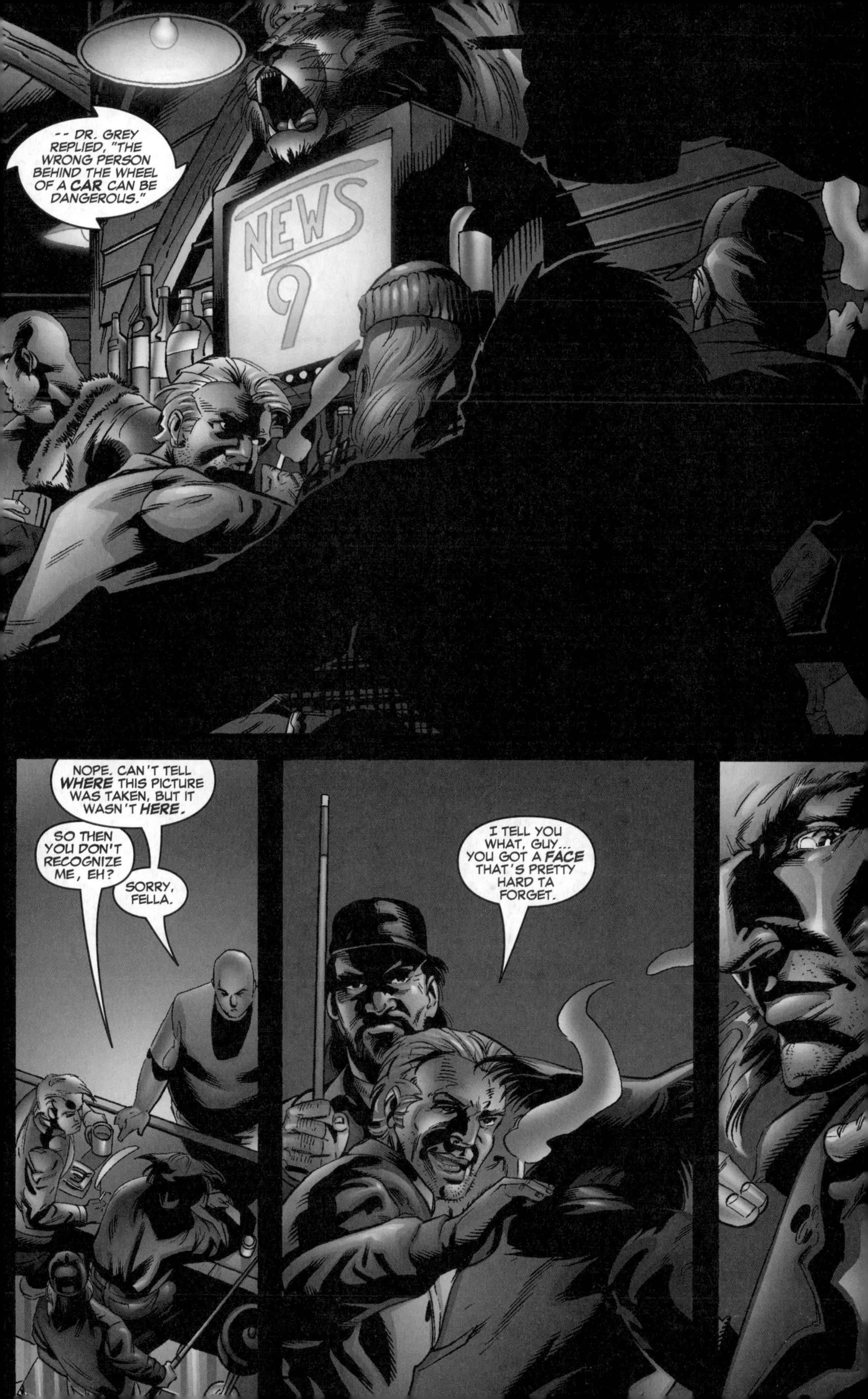
-- DR. GREY REPLIED, "THE WRONG PERSON BEHIND THE WHEEL OF A CAR CAN BE DANGEROUS."
NEWS 9
NOPE. CAN'T TELL WHERE THIS PICTURE WAS TAKEN, BUT IT WASN'T HERE.
SO THEN YOU DON'T RECOGNIZE ME, EH?
SORRY, FELLA.
I TELL YOU WHAT, GUY... YOU GOT A FACE THAT'S PRETTY HARD TA FORGET.

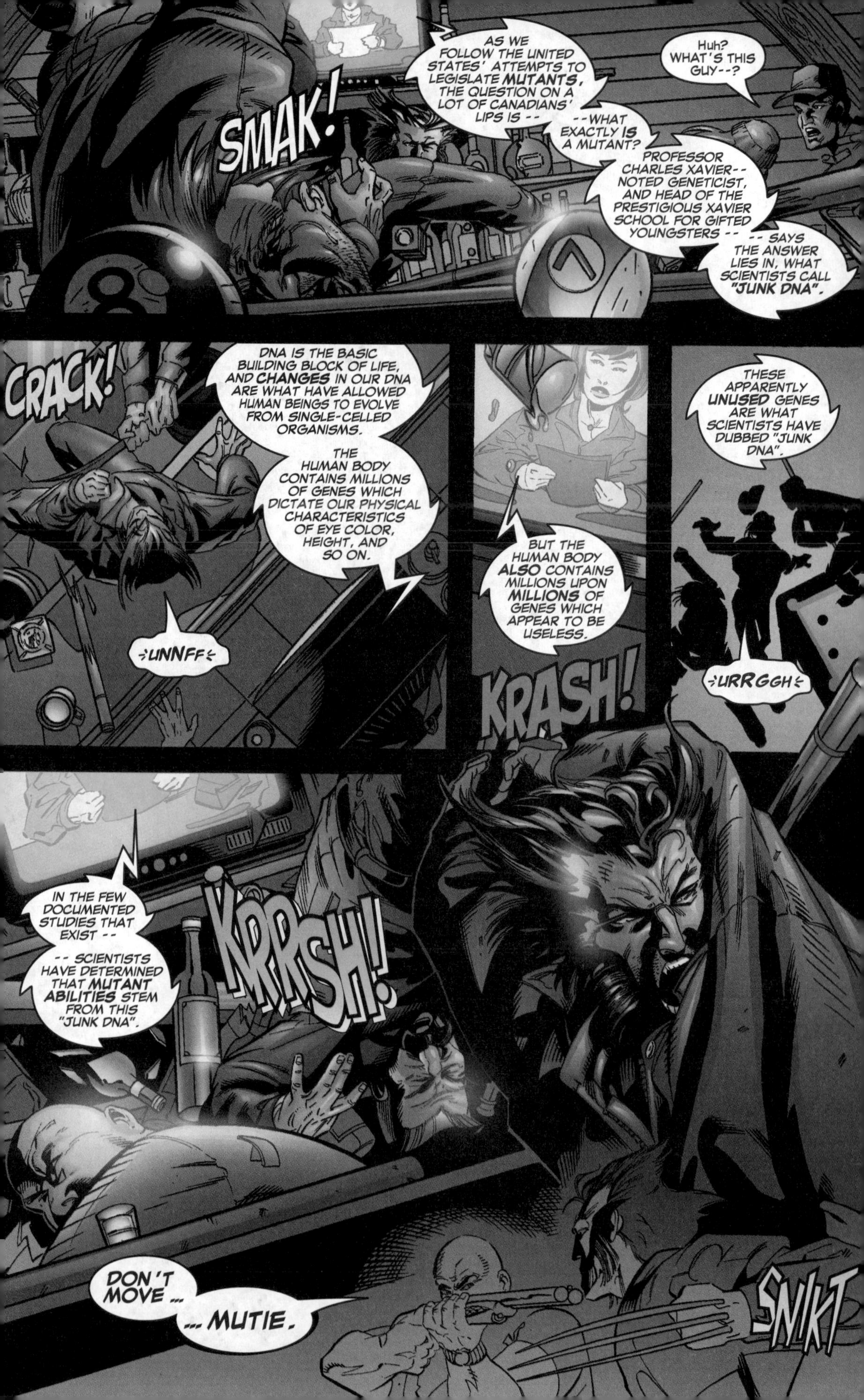
AS WE FOLLOW THE UNITED STATES' ATTEMPTS TO LEGISLATE MUTANTS, THE QUESTION ON A LOT OF CANADIANS' LIPS IS --
Huh? WHAT'S THIS GUY--?
SMAK!
--WHAT EXACTLY IS A MUTANT?
PROFESSOR CHARLES XAVIER-- NOTED GENETICIST, AND HEAD OF THE PRESTIGIOUS XAVIER SCHOOL FOR GIFTED YOUNGSTERS --
-- SAYS THE ANSWER LIES IN, WHAT SCIENTISTS CALL "JUNK DNA".
CRACK!
DNA IS THE BASIC BUILDING BLOCK OF LIFE, AND CHANGES IN OUR DNA ARE WHAT HAVE ALLOWED HUMAN BEINGS TO EVOLVE FROM SINGLE-CELLED ORGANISMS.
THE HUMAN BODY CONTAINS MILLIONS OF GENES WHICH DICTATE OUR PHYSICAL CHARACTERISTICS OF EYE COLOR, HEIGHT, AND SO ON.
UNNFF
BUT THE HUMAN BODY ALSO CONTAINS MILLIONS UPON MILLIONS OF GENES WHICH APPEAR TO BE USELESS.
KRASH!
THESE APPARENTLY UNUSED GENES ARE WHAT SCIENTISTS HAVE DUBBED "JUNK DNA".
URRGGH
IN THE FEW DOCUMENTED STUDIES THAT EXIST --
-- SCIENTISTS HAVE DETERMINED THAT MUTANT ABILITIES STEM FROM THIS "JUNK DNA".
KRRSH!
DON'T MOVE ...
... MUTIE.
SNIKT

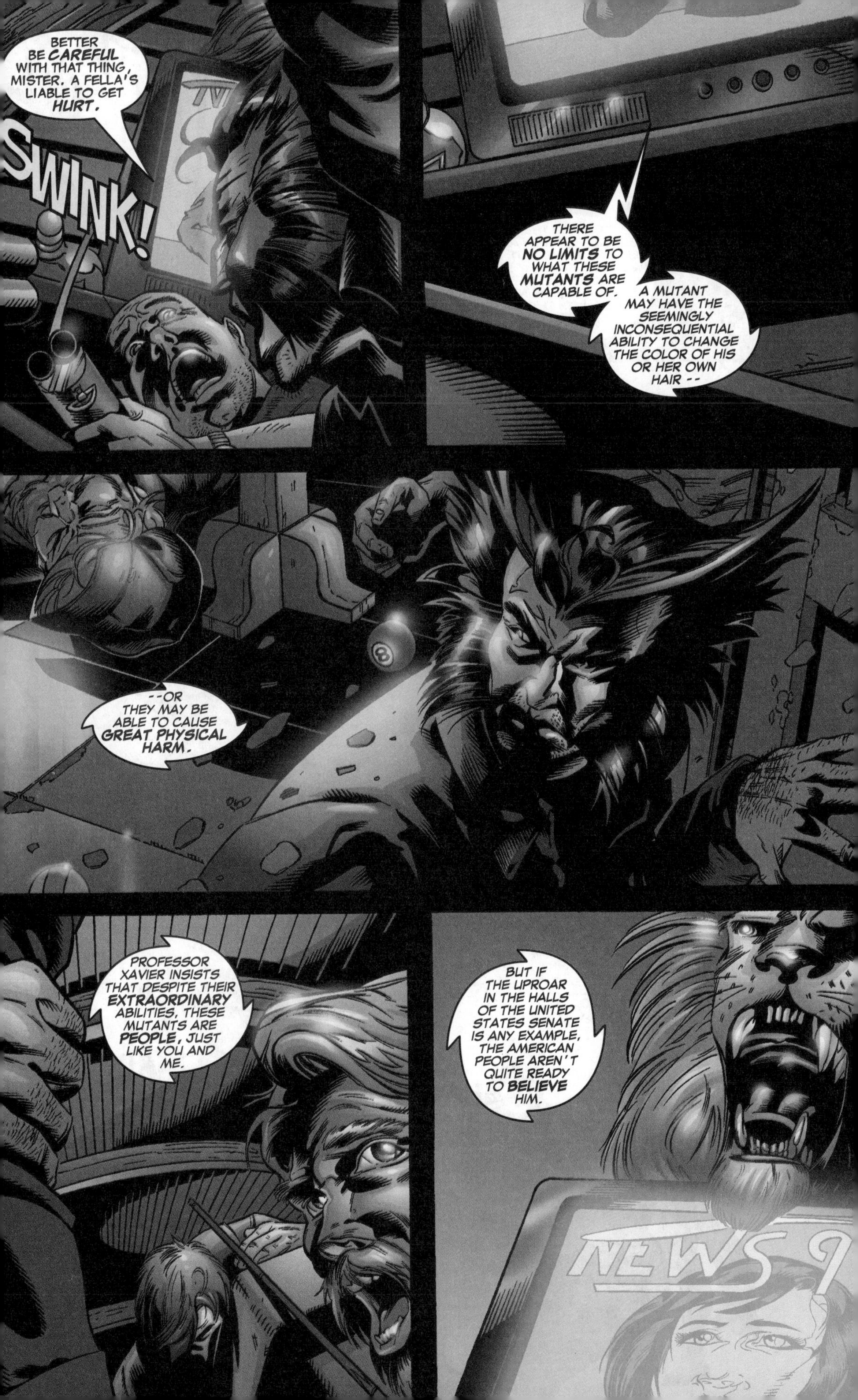
BETTER BE CAREFUL WITH THAT THING, MISTER. A FELLA'S LIABLE TO GET HURT.
SWINK!
THERE APPEAR TO BE NO LIMITS TO WHAT THESE MUTANTS ARE CAPABLE OF.
A MUTANT MAY HAVE THE SEEMINGLY INCONSEQUENTIAL ABILITY TO CHANGE THE COLOR OF HIS OR HER OWN HAIR --
--OR THEY MAY BE ABLE TO CAUSE GREAT PHYSICAL HARM.
PROFESSOR XAVIER INSISTS THAT DESPITE THEIR EXTRAORDINARY ABILITIES, THESE MUTANTS ARE PEOPLE, JUST LIKE YOU AND ME.
BUT IF THE UPROAR IN THE HALLS OF THE UNITED STATES SENATE IS ANY EXAMPLE, THE AMERICAN PEOPLE AREN'T QUITE READY TO BELIEVE HIM.
NEWS 9

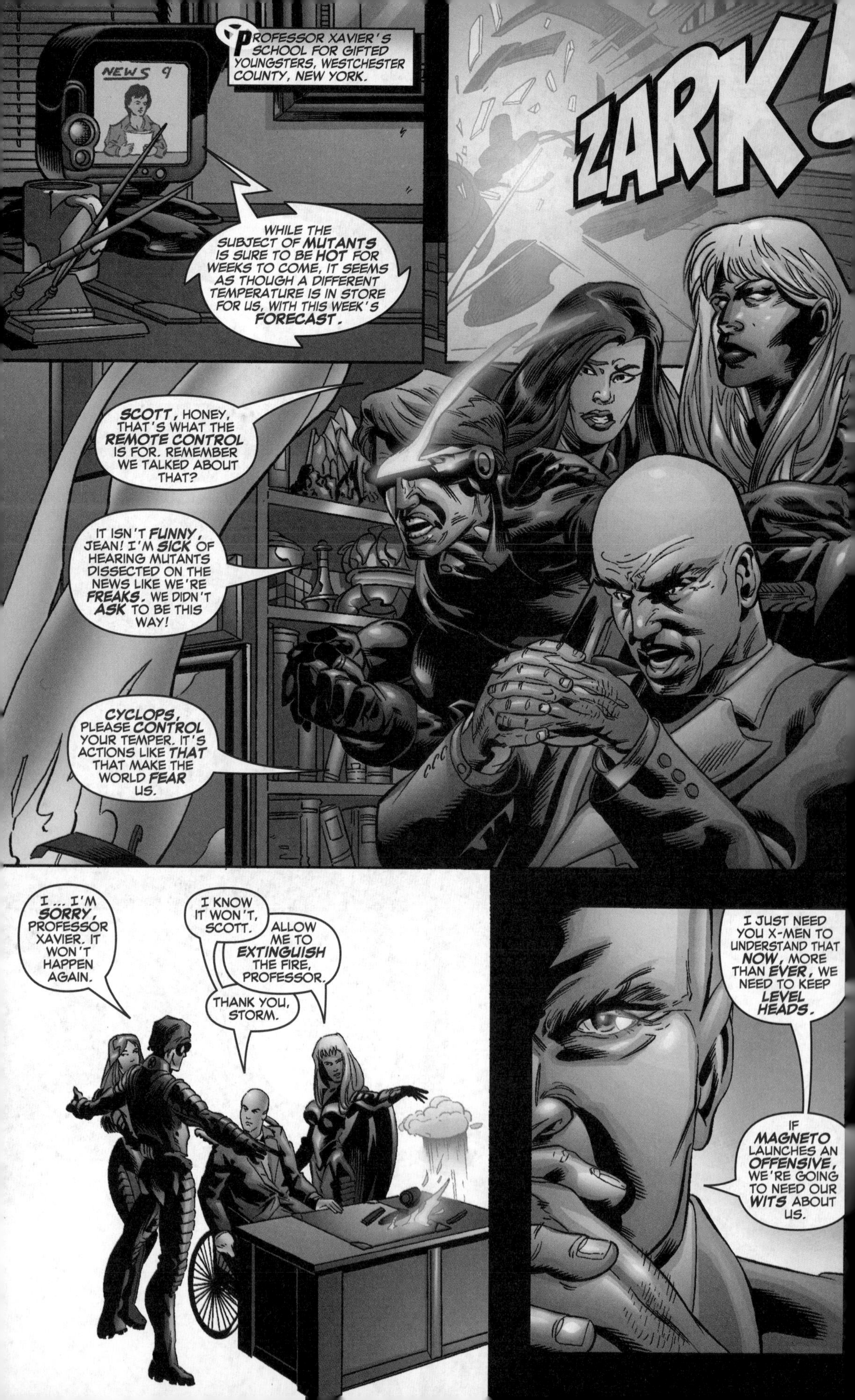
PROFESSOR XAVIER'S SCHOOL FOR GIFTED YOUNGSTERS, WESTCHESTER COUNTY, NEW YORK.
NEWS 9
WHILE THE SUBJECT OF MUTANTS IS SURE TO BE HOT FOR WEEKS TO COME, IT SEEMS AS THOUGH A DIFFERENT TEMPERATURE IS IN STORE FOR US, WITH THIS WEEK'S FORECAST.
ZARK!
SCOTT, HONEY, THAT'S WHAT THE REMOTE CONTROL IS FOR. REMEMBER WE TALKED ABOUT THAT?
IT ISN'T FUNNY, JEAN! I'M SICK OF HEARING MUTANTS DISSECTED ON THE NEWS LIKE WE'RE FREAKS. WE DIDN'T ASK TO BE THIS WAY!
CYCLOPS, PLEASE CONTROL YOUR TEMPER. IT'S ACTIONS LIKE THAT THAT MAKE THE WORLD FEAR US.
I ... I'M SORRY, PROFESSOR XAVIER. IT WON'T HAPPEN AGAIN.
I KNOW IT WON'T, SCOTT.
ALLOW ME TO EXTINGUISH THE FIRE, PROFESSOR.
THANK YOU, STORM.
I JUST NEED YOU X-MEN TO UNDERSTAND THAT NOW, MORE THAN EVER, WE NEED TO KEEP LEVEL HEADS.
IF MAGNETO LAUNCHES AN OFFENSIVE, WE'RE GOING TO NEED OUR WITS ABOUT US.

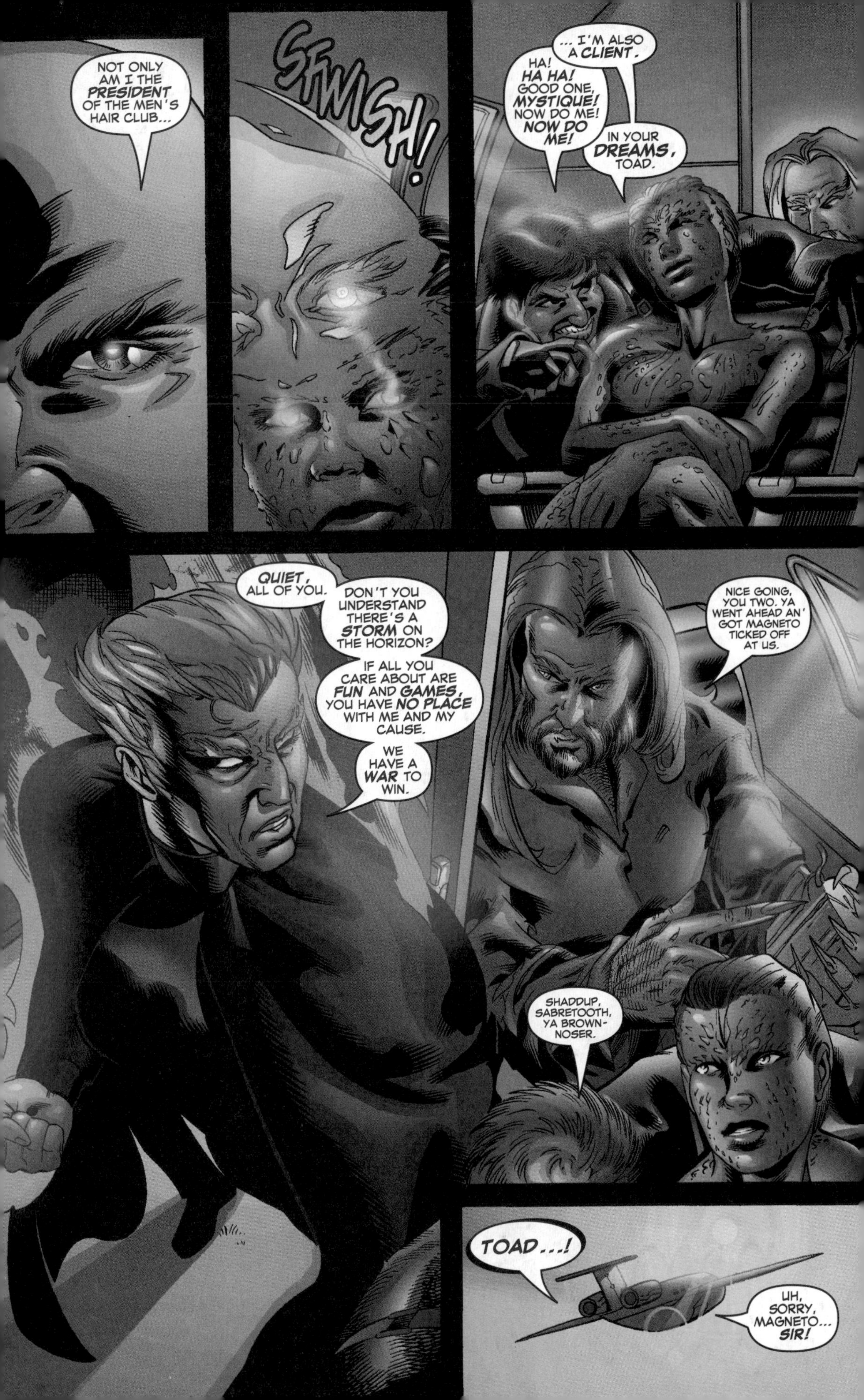
NOT ONLY AM I THE PRESIDENT OF THE MEN'S HAIR CLUB...
SFWISH!
... I'M ALSO A CLIENT.
HA! HA HA! GOOD ONE, MYSTIQUE! NOW DO ME! NOW DO ME!
IN YOUR DREAMS, TOAD.
QUIET, ALL OF YOU.
DON'T YOU UNDERSTAND THERE'S A STORM ON THE HORIZON?
IF ALL YOU CARE ABOUT ARE FUN AND GAMES, YOU HAVE NO PLACE WITH ME AND MY CAUSE.
WE HAVE A WAR TO WIN.
NICE GOING, YOU TWO. YA WENT AHEAD AN' GOT MAGNETO TICKED OFF AT US.
SHADDUP, SABRETOOTH, YA BROWN-NOSER.
TOAD...!
UH, SORRY, MAGNETO... SIR!

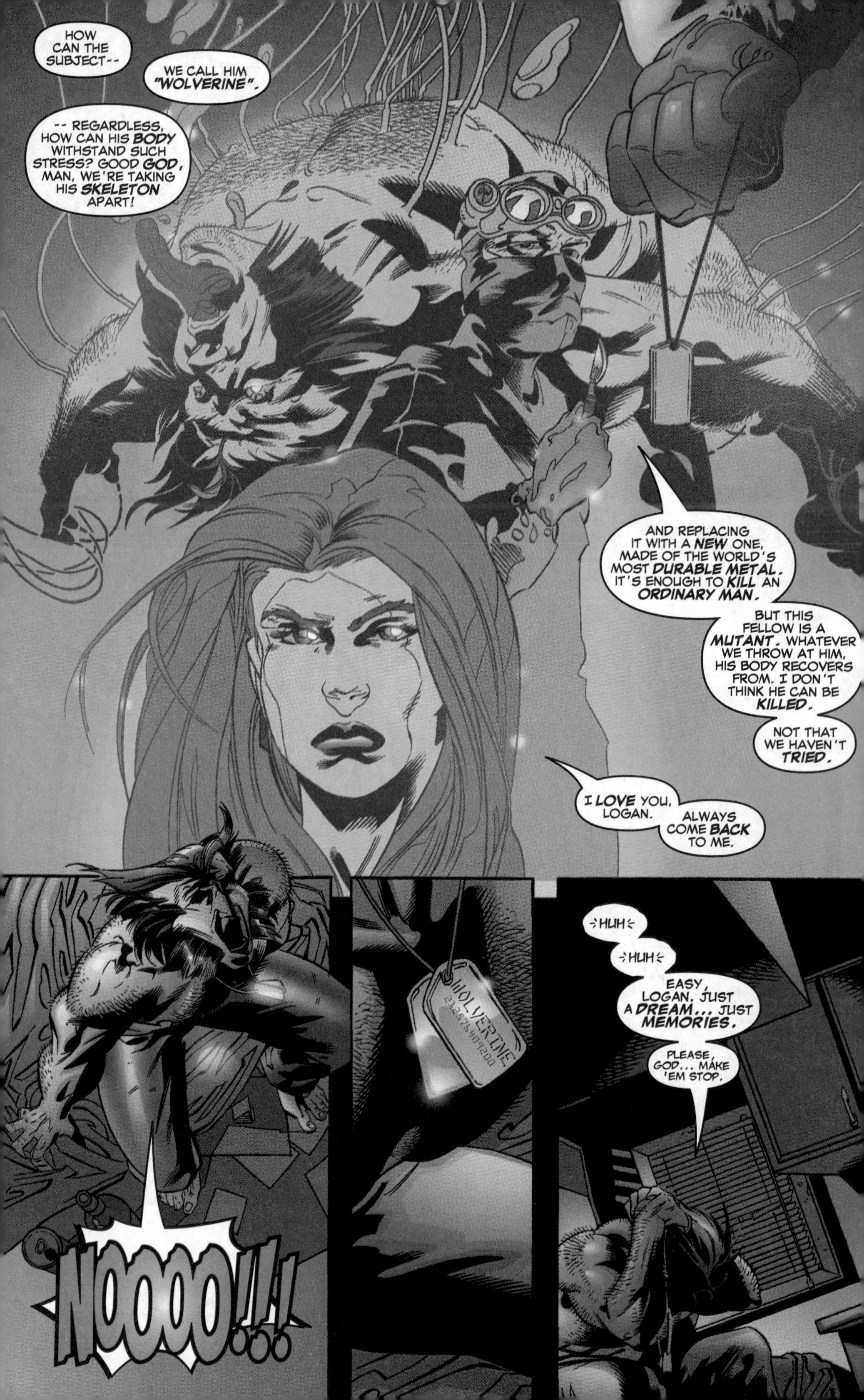
HOW CAN THE SUBJECT--
WE CALL HIM "WOLVERINE".
-- REGARDLESS, HOW CAN HIS BODY WITHSTAND SUCH STRESS? GOOD GOD, MAN, WE'RE TAKING HIS SKELETON APART!
AND REPLACING IT WITH A NEW ONE, MADE OF THE WORLD'S MOST DURABLE METAL. IT'S ENOUGH TO KILL AN ORDINARY MAN.
BUT THIS FELLOW IS A MUTANT. WHATEVER WE THROW AT HIM, HIS BODY RECOVERS FROM. I DON'T THINK HE CAN BE KILLED.
NOT THAT WE HAVEN'T TRIED.
I LOVE YOU, LOGAN.
ALWAYS COME BACK TO ME.
NOOOO!!!
WOLVERINE
HUH
HUH
EASY, LOGAN. JUST A DREAM... JUST MEMORIES.
PLEASE, GOD... MAKE 'EM STOP.

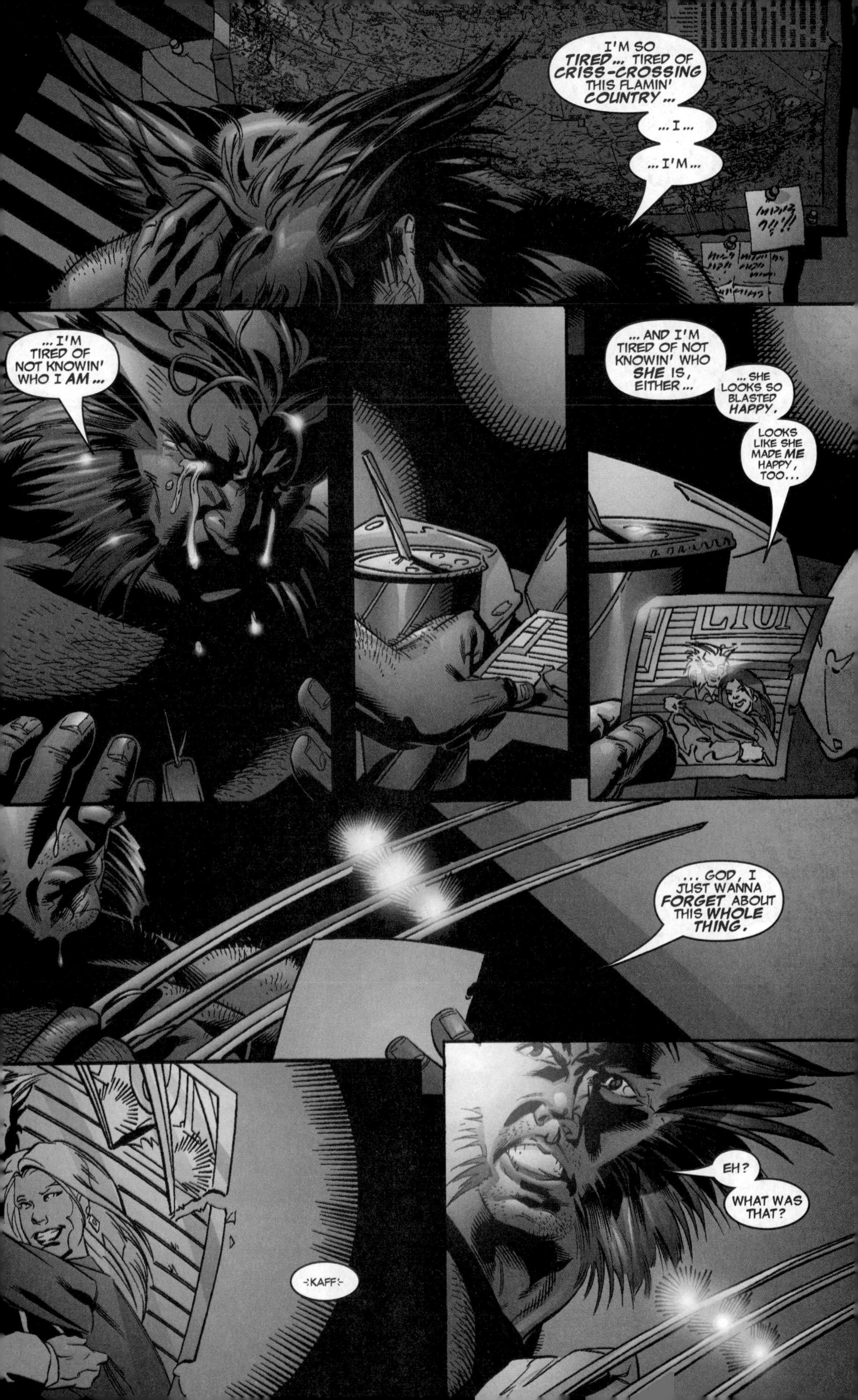

I'M SO TIRED... TIRED OF CRISS-CROSSING THIS FLAMIN' COUNTRY...
...I...
...I'M...
...I'M TIRED OF NOT KNOWIN' WHO I AM...
...AND I'M TIRED OF NOT KNOWIN' WHO SHE IS, EITHER...
...SHE LOOKS SO BLASTED HAPPY.
LOOKS LIKE SHE MADE ME HAPPY, TOO...
...GOD, I JUST WANNA FORGET ABOUT THIS WHOLE THING.
KAFF
EH?
WHAT WAS THAT?

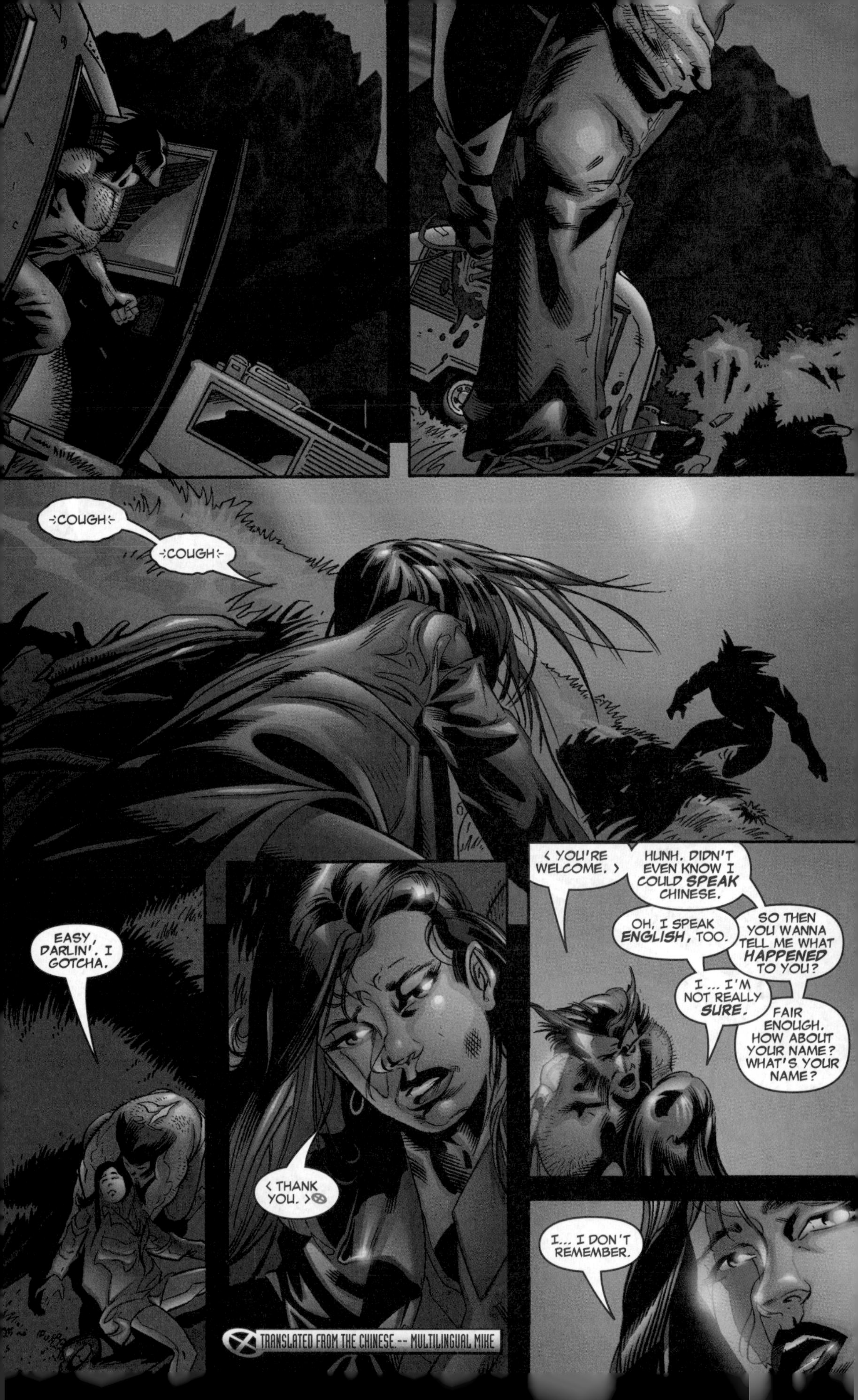
-:COUGH:-
-:COUGH:-
EASY, DARLIN'. I GOTCHA.
‹ THANK YOU. ›
‹ YOU'RE WELCOME. ›
HUNH. DIDN'T EVEN KNOW I COULD SPEAK CHINESE.
OH, I SPEAK ENGLISH, TOO.
SO THEN YOU WANNA TELL ME WHAT HAPPENED TO YOU?
I ... I'M NOT REALLY SURE.
FAIR ENOUGH. HOW ABOUT YOUR NAME? WHAT'S YOUR NAME?
I... I DON'T REMEMBER.
TRANSLATED FROM THE CHINESE.-- MULTILINGUAL MIKE

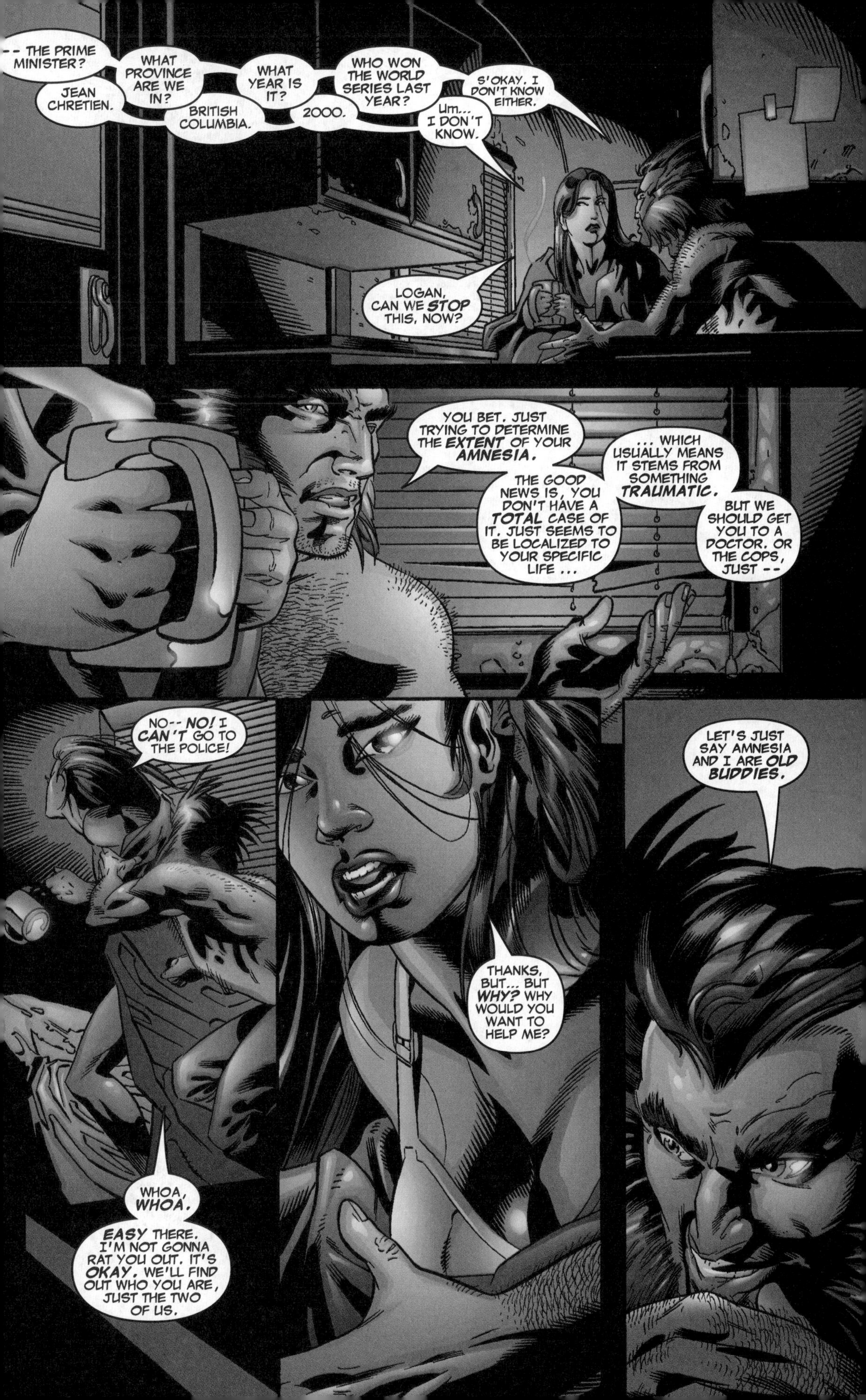
-- THE PRIME MINISTER?
JEAN CHRETIEN.
WHAT PROVINCE ARE WE IN?
BRITISH COLUMBIA.
WHAT YEAR IS IT?
2000.
WHO WON THE WORLD SERIES LAST YEAR?
Um... I DON'T KNOW.
S'OKAY. I DON'T KNOW EITHER.
LOGAN, CAN WE STOP THIS, NOW?
YOU BET. JUST TRYING TO DETERMINE THE EXTENT OF YOUR AMNESIA.
THE GOOD NEWS IS, YOU DON'T HAVE A TOTAL CASE OF IT. JUST SEEMS TO BE LOCALIZED TO YOUR SPECIFIC LIFE ...
... WHICH USUALLY MEANS IT STEMS FROM SOMETHING TRAUMATIC.
BUT WE SHOULD GET YOU TO A DOCTOR. OR THE COPS, JUST --
NO-- NO! I CAN'T GO TO THE POLICE!
WHOA, WHOA.
EASY THERE. I'M NOT GONNA RAT YOU OUT. IT'S OKAY. WE'LL FIND OUT WHO YOU ARE, JUST THE TWO OF US.
THANKS, BUT... BUT WHY? WHY WOULD YOU WANT TO HELP ME?
LET'S JUST SAY AMNESIA AND I ARE OLD BUDDIES.

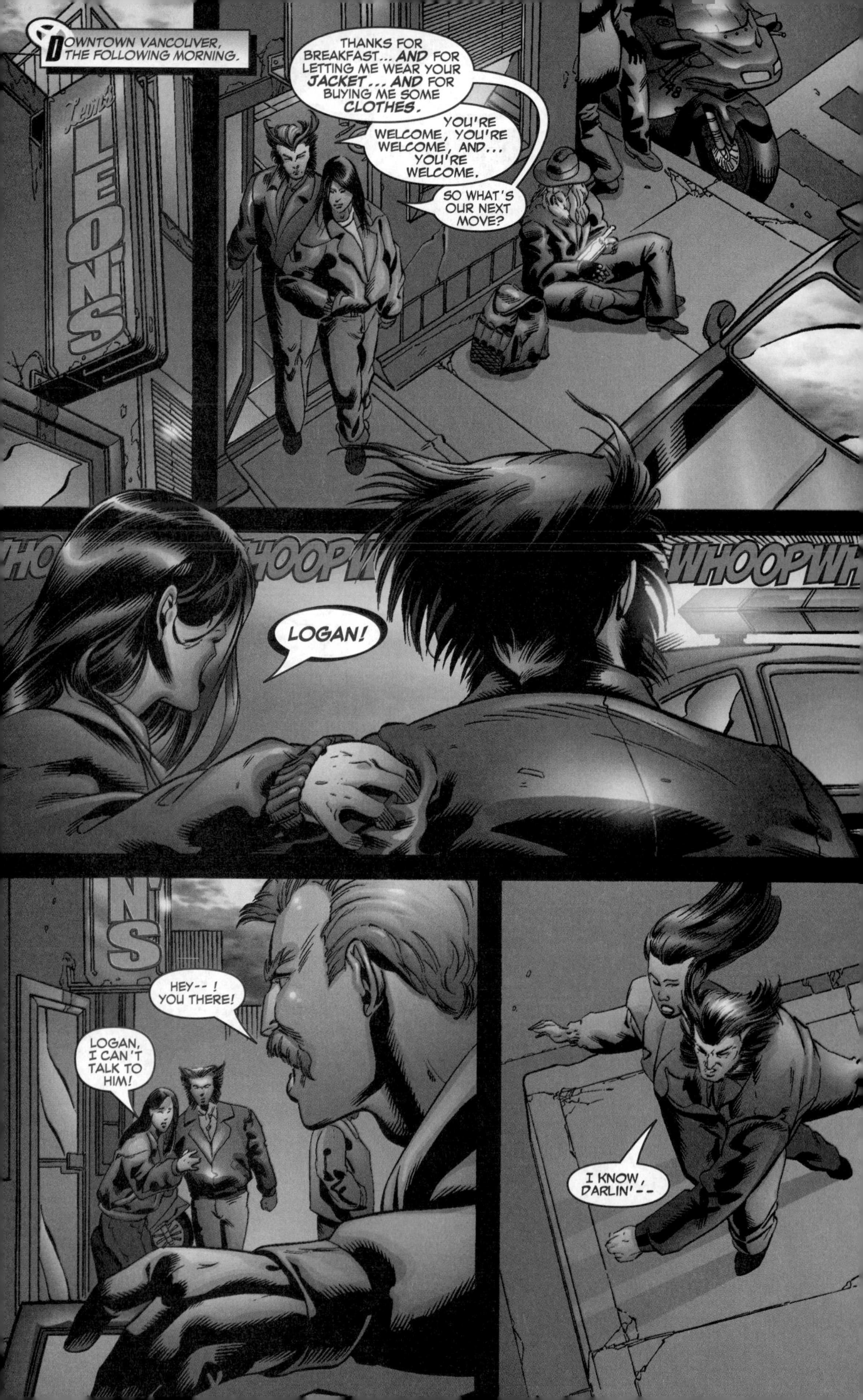
DOWNTOWN VANCOUVER, THE FOLLOWING MORNING.
LEON'S
THANKS FOR BREAKFAST... AND FOR LETTING ME WEAR YOUR JACKET... AND FOR BUYING ME SOME CLOTHES.
YOU'RE WELCOME, YOU'RE WELCOME, AND... YOU'RE WELCOME.
SO WHAT'S OUR NEXT MOVE?
WHOOPWHOOPWHOOPWH
LOGAN!
HEY-- ! YOU THERE!
LOGAN, I CAN'T TALK TO HIM!
I KNOW, DARLIN'--

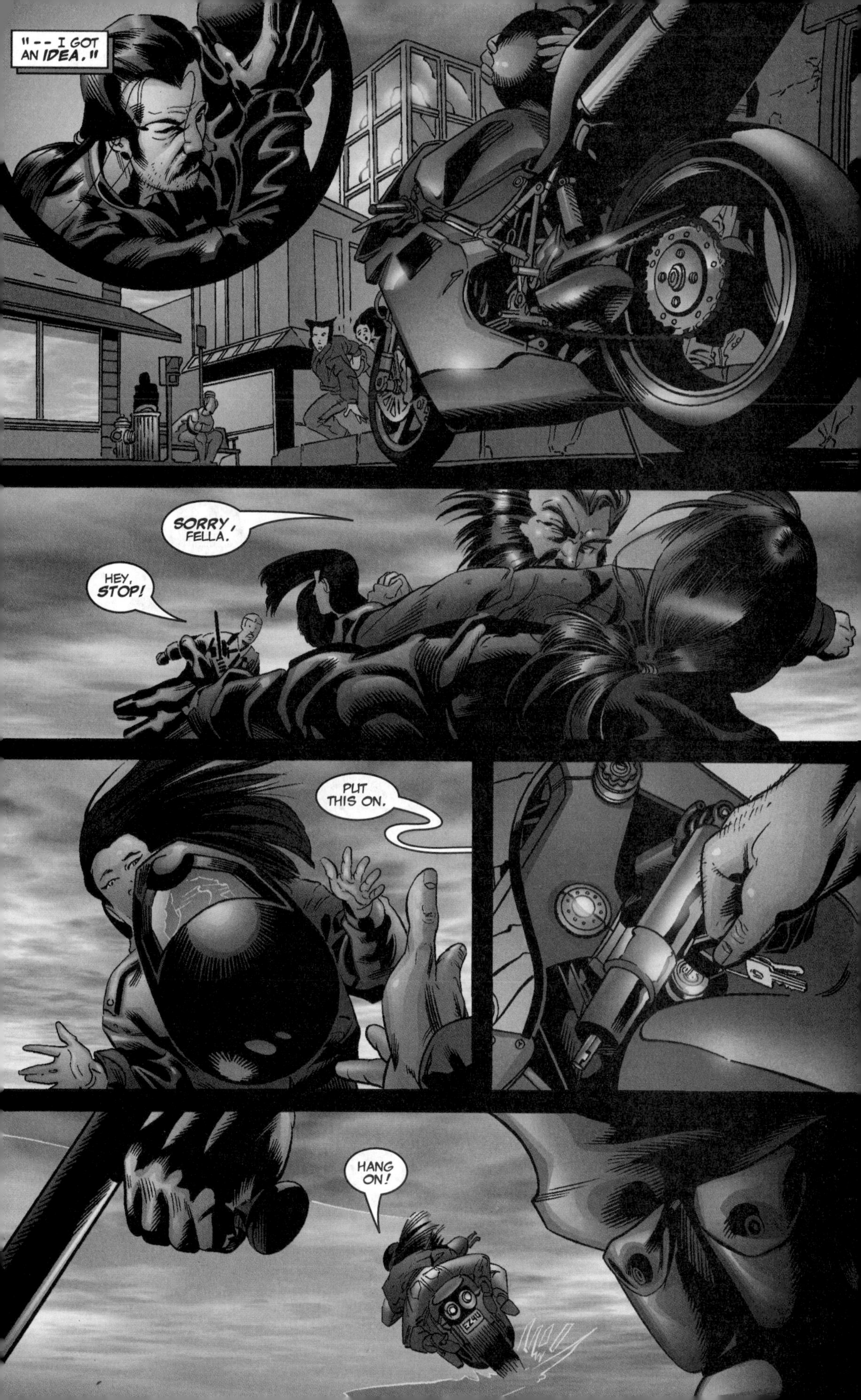
"-- I GOT AN IDEA."
SORRY, FELLA.
HEY, STOP!
PUT THIS ON.
HANG ON!

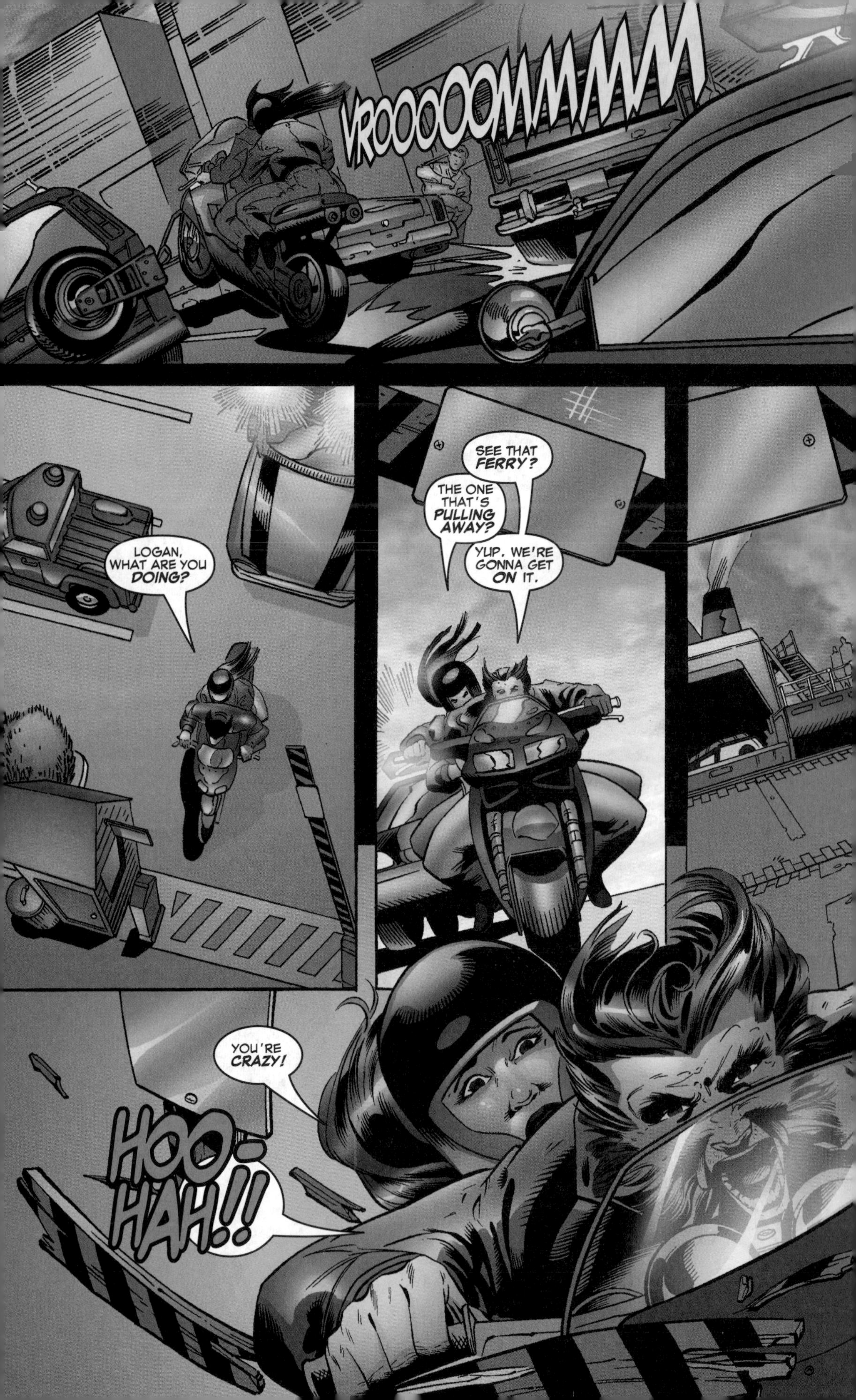
VROOOOOMMMMM
LOGAN, WHAT ARE YOU DOING?
SEE THAT FERRY?
THE ONE THAT'S PULLING AWAY?
YUP. WE'RE GONNA GET ON IT.
YOU'RE CRAZY!
HOO-HAH!!

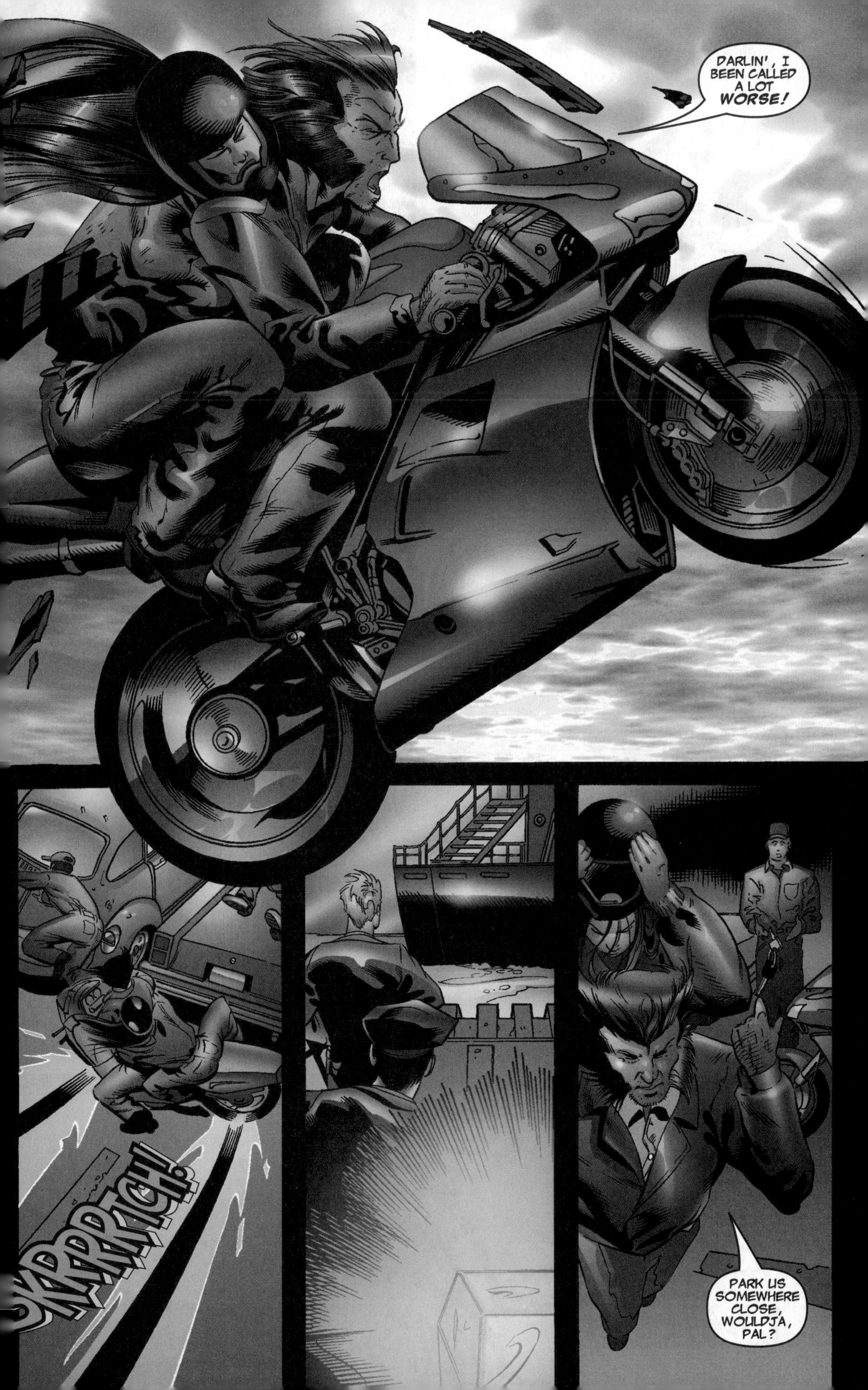
DARLIN', I BEEN CALLED A LOT WORSE!
SKRRRITCH!
PARK US SOMEWHERE CLOSE, WOULDJA, PAL?

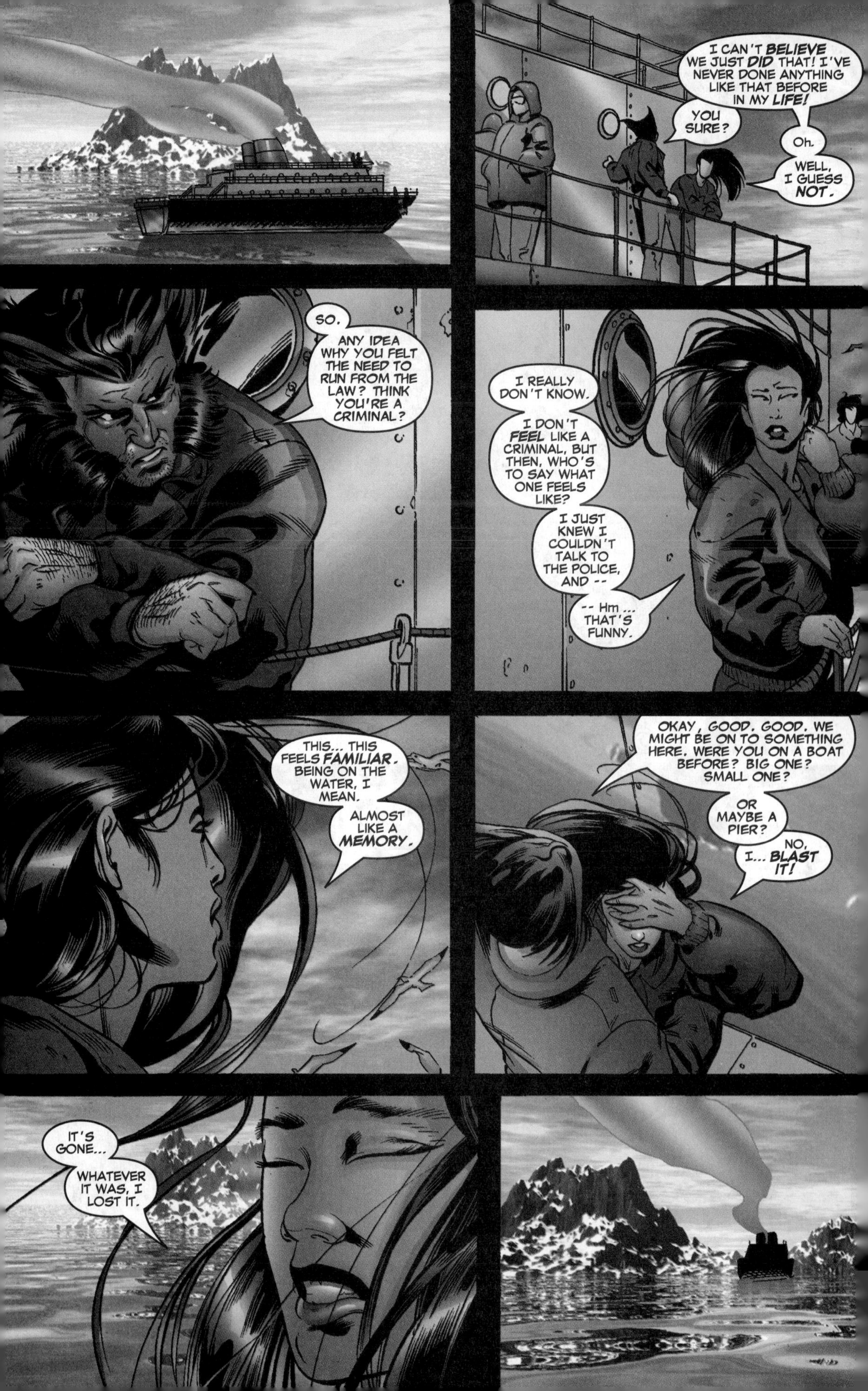
I CAN'T BELIEVE WE JUST DID THAT! I'VE NEVER DONE ANYTHING LIKE THAT BEFORE IN MY LIFE!
YOU SURE?
Oh.
WELL, I GUESS NOT.
SO.
ANY IDEA WHY YOU FELT THE NEED TO RUN FROM THE LAW? THINK YOU'RE A CRIMINAL?
I REALLY DON'T KNOW.
I DON'T FEEL LIKE A CRIMINAL, BUT THEN, WHO'S TO SAY WHAT ONE FEELS LIKE?
I JUST KNEW I COULDN'T TALK TO THE POLICE, AND --
-- Hm ... THAT'S FUNNY.
THIS... THIS FEELS FAMILIAR. BEING ON THE WATER, I MEAN.
ALMOST LIKE A MEMORY.
OKAY, GOOD. GOOD. WE MIGHT BE ON TO SOMETHING HERE. WERE YOU ON A BOAT BEFORE? BIG ONE? SMALL ONE?
OR MAYBE A PIER?
NO, I... BLAST IT!
IT'S GONE...
WHATEVER IT WAS, I LOST IT.

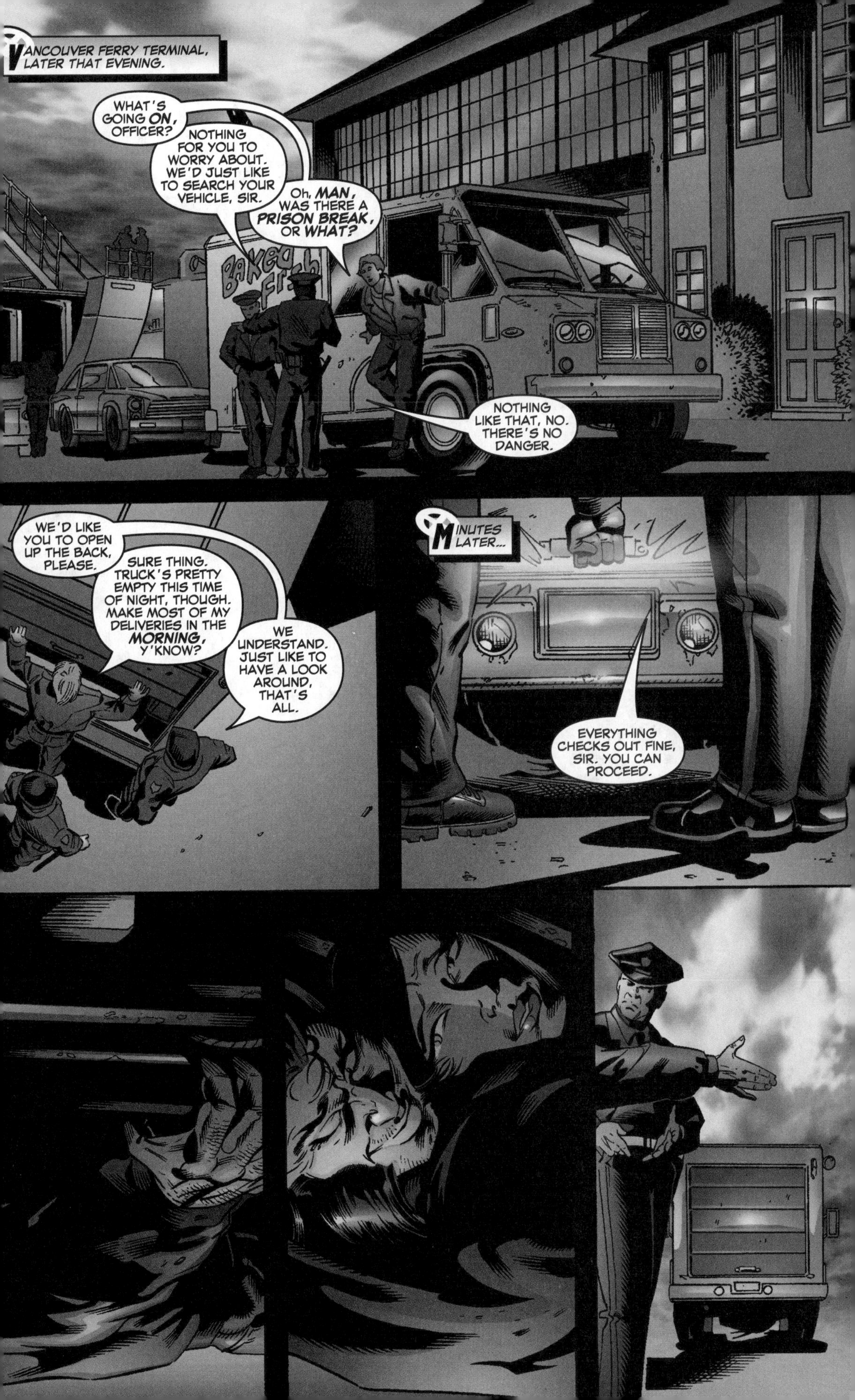
VANCOUVER FERRY TERMINAL, LATER THAT EVENING.
WHAT'S GOING ON, OFFICER?
NOTHING FOR YOU TO WORRY ABOUT. WE'D JUST LIKE TO SEARCH YOUR VEHICLE, SIR.
Oh, MAN, WAS THERE A PRISON BREAK, OR WHAT?
NOTHING LIKE THAT, NO. THERE'S NO DANGER.
WE'D LIKE YOU TO OPEN UP THE BACK, PLEASE.
SURE THING. TRUCK'S PRETTY EMPTY THIS TIME OF NIGHT, THOUGH. MAKE MOST OF MY DELIVERIES IN THE MORNING, Y'KNOW?
WE UNDERSTAND. JUST LIKE TO HAVE A LOOK AROUND, THAT'S ALL.
MINUTES LATER...
EVERYTHING CHECKS OUT FINE, SIR. YOU CAN PROCEED.

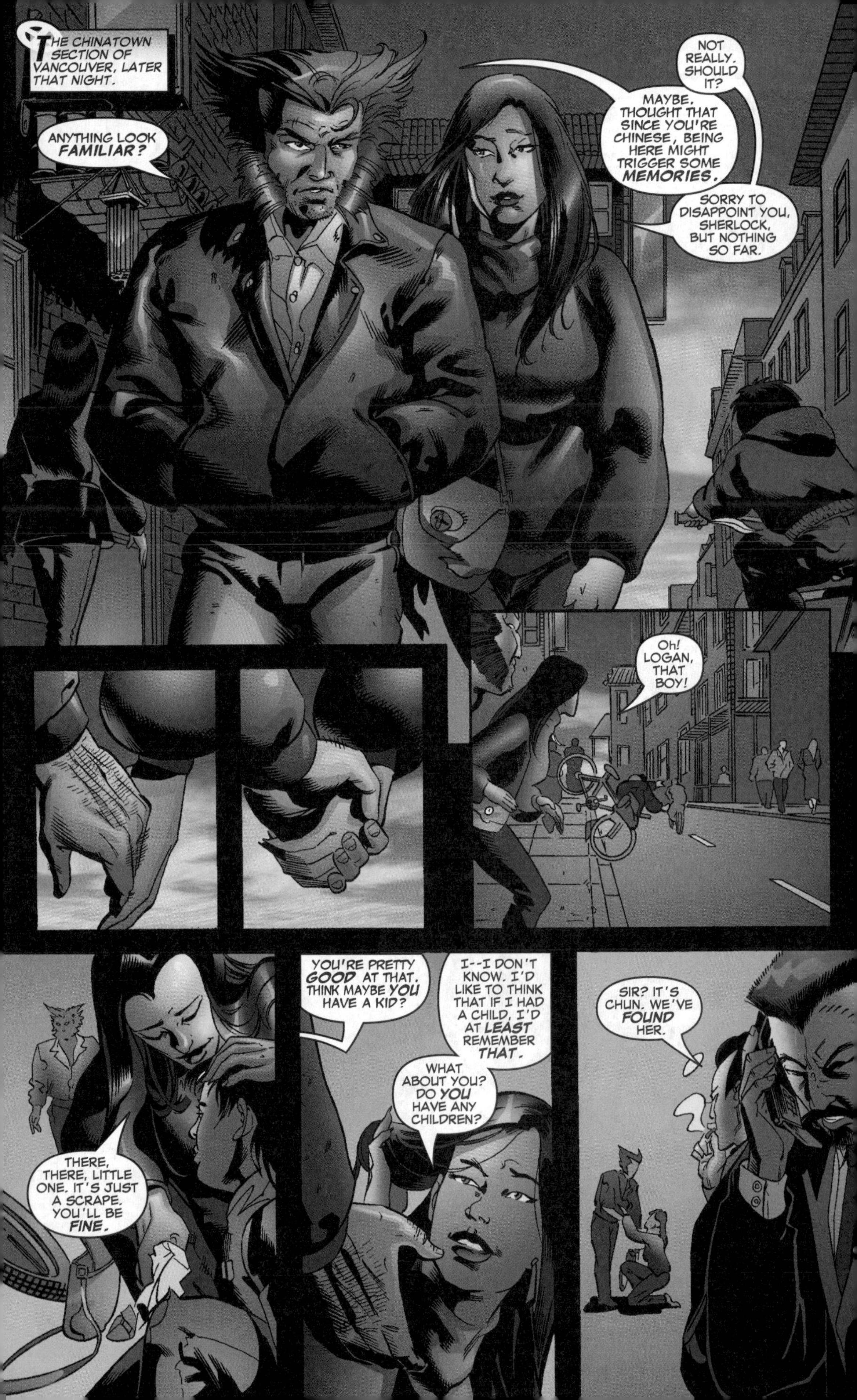
THE CHINATOWN SECTION OF VANCOUVER, LATER THAT NIGHT.
ANYTHING LOOK FAMILIAR?
NOT REALLY. SHOULD IT?
MAYBE. THOUGHT THAT SINCE YOU'RE CHINESE, BEING HERE MIGHT TRIGGER SOME MEMORIES.
SORRY TO DISAPPOINT YOU, SHERLOCK, BUT NOTHING SO FAR.
Oh! LOGAN, THAT BOY!
THERE, THERE, LITTLE ONE. IT'S JUST A SCRAPE. YOU'LL BE FINE.
YOU'RE PRETTY GOOD AT THAT. THINK MAYBE YOU HAVE A KID?
I--I DON'T KNOW. I'D LIKE TO THINK THAT IF I HAD A CHILD, I'D AT LEAST REMEMBER THAT.
WHAT ABOUT YOU? DO YOU HAVE ANY CHILDREN?
SIR? IT'S CHUN. WE'VE FOUND HER.

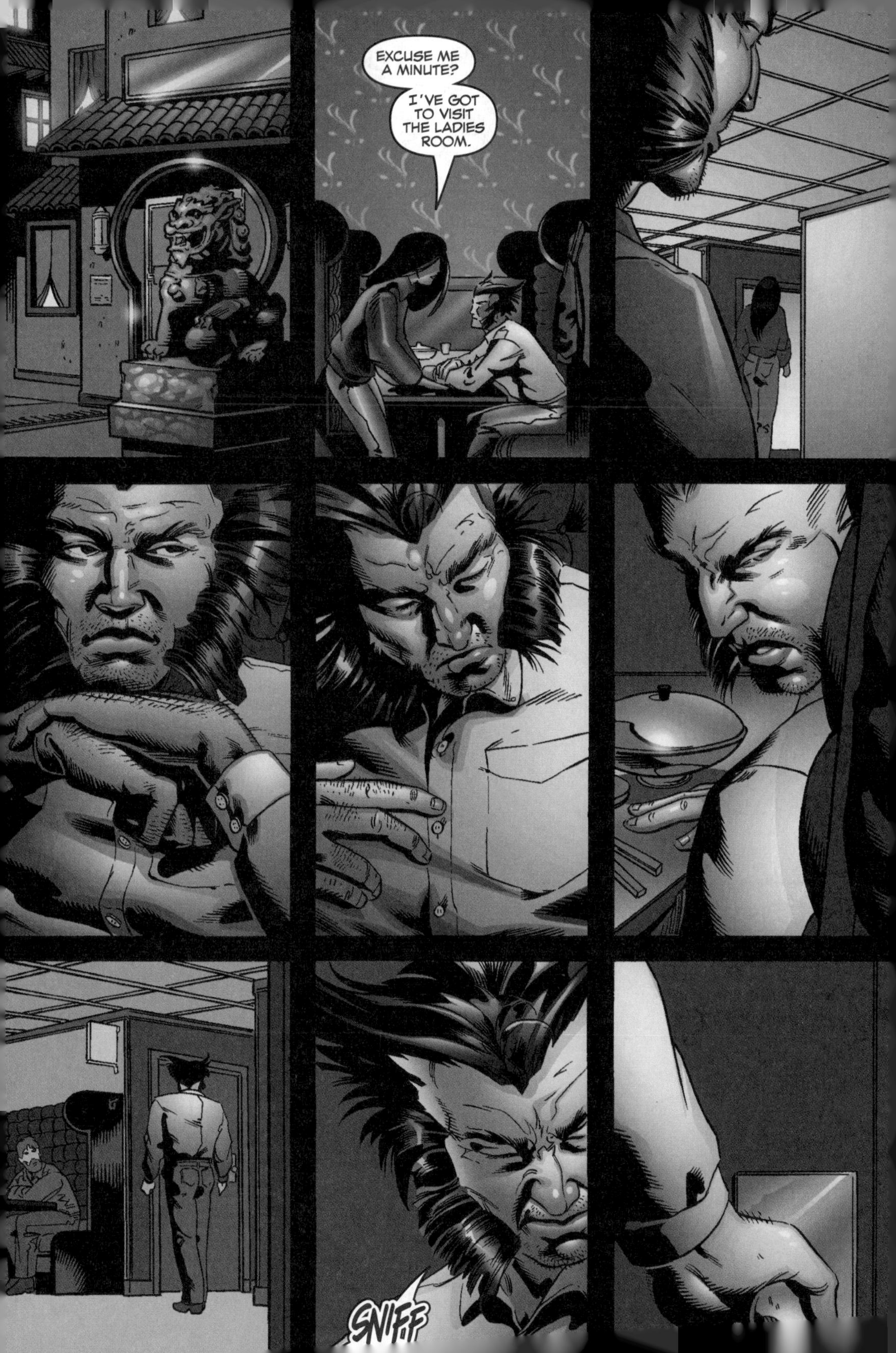
EXCUSE ME A MINUTE?
I'VE GOT TO VISIT THE LADIES ROOM.
SNIFF

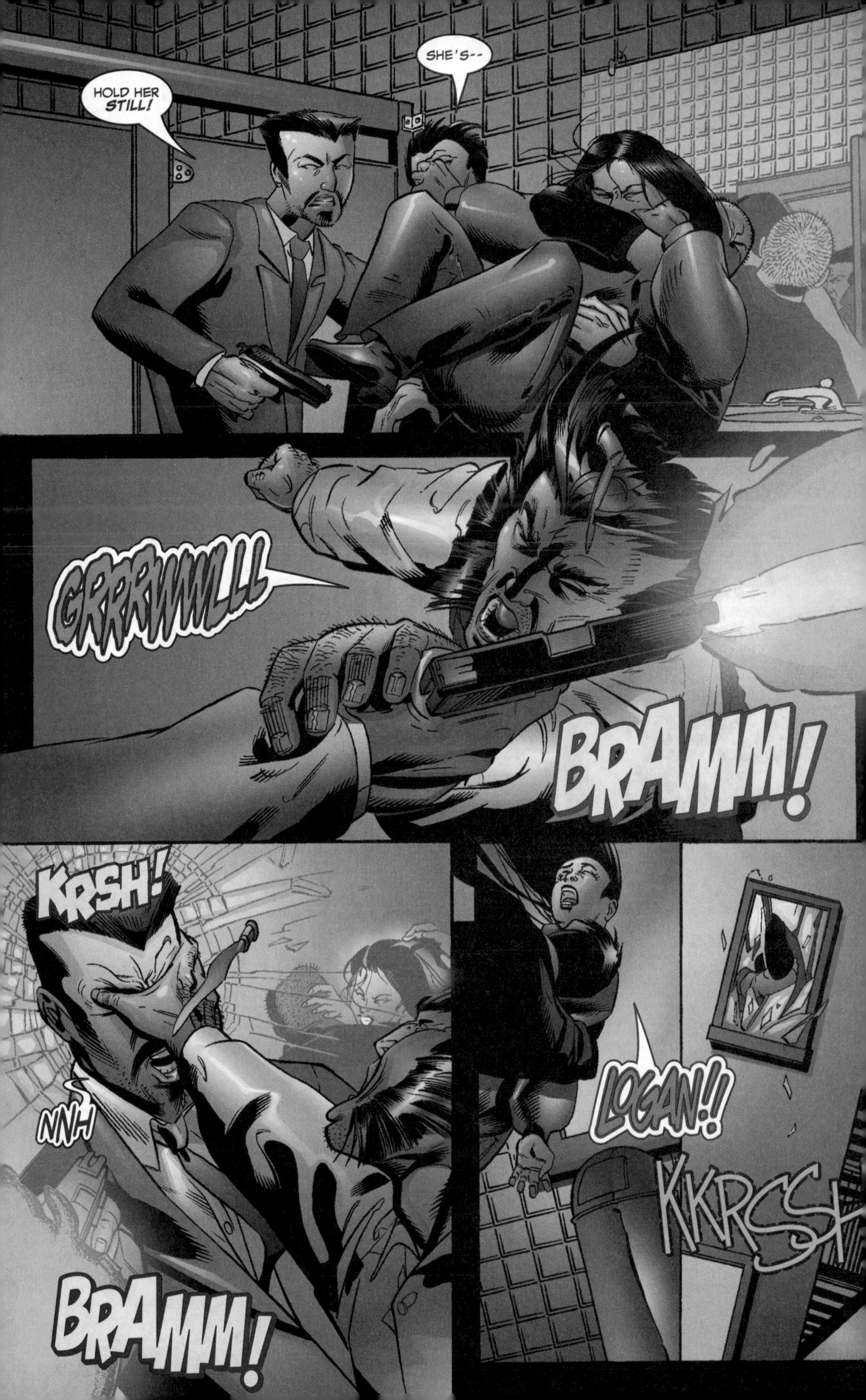
HOLD HER STILL!
SHE'S--
GRRRWWLLL
BRAMM!
KRSH!
NNH
BRAMM!
LOGAN!!
KKRSH

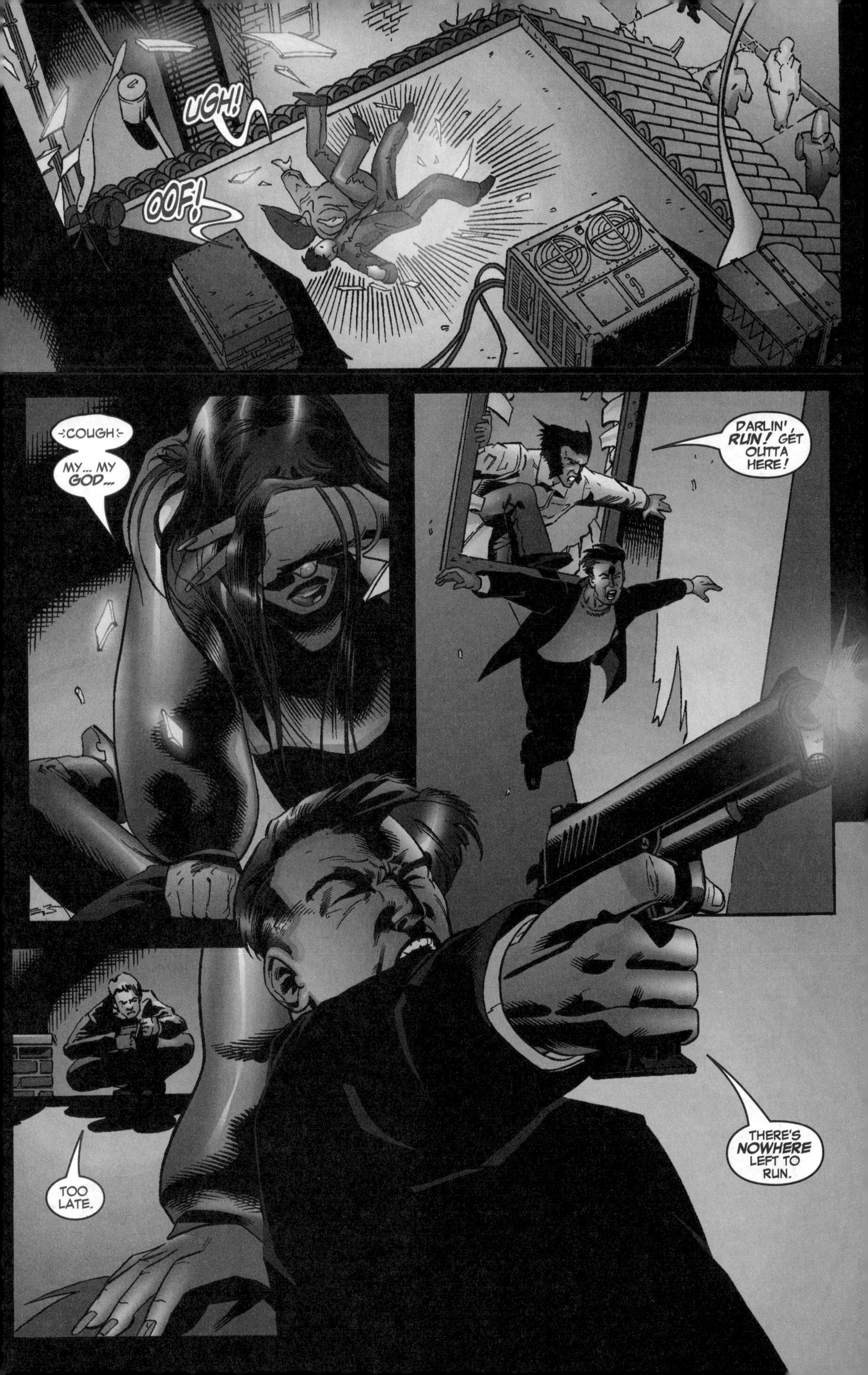
UGH!
OOF!
-COUGH-
MY... MY GOD...
DARLIN', RUN! GET OUTTA HERE!
THERE'S NOWHERE LEFT TO RUN.
TOO LATE.

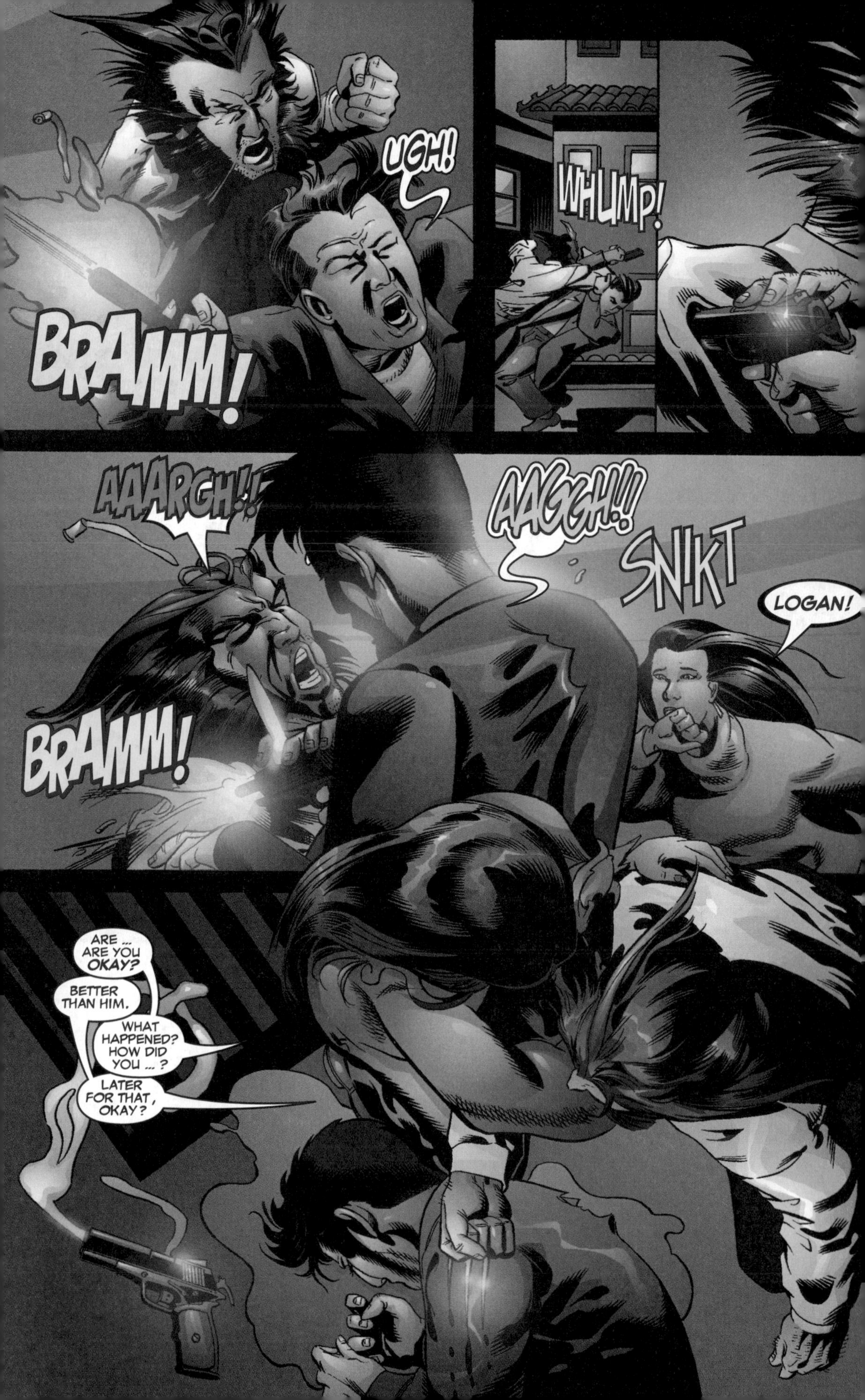
UGH!
BRAMM!
WHUMP!
AAARGH!!
AAGGH!!
SNIKT
LOGAN!
BRAMM!
ARE ... ARE YOU OKAY?
BETTER THAN HIM.
WHAT HAPPENED? HOW DID YOU ... ?
LATER FOR THAT, OKAY?

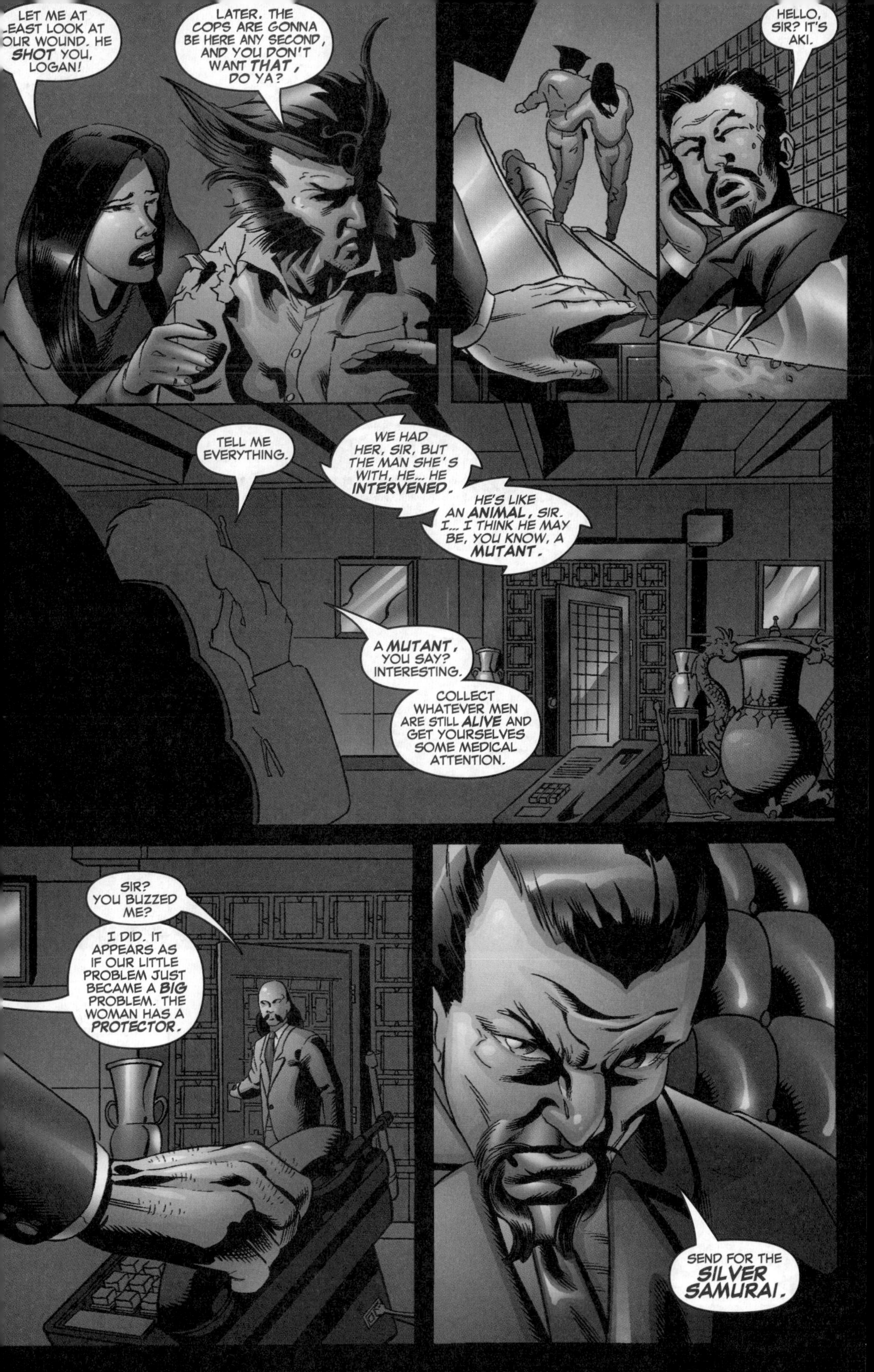

LET ME AT LEAST LOOK AT OUR WOUND. HE SHOT YOU, LOGAN!
LATER. THE COPS ARE GONNA BE HERE ANY SECOND, AND YOU DON'T WANT THAT, DO YA?
HELLO, SIR? IT'S AKI.
TELL ME EVERYTHING.
WE HAD HER, SIR, BUT THE MAN SHE'S WITH, HE... HE INTERVENED.
HE'S LIKE AN ANIMAL, SIR. I... I THINK HE MAY BE, YOU KNOW, A MUTANT.
A MUTANT, YOU SAY? INTERESTING.
COLLECT WHATEVER MEN ARE STILL ALIVE AND GET YOURSELVES SOME MEDICAL ATTENTION.
SIR? YOU BUZZED ME?
I DID. IT APPEARS AS IF OUR LITTLE PROBLEM JUST BECAME A BIG PROBLEM. THE WOMAN HAS A PROTECTOR.
SEND FOR THE SILVER SAMURAI.

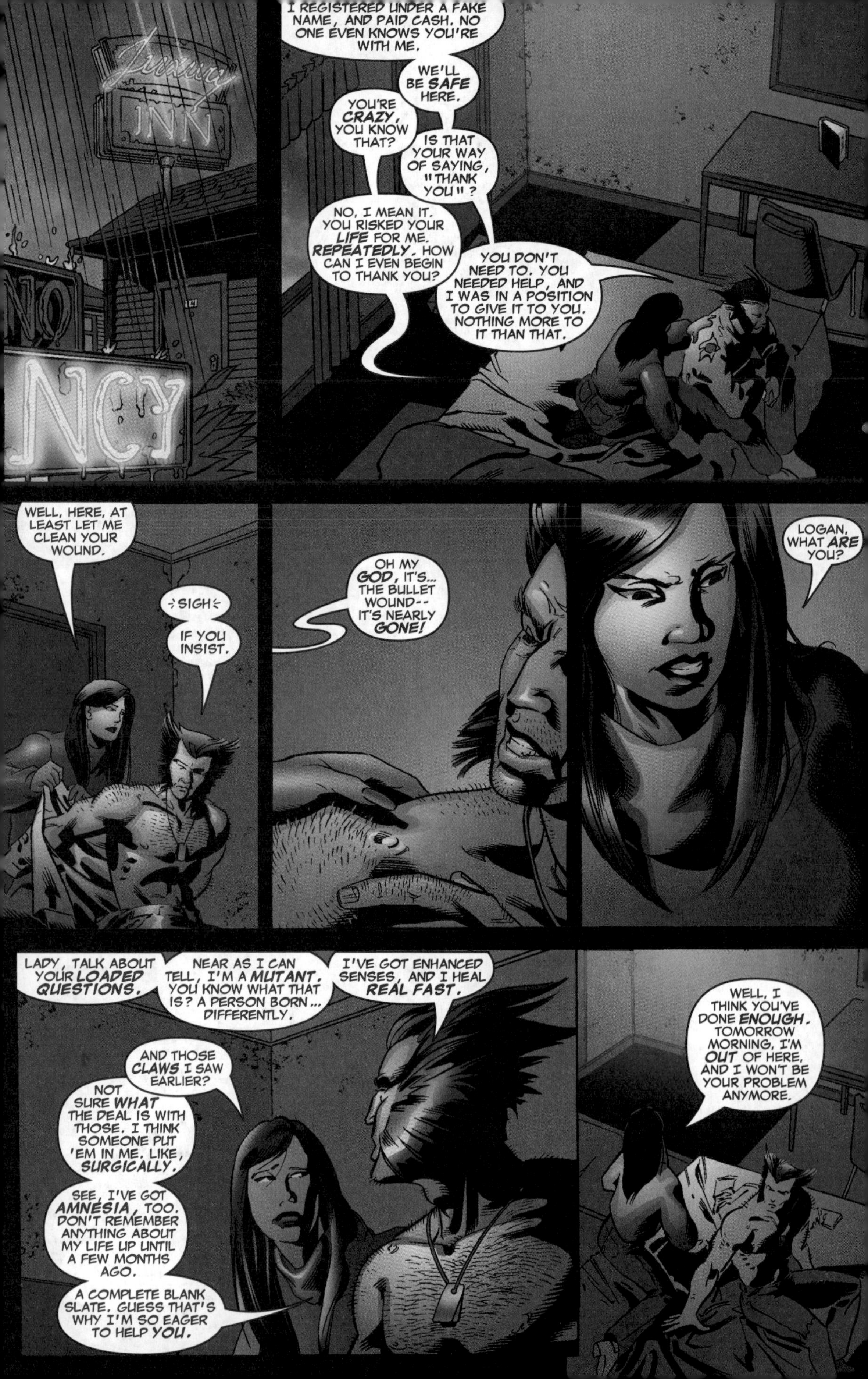
Luxury
INN
NCY
I REGISTERED UNDER A FAKE NAME, AND PAID CASH. NO ONE EVEN KNOWS YOU'RE WITH ME.
WE'LL BE SAFE HERE.
YOU'RE CRAZY, YOU KNOW THAT?
IS THAT YOUR WAY OF SAYING, "THANK YOU"?
NO, I MEAN IT. YOU RISKED YOUR LIFE FOR ME. REPEATEDLY. HOW CAN I EVEN BEGIN TO THANK YOU?
YOU DON'T NEED TO. YOU NEEDED HELP, AND I WAS IN A POSITION TO GIVE IT TO YOU. NOTHING MORE TO IT THAN THAT.
WELL, HERE, AT LEAST LET ME CLEAN YOUR WOUND.
SIGH
IF YOU INSIST.
OH MY GOD, IT'S... THE BULLET WOUND-- IT'S NEARLY GONE!
LOGAN, WHAT ARE YOU?
LADY, TALK ABOUT YOUR LOADED QUESTIONS.
NEAR AS I CAN TELL, I'M A MUTANT. YOU KNOW WHAT THAT IS? A PERSON BORN... DIFFERENTLY.
I'VE GOT ENHANCED SENSES, AND I HEAL REAL FAST.
AND THOSE CLAWS I SAW EARLIER?
NOT SURE WHAT THE DEAL IS WITH THOSE. I THINK SOMEONE PUT 'EM IN ME. LIKE, SURGICALLY.
SEE, I'VE GOT AMNESIA, TOO. DON'T REMEMBER ANYTHING ABOUT MY LIFE UP UNTIL A FEW MONTHS AGO.
A COMPLETE BLANK SLATE. GUESS THAT'S WHY I'M SO EAGER TO HELP YOU.
WELL, I THINK YOU'VE DONE ENOUGH. TOMORROW MORNING, I'M OUT OF HERE, AND I WON'T BE YOUR PROBLEM ANYMORE.

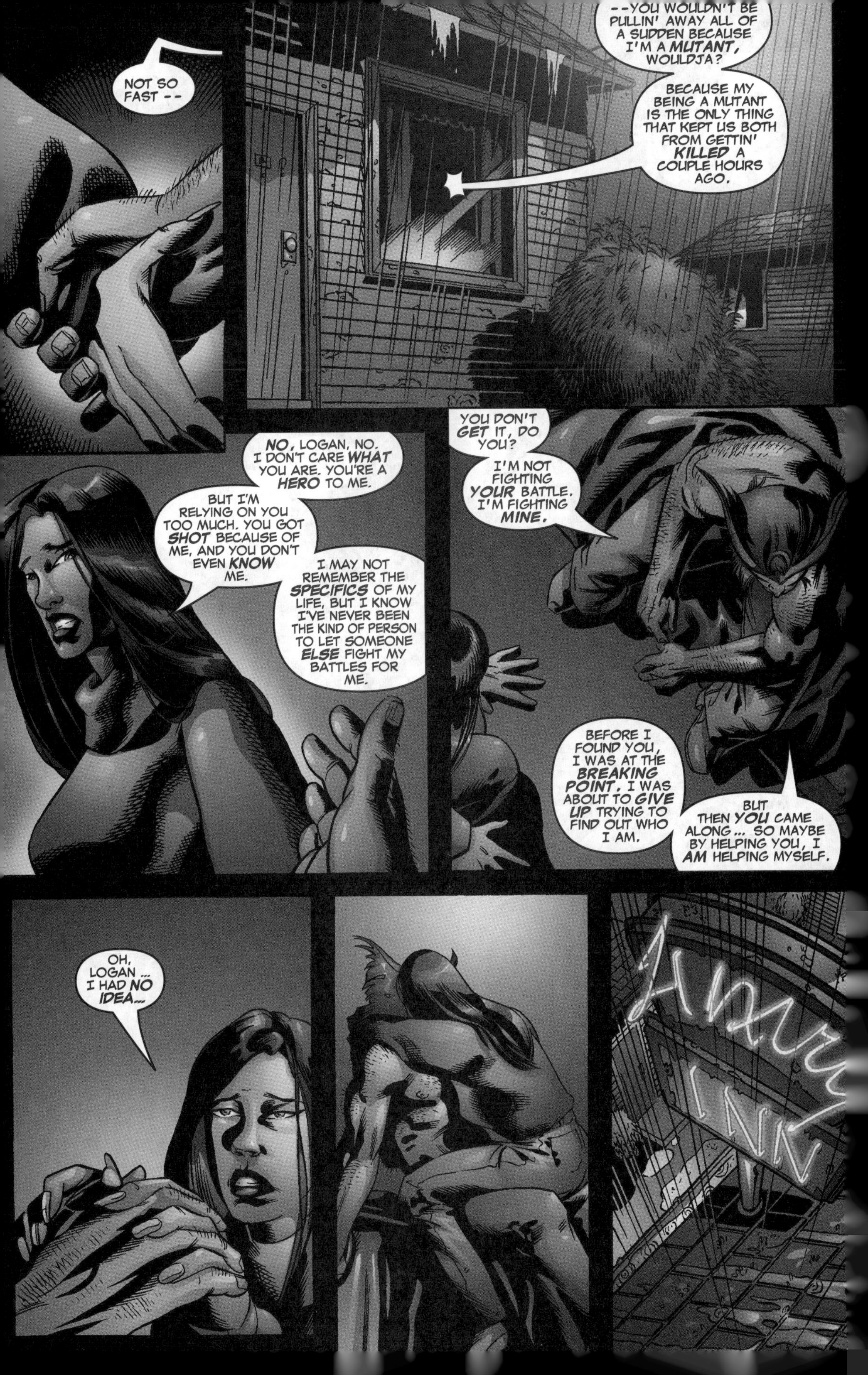
NOT SO FAST --
--YOU WOULDN'T BE PULLIN' AWAY ALL OF A SUDDEN BECAUSE I'M A MUTANT, WOULDJA?
BECAUSE MY BEING A MUTANT IS THE ONLY THING THAT KEPT US BOTH FROM GETTIN' KILLED A COUPLE HOURS AGO.
NO, LOGAN, NO. I DON'T CARE WHAT YOU ARE. YOU'RE A HERO TO ME.
BUT I'M RELYING ON YOU TOO MUCH. YOU GOT SHOT BECAUSE OF ME, AND YOU DON'T EVEN KNOW ME.
I MAY NOT REMEMBER THE SPECIFICS OF MY LIFE, BUT I KNOW I'VE NEVER BEEN THE KIND OF PERSON TO LET SOMEONE ELSE FIGHT MY BATTLES FOR ME.
YOU DON'T GET IT, DO YOU?
I'M NOT FIGHTING YOUR BATTLE. I'M FIGHTING MINE.
BEFORE I FOUND YOU, I WAS AT THE BREAKING POINT. I WAS ABOUT TO GIVE UP TRYING TO FIND OUT WHO I AM.
BUT THEN YOU CAME ALONG... SO MAYBE BY HELPING YOU, I AM HELPING MYSELF.
OH, LOGAN... I HAD NO IDEA...

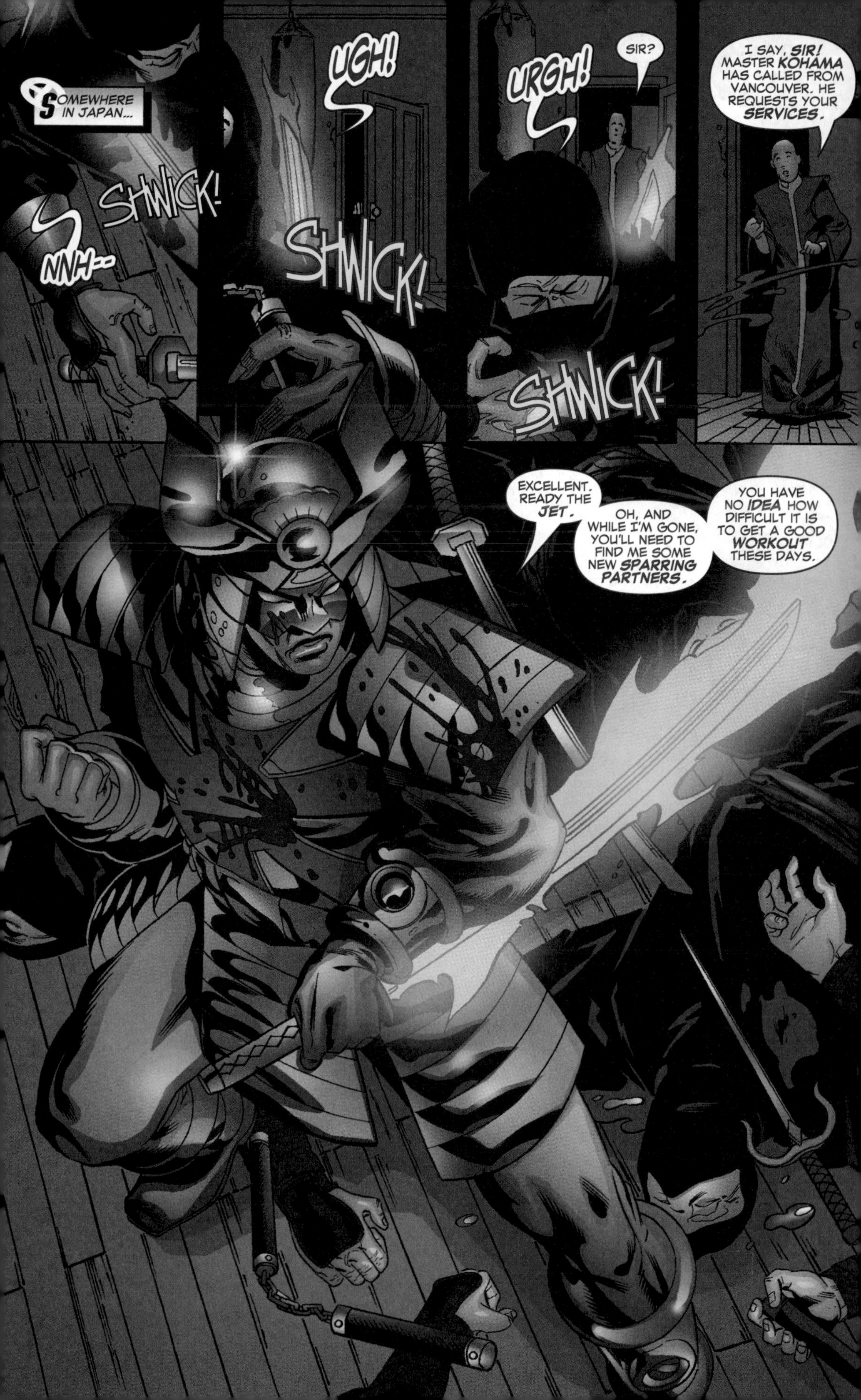
SOMEWHERE IN JAPAN...
SHWICK!
NNH--
UGH!
SHWICK!
URGH!
SIR?
SHWICK!
I SAY, SIR! MASTER KOHAMA HAS CALLED FROM VANCOUVER. HE REQUESTS YOUR SERVICES.
EXCELLENT. READY THE JET.
OH, AND WHILE I'M GONE, YOU'LL NEED TO FIND ME SOME NEW SPARRING PARTNERS.
YOU HAVE NO IDEA HOW DIFFICULT IT IS TO GET A GOOD WORKOUT THESE DAYS.

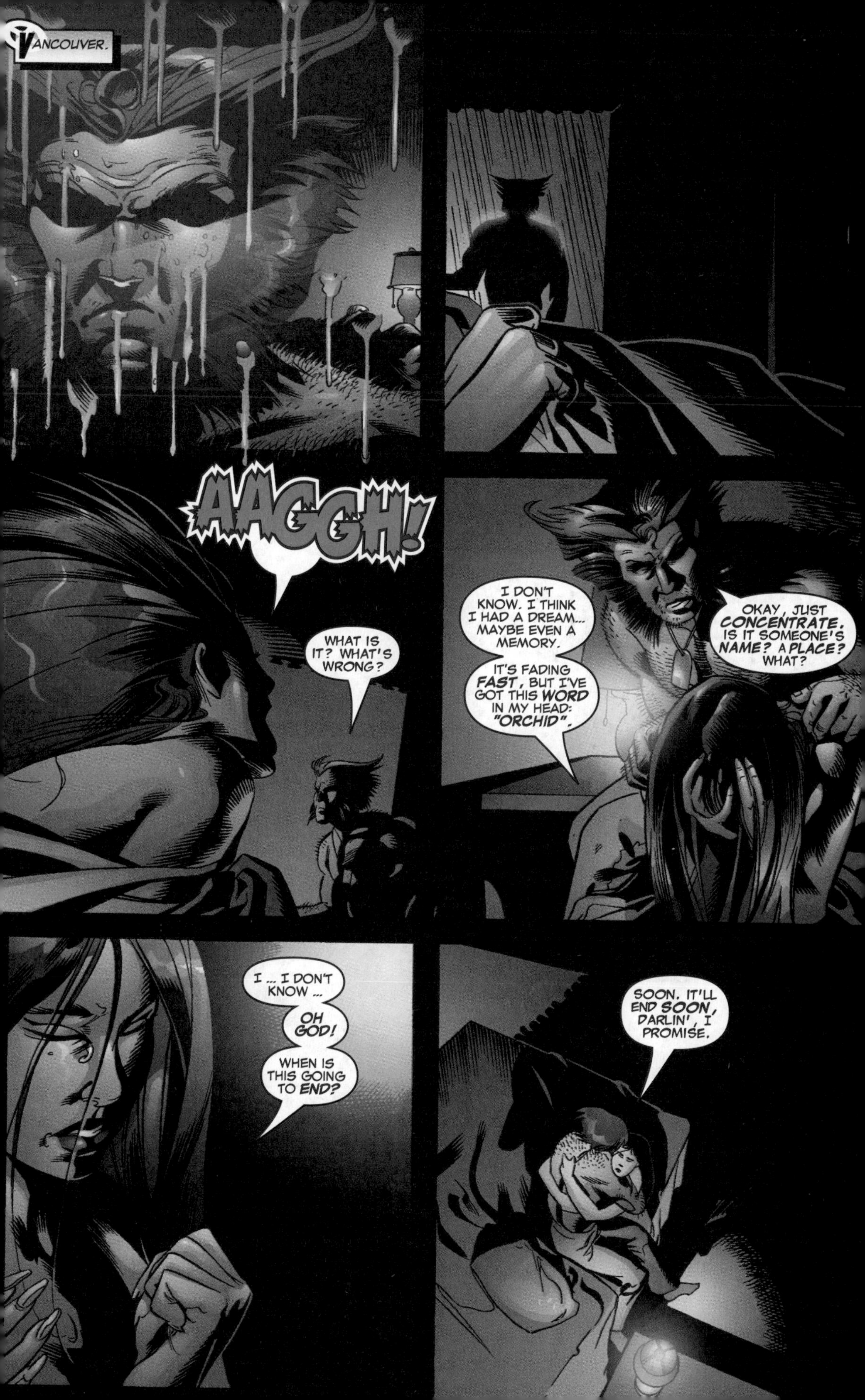
VANCOUVER.
AAGGH!
WHAT IS IT? WHAT'S WRONG?
I DON'T KNOW. I THINK I HAD A DREAM... MAYBE EVEN A MEMORY.
IT'S FADING FAST, BUT I'VE GOT THIS WORD IN MY HEAD: "ORCHID".
OKAY, JUST CONCENTRATE. IS IT SOMEONE'S NAME? A PLACE? WHAT?
I ... I DON'T KNOW ...
OH GOD!
WHEN IS THIS GOING TO END?
SOON. IT'LL END SOON, DARLIN', I PROMISE.

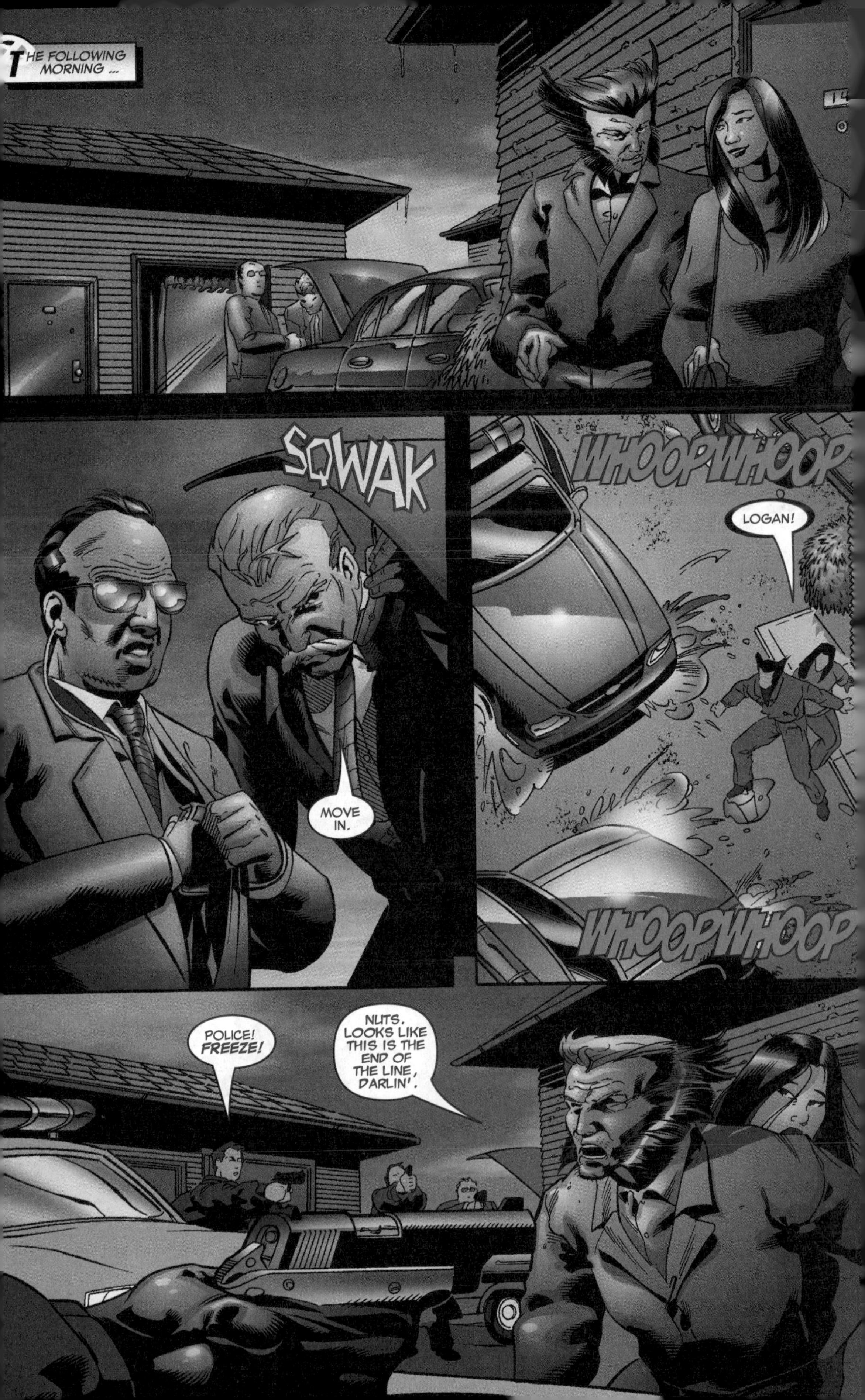
THE FOLLOWING MORNING ...
SQWAK
MOVE IN.
WHOOPWHOOP
LOGAN!
WHOOPWHOOP
POLICE! FREEZE!
NUTS. LOOKS LIKE THIS IS THE END OF THE LINE, DARLIN'.

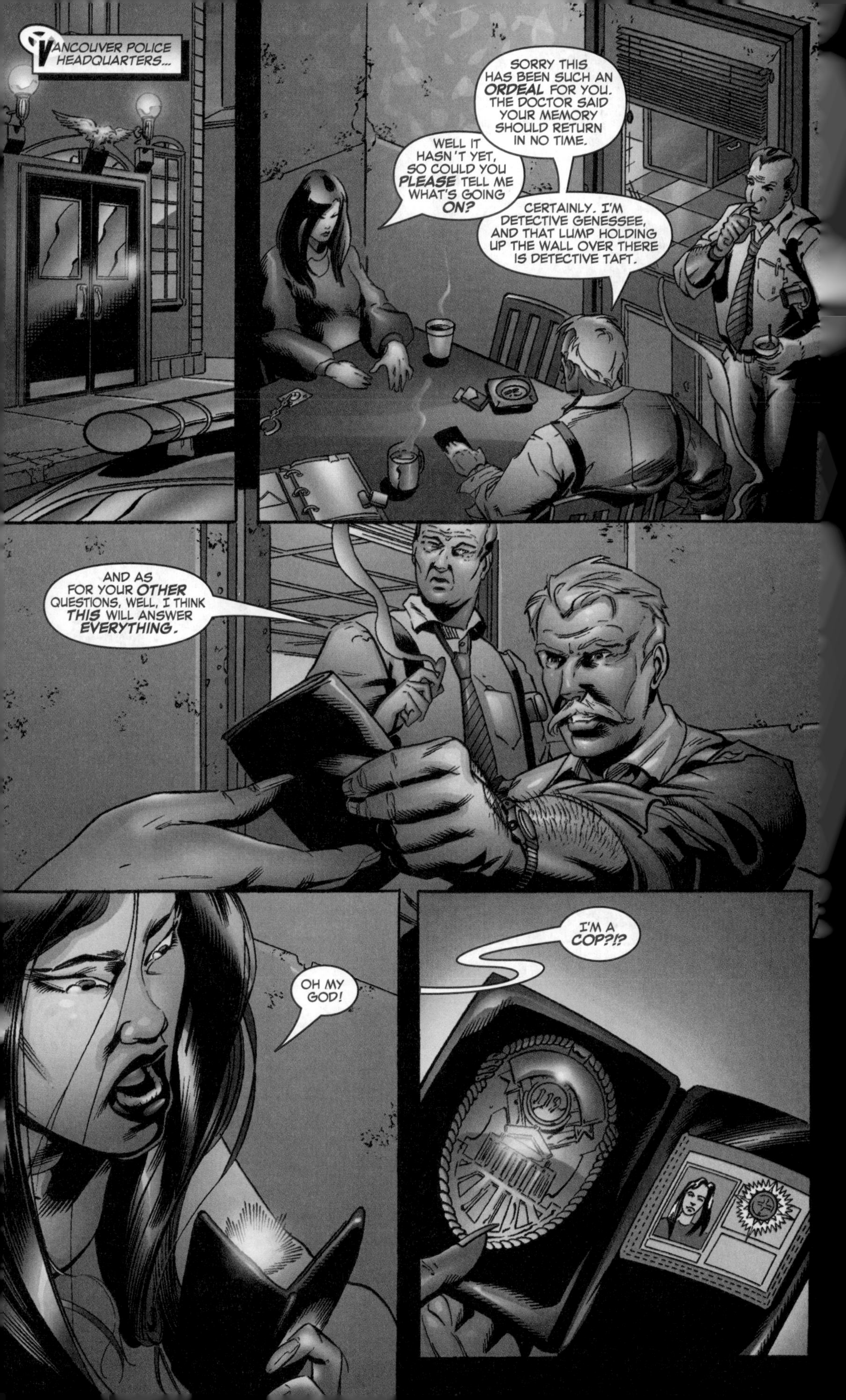
VANCOUVER POLICE HEADQUARTERS...
SORRY THIS HAS BEEN SUCH AN ORDEAL FOR YOU. THE DOCTOR SAID YOUR MEMORY SHOULD RETURN IN NO TIME.
WELL IT HASN'T YET, SO COULD YOU PLEASE TELL ME WHAT'S GOING ON?
CERTAINLY. I'M DETECTIVE GENESSEE, AND THAT LUMP HOLDING UP THE WALL OVER THERE IS DETECTIVE TAFT.
AND AS FOR YOUR OTHER QUESTIONS, WELL, I THINK THIS WILL ANSWER EVERYTHING.
OH MY GOD!
I'M A COP?!?

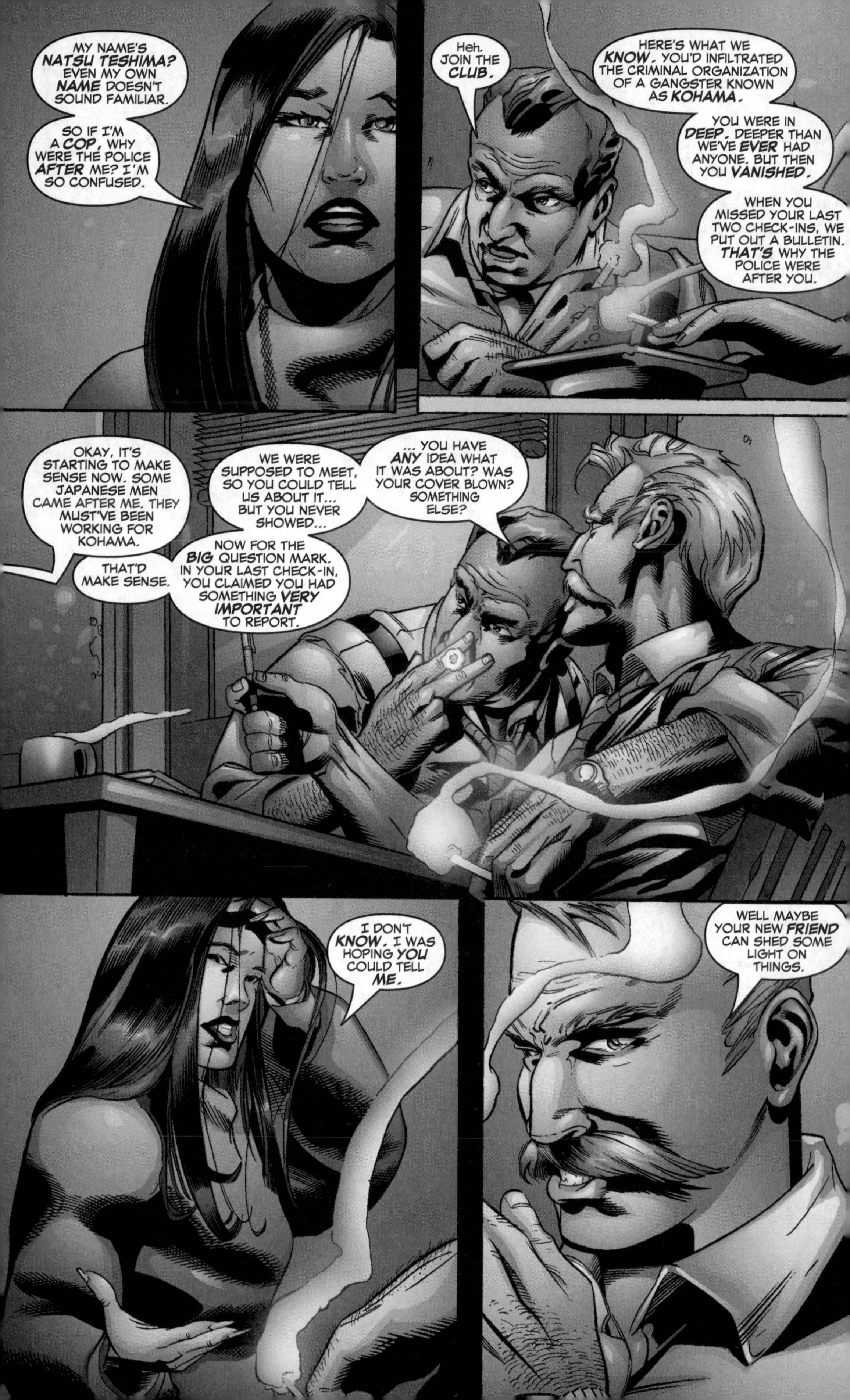
MY NAME'S NATSU TESHIMA? EVEN MY OWN NAME DOESN'T SOUND FAMILIAR.
SO IF I'M A COP, WHY WERE THE POLICE AFTER ME? I'M SO CONFUSED.
Heh. JOIN THE CLUB.
HERE'S WHAT WE KNOW. YOU'D INFILTRATED THE CRIMINAL ORGANIZATION OF A GANGSTER KNOWN AS KOHAMA.
YOU WERE IN DEEP. DEEPER THAN WE'VE EVER HAD ANYONE. BUT THEN YOU VANISHED.
WHEN YOU MISSED YOUR LAST TWO CHECK-INS, WE PUT OUT A BULLETIN. THAT'S WHY THE POLICE WERE AFTER YOU.
OKAY, IT'S STARTING TO MAKE SENSE NOW. SOME JAPANESE MEN CAME AFTER ME. THEY MUST'VE BEEN WORKING FOR KOHAMA.
THAT'D MAKE SENSE.
NOW FOR THE BIG QUESTION MARK. IN YOUR LAST CHECK-IN, YOU CLAIMED YOU HAD SOMETHING VERY IMPORTANT TO REPORT.
WE WERE SUPPOSED TO MEET, SO YOU COULD TELL US ABOUT IT... BUT YOU NEVER SHOWED...
... YOU HAVE ANY IDEA WHAT IT WAS ABOUT? WAS YOUR COVER BLOWN? SOMETHING ELSE?
I DON'T KNOW. I WAS HOPING YOU COULD TELL ME.
WELL MAYBE YOUR NEW FRIEND CAN SHED SOME LIGHT ON THINGS.

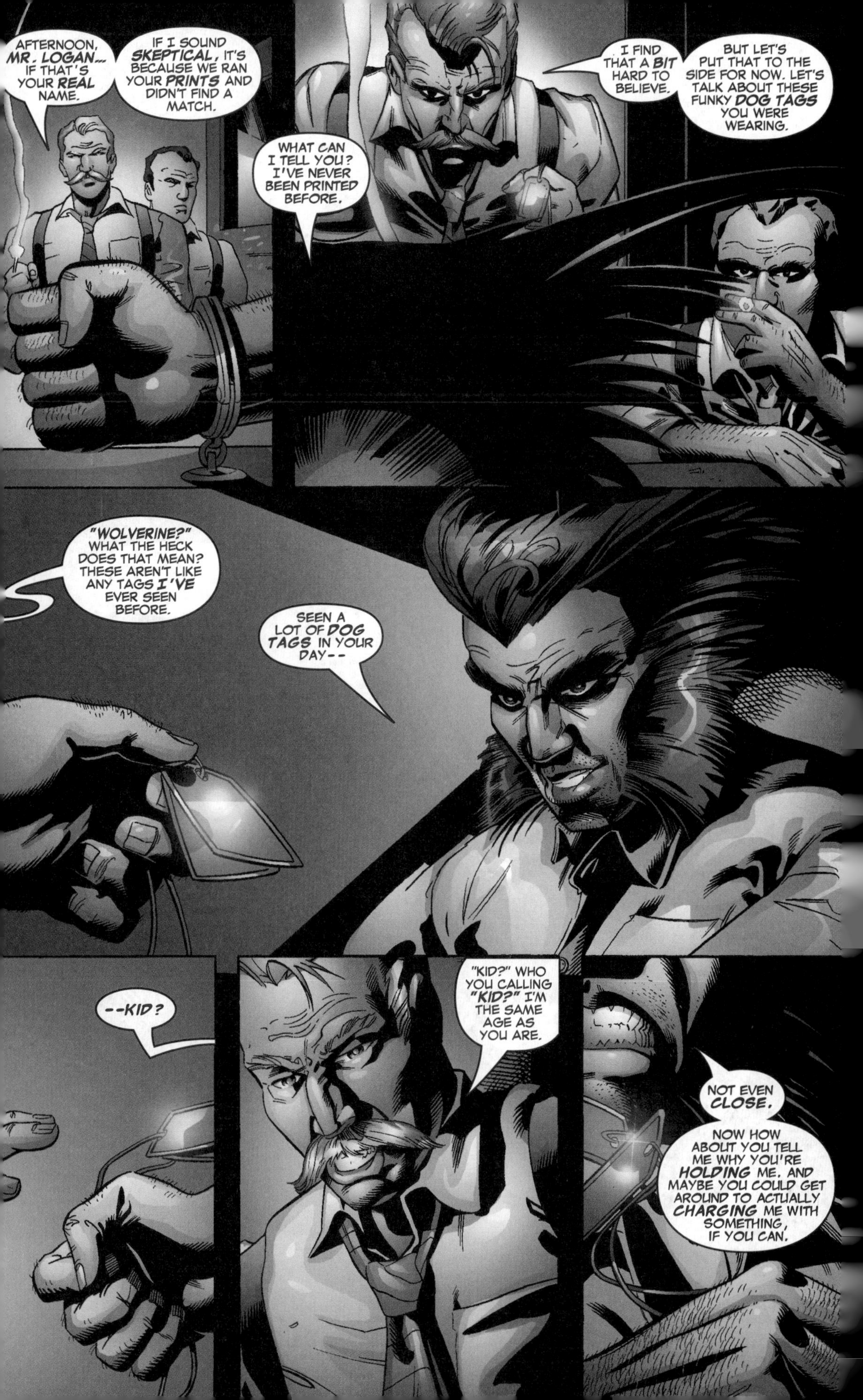

AFTERNOON, MR. LOGAN... IF THAT'S YOUR REAL NAME.
IF I SOUND SKEPTICAL, IT'S BECAUSE WE RAN YOUR PRINTS AND DIDN'T FIND A MATCH.
WHAT CAN I TELL YOU? I'VE NEVER BEEN PRINTED BEFORE.
I FIND THAT A BIT HARD TO BELIEVE.
BUT LET'S PUT THAT TO THE SIDE FOR NOW. LET'S TALK ABOUT THESE FUNKY DOG TAGS YOU WERE WEARING.
"WOLVERINE?" WHAT THE HECK DOES THAT MEAN? THESE AREN'T LIKE ANY TAGS I'VE EVER SEEN BEFORE.
SEEN A LOT OF DOG TAGS IN YOUR DAY--
--KID?
"KID?" WHO YOU CALLING "KID?" I'M THE SAME AGE AS YOU ARE.
NOT EVEN CLOSE.
NOW HOW ABOUT YOU TELL ME WHY YOU'RE HOLDING ME. AND MAYBE YOU COULD GET AROUND TO ACTUALLY CHARGING ME WITH SOMETHING, IF YOU CAN.

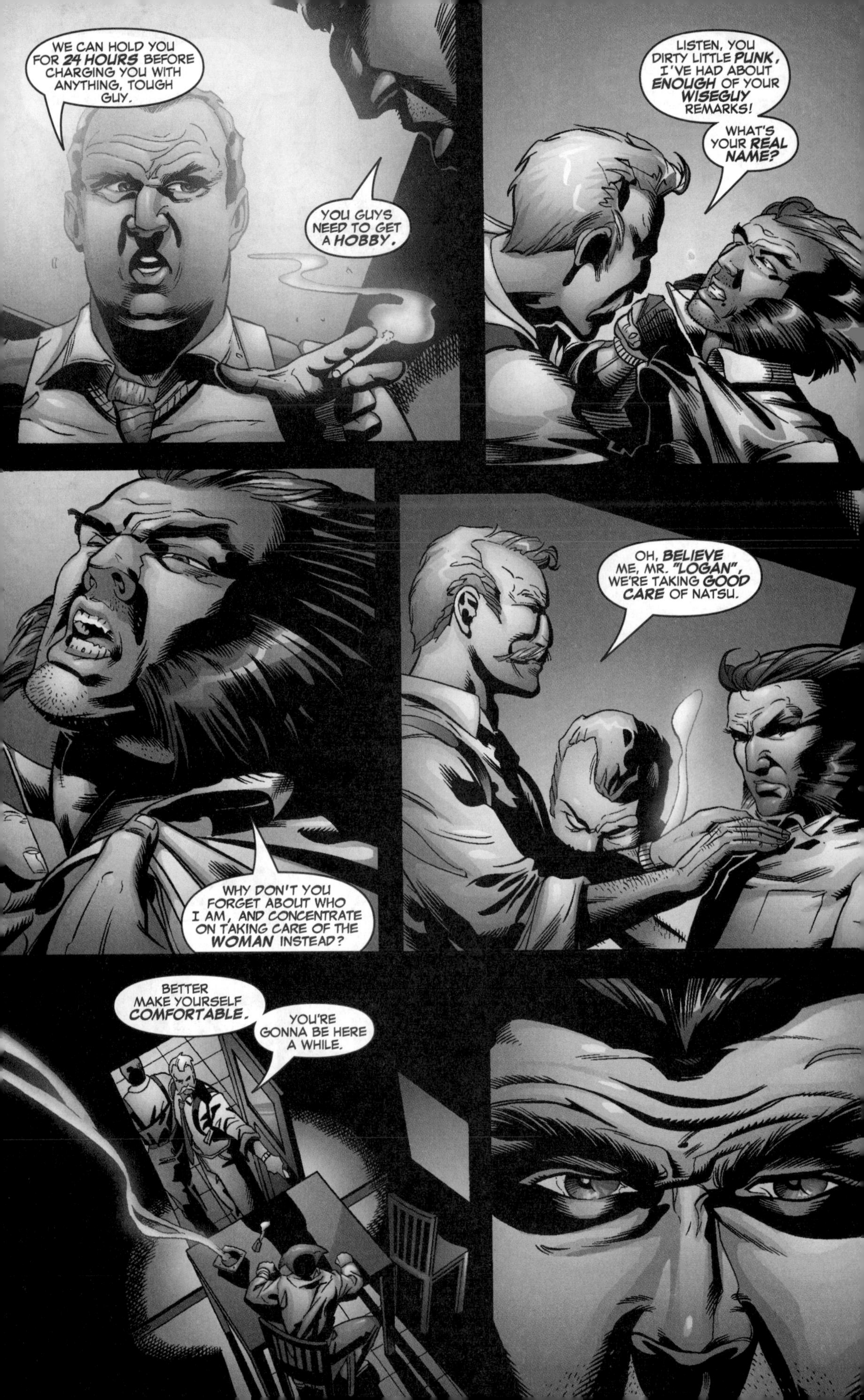
WE CAN HOLD YOU FOR 24 HOURS BEFORE CHARGING YOU WITH ANYTHING, TOUGH GUY.
YOU GUYS NEED TO GET A HOBBY.
LISTEN, YOU DIRTY LITTLE PUNK, I'VE HAD ABOUT ENOUGH OF YOUR WISEGUY REMARKS!
WHAT'S YOUR REAL NAME?
WHY DON'T YOU FORGET ABOUT WHO I AM, AND CONCENTRATE ON TAKING CARE OF THE WOMAN INSTEAD?
OH, BELIEVE ME, MR. "LOGAN", WE'RE TAKING GOOD CARE OF NATSU.
BETTER MAKE YOURSELF COMFORTABLE.
YOU'RE GONNA BE HERE A WHILE.

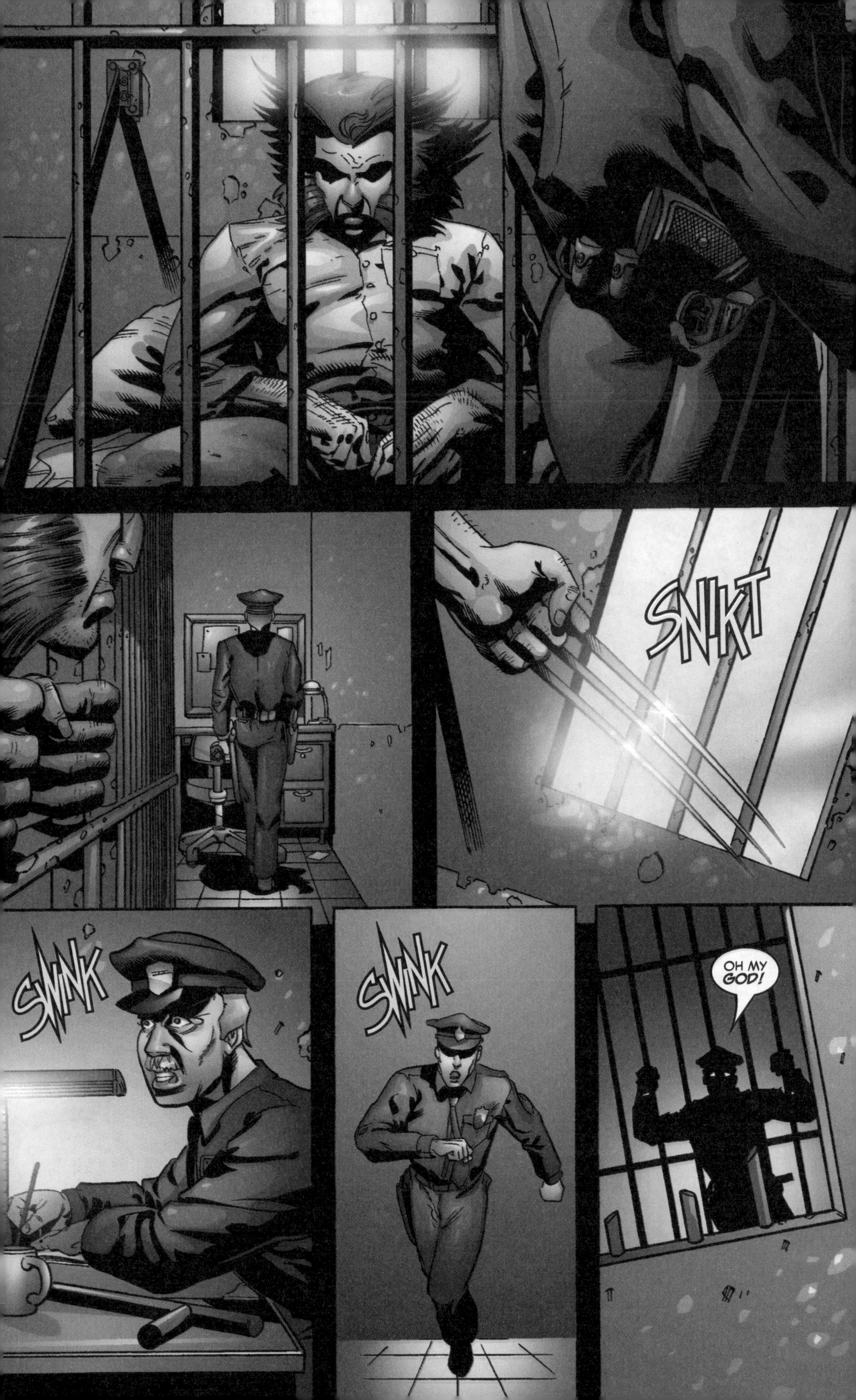
SNIKT
SWINK
SWINK
OH MY GOD!

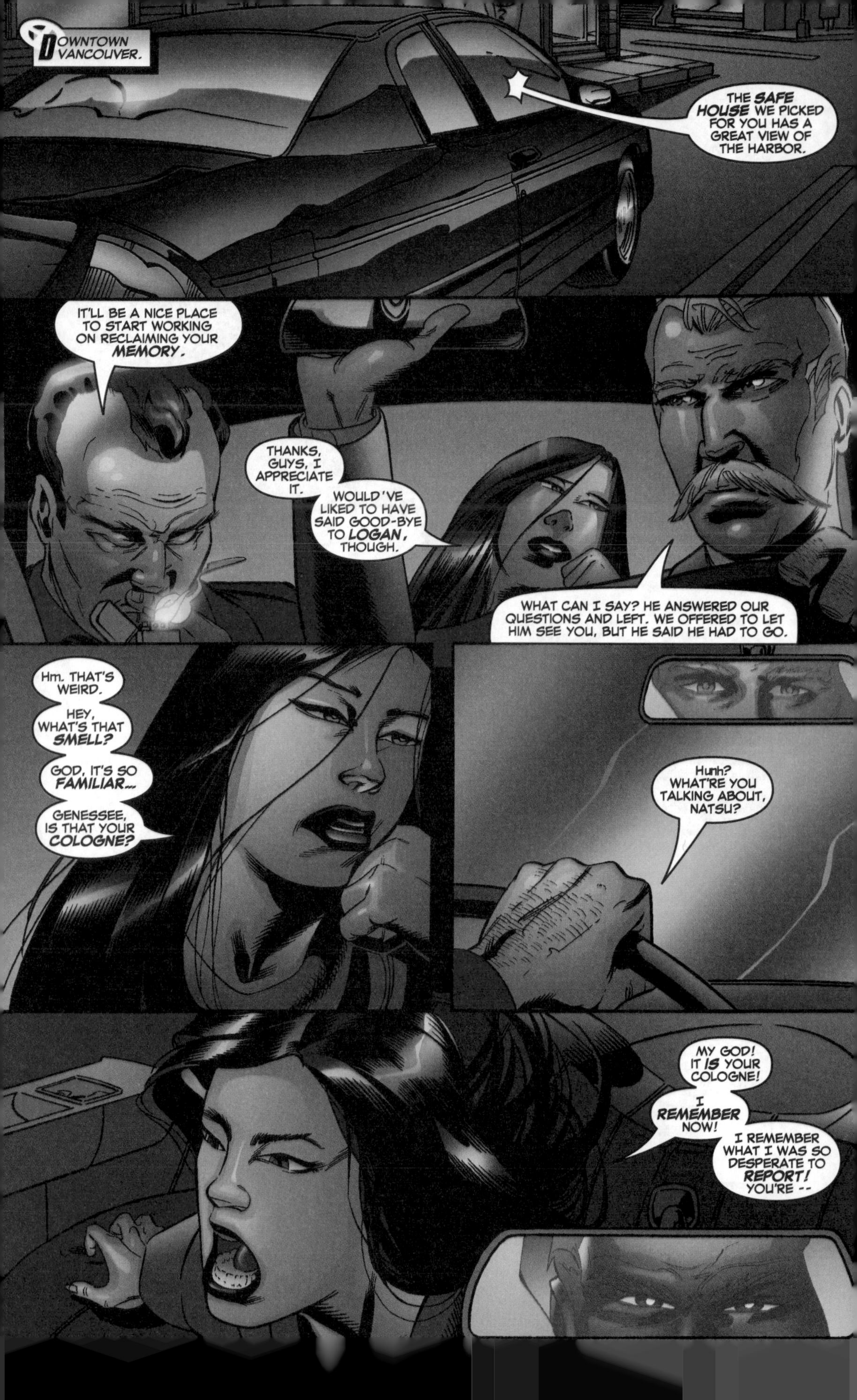
DOWNTOWN VANCOUVER.
THE SAFE HOUSE WE PICKED FOR YOU HAS A GREAT VIEW OF THE HARBOR.
IT'LL BE A NICE PLACE TO START WORKING ON RECLAIMING YOUR MEMORY.
THANKS, GUYS, I APPRECIATE IT.
WOULD'VE LIKED TO HAVE SAID GOOD-BYE TO LOGAN, THOUGH.
WHAT CAN I SAY? HE ANSWERED OUR QUESTIONS AND LEFT. WE OFFERED TO LET HIM SEE YOU, BUT HE SAID HE HAD TO GO.
Hm. THAT'S WEIRD.
HEY, WHAT'S THAT SMELL?
GOD, IT'S SO FAMILIAR...
GENESSEE, IS THAT YOUR COLOGNE?
Hunh? WHAT'RE YOU TALKING ABOUT, NATSU?
MY GOD! IT IS YOUR COLOGNE!
I REMEMBER NOW!
I REMEMBER WHAT I WAS SO DESPERATE TO REPORT! YOU'RE --

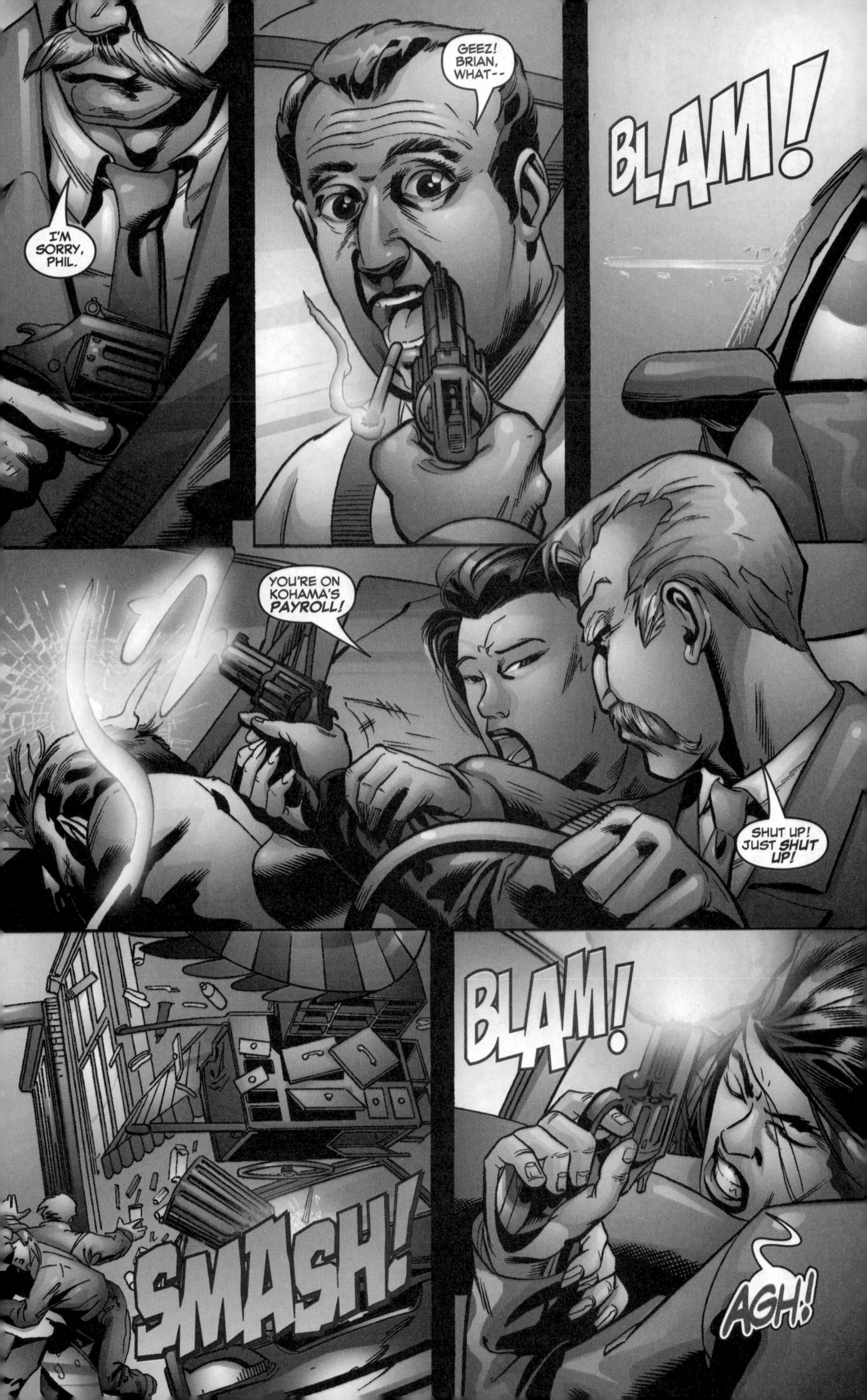
I'M SORRY, PHIL.
GEEZ! BRIAN, WHAT--
BLAM!
YOU'RE ON KOHAMA'S PAYROLL!
SHUT UP! JUST SHUT UP!
SMASH!
BLAM!
AGH!

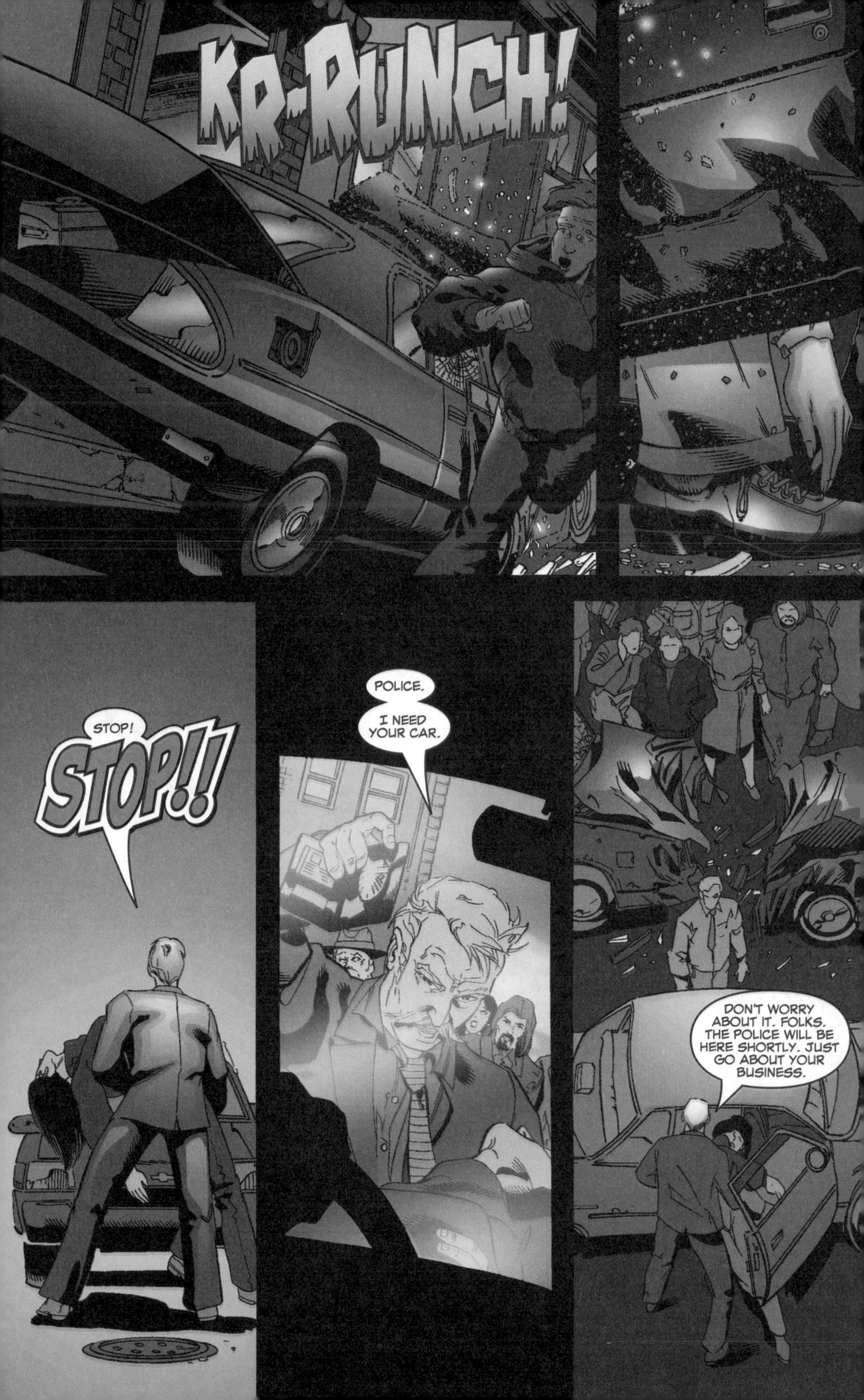
KR-RUNCH!
STOP!
STOP!!
POLICE.
I NEED YOUR CAR.
DON'T WORRY ABOUT IT, FOLKS. THE POLICE WILL BE HERE SHORTLY. JUST GO ABOUT YOUR BUSINESS.

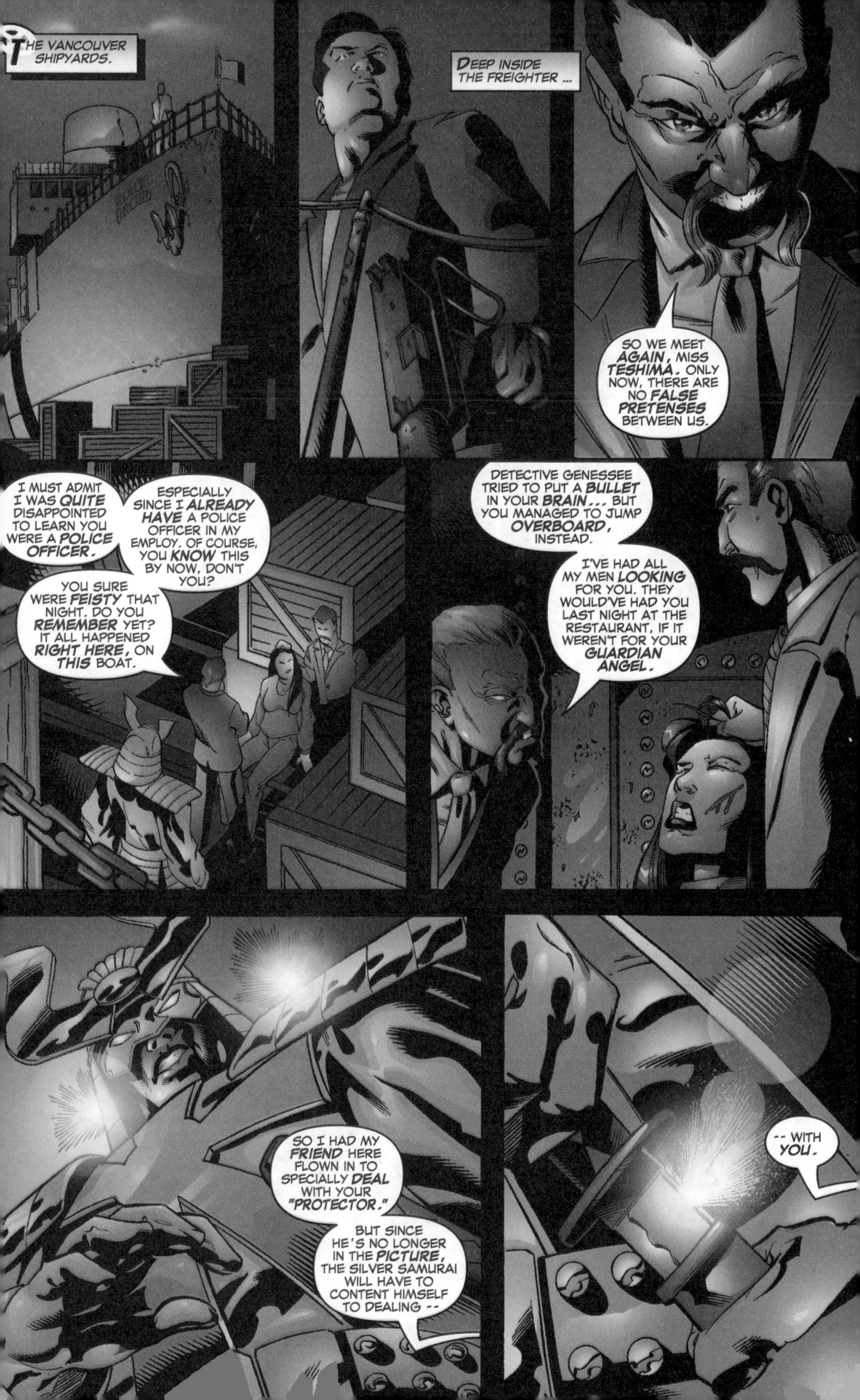
THE VANCOUVER SHIPYARDS.
DEEP INSIDE THE FREIGHTER ...
SO WE MEET AGAIN, MISS TESHIMA. ONLY NOW, THERE ARE NO FALSE PRETENSES BETWEEN US.
I MUST ADMIT I WAS QUITE DISAPPOINTED TO LEARN YOU WERE A POLICE OFFICER.
ESPECIALLY SINCE I ALREADY HAVE A POLICE OFFICER IN MY EMPLOY. OF COURSE, YOU KNOW THIS BY NOW, DON'T YOU?
YOU SURE WERE FEISTY THAT NIGHT. DO YOU REMEMBER YET? IT ALL HAPPENED RIGHT HERE, ON THIS BOAT.
DETECTIVE GENESSEE TRIED TO PUT A BULLET IN YOUR BRAIN... BUT YOU MANAGED TO JUMP OVERBOARD, INSTEAD.
I'VE HAD ALL MY MEN LOOKING FOR YOU. THEY WOULD'VE HAD YOU LAST NIGHT AT THE RESTAURANT, IF IT WEREN'T FOR YOUR GUARDIAN ANGEL.
SO I HAD MY FRIEND HERE FLOWN IN TO SPECIALLY DEAL WITH YOUR "PROTECTOR."
BUT SINCE HE'S NO LONGER IN THE PICTURE, THE SILVER SAMURAI WILL HAVE TO CONTENT HIMSELF TO DEALING --
-- WITH YOU.

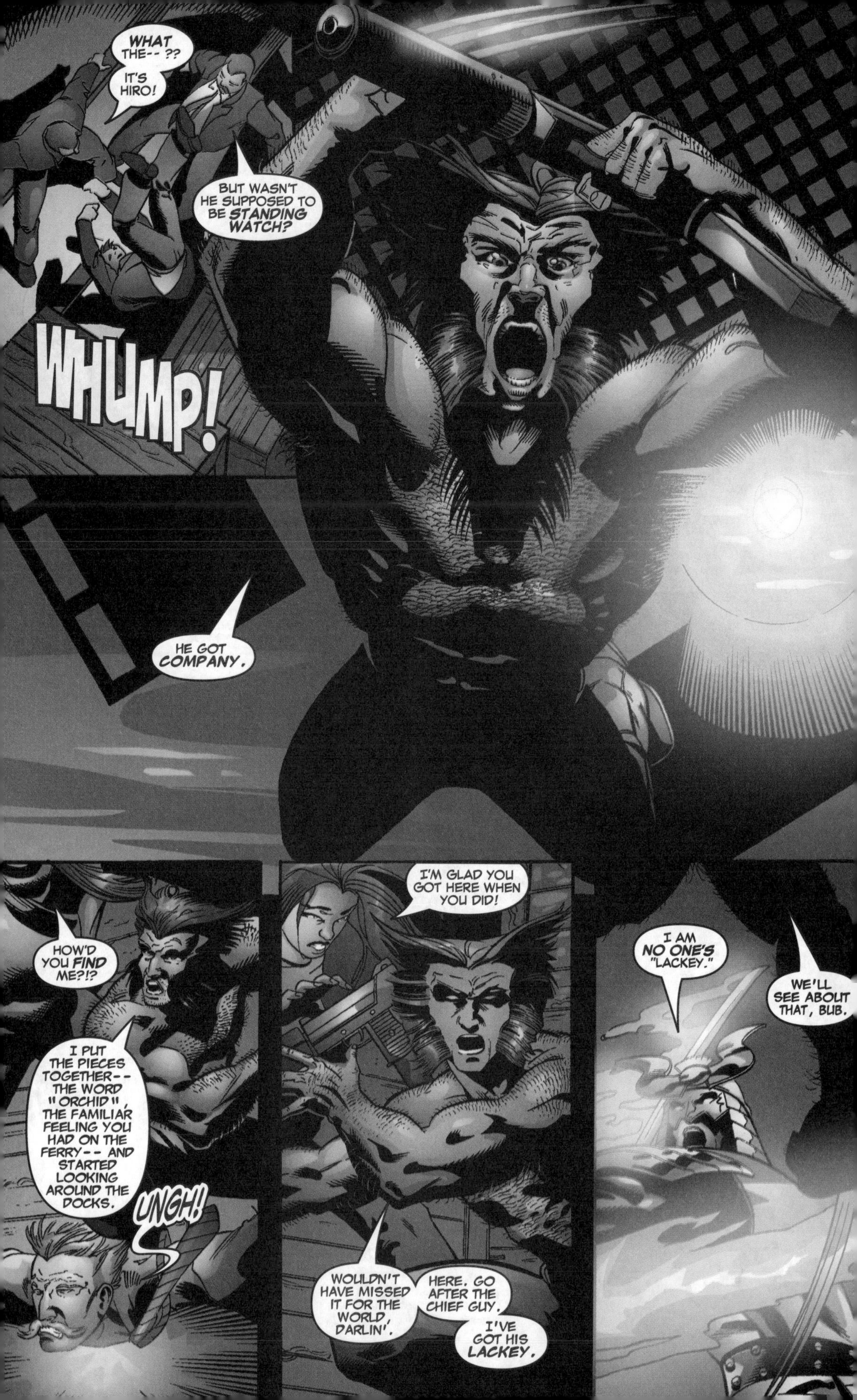
WHAT THE-- ??
IT'S HIRO!
BUT WASN'T HE SUPPOSED TO BE STANDING WATCH?
WHUMP!
HE GOT COMPANY.
HOW'D YOU FIND ME?!?
I PUT THE PIECES TOGETHER-- THE WORD "ORCHID", THE FAMILIAR FEELING YOU HAD ON THE FERRY-- AND STARTED LOOKING AROUND THE DOCKS.
UNGH!
I'M GLAD YOU GOT HERE WHEN YOU DID!
WOULDN'T HAVE MISSED IT FOR THE WORLD, DARLIN'.
HERE. GO AFTER THE CHIEF GUY.
I'VE GOT HIS LACKEY.
I AM NO ONE'S "LACKEY."
WE'LL SEE ABOUT THAT, BUB.

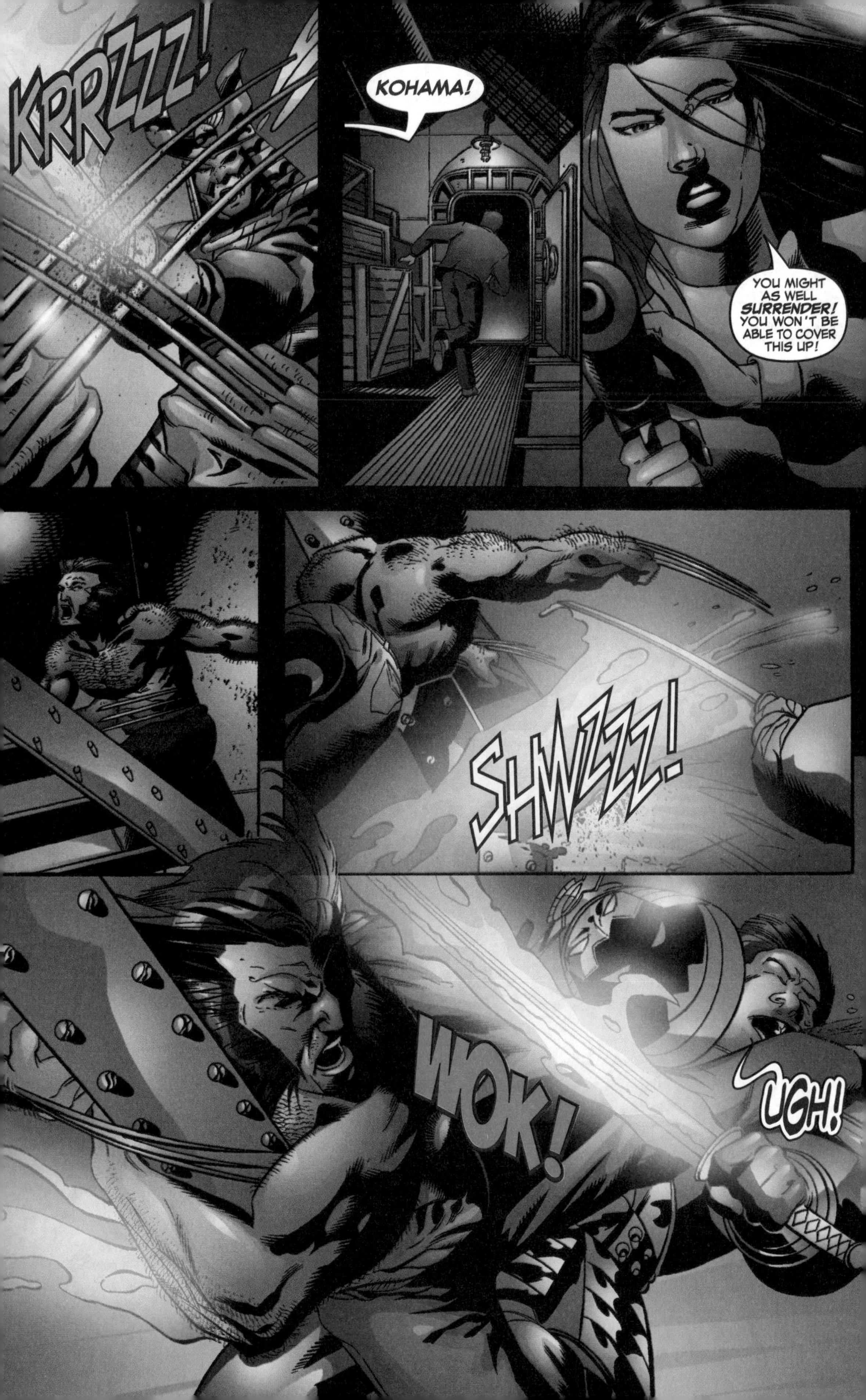
KRRZZZ!
KOHAMA!
YOU MIGHT AS WELL SURRENDER! YOU WON'T BE ABLE TO COVER THIS UP!
SHWZZZ!
WOK!
UGH!

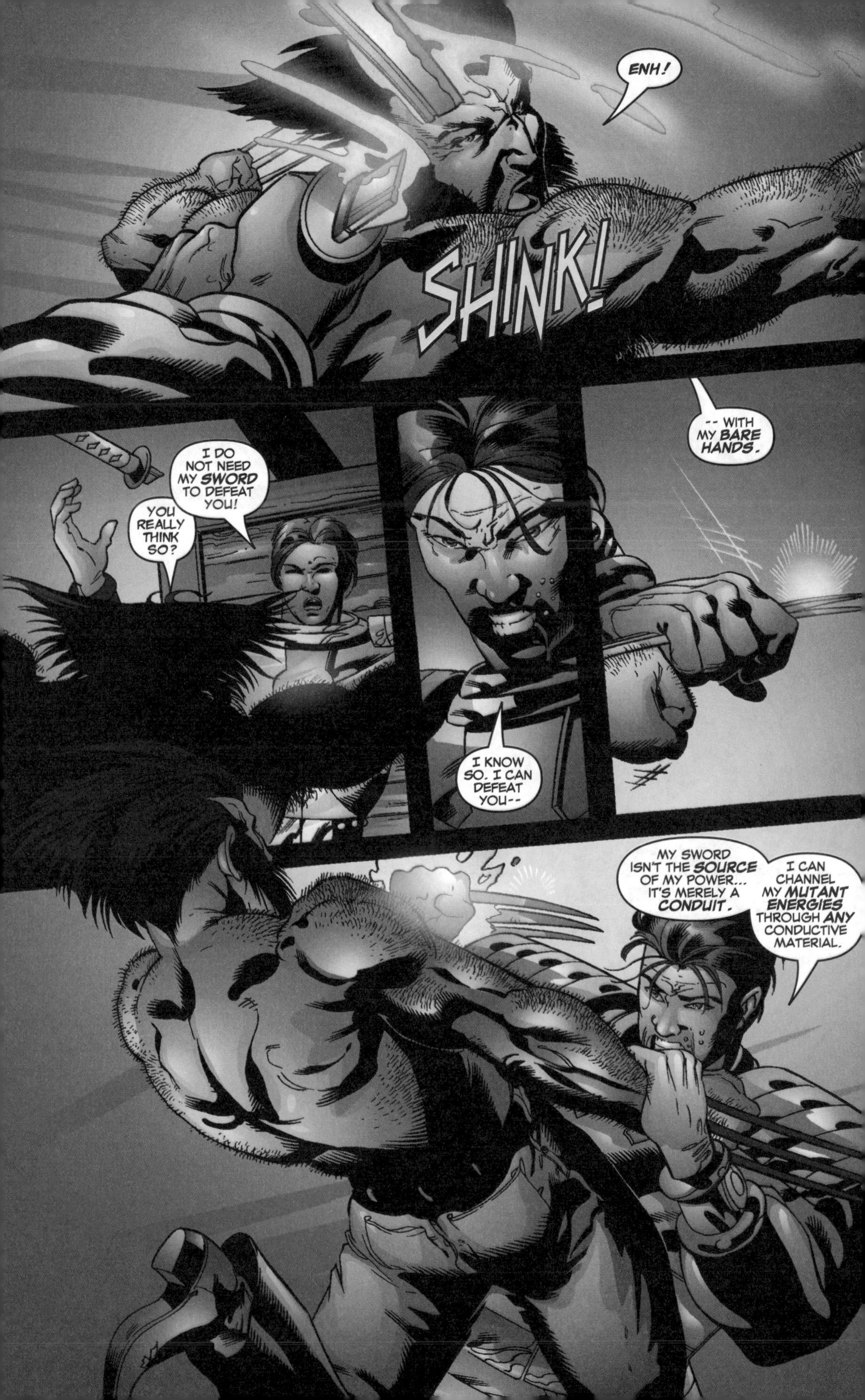
ENH!
SHINK!
I DO NOT NEED MY SWORD TO DEFEAT YOU!
YOU REALLY THINK SO?
I KNOW SO. I CAN DEFEAT YOU--
-- WITH MY BARE HANDS.
MY SWORD ISN'T THE SOURCE OF MY POWER... IT'S MERELY A CONDUIT.
I CAN CHANNEL MY MUTANT ENERGIES THROUGH ANY CONDUCTIVE MATERIAL.

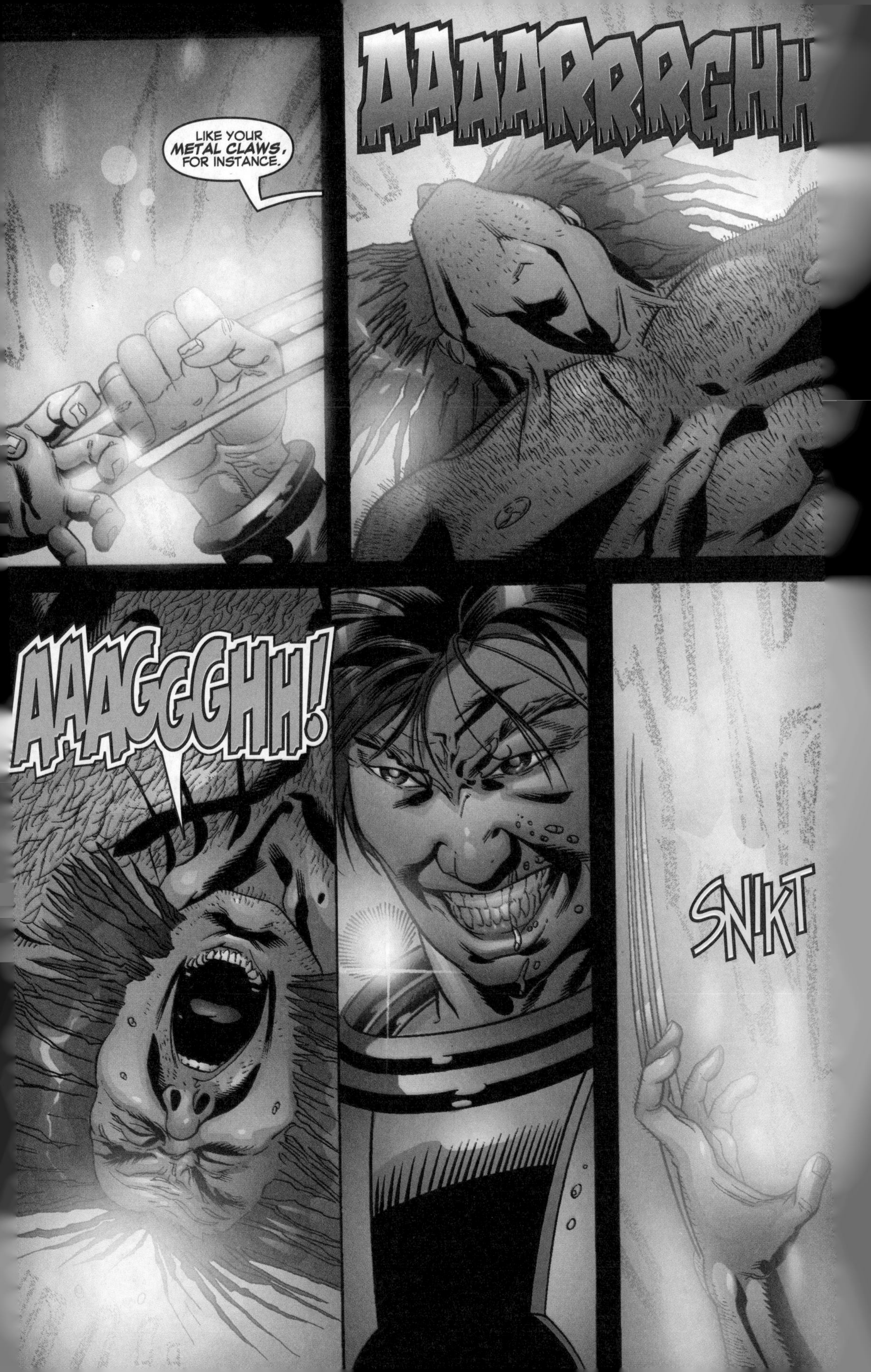

LIKE YOUR METAL CLAWS, FOR INSTANCE.
AAAARRRGHH
AAAGGGHH!
SNIKT

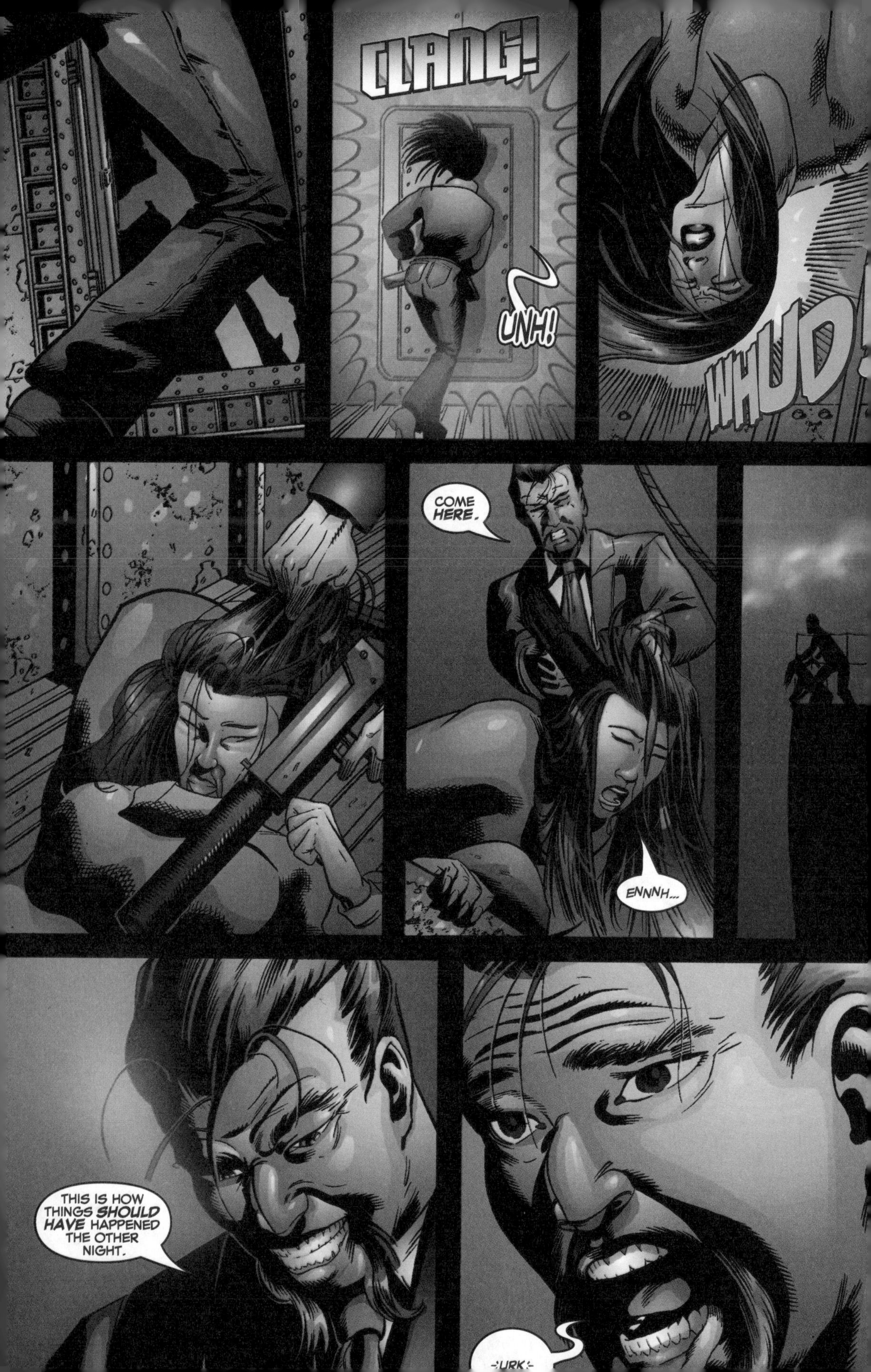
CLANG!
UNH!
WHUD!
COME HERE.
ENNNH...
THIS IS HOW THINGS SHOULD HAVE HAPPENED THE OTHER NIGHT.
-URK-

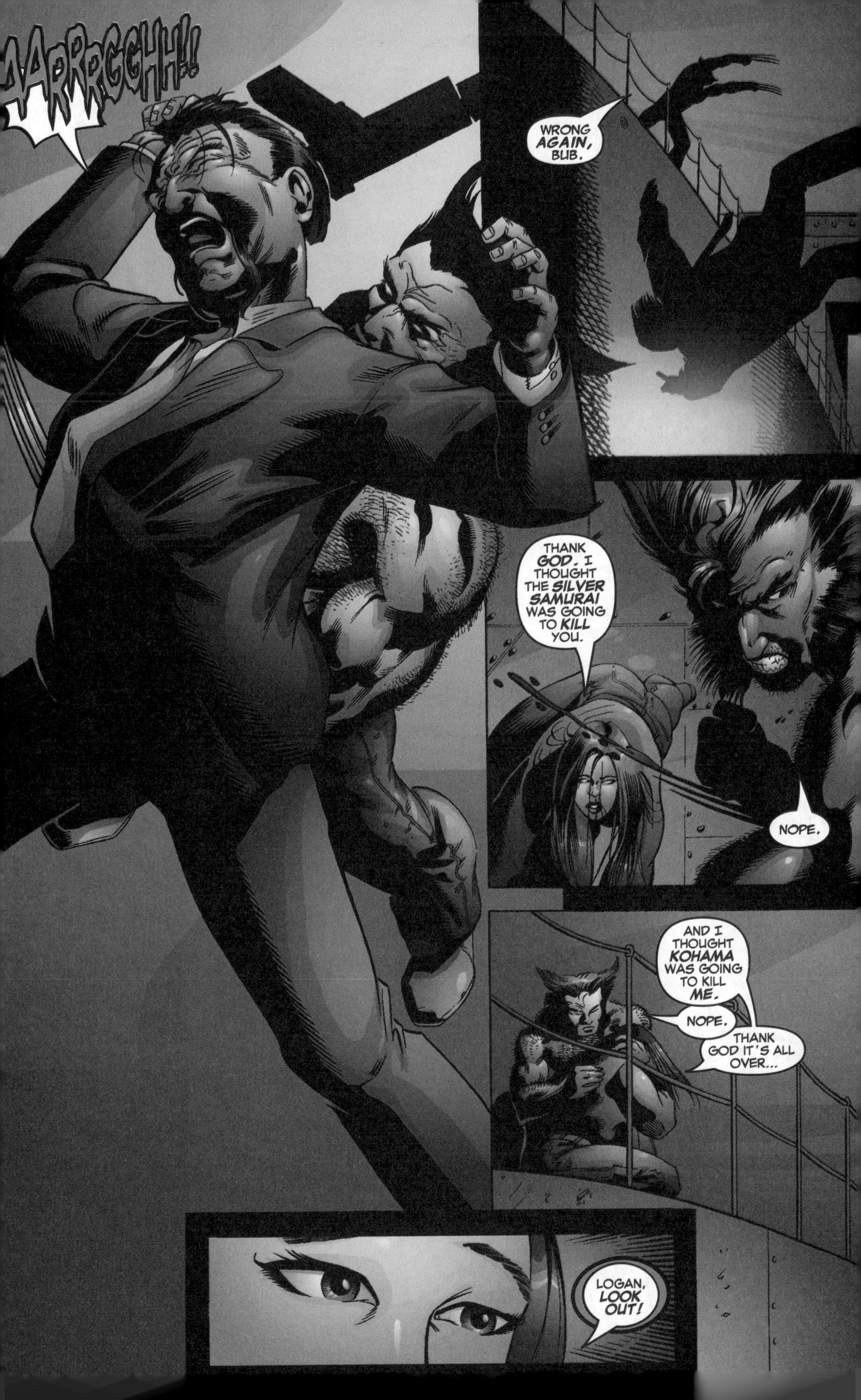
AARRRGCHH!!
WRONG AGAIN, BUB.
THANK GOD. I THOUGHT THE SILVER SAMURAI WAS GOING TO KILL YOU.
NOPE.
AND I THOUGHT KOHAMA WAS GOING TO KILL ME.
NOPE.
THANK GOD IT'S ALL OVER...
LOGAN, LOOK OUT!

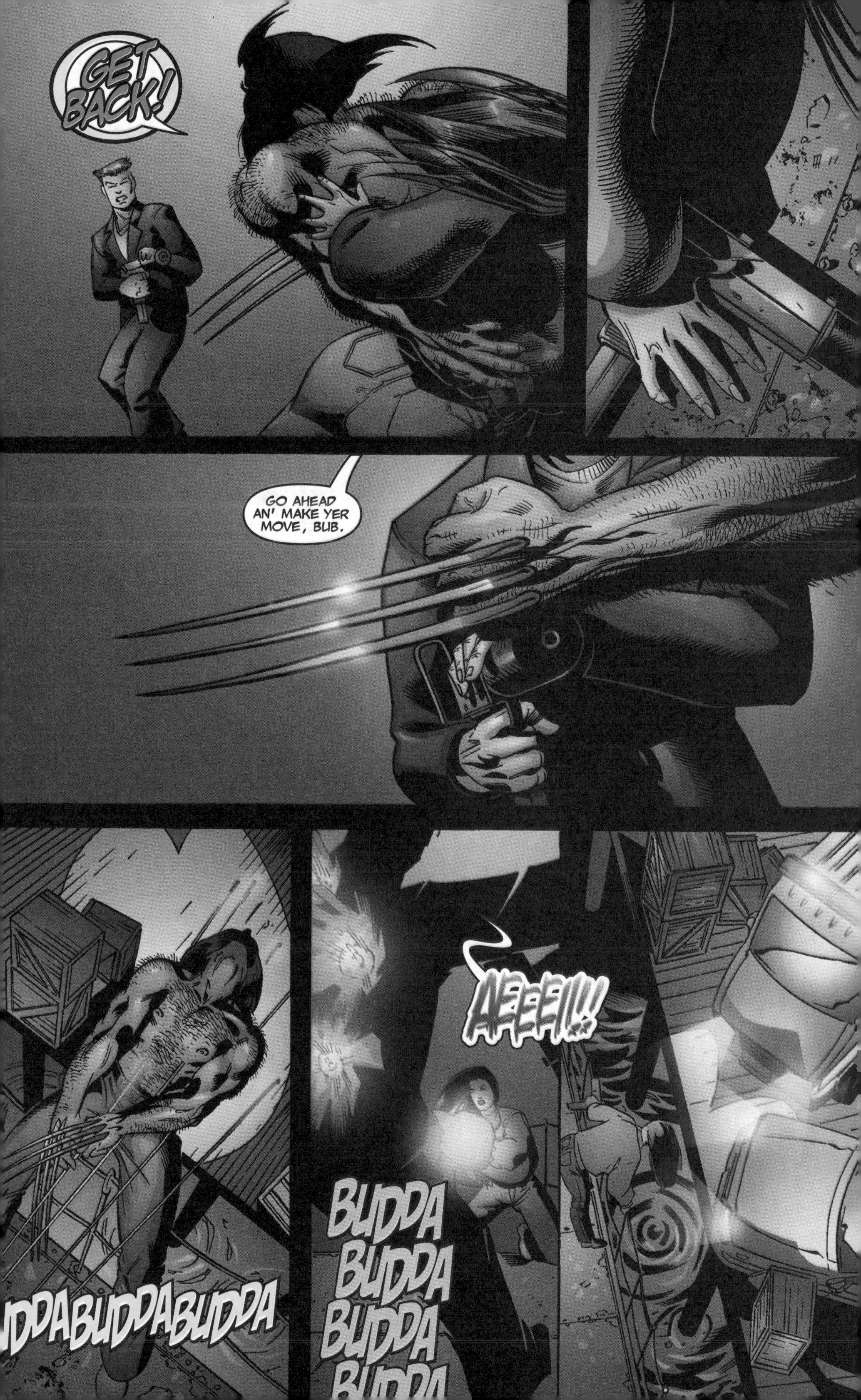
GET BACK!
GO AHEAD AN' MAKE YER MOVE, BUB.
AEEEII!!
DDABUDDABUDDA
BUDDA BUDDA BUDDA

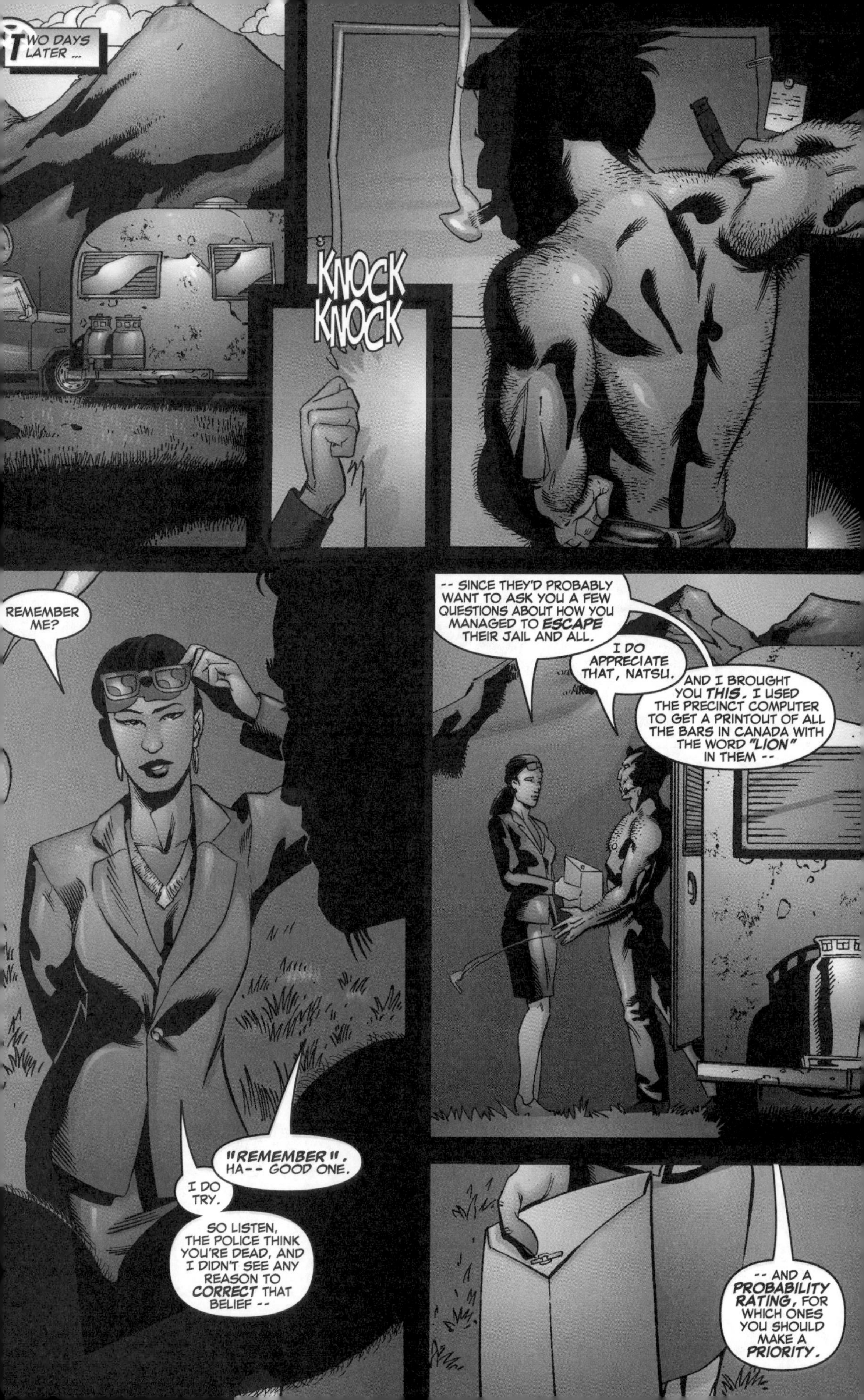
TWO DAYS LATER ...
KNOCK KNOCK
REMEMBER ME?
"REMEMBER", HA-- GOOD ONE.
I DO TRY.
SO LISTEN, THE POLICE THINK YOU'RE DEAD, AND I DIDN'T SEE ANY REASON TO CORRECT THAT BELIEF --
-- SINCE THEY'D PROBABLY WANT TO ASK YOU A FEW QUESTIONS ABOUT HOW YOU MANAGED TO ESCAPE THEIR JAIL AND ALL.
I DO APPRECIATE THAT, NATSU.
AND I BROUGHT YOU THIS. I USED THE PRECINCT COMPUTER TO GET A PRINTOUT OF ALL THE BARS IN CANADA WITH THE WORD "LION" IN THEM --
-- AND A PROBABILITY RATING, FOR WHICH ONES YOU SHOULD MAKE A PRIORITY.

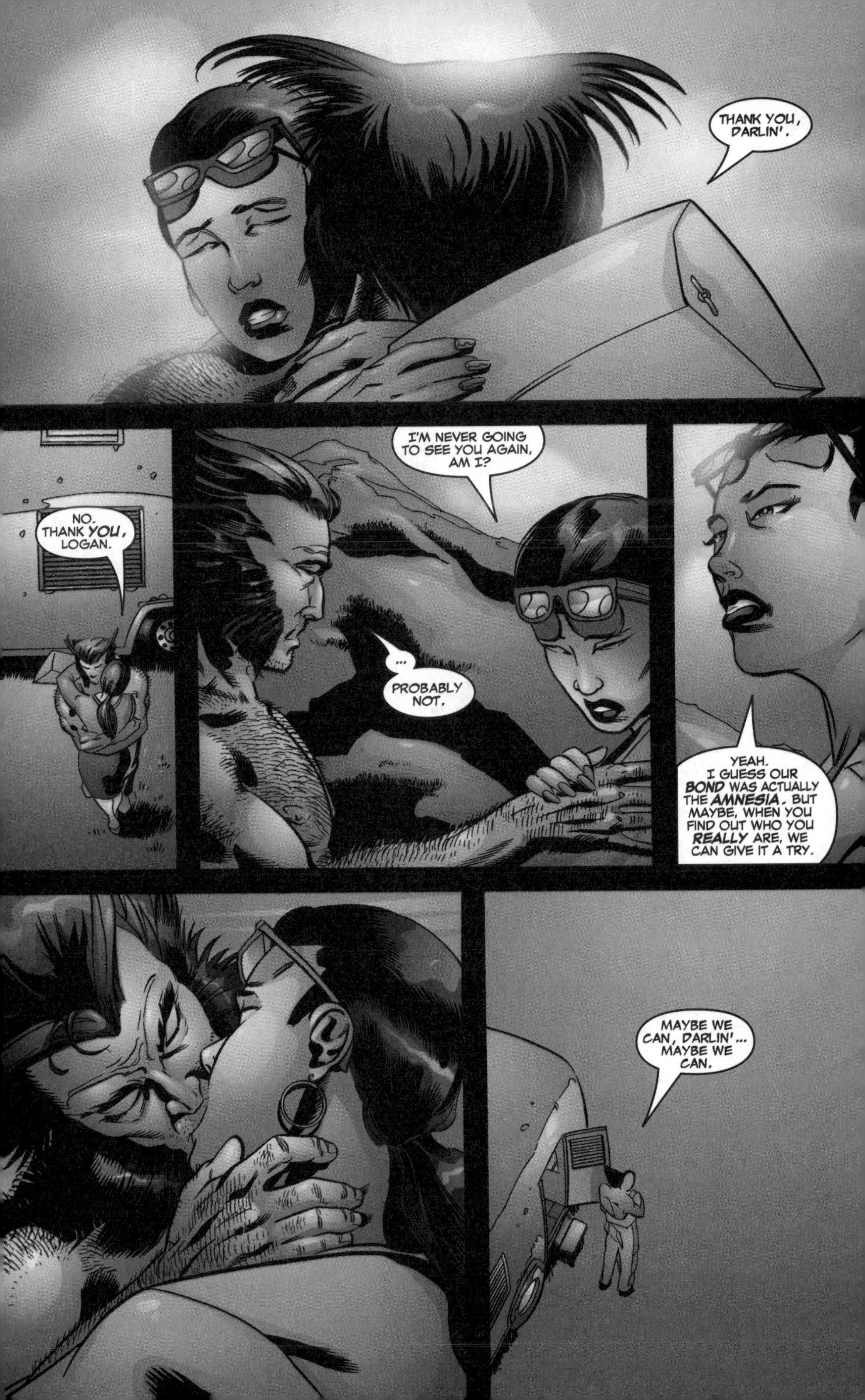
THANK YOU, DARLIN'.
NO. THANK YOU, LOGAN.
I'M NEVER GOING TO SEE YOU AGAIN, AM I?
... PROBABLY NOT.
YEAH. I GUESS OUR BOND WAS ACTUALLY THE AMNESIA. BUT MAYBE, WHEN YOU FIND OUT WHO YOU REALLY ARE, WE CAN GIVE IT A TRY.
MAYBE WE CAN, DARLIN'... MAYBE WE CAN.

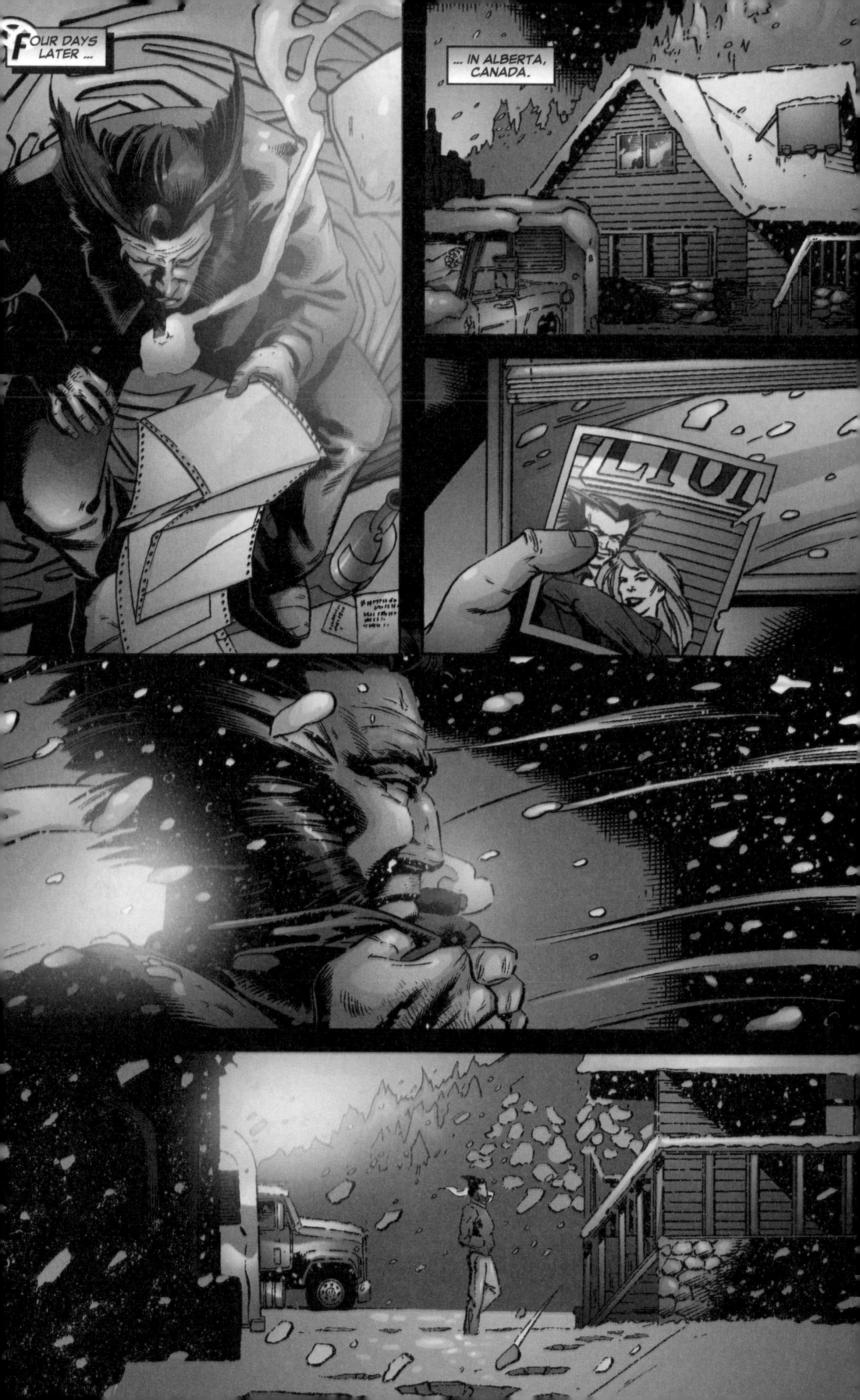
FOUR DAYS LATER ...
... IN ALBERTA, CANADA.

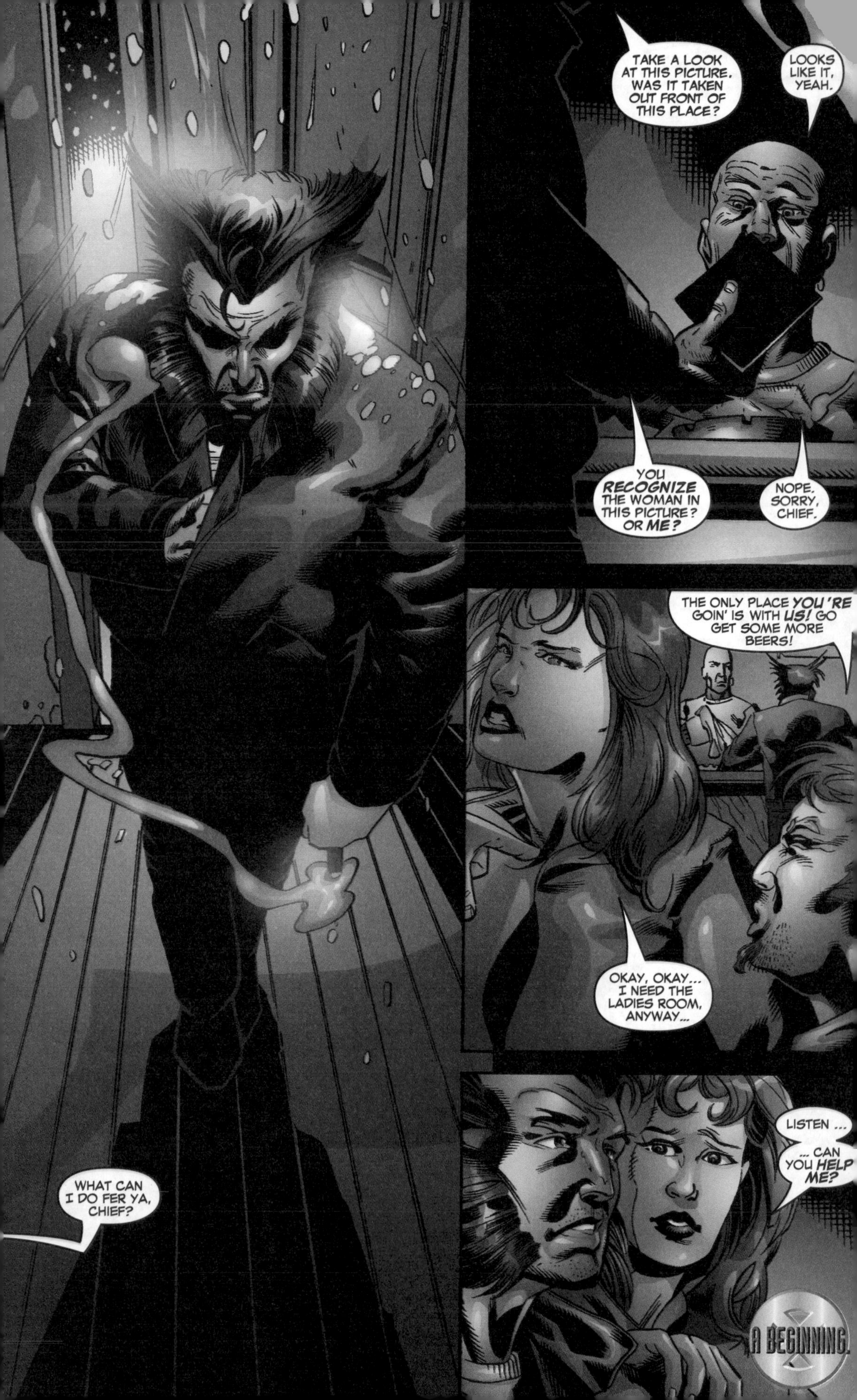
TAKE A LOOK AT THIS PICTURE. WAS IT TAKEN OUT FRONT OF THIS PLACE?
LOOKS LIKE IT, YEAH.
YOU RECOGNIZE THE WOMAN IN THIS PICTURE? OR ME?
NOPE. SORRY, CHIEF.
THE ONLY PLACE YOU'RE GOIN' IS WITH US! GO GET SOME MORE BEERS!
OKAY, OKAY... I NEED THE LADIES ROOM, ANYWAY...
WHAT CAN I DO FER YA, CHIEF?
LISTEN ...
... CAN YOU HELP ME?
A BEGINNING.

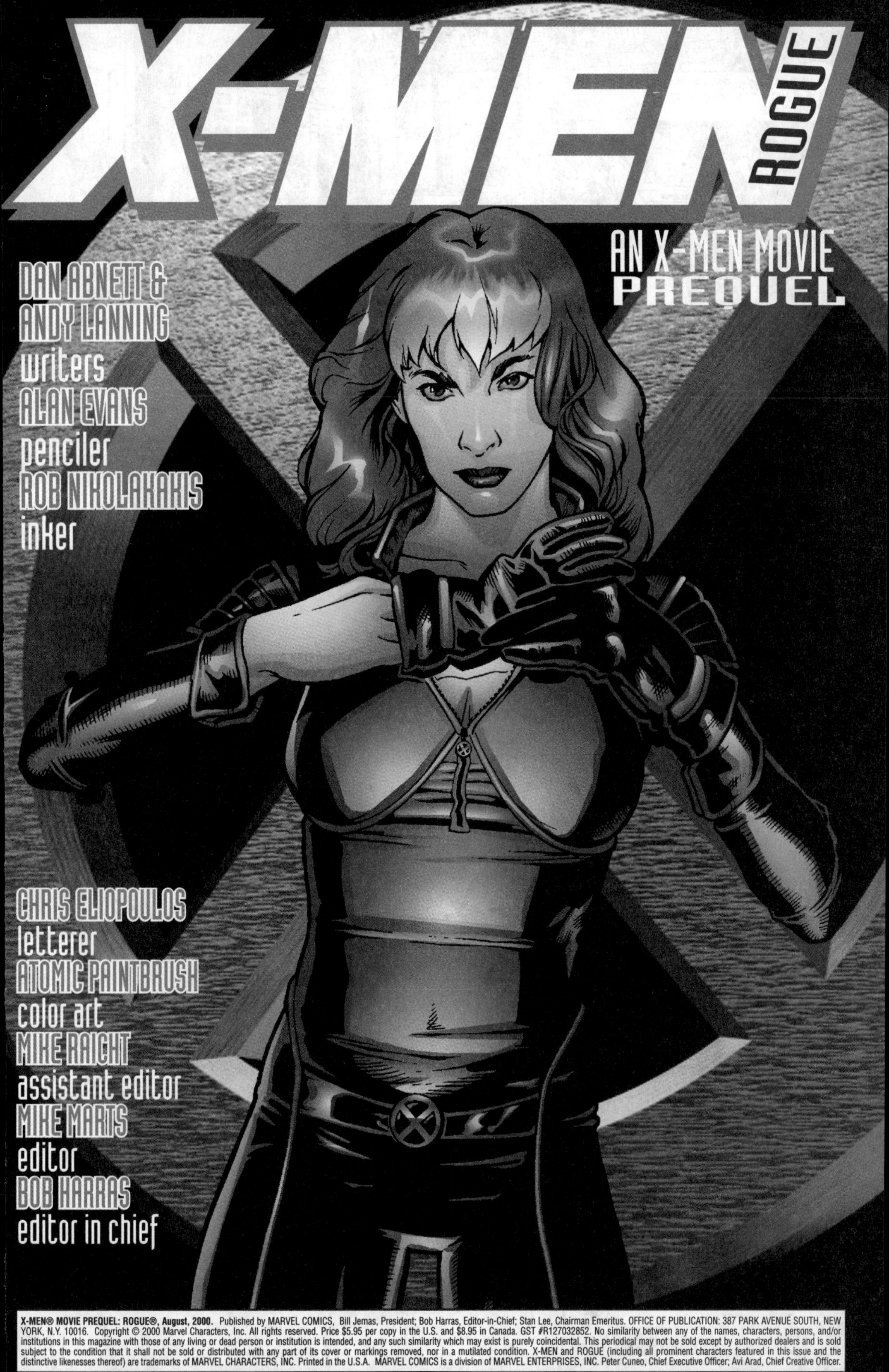
X-MEN
ROGUE
AN X-MEN MOVIE PREQUEL
DAN ABNETT & ANDY LANNING
writers
ALAN EVANS
penciler
ROB NIKOLAKAKIS
inker
CHRIS ELIOPOULOS
letterer
ATOMIC PAINTBRUSH
color art
MIKE RAICHT
assistant editor
MIKE MARTS
editor
BOB HARRAS
editor in chief

X-MEN® MOVIE PREQUEL: ROGUE®, August, 2000. Published by MARVEL COMICS, Bill Jemas, President; Bob Harras, Editor-in-Chief; Stan Lee, Chairman Emeritus. OFFICE OF PUBLICATION: 387 PARK AVENUE SOUTH, NEW YORK, N.Y. 10016.

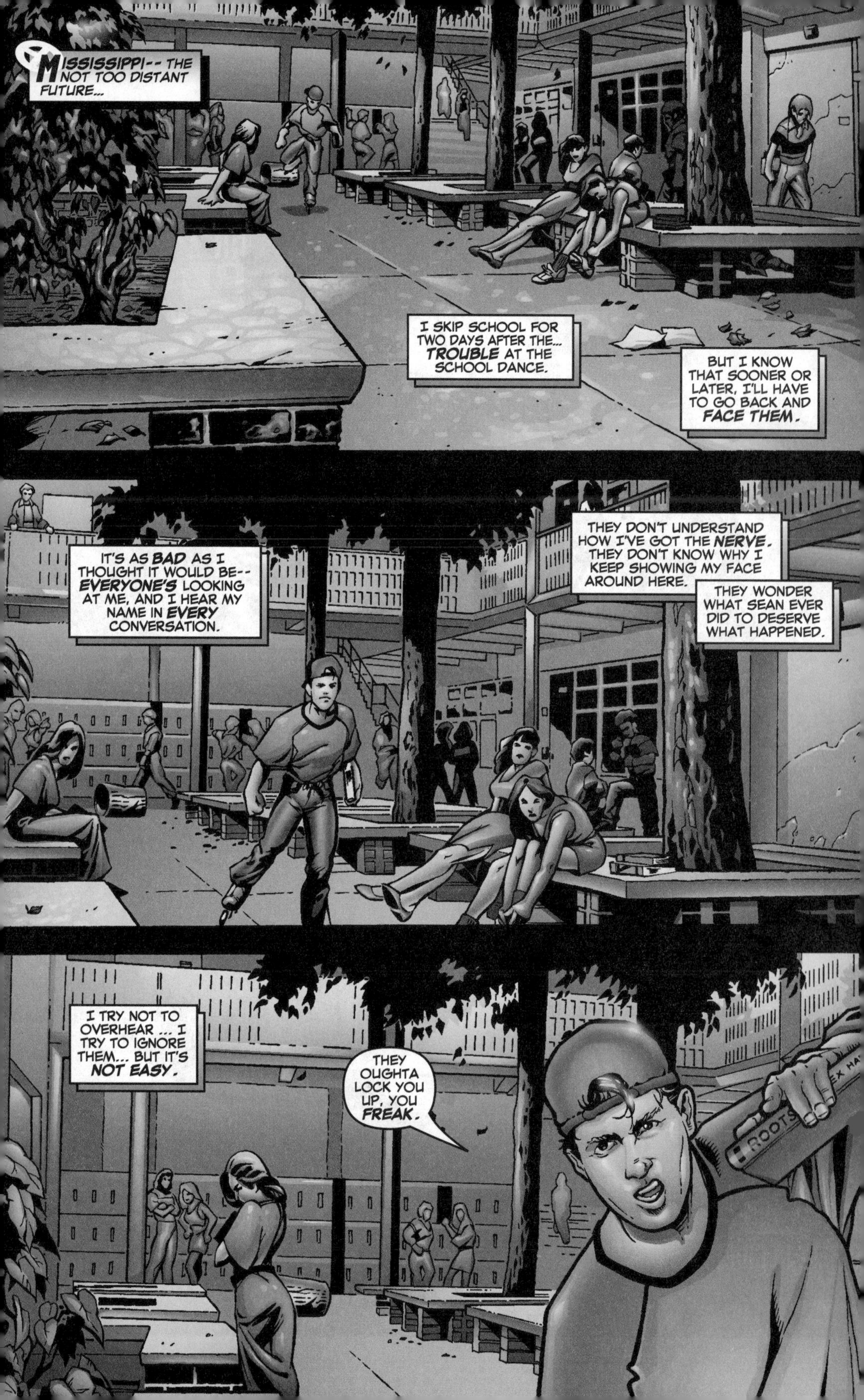
MISSISSIPPI-- THE NOT TOO DISTANT FUTURE...
I SKIP SCHOOL FOR TWO DAYS AFTER THE... TROUBLE AT THE SCHOOL DANCE.
BUT I KNOW THAT SOONER OR LATER, I'LL HAVE TO GO BACK AND FACE THEM.
IT'S AS BAD AS I THOUGHT IT WOULD BE-- EVERYONE'S LOOKING AT ME, AND I HEAR MY NAME IN EVERY CONVERSATION.
THEY DON'T UNDERSTAND HOW I'VE GOT THE NERVE. THEY DON'T KNOW WHY I KEEP SHOWING MY FACE AROUND HERE.
THEY WONDER WHAT SEAN EVER DID TO DESERVE WHAT HAPPENED.
I TRY NOT TO OVERHEAR ... I TRY TO IGNORE THEM... BUT IT'S NOT EASY.
THEY OUGHTA LOCK YOU UP, YOU FREAK.
ROOTS

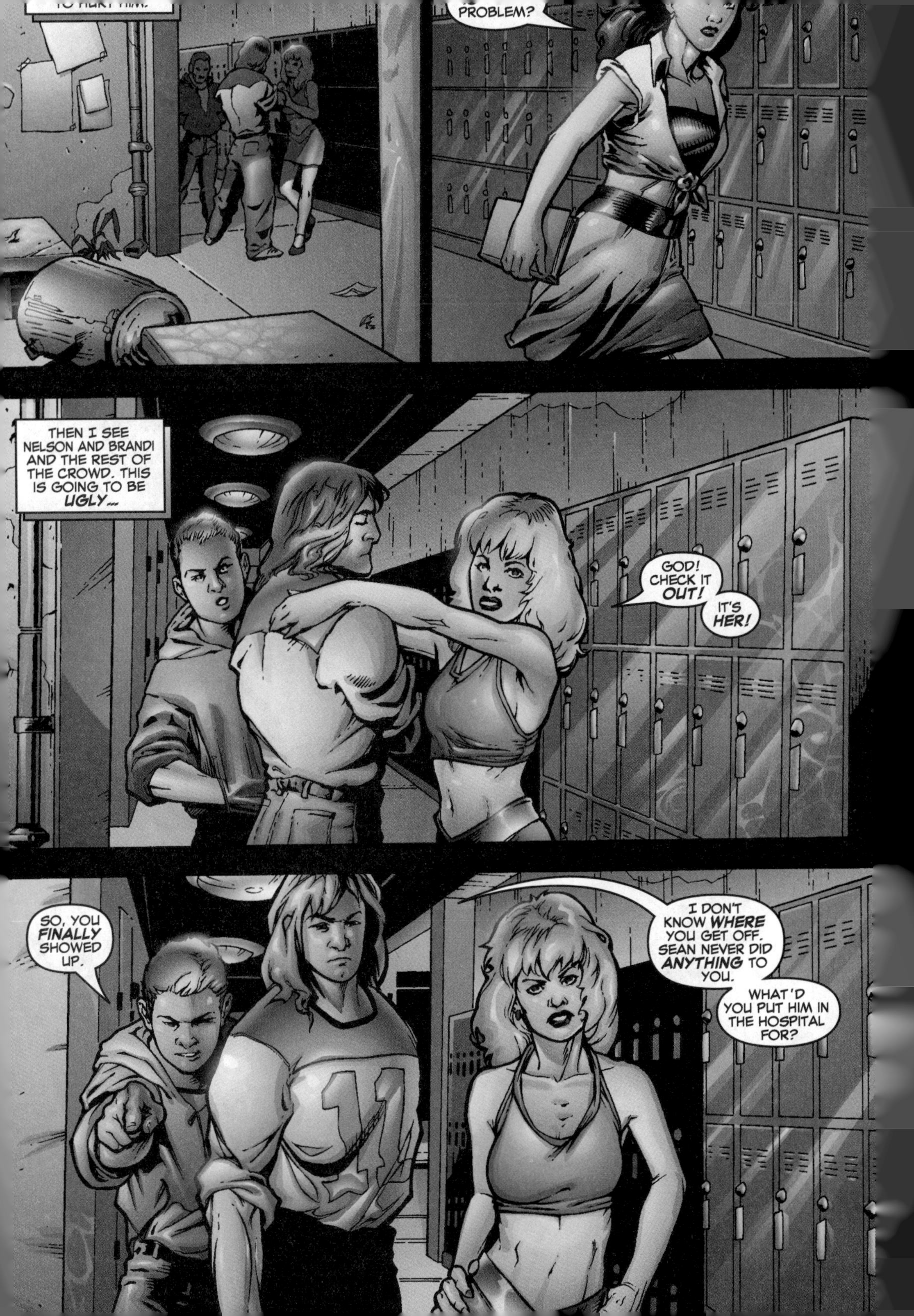
PROBLEM?
THEN I SEE NELSON AND BRANDI AND THE REST OF THE CROWD. THIS IS GOING TO BE *UGLY...*
GOD! CHECK IT *OUT!*
IT'S *HER!*
SO, YOU *FINALLY* SHOWED UP.
I DON'T KNOW *WHERE* YOU GET OFF. SEAN NEVER DID *ANYTHING* TO YOU.
WHAT'D YOU PUT HIM IN THE HOSPITAL FOR?

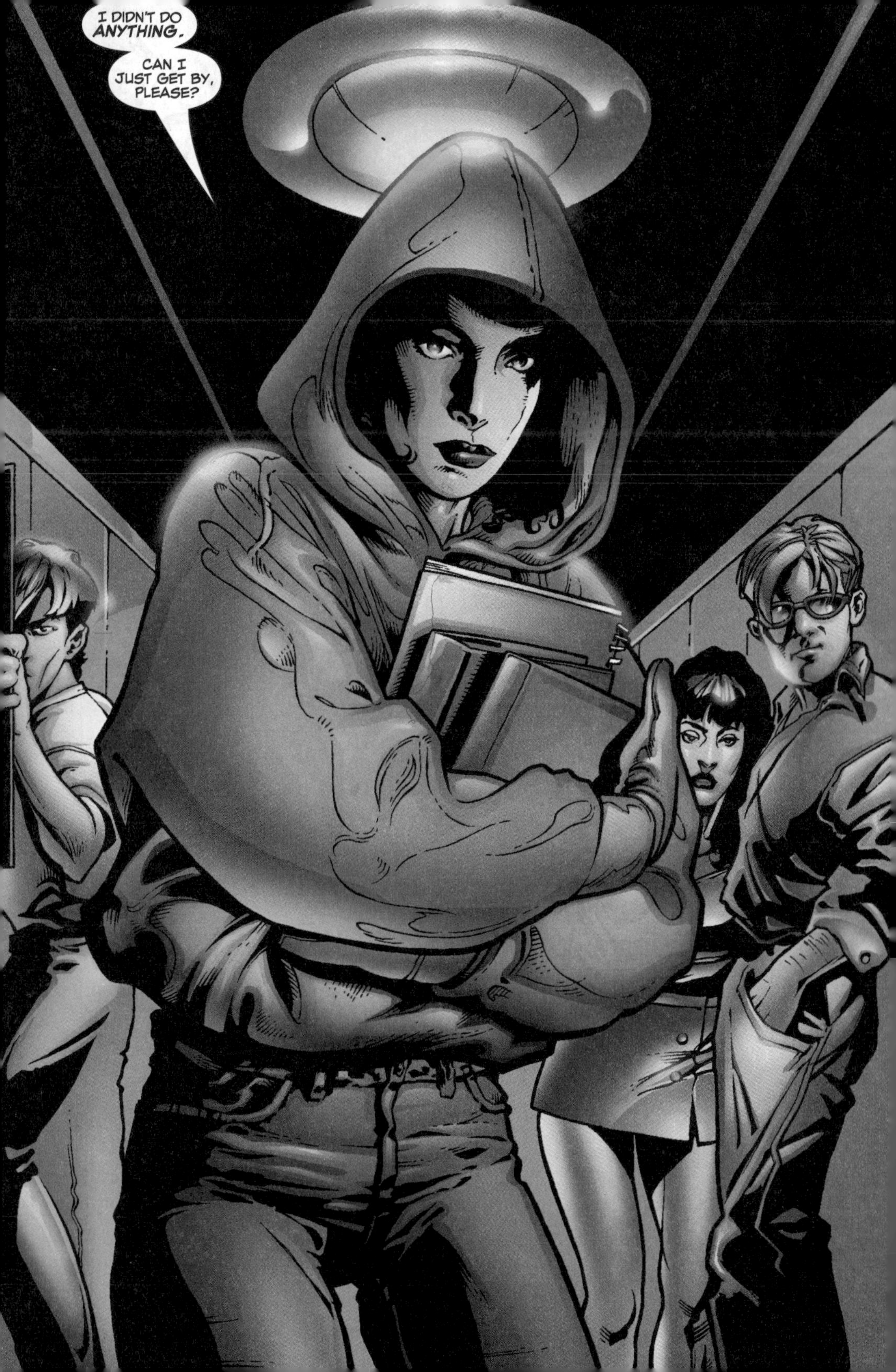
I DIDN'T DO ANYTHING.
CAN I JUST GET BY, PLEASE?

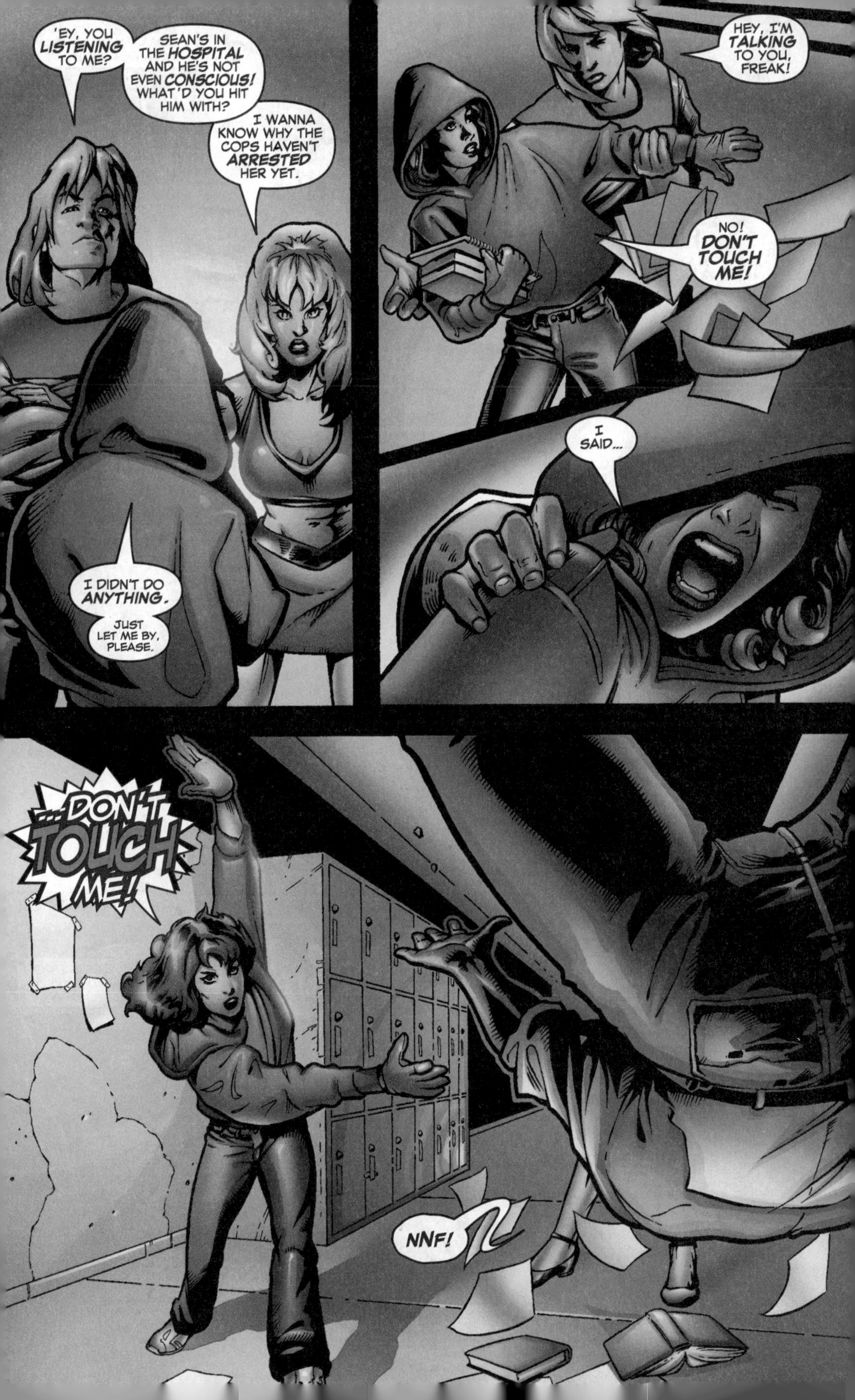
'EY, YOU LISTENING TO ME?
SEAN'S IN THE HOSPITAL AND HE'S NOT EVEN CONSCIOUS! WHAT'D YOU HIT HIM WITH?
I WANNA KNOW WHY THE COPS HAVEN'T ARRESTED HER YET.
I DIDN'T DO ANYTHING.
JUST LET ME BY, PLEASE.
HEY, I'M TALKING TO YOU, FREAK!
NO! DON'T TOUCH ME!
I SAID...
...DON'T TOUCH ME!
NNF!

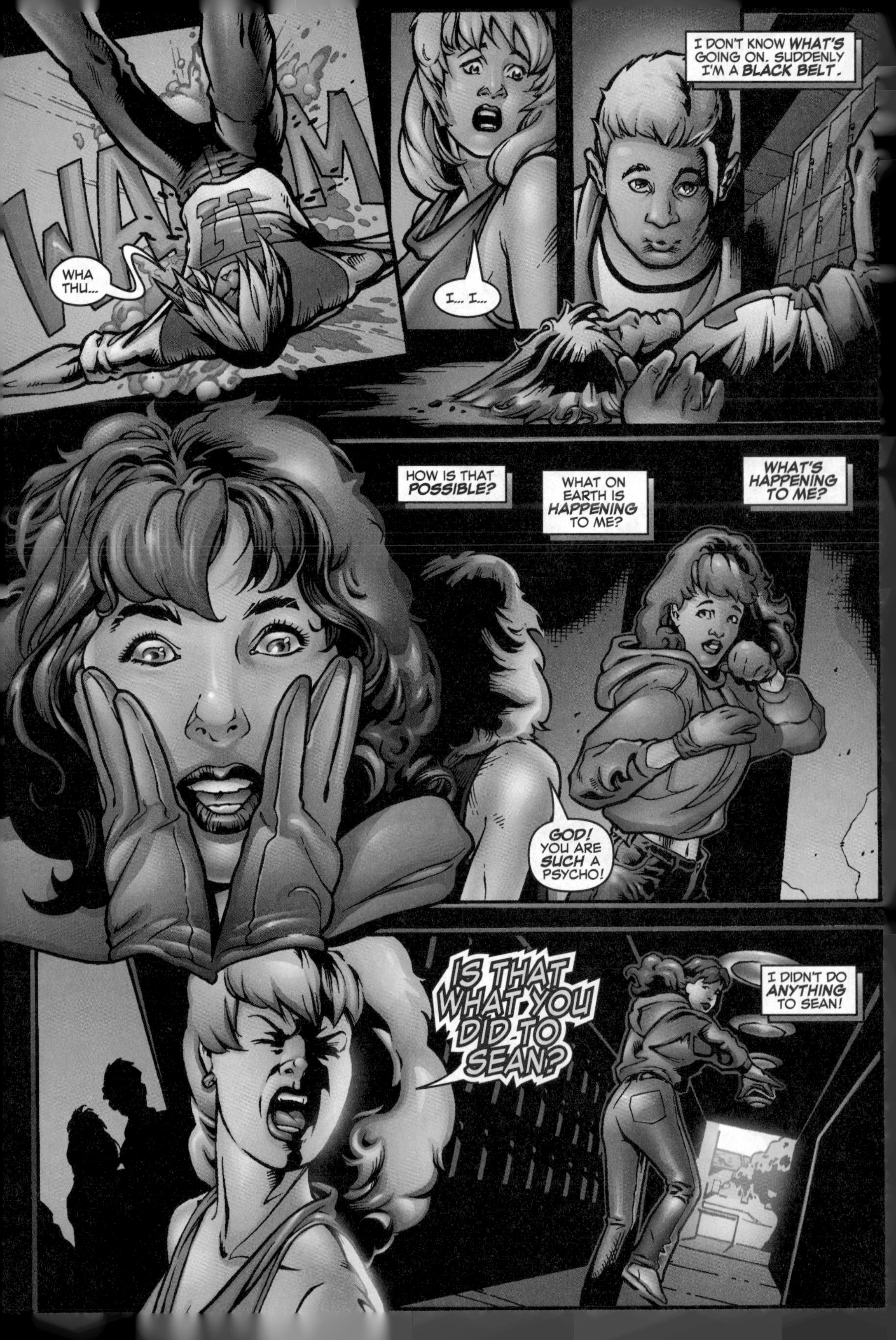
WHAM
WHA THU...
I... I...
I DON'T KNOW WHAT'S GOING ON. SUDDENLY I'M A BLACK BELT.
HOW IS THAT POSSIBLE?
WHAT ON EARTH IS HAPPENING TO ME?
WHAT'S HAPPENING TO ME?
GOD! YOU ARE SUCH A PSYCHO!
IS THAT WHAT YOU DID TO SEAN?
I DIDN'T DO ANYTHING TO SEAN!

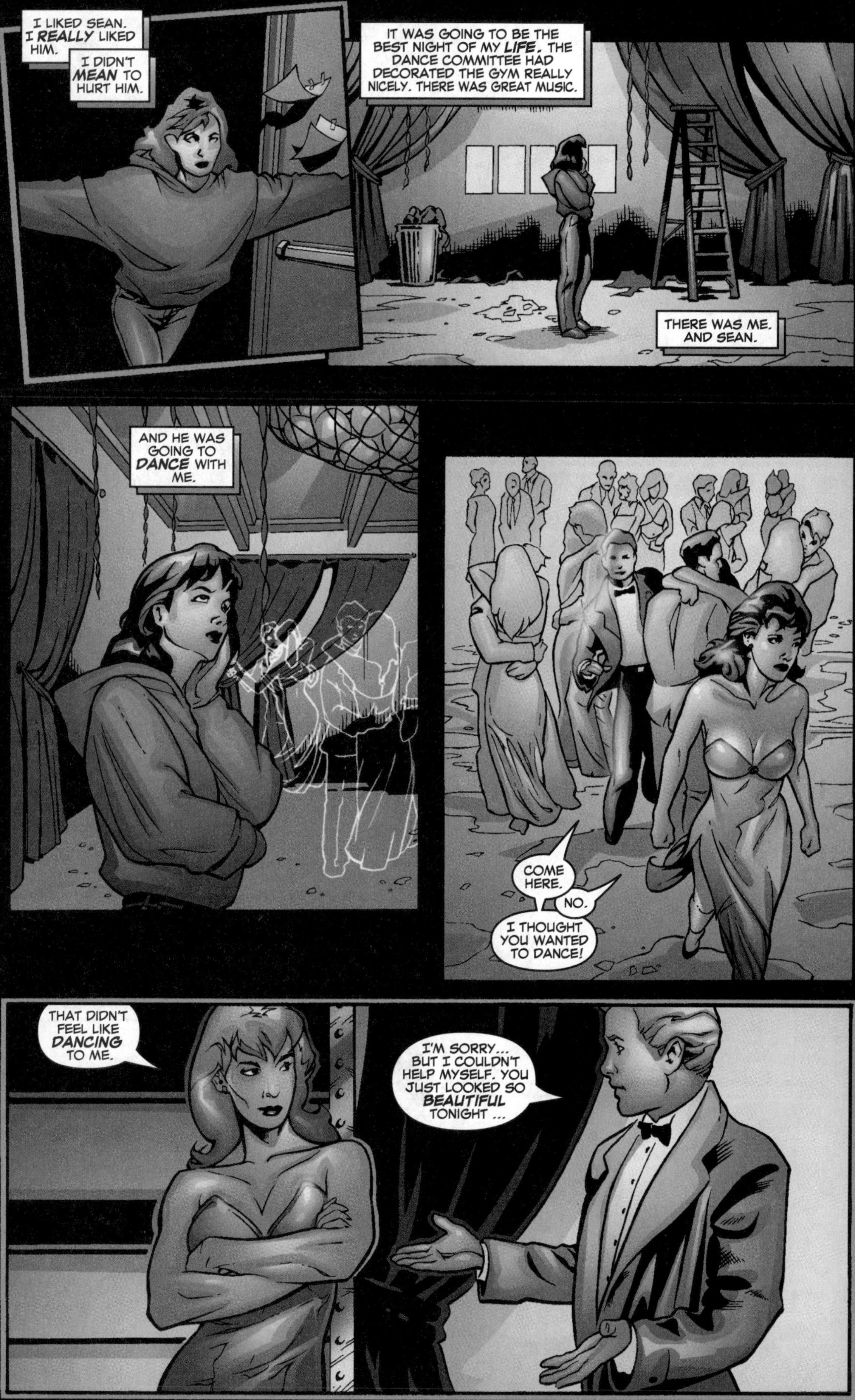
I LIKED SEAN. I REALLY LIKED HIM.
I DIDN'T MEAN TO HURT HIM.
IT WAS GOING TO BE THE BEST NIGHT OF MY LIFE. THE DANCE COMMITTEE HAD DECORATED THE GYM REALLY NICELY. THERE WAS GREAT MUSIC.
THERE WAS ME. AND SEAN.
AND HE WAS GOING TO DANCE WITH ME.
COME HERE.
NO.
I THOUGHT YOU WANTED TO DANCE!
THAT DIDN'T FEEL LIKE DANCING TO ME.
I'M SORRY... BUT I COULDN'T HELP MYSELF. YOU JUST LOOKED SO BEAUTIFUL TONIGHT ...

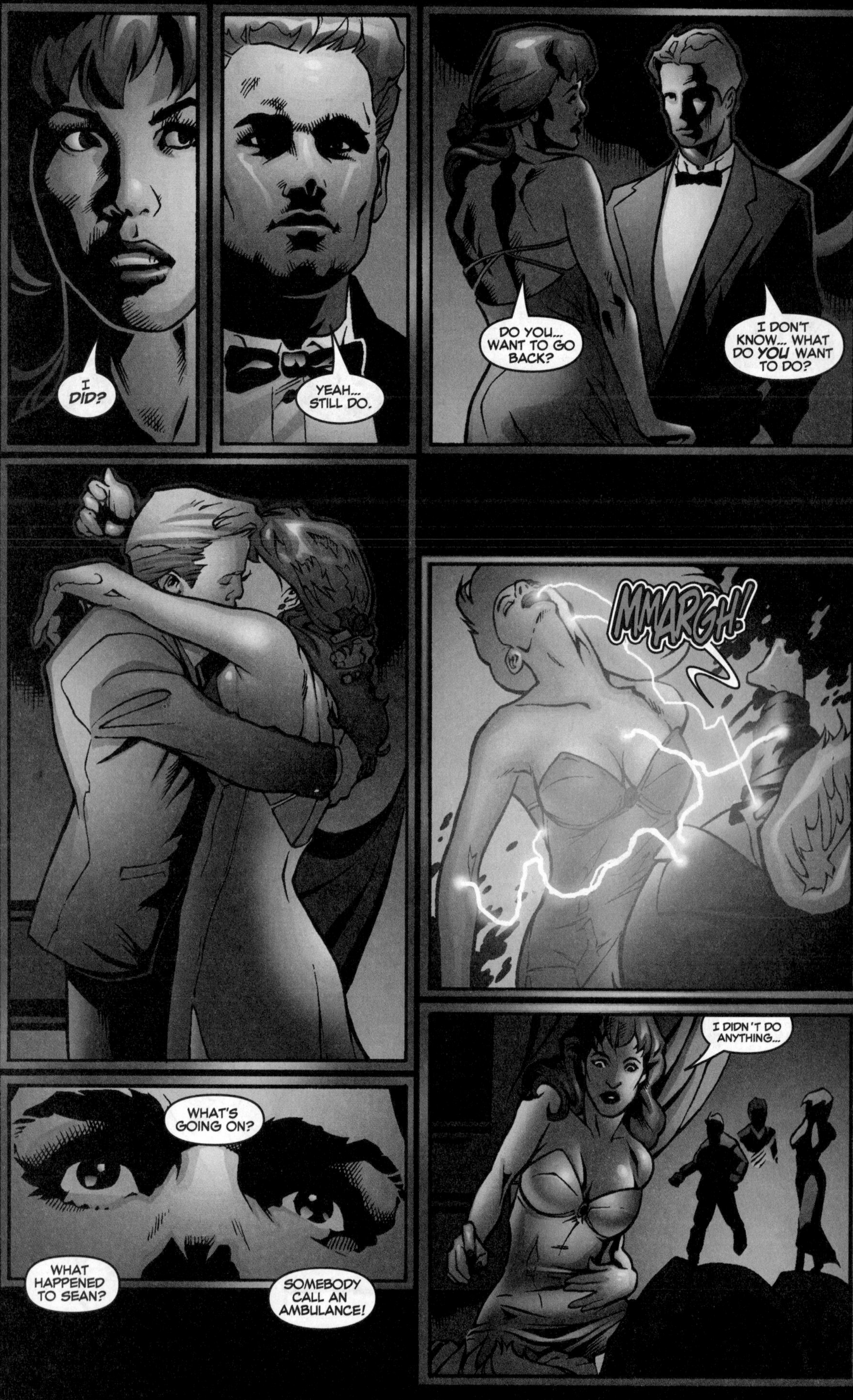
I DID?
YEAH... STILL DO.
DO YOU... WANT TO GO BACK?
I DON'T KNOW... WHAT DO YOU WANT TO DO?
MMARGH!
I DIDN'T DO ANYTHING...
WHAT'S GOING ON?
WHAT HAPPENED TO SEAN?
SOMEBODY CALL AN AMBULANCE!

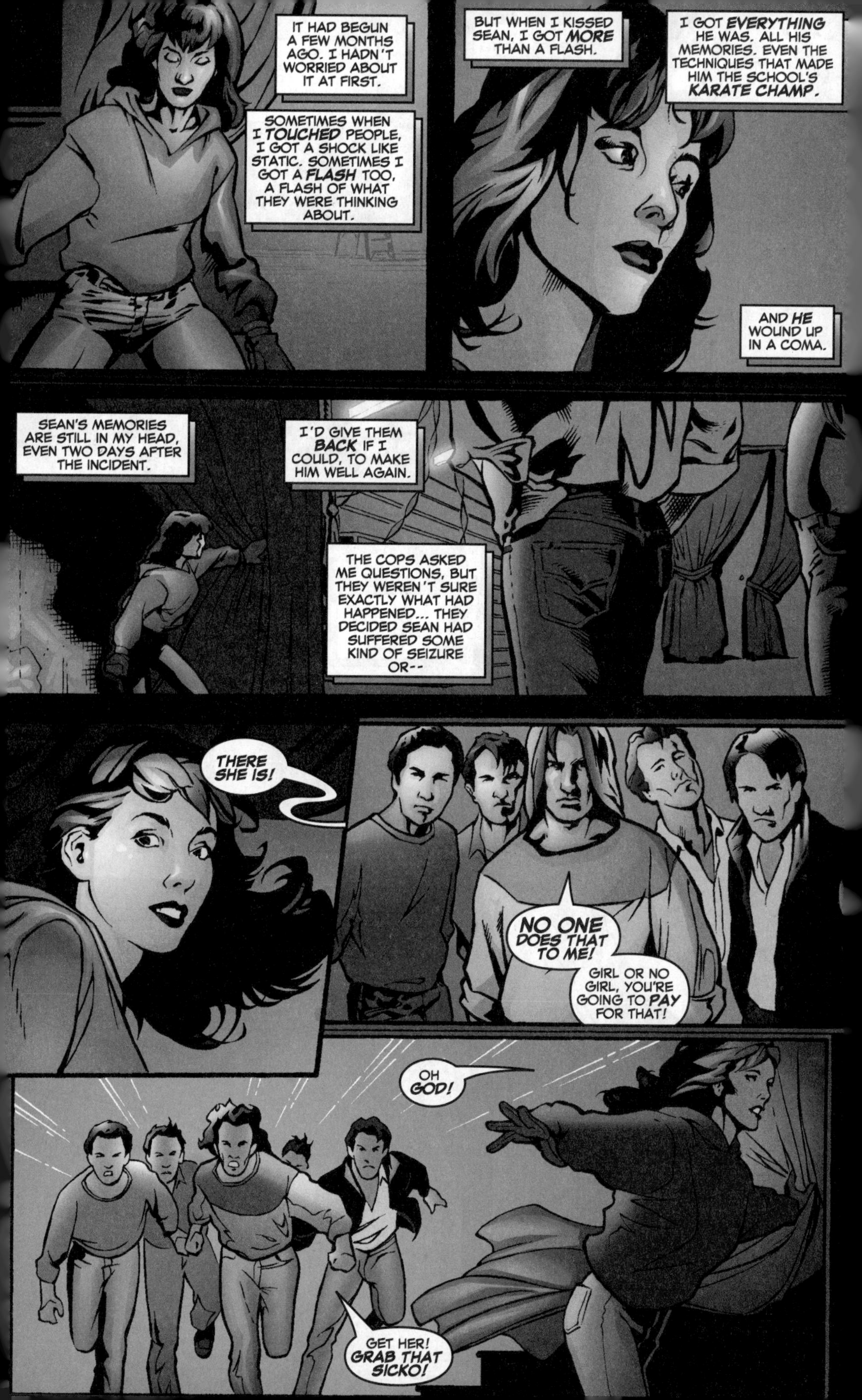

IT HAD BEGUN A FEW MONTHS AGO. I HADN'T WORRIED ABOUT IT AT FIRST.
SOMETIMES WHEN I TOUCHED PEOPLE, I GOT A SHOCK LIKE STATIC. SOMETIMES I GOT A FLASH TOO, A FLASH OF WHAT THEY WERE THINKING ABOUT.
BUT WHEN I KISSED SEAN, I GOT MORE THAN A FLASH.
I GOT EVERYTHING HE WAS. ALL HIS MEMORIES. EVEN THE TECHNIQUES THAT MADE HIM THE SCHOOL'S KARATE CHAMP.
AND HE WOUND UP IN A COMA.
SEAN'S MEMORIES ARE STILL IN MY HEAD, EVEN TWO DAYS AFTER THE INCIDENT.
I'D GIVE THEM BACK IF I COULD, TO MAKE HIM WELL AGAIN.
THE COPS ASKED ME QUESTIONS, BUT THEY WEREN'T SURE EXACTLY WHAT HAD HAPPENED... THEY DECIDED SEAN HAD SUFFERED SOME KIND OF SEIZURE OR--
THERE SHE IS!
NO ONE DOES THAT TO ME!
GIRL OR NO GIRL, YOU'RE GOING TO PAY FOR THAT!
OH GOD!
GET HER! GRAB THAT SICKO!

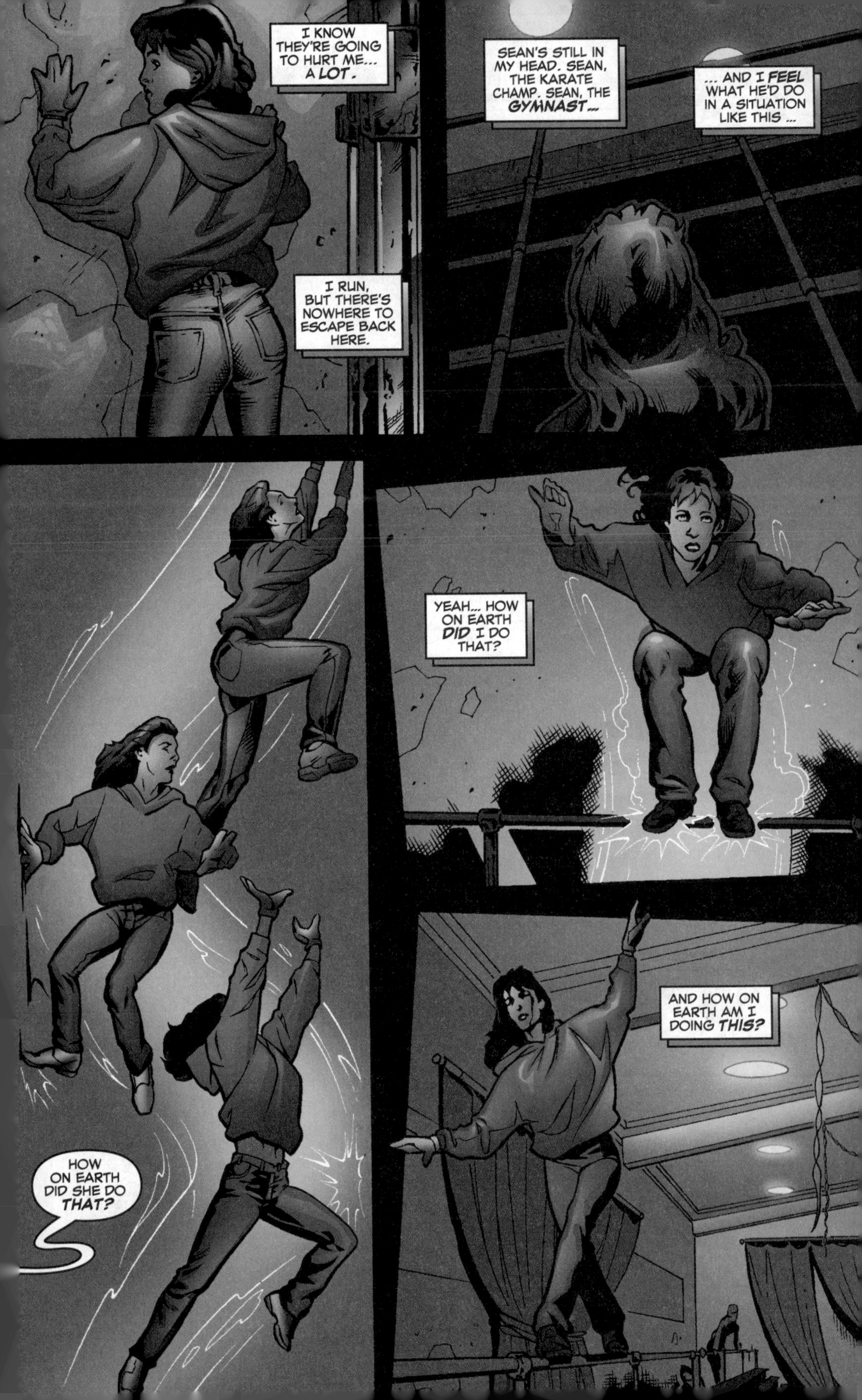
I KNOW THEY'RE GOING TO HURT ME... A LOT.
I RUN, BUT THERE'S NOWHERE TO ESCAPE BACK HERE.
SEAN'S STILL IN MY HEAD. SEAN, THE KARATE CHAMP. SEAN, THE GYMNAST...
... AND I FEEL WHAT HE'D DO IN A SITUATION LIKE THIS ...
HOW ON EARTH DID SHE DO THAT?
YEAH... HOW ON EARTH DID I DO THAT?
AND HOW ON EARTH AM I DOING THIS?

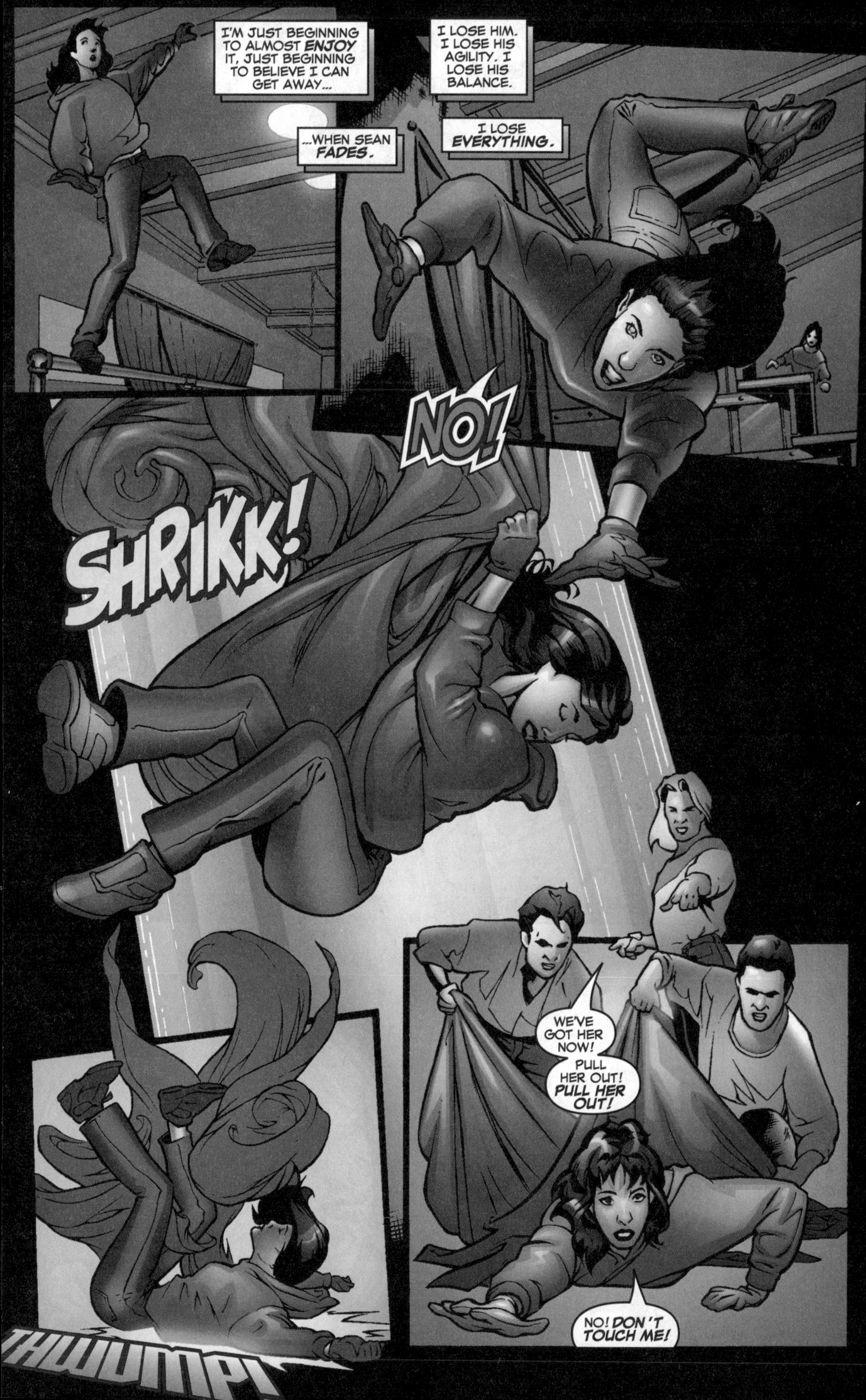
I'M JUST BEGINNING TO ALMOST ENJOY IT, JUST BEGINNING TO BELIEVE I CAN GET AWAY...
...WHEN SEAN FADES.
I LOSE HIM. I LOSE HIS AGILITY. I LOSE HIS BALANCE.
I LOSE EVERYTHING.
NO!
SHRIKK!
THWUMP!
WE'VE GOT HER NOW!
PULL HER OUT! PULL HER OUT!
NO! DON'T TOUCH ME!

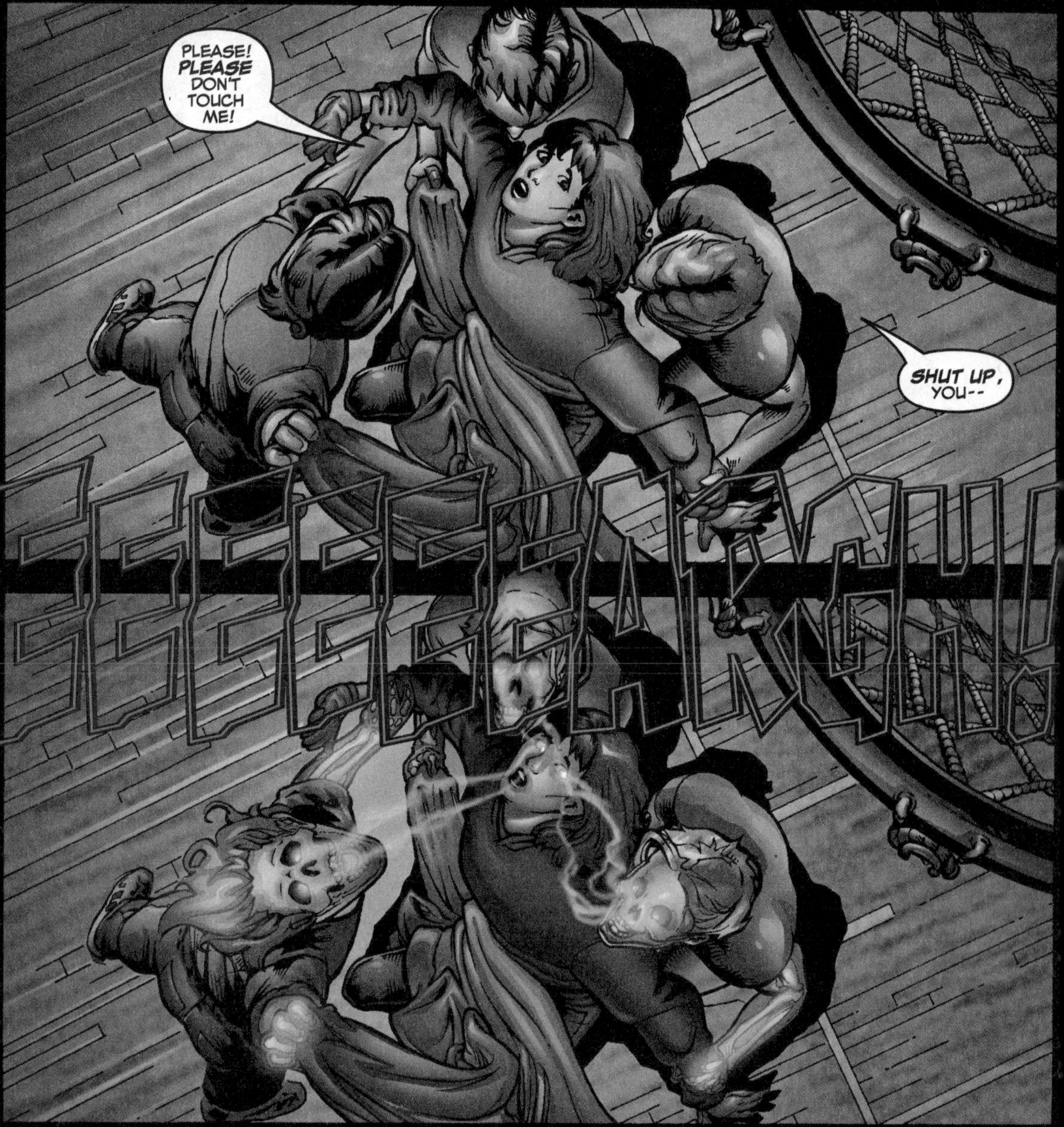
PLEASE! PLEASE DON'T TOUCH ME!
SHUT UP, YOU--

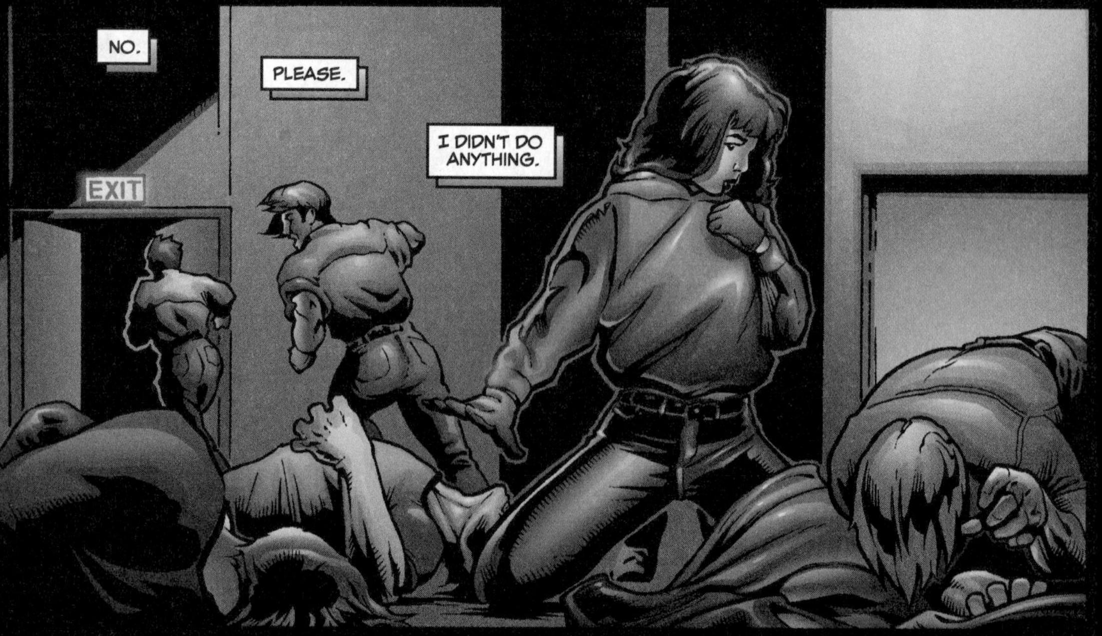
NO.
PLEASE.
I DIDN'T DO ANYTHING.
EXIT

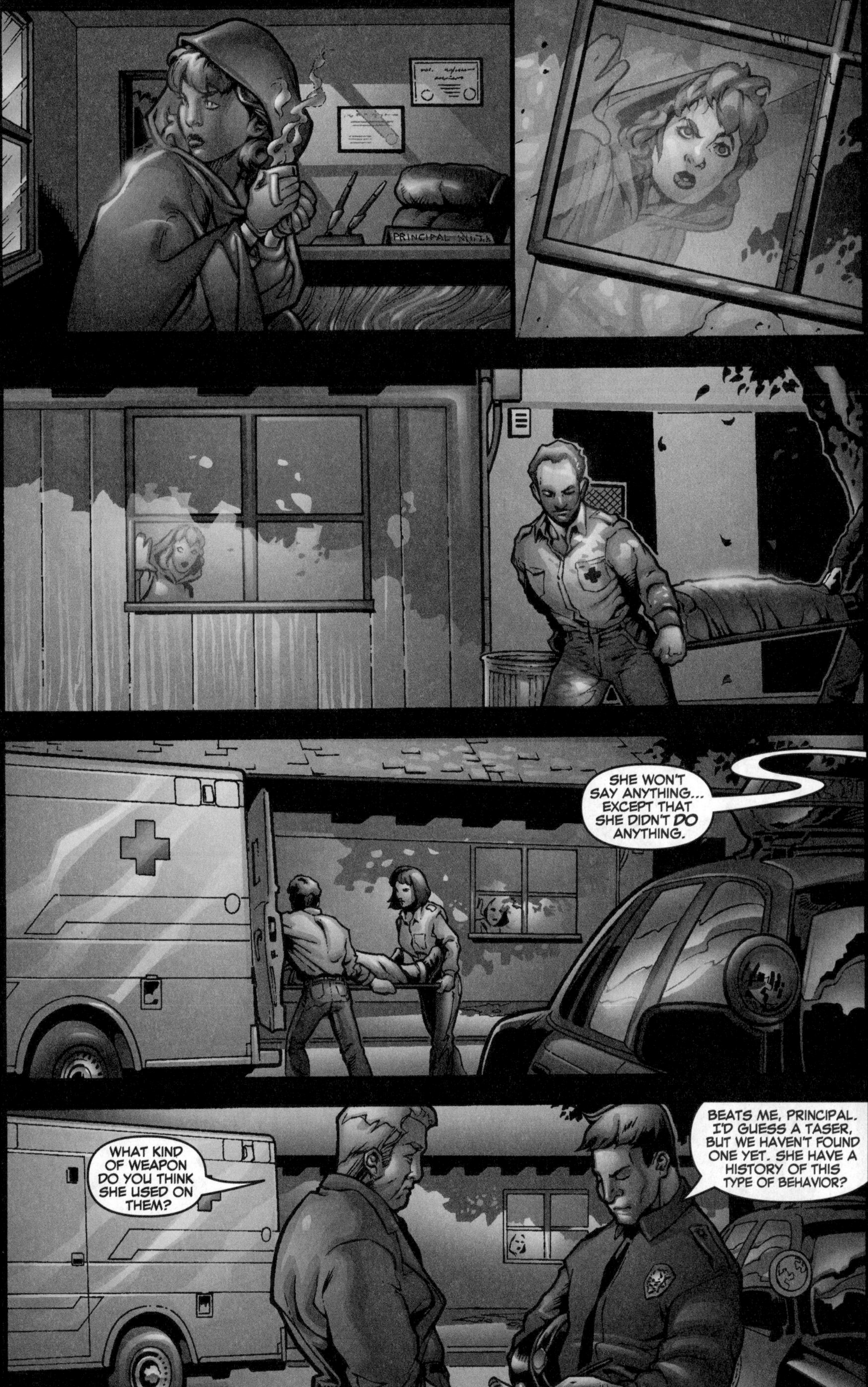
PRINCIPAL NUTA
SHE WON'T SAY ANYTHING... EXCEPT THAT SHE DIDN'T DO ANYTHING.
WHAT KIND OF WEAPON DO YOU THINK SHE USED ON THEM?
BEATS ME, PRINCIPAL. I'D GUESS A TASER, BUT WE HAVEN'T FOUND ONE YET. SHE HAVE A HISTORY OF THIS TYPE OF BEHAVIOR?

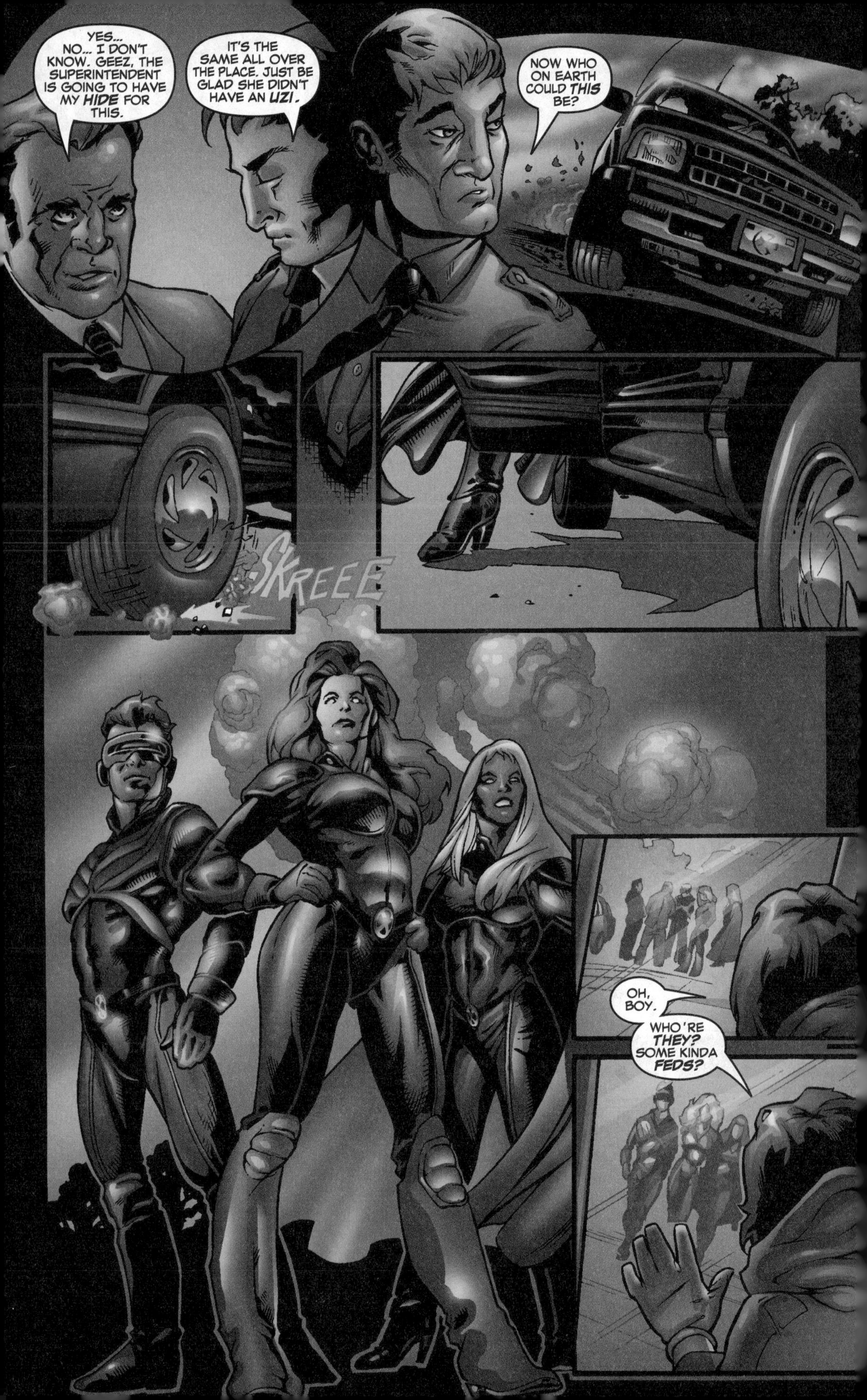
YES... NO... I DON'T KNOW. GEEZ, THE SUPERINTENDENT IS GOING TO HAVE MY HIDE FOR THIS.
IT'S THE SAME ALL OVER THE PLACE. JUST BE GLAD SHE DIDN'T HAVE AN UZI.
NOW WHO ON EARTH COULD THIS BE?
SKREEE
OH, BOY.
WHO'RE THEY? SOME KINDA FEDS?

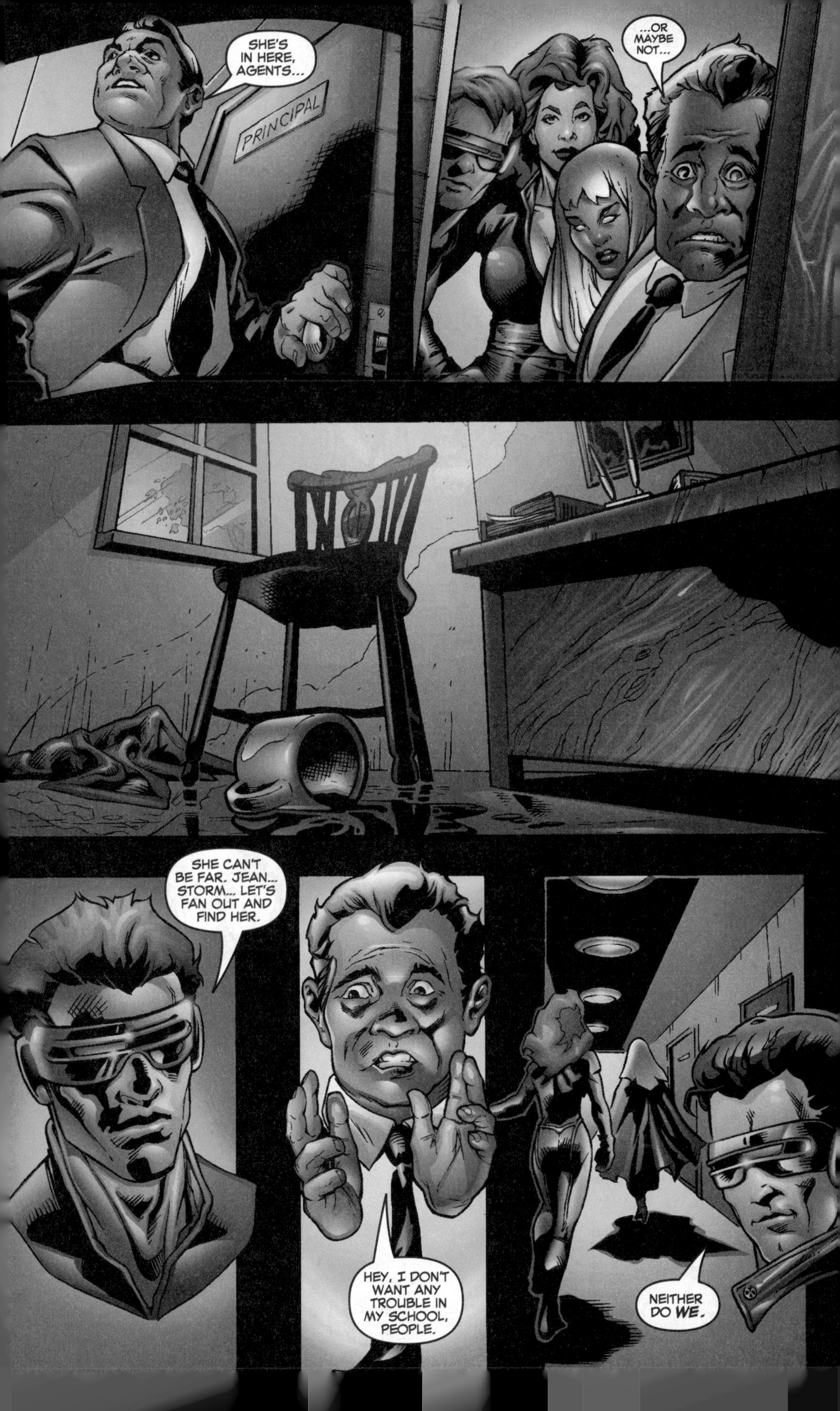
SHE'S IN HERE, AGENTS...
PRINCIPAL
...OR MAYBE NOT...
SHE CAN'T BE FAR. JEAN... STORM... LET'S FAN OUT AND FIND HER.
HEY, I DON'T WANT ANY TROUBLE IN MY SCHOOL, PEOPLE.
NEITHER DO **WE**.

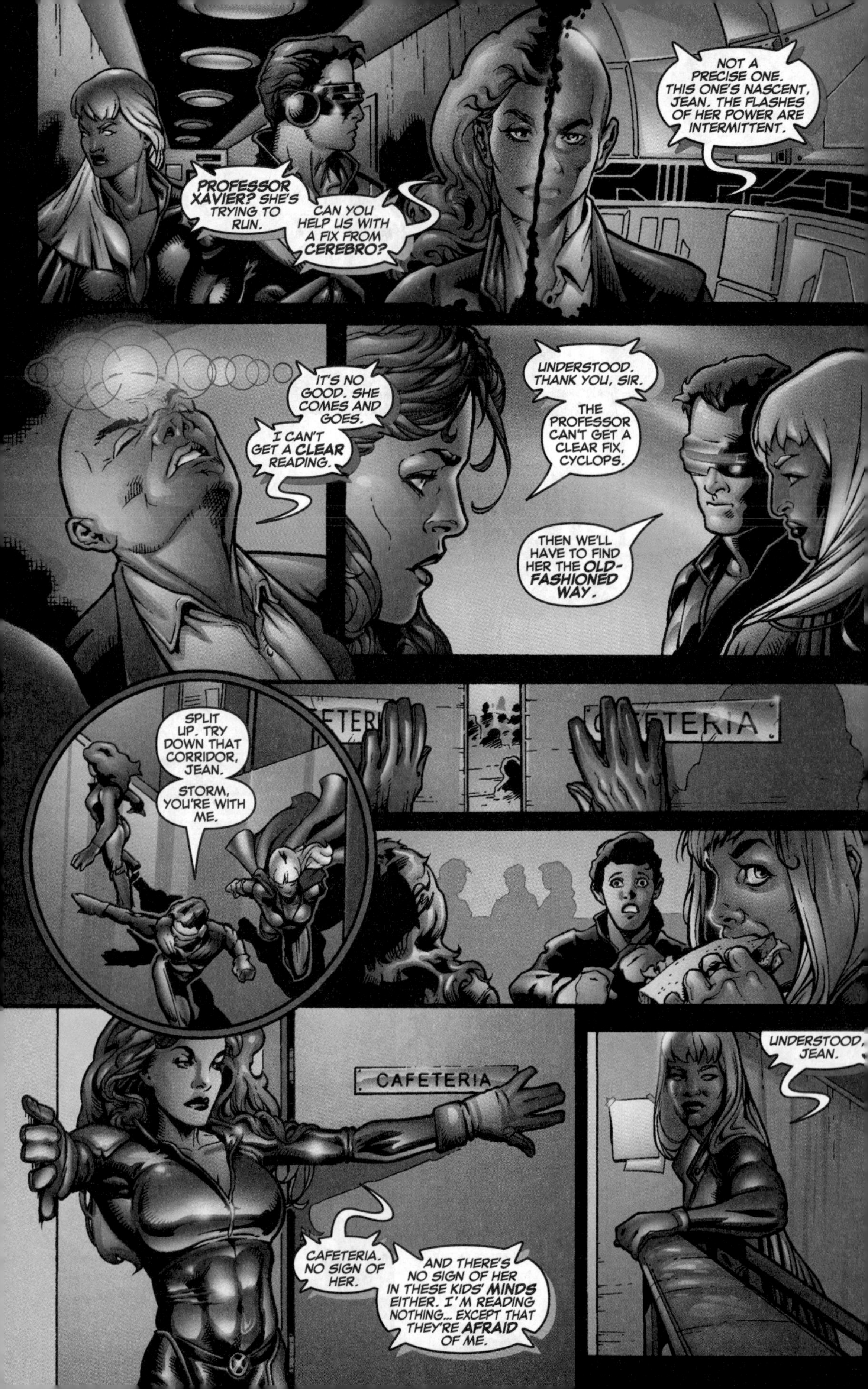
PROFESSOR XAVIER? SHE'S TRYING TO RUN.
CAN YOU HELP US WITH A FIX FROM CEREBRO?
NOT A PRECISE ONE. THIS ONE'S NASCENT, JEAN. THE FLASHES OF HER POWER ARE INTERMITTENT.
IT'S NO GOOD. SHE COMES AND GOES.
I CAN'T GET A CLEAR READING.
UNDERSTOOD. THANK YOU, SIR.
THE PROFESSOR CAN'T GET A CLEAR FIX, CYCLOPS.
THEN WE'LL HAVE TO FIND HER THE OLD-FASHIONED WAY.
SPLIT UP. TRY DOWN THAT CORRIDOR, JEAN.
STORM, YOU'RE WITH ME.
CAFETERIA
CAFETERIA
CAFETERIA. NO SIGN OF HER.
AND THERE'S NO SIGN OF HER IN THESE KIDS' MINDS EITHER. I'M READING NOTHING... EXCEPT THAT THEY'RE AFRAID OF ME.
UNDERSTOOD, JEAN.

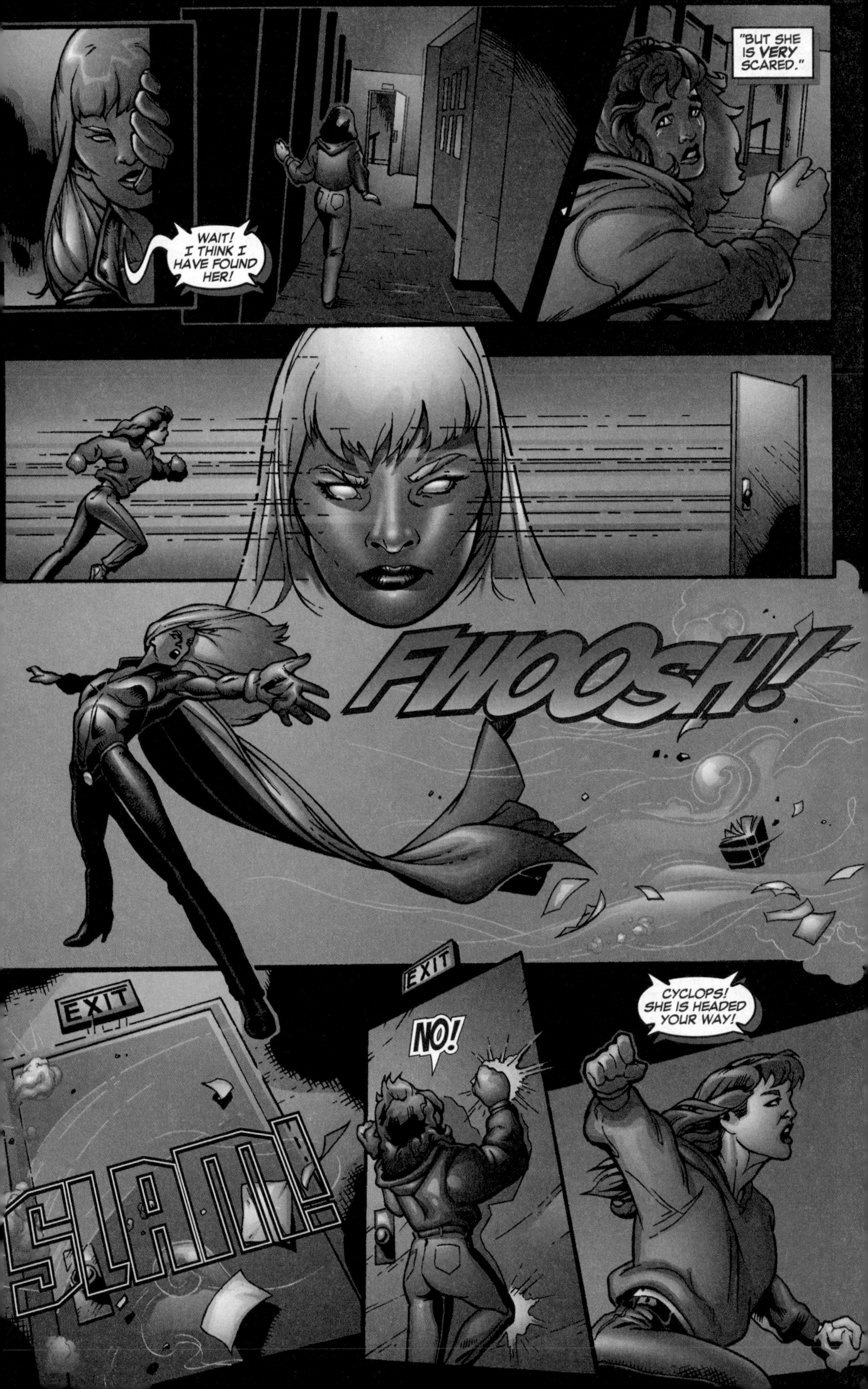
WAIT! I THINK I HAVE FOUND HER!
"BUT SHE IS VERY SCARED."
FWOOSH!
EXIT
SLAM!
EXIT
NO!
CYCLOPS! SHE IS HEADED YOUR WAY!

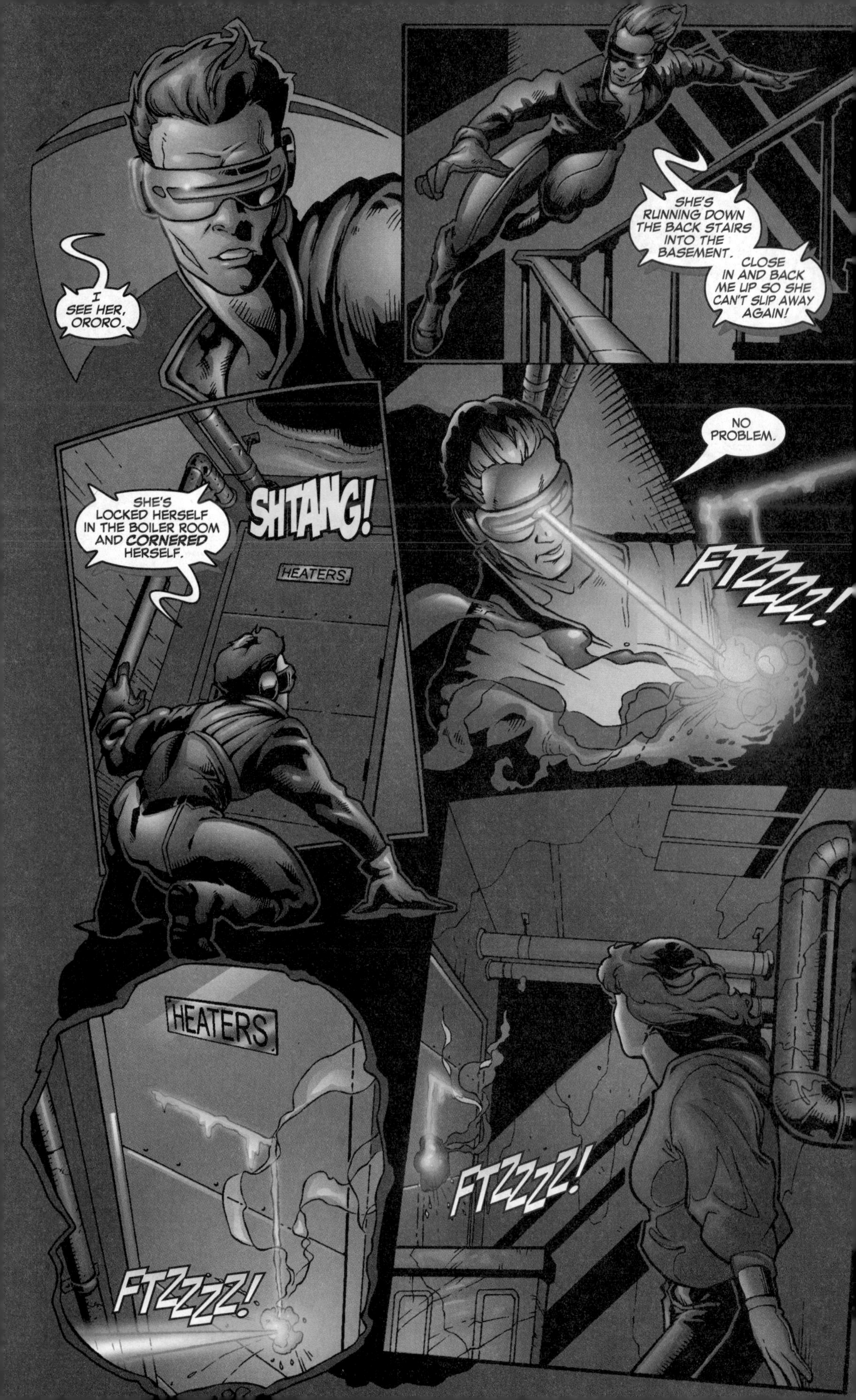
I SEE HER, ORORO.
SHE'S RUNNING DOWN THE BACK STAIRS INTO THE BASEMENT.
CLOSE IN AND BACK ME UP SO SHE CAN'T SLIP AWAY AGAIN!
NO PROBLEM.
SHE'S LOCKED HERSELF IN THE BOILER ROOM AND CORNERED HERSELF.
SHTANG!
HEATERS
FTZZZZ!
HEATERS
FTZZZZ!
FTZZZZ!

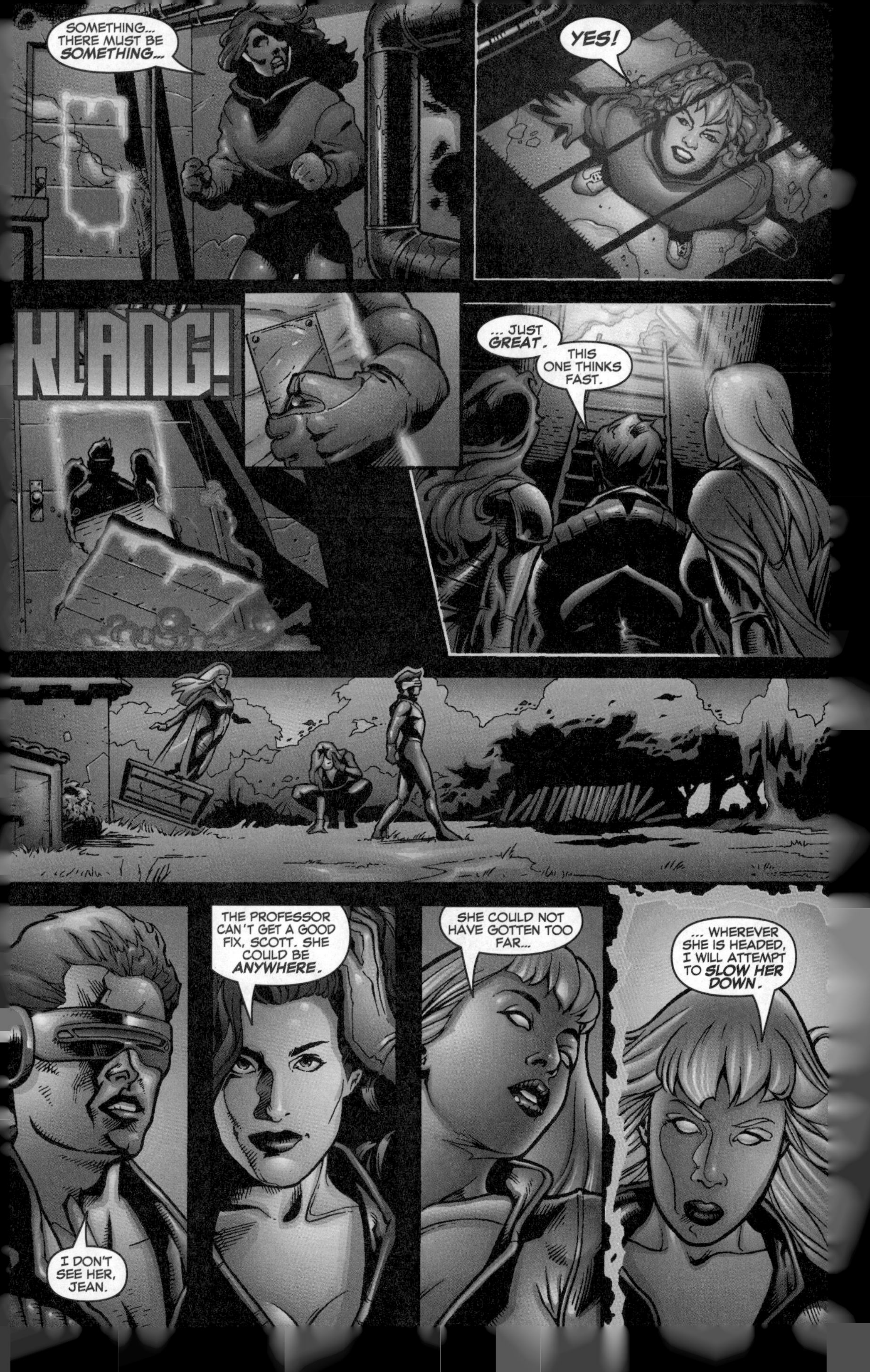

SOMETHING... THERE MUST BE SOMETHING...
YES!
KLANG!
... JUST GREAT.
THIS ONE THINKS FAST.
I DON'T SEE HER, JEAN.
THE PROFESSOR CAN'T GET A GOOD FIX, SCOTT. SHE COULD BE ANYWHERE.
SHE COULD NOT HAVE GOTTEN TOO FAR...
... WHEREVER SHE IS HEADED, I WILL ATTEMPT TO SLOW HER DOWN.

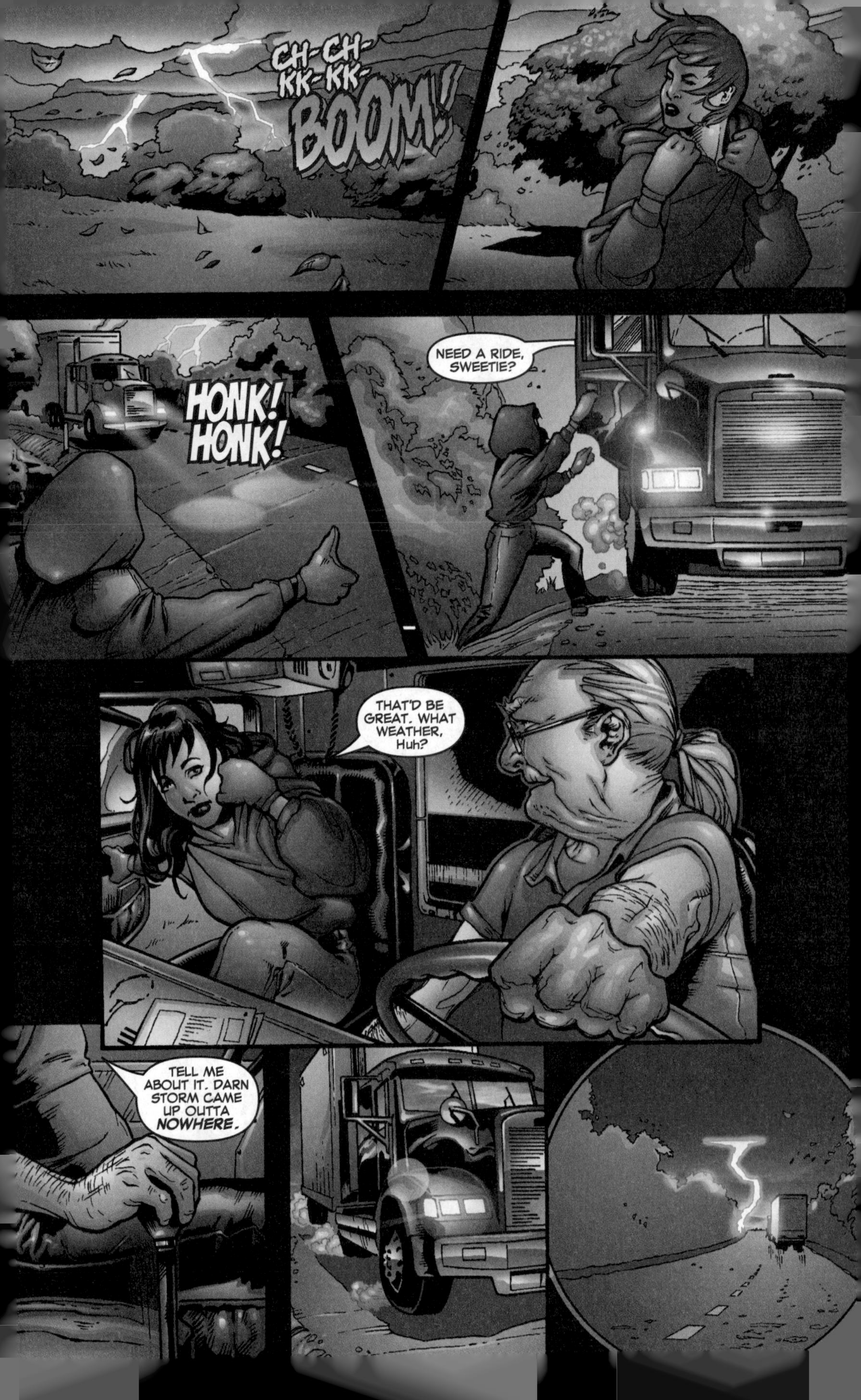
CH-CH-
KK-KK-
BOOM!
HONK!
HONK!
NEED A RIDE, SWEETIE?
THAT'D BE GREAT. WHAT WEATHER, Huh?
TELL ME ABOUT IT. DARN STORM CAME UP OUTTA NOWHERE.

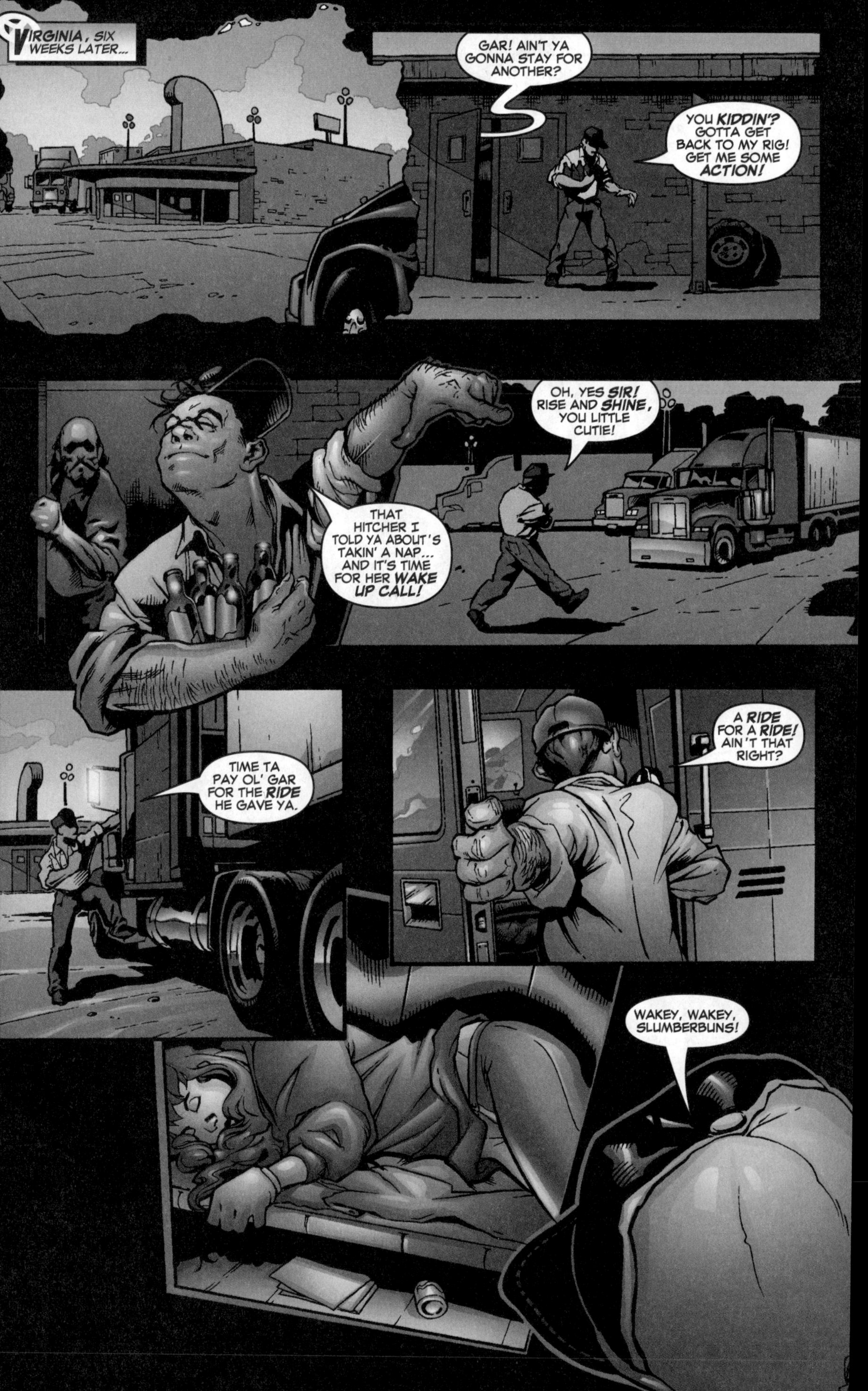
VIRGINIA, SIX WEEKS LATER...
GAR! AIN'T YA GONNA STAY FOR ANOTHER?
YOU KIDDIN'? GOTTA GET BACK TO MY RIG! GET ME SOME ACTION!
THAT HITCHER I TOLD YA ABOUT'S TAKIN' A NAP... AND IT'S TIME FOR HER WAKE UP CALL!
OH, YES SIR! RISE AND SHINE, YOU LITTLE CUTIE!
TIME TA PAY OL' GAR FOR THE RIDE HE GAVE YA.
A RIDE FOR A RIDE! AIN'T THAT RIGHT?
WAKEY, WAKEY, SLUMBERBUNS!

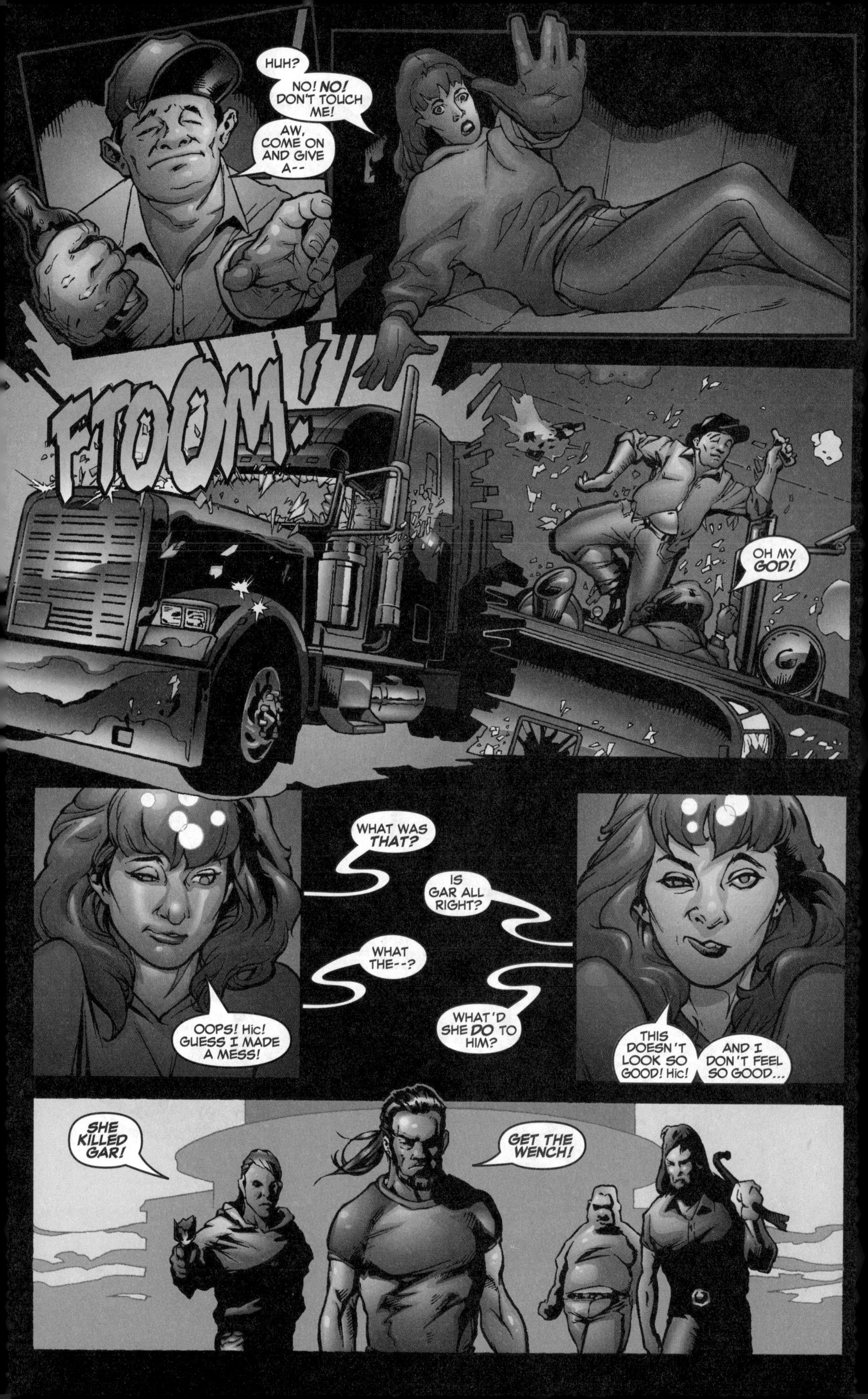
HUH?
NO! NO! DON'T TOUCH ME!
AW, COME ON AND GIVE A--
FTOOM!
OH MY GOD!
OOPS! Hic! GUESS I MADE A MESS!
WHAT WAS THAT?
IS GAR ALL RIGHT?
WHAT THE--?
WHAT'D SHE DO TO HIM?
THIS DOESN'T LOOK SO GOOD! Hic!
AND I DON'T FEEL SO GOOD...
SHE KILLED GAR!
GET THE WENCH!

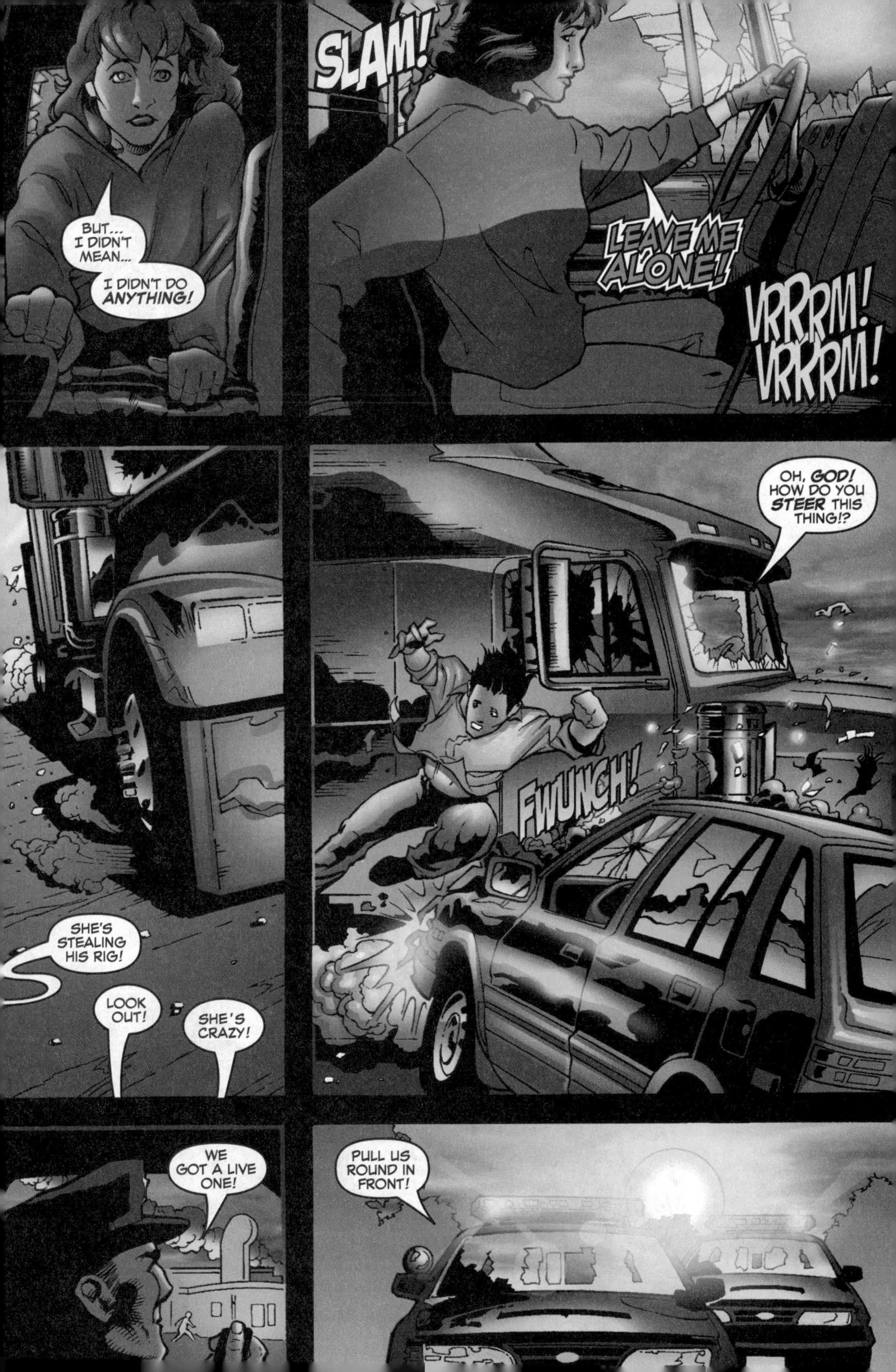
BUT... I DIDN'T MEAN...
I DIDN'T DO ANYTHING!
SLAM!
LEAVE ME ALONE!
VRRRM! VRRRM!
OH, GOD! HOW DO YOU STEER THIS THING!?
FWUNCH!
SHE'S STEALING HIS RIG!
LOOK OUT!
SHE'S CRAZY!
WE GOT A LIVE ONE!
PULL US ROUND IN FRONT!

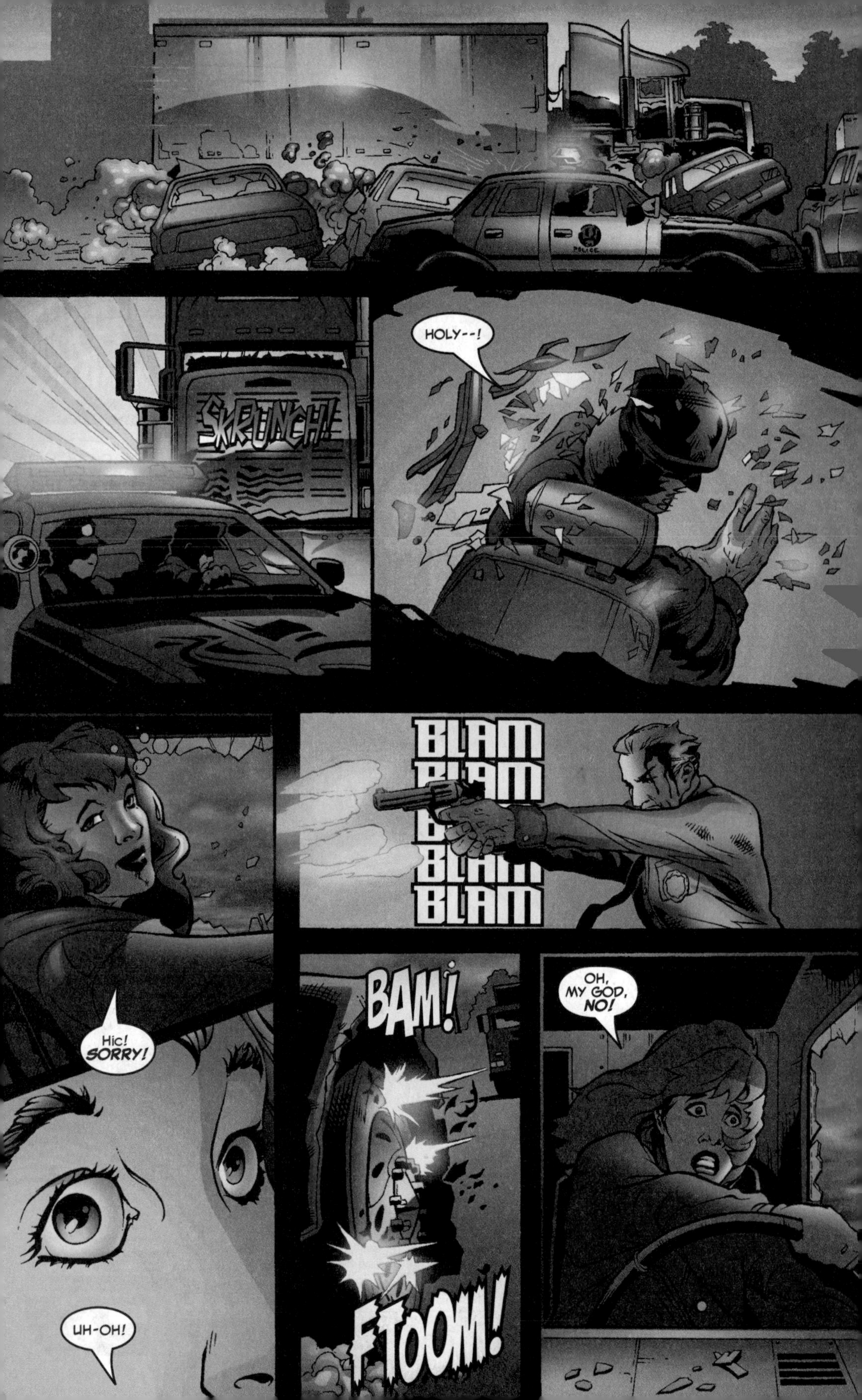
SKRUNCH!
HOLY--!
Hic! SORRY!
UH-OH!
BLAM
BLAM
BLAM
BLAM
BLAM
BAM!
FTOOM!
OH, MY GOD, NO!

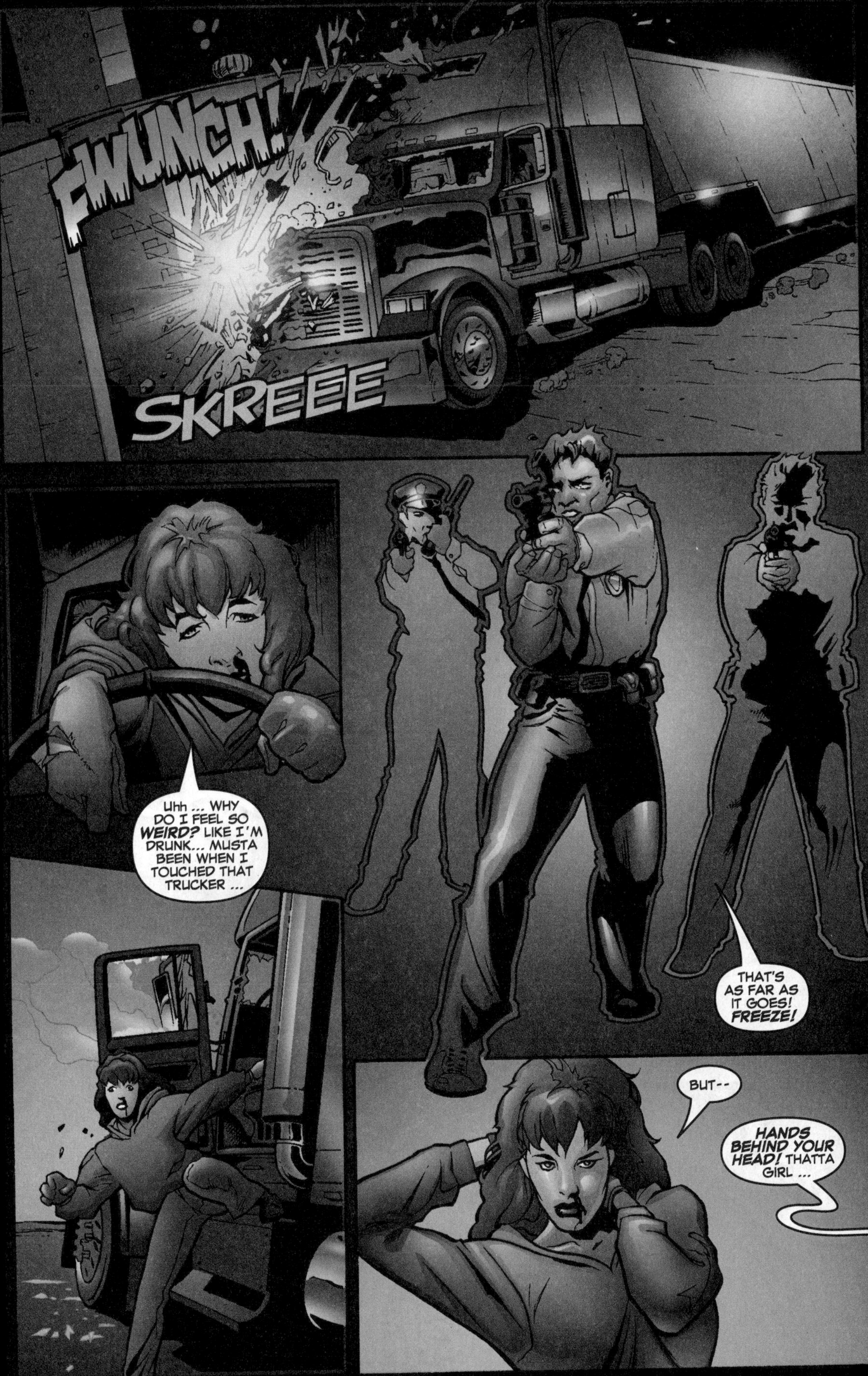
FWUNCH!
SKREEE
Uhh ... WHY DO I FEEL SO WEIRD? LIKE I'M DRUNK... MUSTA BEEN WHEN I TOUCHED THAT TRUCKER ...
THAT'S AS FAR AS IT GOES! FREEZE!
BUT--
HANDS BEHIND YOUR HEAD! THATTA GIRL ...

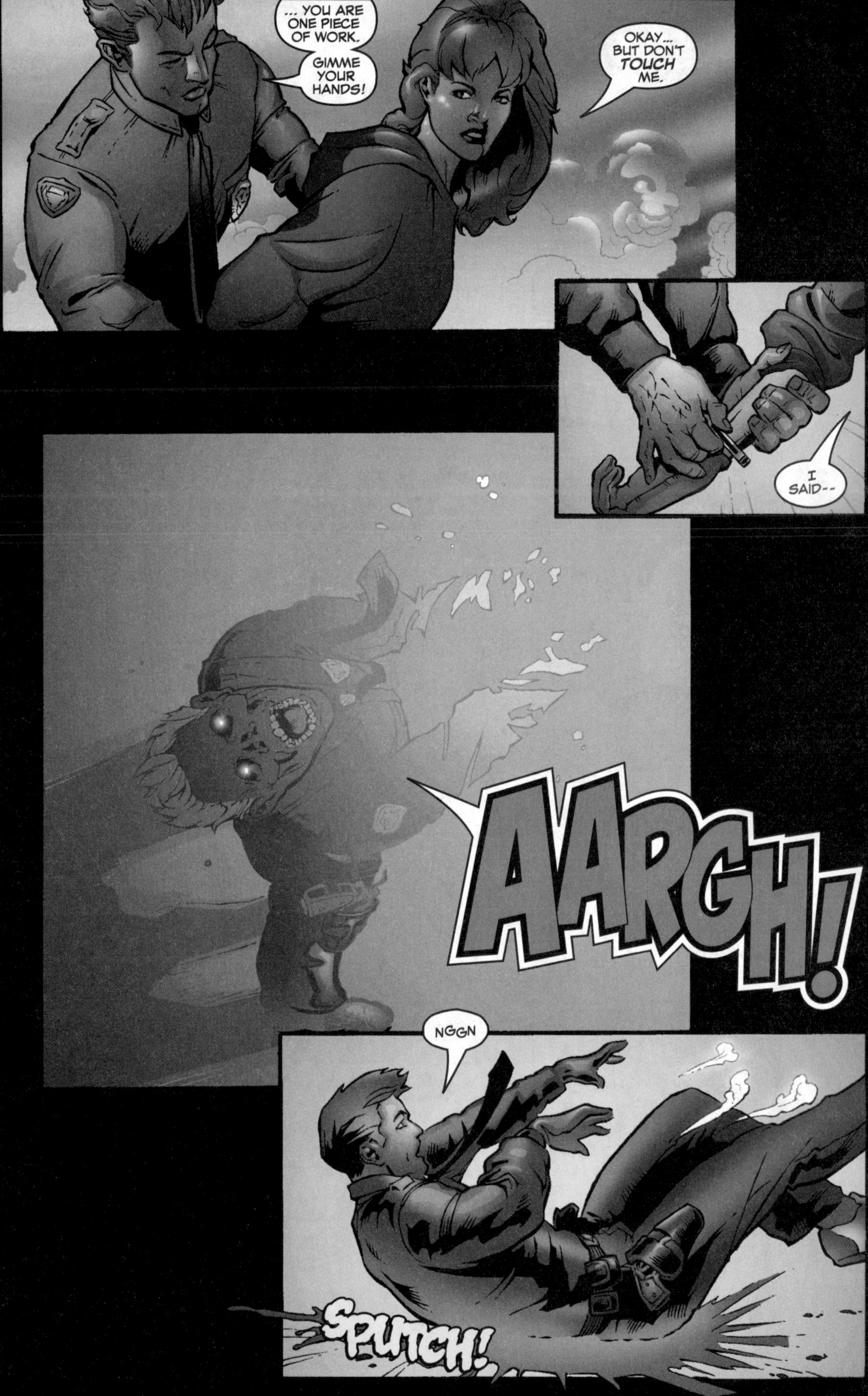
... YOU ARE ONE PIECE OF WORK.
GIMME YOUR HANDS!
OKAY... BUT DON'T *TOUCH* ME.
I SAID--
AARGH!
NGGN
SPLUTCH!

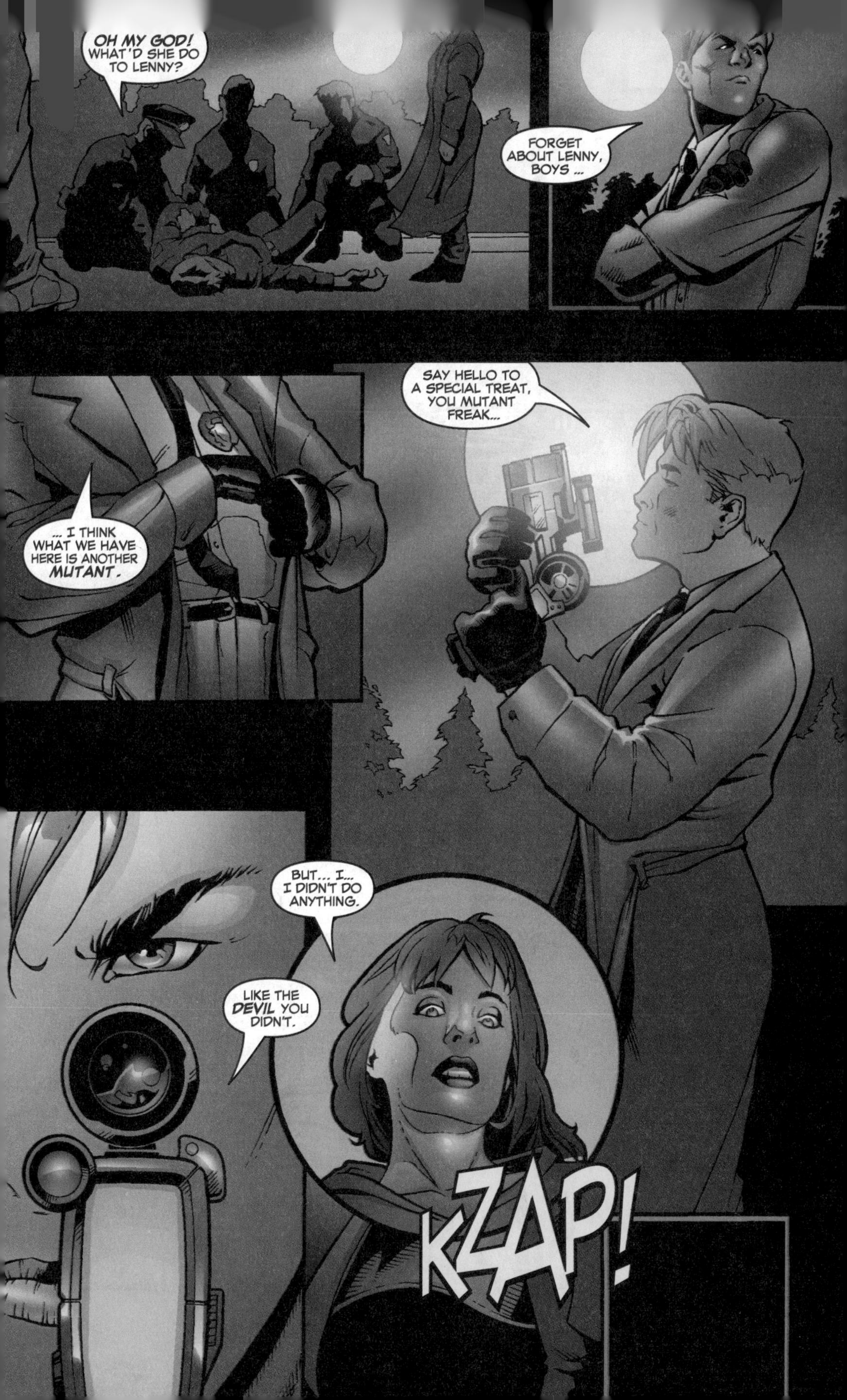
OH MY GOD! WHAT'D SHE DO TO LENNY?
FORGET ABOUT LENNY, BOYS ...
... I THINK WHAT WE HAVE HERE IS ANOTHER MUTANT.
SAY HELLO TO A SPECIAL TREAT, YOU MUTANT FREAK...
BUT... I... I DIDN'T DO ANYTHING.
LIKE THE DEVIL YOU DIDN'T.
KZAP!

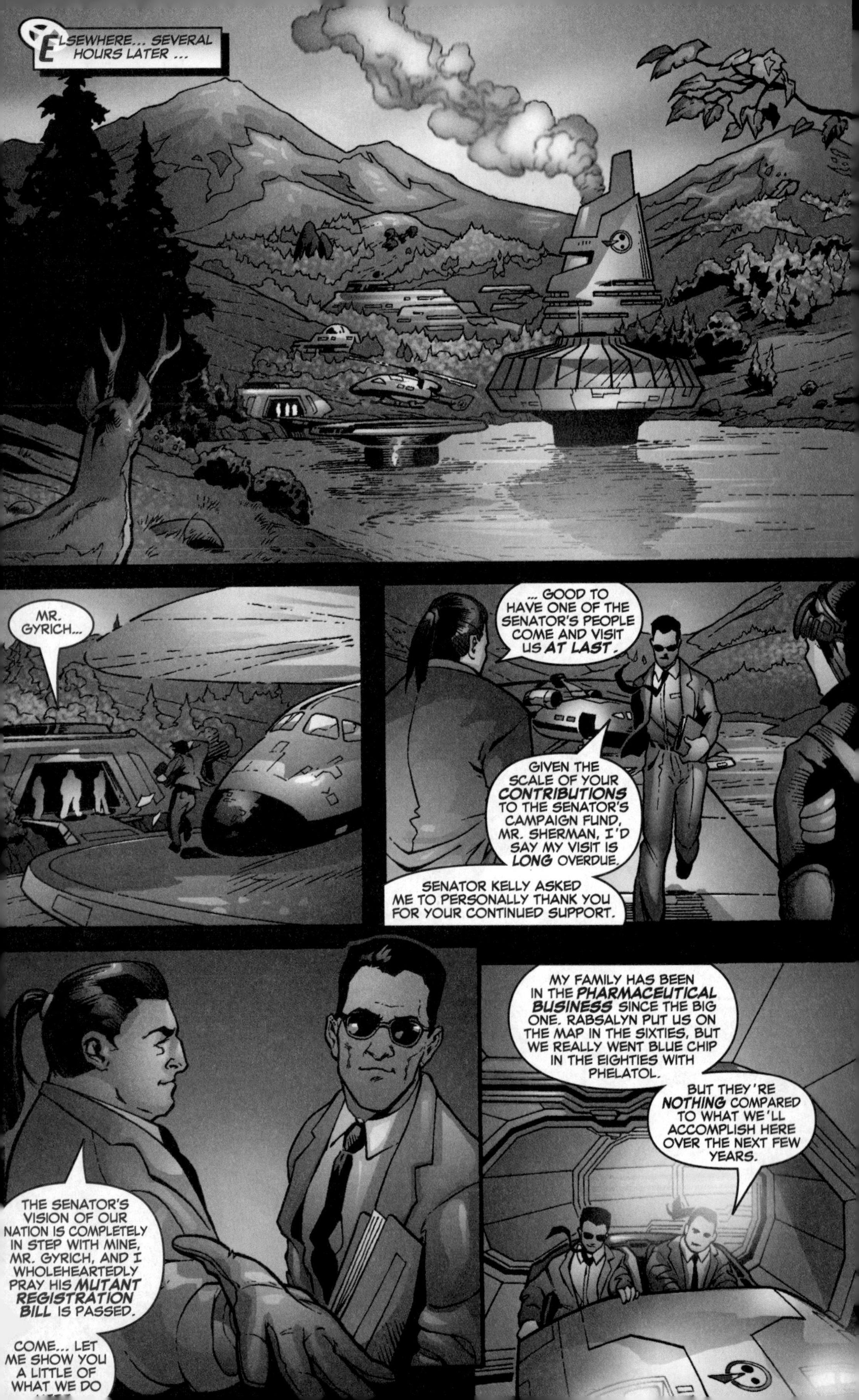
ELSEWHERE... SEVERAL HOURS LATER ...
MR. GYRICH...
... GOOD TO HAVE ONE OF THE SENATOR'S PEOPLE COME AND VISIT US AT LAST.
GIVEN THE SCALE OF YOUR CONTRIBUTIONS TO THE SENATOR'S CAMPAIGN FUND, MR. SHERMAN, I'D SAY MY VISIT IS LONG OVERDUE.
SENATOR KELLY ASKED ME TO PERSONALLY THANK YOU FOR YOUR CONTINUED SUPPORT.
THE SENATOR'S VISION OF OUR NATION IS COMPLETELY IN STEP WITH MINE, MR. GYRICH, AND I WHOLEHEARTEDLY PRAY HIS MUTANT REGISTRATION BILL IS PASSED.
COME... LET ME SHOW YOU A LITTLE OF WHAT WE DO
MY FAMILY HAS BEEN IN THE PHARMACEUTICAL BUSINESS SINCE THE BIG ONE. RABSALYN PUT US ON THE MAP IN THE SIXTIES, BUT WE REALLY WENT BLUE CHIP IN THE EIGHTIES WITH PHELATOL.
BUT THEY'RE NOTHING COMPARED TO WHAT WE'LL ACCOMPLISH HERE OVER THE NEXT FEW YEARS.

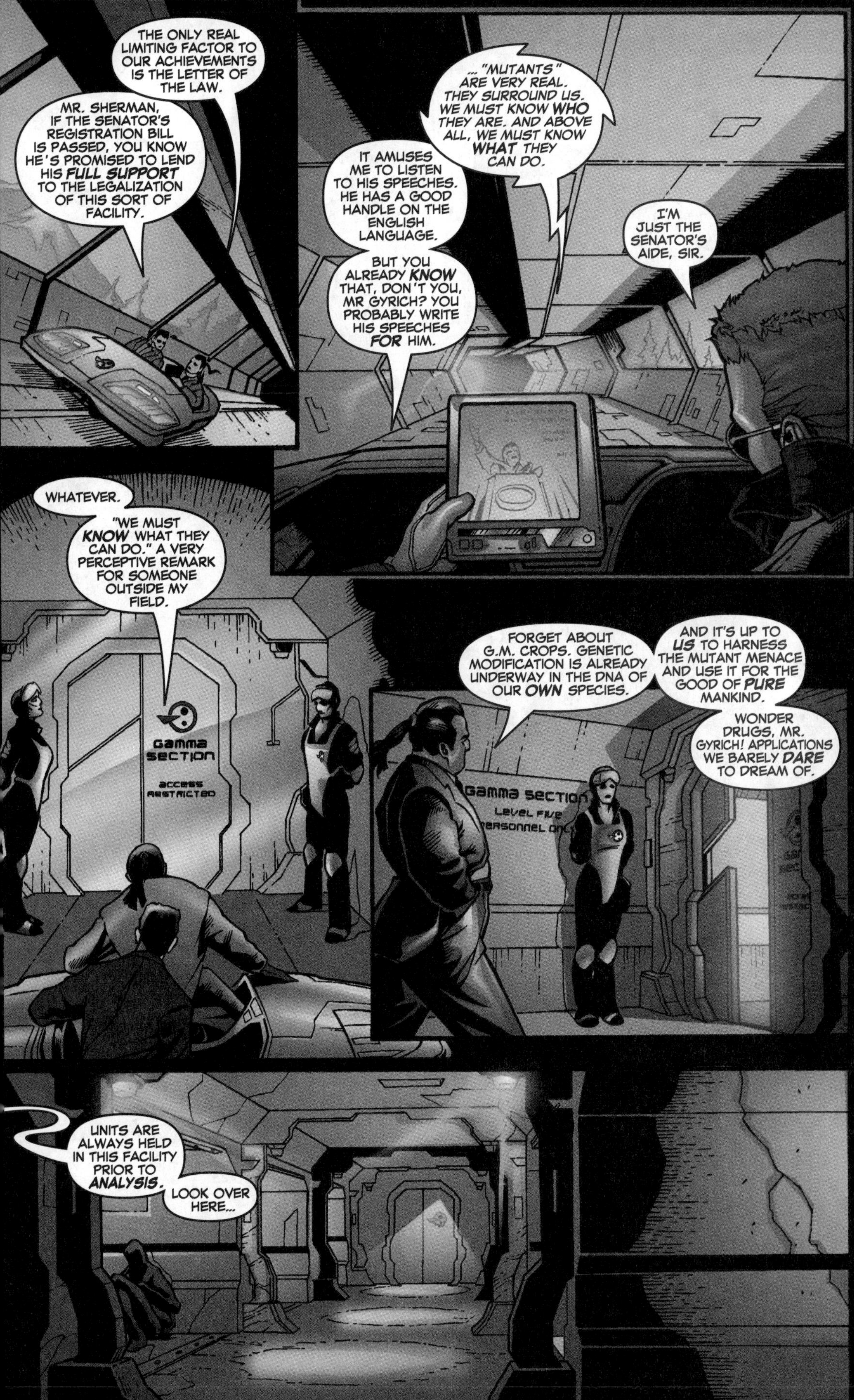
MR. SHERMAN, IF THE SENATOR'S REGISTRATION BILL IS PASSED, YOU KNOW HE'S PROMISED TO LEND HIS FULL SUPPORT TO THE LEGALIZATION OF THIS SORT OF FACILITY.
THE ONLY REAL LIMITING FACTOR TO OUR ACHIEVEMENTS IS THE LETTER OF THE LAW.
..."MUTANTS" ARE VERY REAL. THEY SURROUND US. WE MUST KNOW WHO THEY ARE. AND ABOVE ALL, WE MUST KNOW WHAT THEY CAN DO.
IT AMUSES ME TO LISTEN TO HIS SPEECHES. HE HAS A GOOD HANDLE ON THE ENGLISH LANGUAGE.
BUT YOU ALREADY KNOW THAT, DON'T YOU, MR GYRICH? YOU PROBABLY WRITE HIS SPEECHES FOR HIM.
I'M JUST THE SENATOR'S AIDE, SIR.
WHATEVER.
"WE MUST KNOW WHAT THEY CAN DO." A VERY PERCEPTIVE REMARK FOR SOMEONE OUTSIDE MY FIELD.
GAMMA SECTION
ACCESS RESTRICTED
FORGET ABOUT G.M. CROPS. GENETIC MODIFICATION IS ALREADY UNDERWAY IN THE DNA OF OUR OWN SPECIES.
AND IT'S UP TO US TO HARNESS THE MUTANT MENACE AND USE IT FOR THE GOOD OF PURE MANKIND.
WONDER DRUGS, MR. GYRICH! APPLICATIONS WE BARELY DARE TO DREAM OF.
GAMMA SECTION
LEVEL FIVE
UNITS ARE ALWAYS HELD IN THIS FACILITY PRIOR TO ANALYSIS.
LOOK OVER HERE...

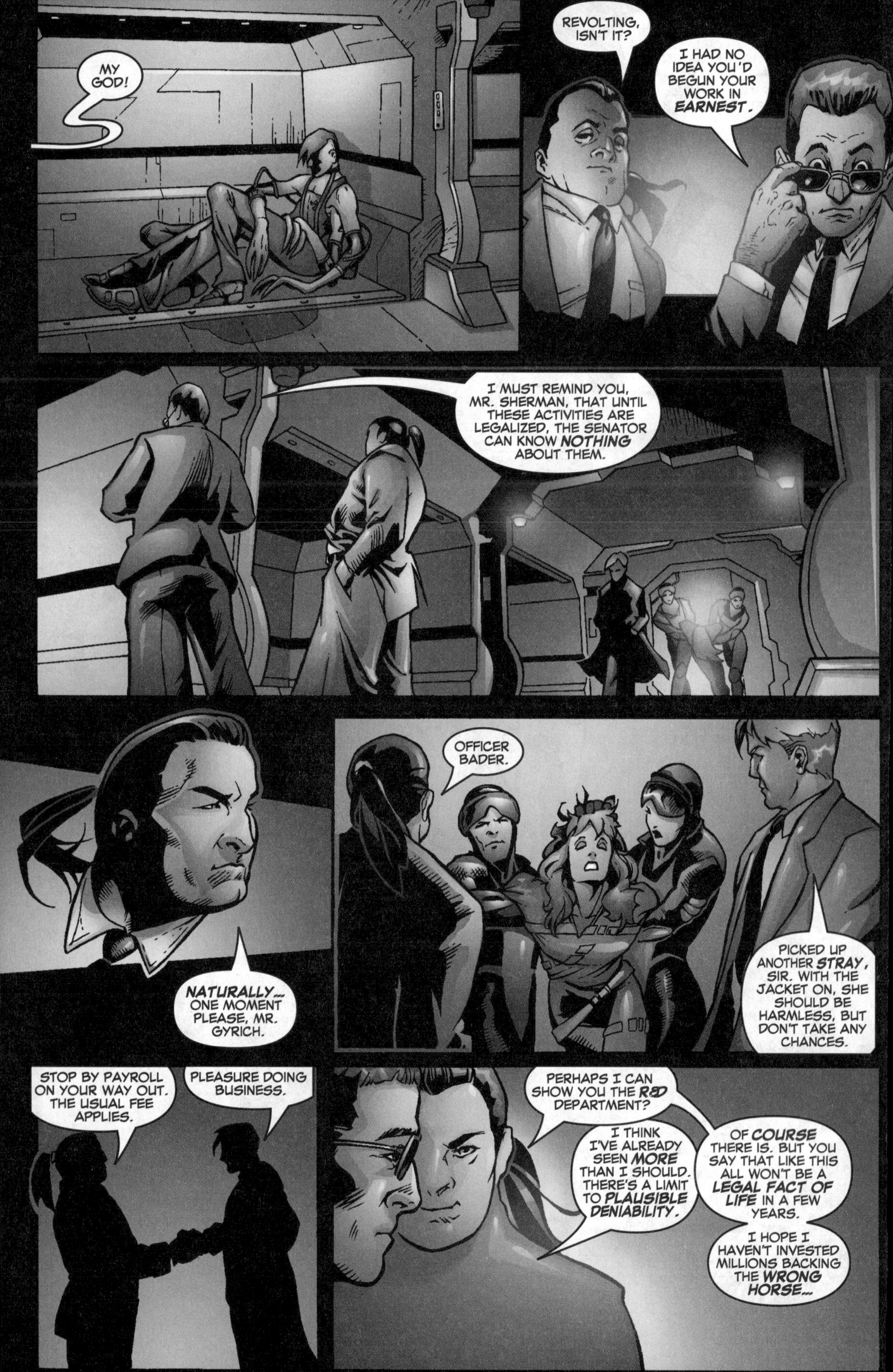
MY GOD!
REVOLTING, ISN'T IT?
I HAD NO IDEA YOU'D BEGUN YOUR WORK IN EARNEST.
I MUST REMIND YOU, MR. SHERMAN, THAT UNTIL THESE ACTIVITIES ARE LEGALIZED, THE SENATOR CAN KNOW NOTHING ABOUT THEM.
NATURALLY... ONE MOMENT PLEASE, MR. GYRICH.
OFFICER BADER.
PICKED UP ANOTHER STRAY, SIR. WITH THE JACKET ON, SHE SHOULD BE HARMLESS, BUT DON'T TAKE ANY CHANCES.
STOP BY PAYROLL ON YOUR WAY OUT. THE USUAL FEE APPLIES.
PLEASURE DOING BUSINESS.
PERHAPS I CAN SHOW YOU THE R&D DEPARTMENT?
I THINK I'VE ALREADY SEEN MORE THAN I SHOULD. THERE'S A LIMIT TO PLAUSIBLE DENIABILITY.
OF COURSE THERE IS. BUT YOU SAY THAT LIKE THIS ALL WON'T BE A LEGAL FACT OF LIFE IN A FEW YEARS.
I HOPE I HAVEN'T INVESTED MILLIONS BACKING THE WRONG HORSE...

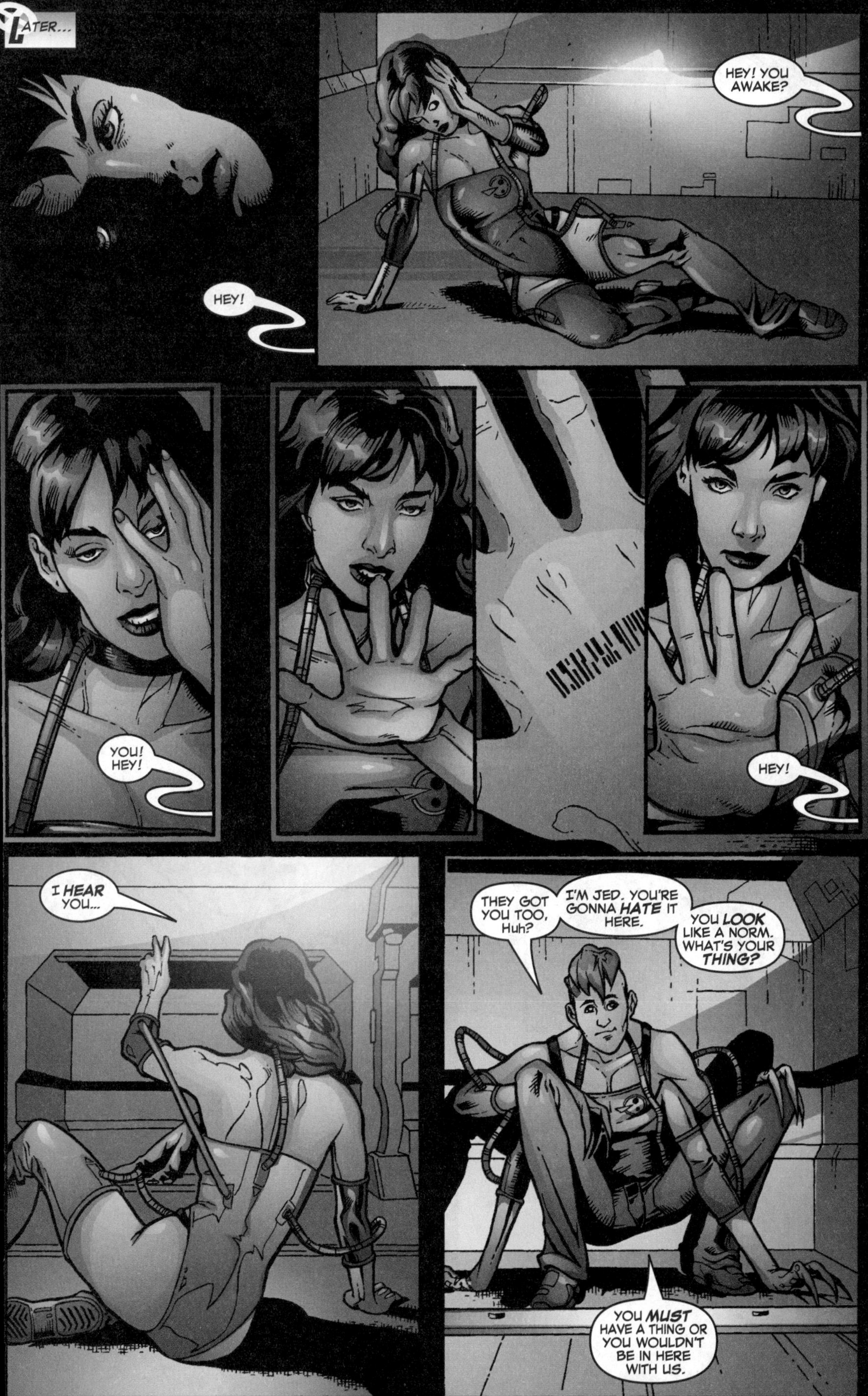
LATER...
HEY!
HEY! YOU AWAKE?
YOU! HEY!
HEY!
I HEAR YOU...
THEY GOT YOU TOO, Huh?
I'M JED. YOU'RE GONNA HATE IT HERE.
YOU LOOK LIKE A NORM. WHAT'S YOUR THING?
YOU MUST HAVE A THING OR YOU WOULDN'T BE IN HERE WITH US.

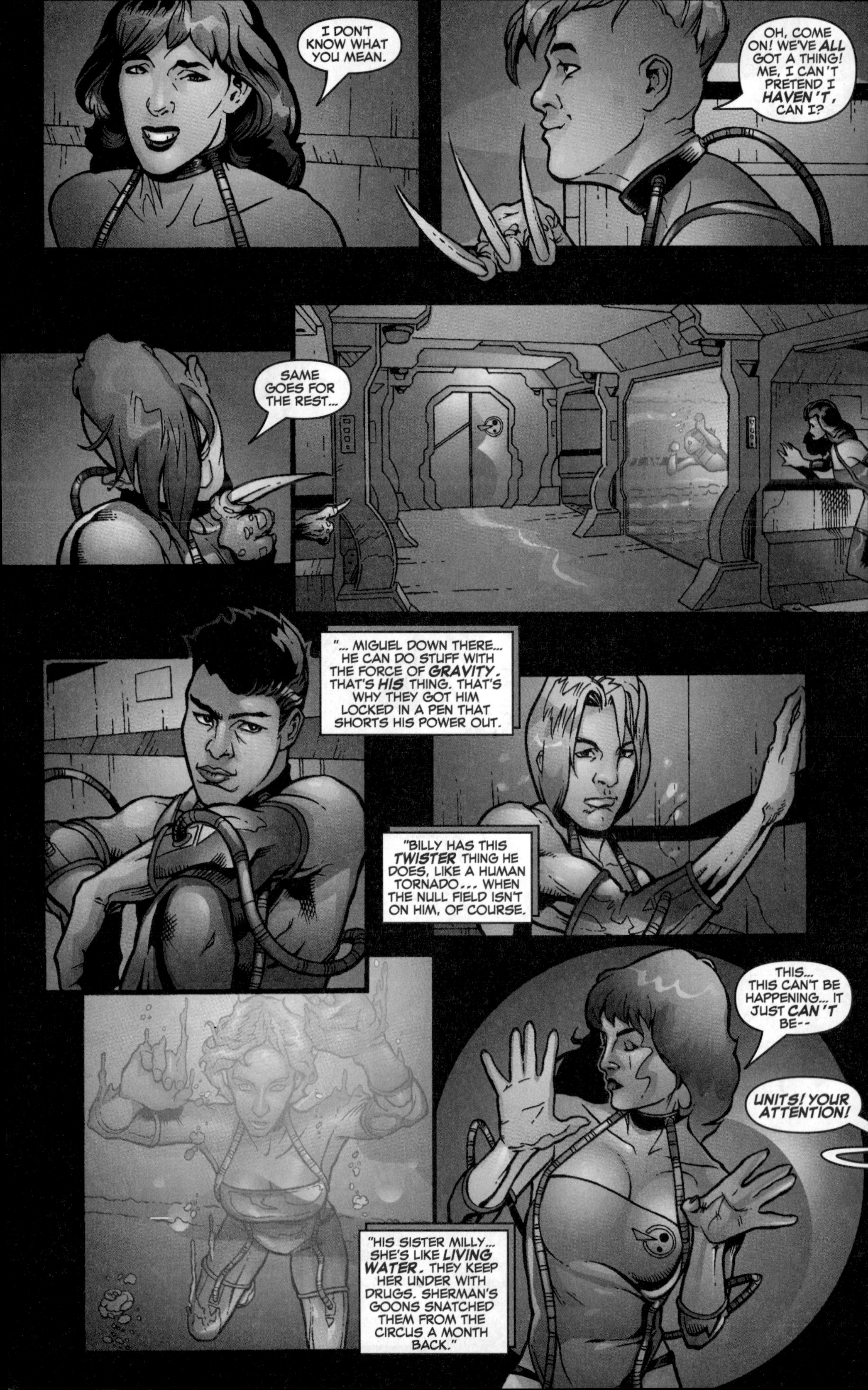

I DON'T KNOW WHAT YOU MEAN.
OH, COME ON! WE'VE ALL GOT A THING! ME, I CAN'T PRETEND I HAVEN'T, CAN I?
SAME GOES FOR THE REST...
"... MIGUEL DOWN THERE... HE CAN DO STUFF WITH THE FORCE OF GRAVITY. THAT'S HIS THING. THAT'S WHY THEY GOT HIM LOCKED IN A PEN THAT SHORTS HIS POWER OUT.
"BILLY HAS THIS TWISTER THING HE DOES, LIKE A HUMAN TORNADO... WHEN THE NULL FIELD ISN'T ON HIM, OF COURSE.
"HIS SISTER MILLY... SHE'S LIKE LIVING WATER. THEY KEEP HER UNDER WITH DRUGS. SHERMAN'S GOONS SNATCHED THEM FROM THE CIRCUS A MONTH BACK."
THIS... THIS CAN'T BE HAPPENING... IT JUST CAN'T BE--
UNITS! YOUR ATTENTION!

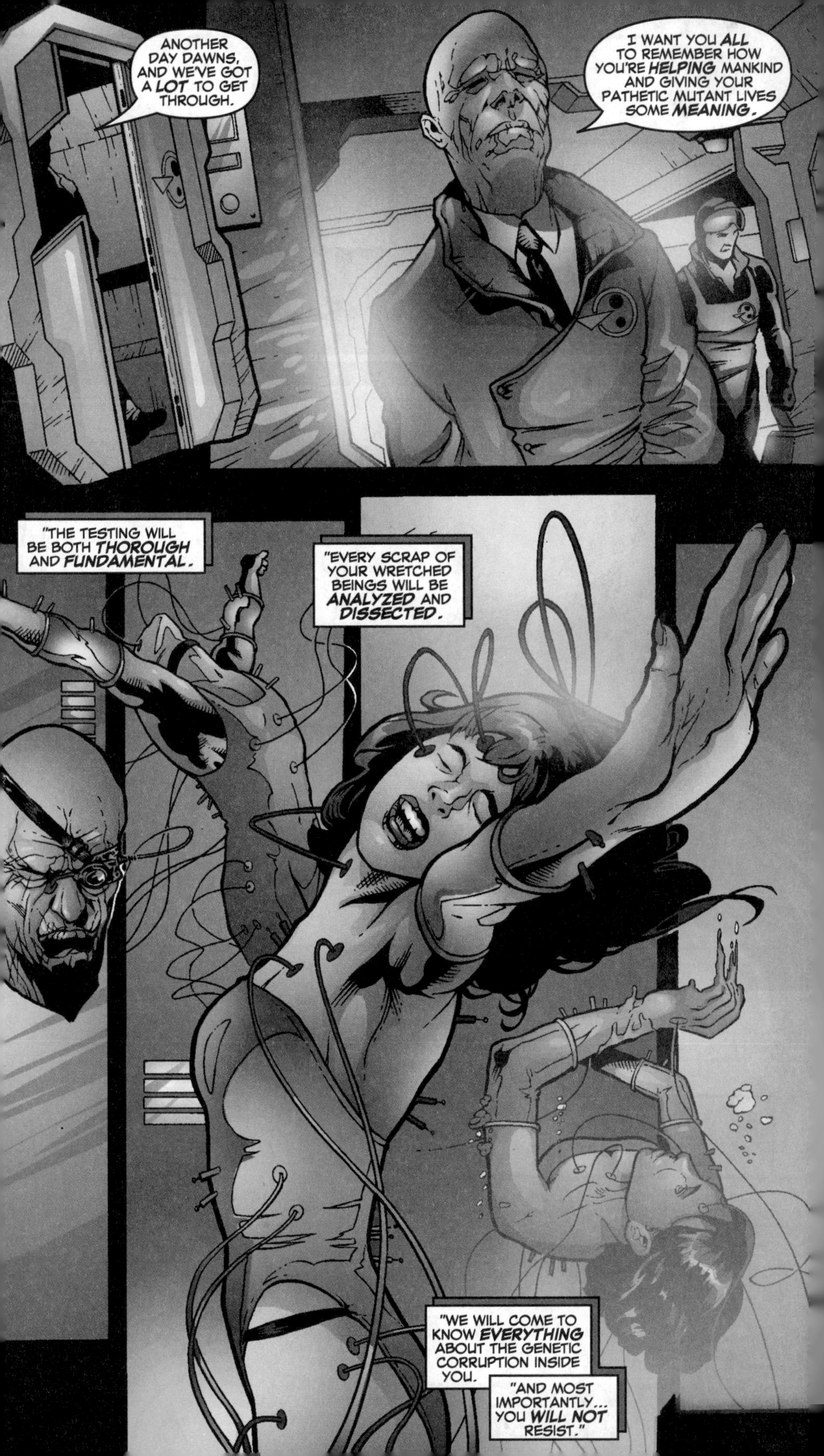
ANOTHER DAY DAWNS, AND WE'VE GOT A LOT TO GET THROUGH.
I WANT YOU ALL TO REMEMBER HOW YOU'RE HELPING MANKIND AND GIVING YOUR PATHETIC MUTANT LIVES SOME MEANING.
"THE TESTING WILL BE BOTH THOROUGH AND FUNDAMENTAL.
"EVERY SCRAP OF YOUR WRETCHED BEINGS WILL BE ANALYZED AND DISSECTED.
"WE WILL COME TO KNOW EVERYTHING ABOUT THE GENETIC CORRUPTION INSIDE YOU.
"AND MOST IMPORTANTLY... YOU WILL NOT RESIST."

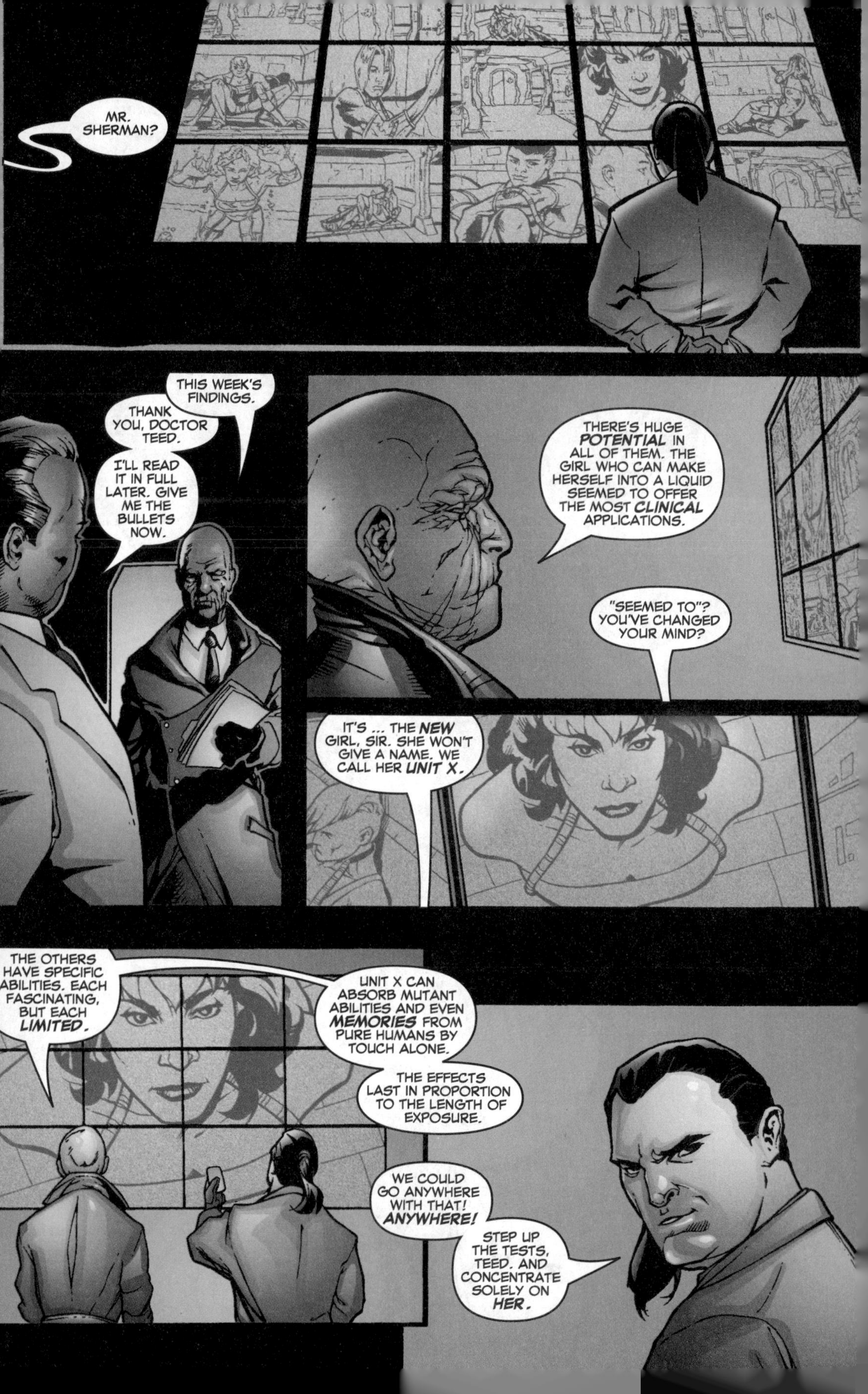
MR. SHERMAN?
THIS WEEK'S FINDINGS.
THANK YOU, DOCTOR TEED.
I'LL READ IT IN FULL LATER. GIVE ME THE BULLETS NOW.
THERE'S HUGE POTENTIAL IN ALL OF THEM. THE GIRL WHO CAN MAKE HERSELF INTO A LIQUID SEEMED TO OFFER THE MOST CLINICAL APPLICATIONS.
"SEEMED TO"? YOU'VE CHANGED YOUR MIND?
IT'S ... THE NEW GIRL, SIR. SHE WON'T GIVE A NAME. WE CALL HER UNIT X.
THE OTHERS HAVE SPECIFIC ABILITIES. EACH FASCINATING, BUT EACH LIMITED.
UNIT X CAN ABSORB MUTANT ABILITIES AND EVEN MEMORIES FROM PURE HUMANS BY TOUCH ALONE.
THE EFFECTS LAST IN PROPORTION TO THE LENGTH OF EXPOSURE.
WE COULD GO ANYWHERE WITH THAT! ANYWHERE!
STEP UP THE TESTS, TEED. AND CONCENTRATE SOLELY ON HER.

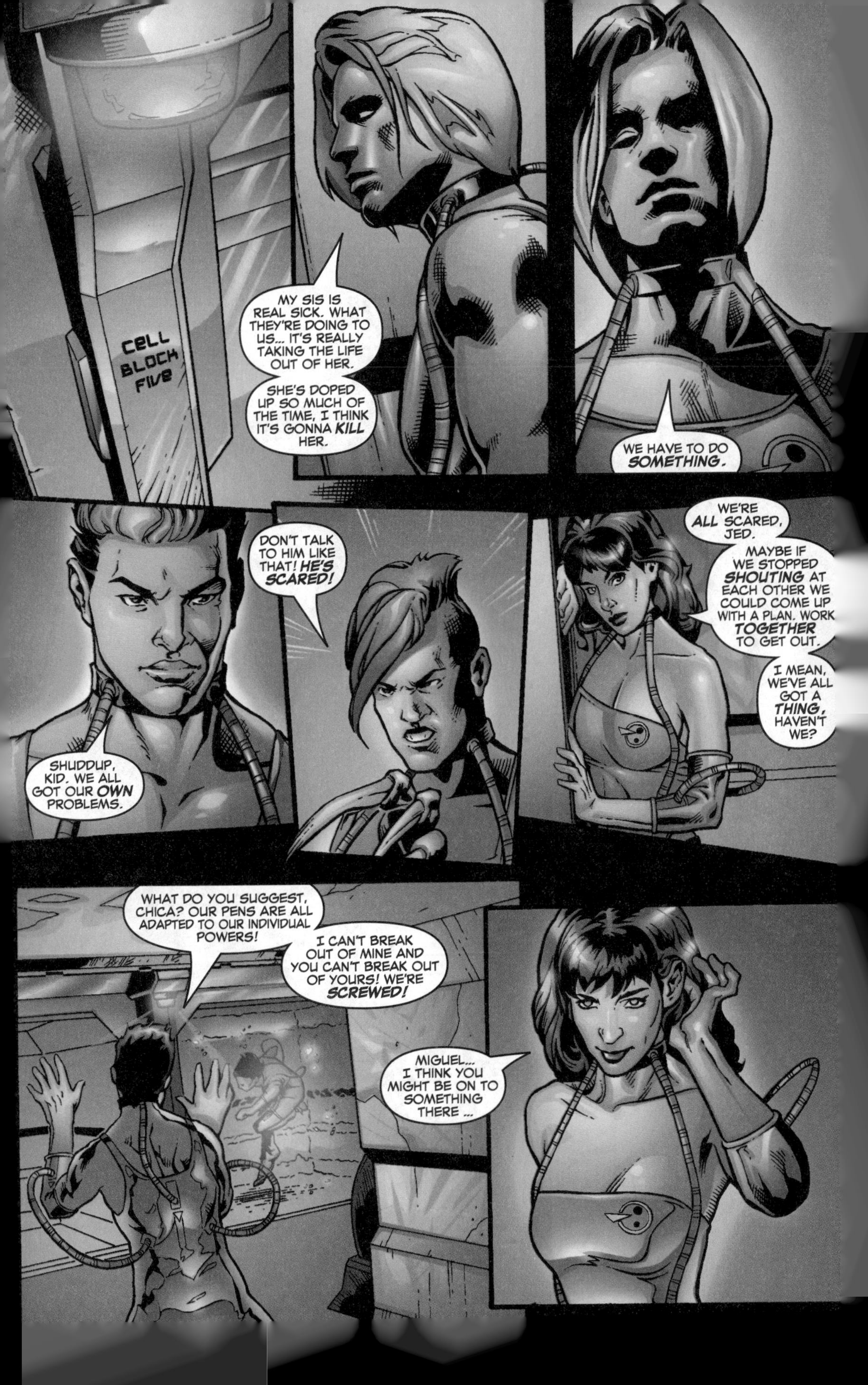
CELL BLOCK FIVE
MY SIS IS REAL SICK. WHAT THEY'RE DOING TO US... IT'S REALLY TAKING THE LIFE OUT OF HER.
SHE'S DOPED UP SO MUCH OF THE TIME, I THINK IT'S GONNA KILL HER.
WE HAVE TO DO SOMETHING.
SHUDDUP, KID. WE ALL GOT OUR OWN PROBLEMS.
DON'T TALK TO HIM LIKE THAT! HE'S SCARED!
WE'RE ALL SCARED, JED.
MAYBE IF WE STOPPED SHOUTING AT EACH OTHER WE COULD COME UP WITH A PLAN. WORK TOGETHER TO GET OUT.
I MEAN, WE'VE ALL GOT A THING, HAVEN'T WE?
WHAT DO YOU SUGGEST, CHICA? OUR PENS ARE ALL ADAPTED TO OUR INDIVIDUAL POWERS!
I CAN'T BREAK OUT OF MINE AND YOU CAN'T BREAK OUT OF YOURS! WE'RE SCREWED!
MIGUEL... I THINK YOU MIGHT BE ON TO SOMETHING THERE ...

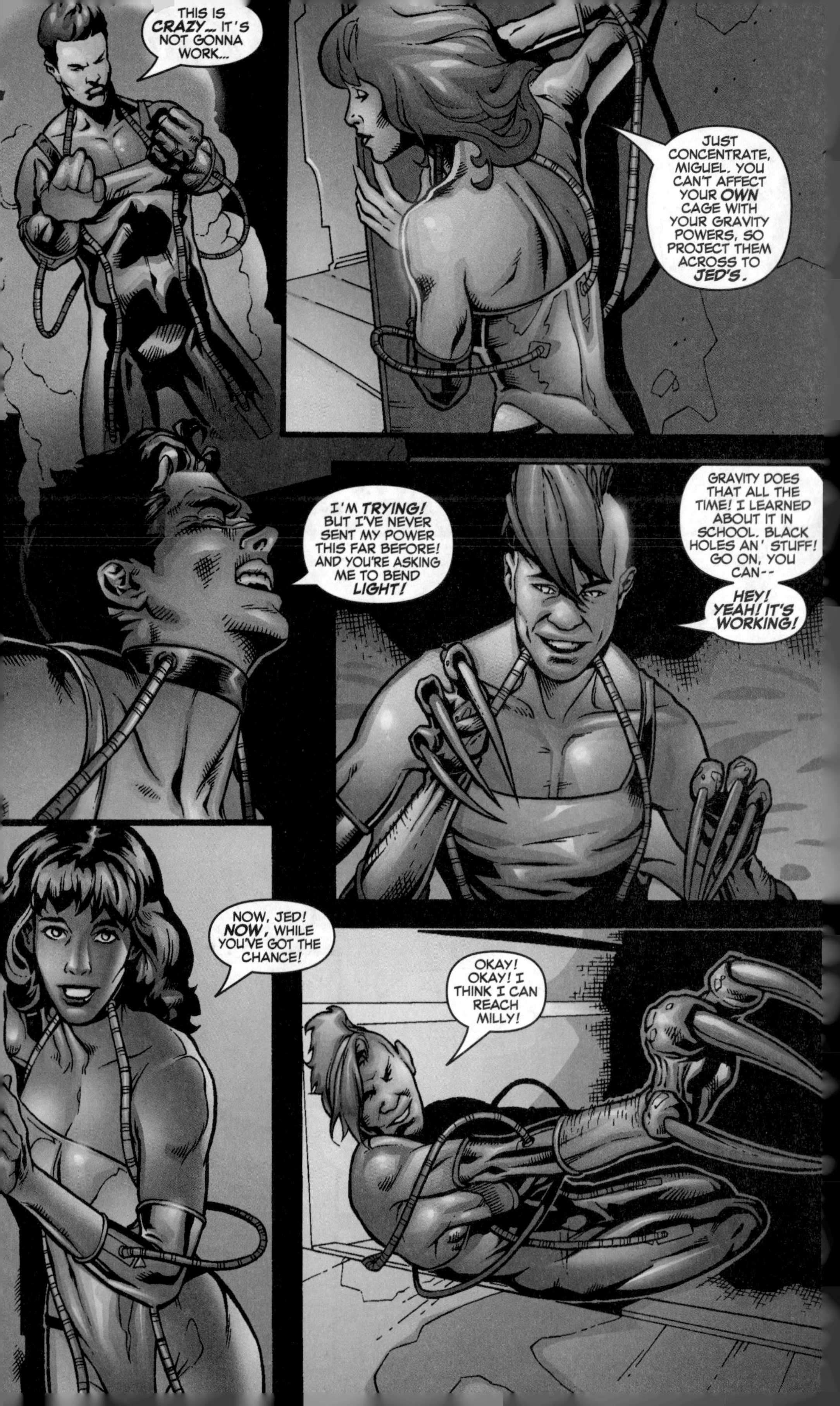
THIS IS CRAZY... IT'S NOT GONNA WORK...
JUST CONCENTRATE, MIGUEL. YOU CAN'T AFFECT YOUR OWN CAGE WITH YOUR GRAVITY POWERS, SO PROJECT THEM ACROSS TO JED'S.
I'M TRYING! BUT I'VE NEVER SENT MY POWER THIS FAR BEFORE! AND YOU'RE ASKING ME TO BEND LIGHT!
GRAVITY DOES THAT ALL THE TIME! I LEARNED ABOUT IT IN SCHOOL. BLACK HOLES AN' STUFF! GO ON, YOU CAN--
HEY! YEAH! IT'S WORKING!
NOW, JED! NOW, WHILE YOU'VE GOT THE CHANCE!
OKAY! OKAY! I THINK I CAN REACH MILLY!

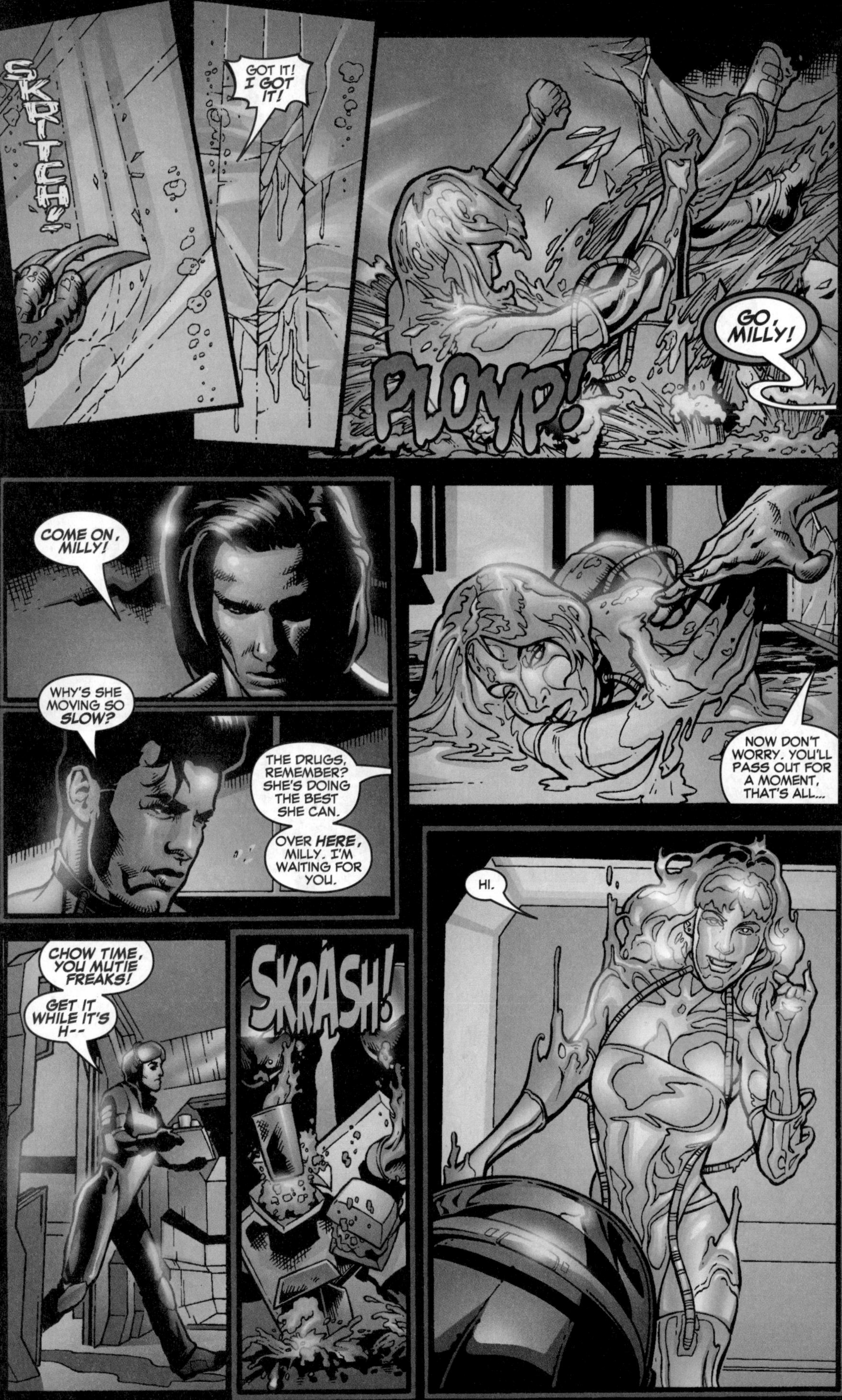
SKRITCH!
GOT IT! I GOT IT!
PLOYP!
GO, MILLY!
COME ON, MILLY!
NOW DON'T WORRY. YOU'LL PASS OUT FOR A MOMENT, THAT'S ALL...
WHY'S SHE MOVING SO SLOW?
THE DRUGS, REMEMBER? SHE'S DOING THE BEST SHE CAN.
OVER HERE, MILLY. I'M WAITING FOR YOU.
CHOW TIME, YOU MUTIE FREAKS!
GET IT WHILE IT'S H--
SKRASH!
HI.

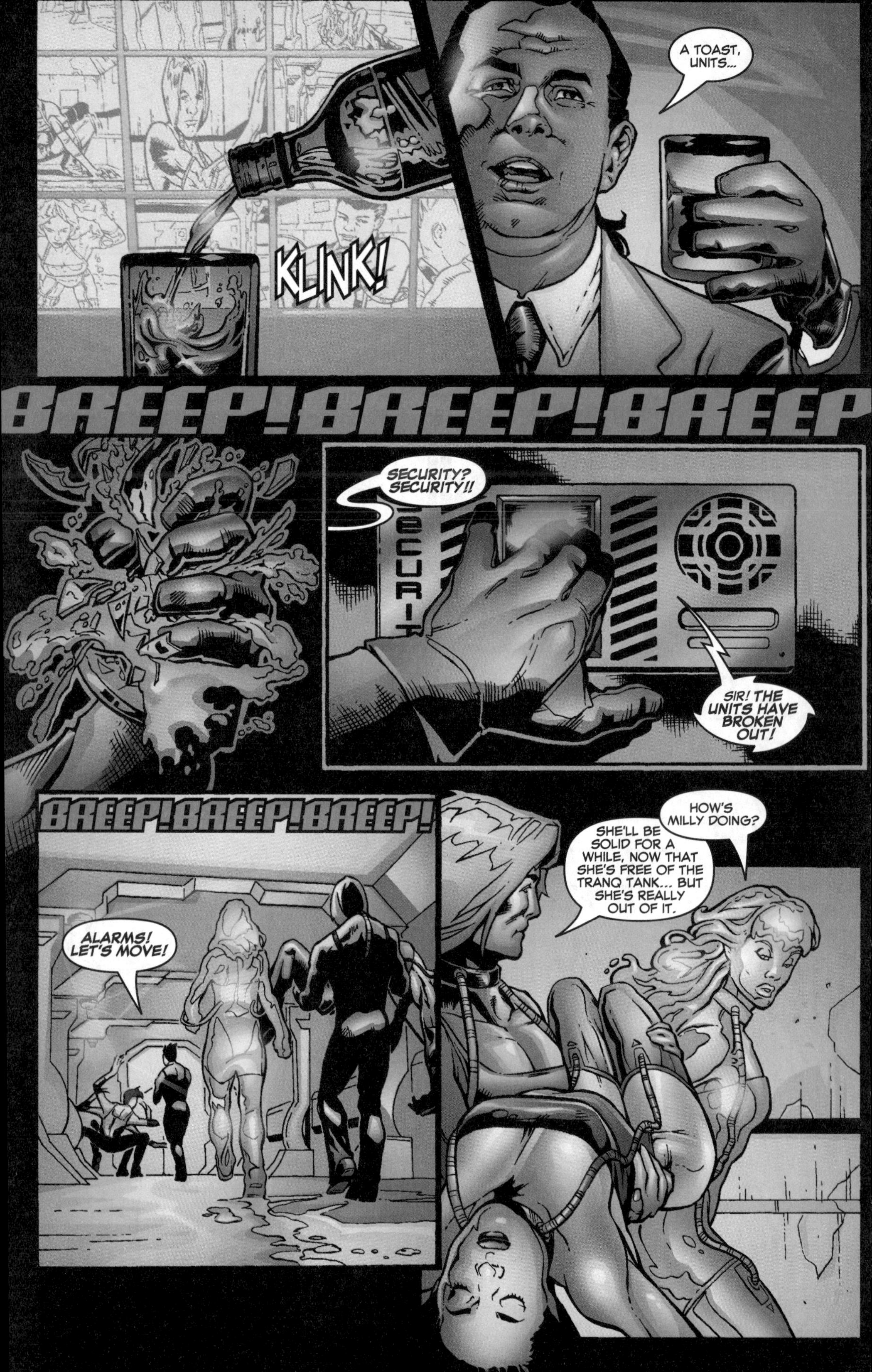
A TOAST, UNITS...
KLINK!
BREEP! BREEP! BREEP
SECURITY? SECURITY!!
SECURIT
SIR! THE UNITS HAVE BROKEN OUT!
BREEP! BREEP! BREEP!
ALARMS! LET'S MOVE!
HOW'S MILLY DOING?
SHE'LL BE SOLID FOR A WHILE, NOW THAT SHE'S FREE OF THE TRANQ TANK... BUT SHE'S REALLY OUT OF IT.

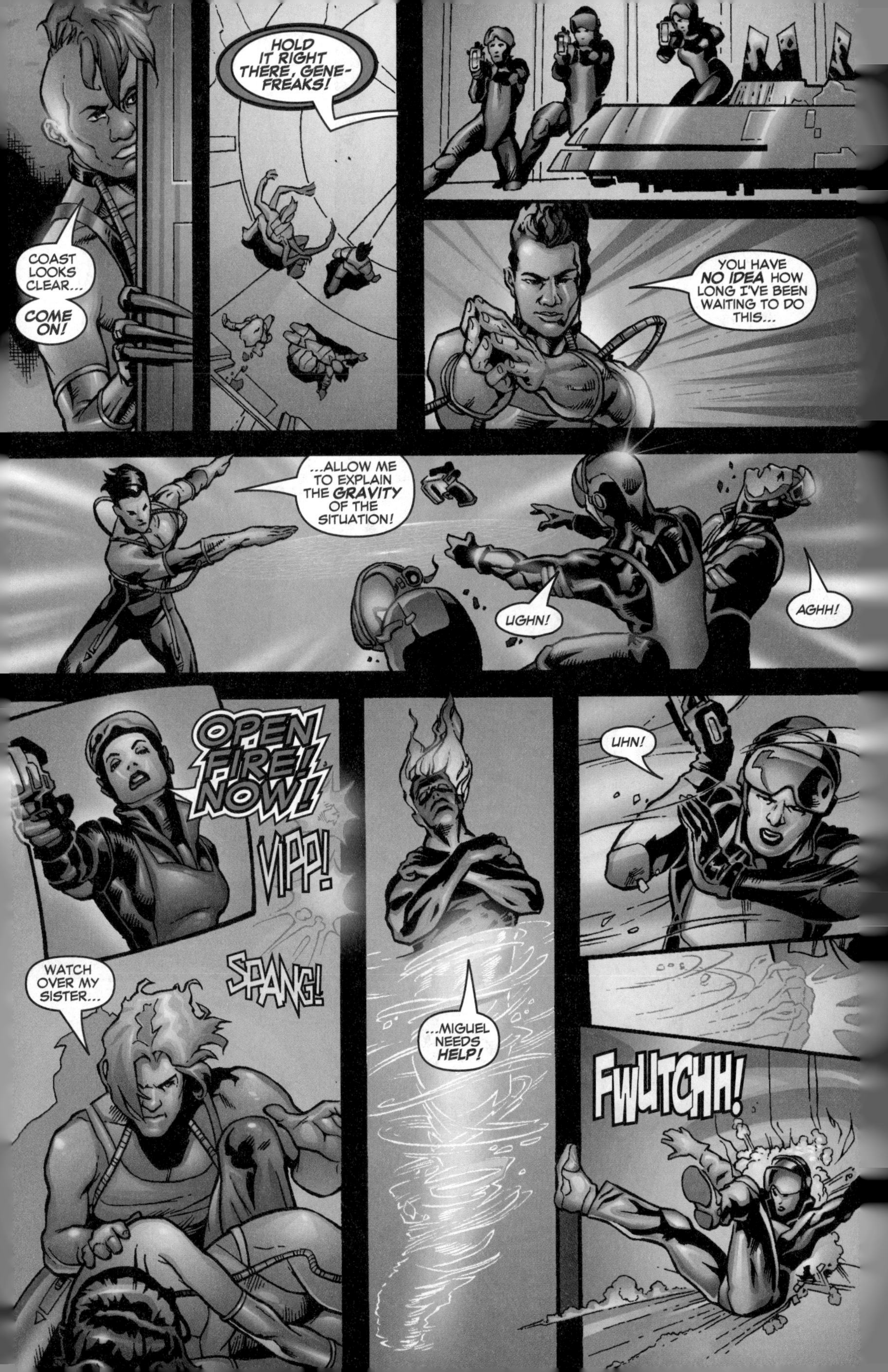
HOLD IT RIGHT THERE, GENE-FREAKS!
COAST LOOKS CLEAR...
COME ON!
YOU HAVE NO IDEA HOW LONG I'VE BEEN WAITING TO DO THIS...
...ALLOW ME TO EXPLAIN THE GRAVITY OF THE SITUATION!
UGHN!
AGHH!
OPEN FIRE! NOW!
VIPP!
SPANG!
WATCH OVER MY SISTER...
...MIGUEL NEEDS HELP!
UHN!
FWUTCHH!

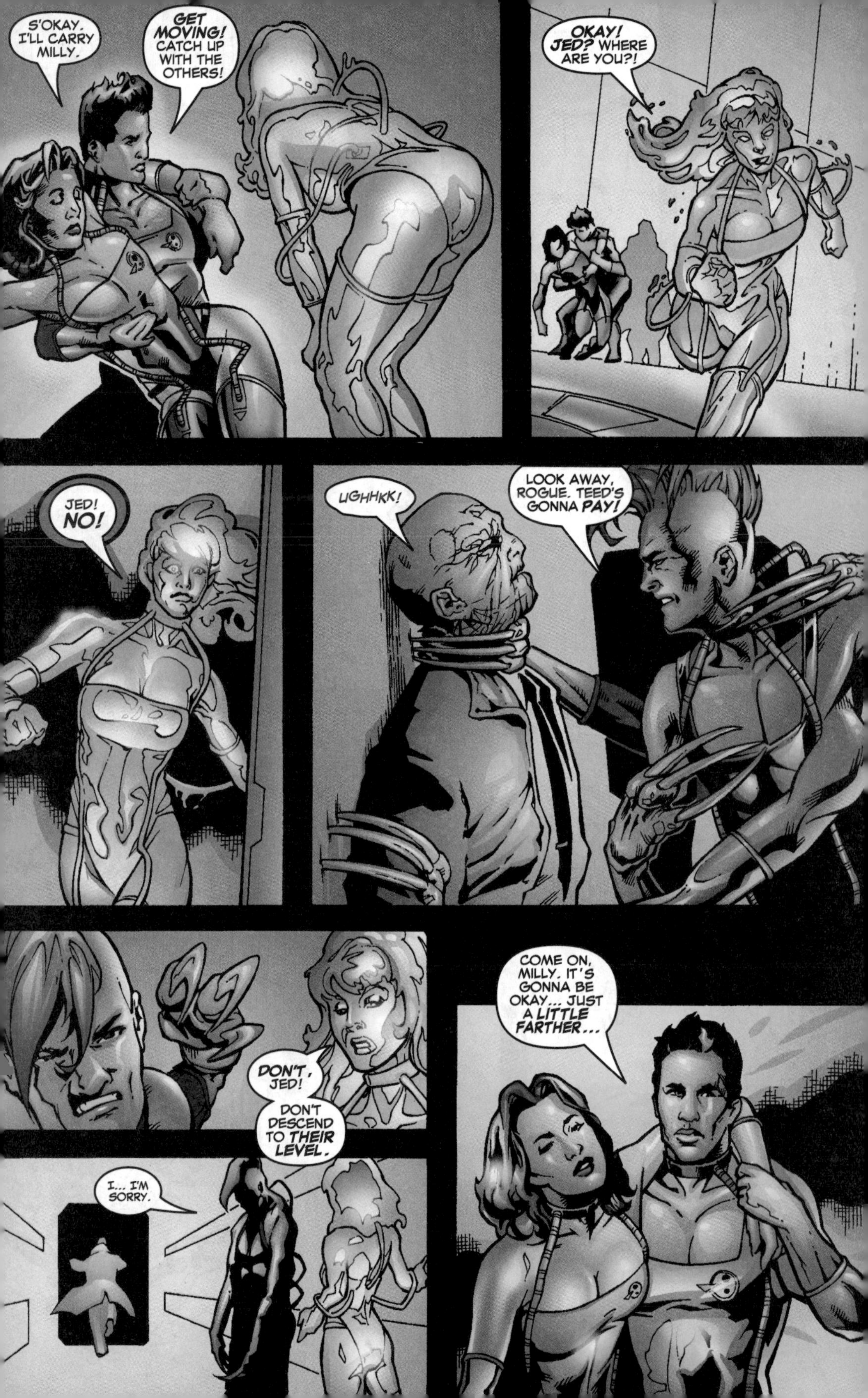
S'OKAY. I'LL CARRY MILLY.
GET MOVING! CATCH UP WITH THE OTHERS!
OKAY! JED? WHERE ARE YOU?!
JED! NO!
UGHHKK!
LOOK AWAY, ROGUE. TEED'S GONNA PAY!
DON'T, JED!
DON'T DESCEND TO THEIR LEVEL.
I... I'M SORRY.
COME ON, MILLY. IT'S GONNA BE OKAY... JUST A LITTLE FARTHER...

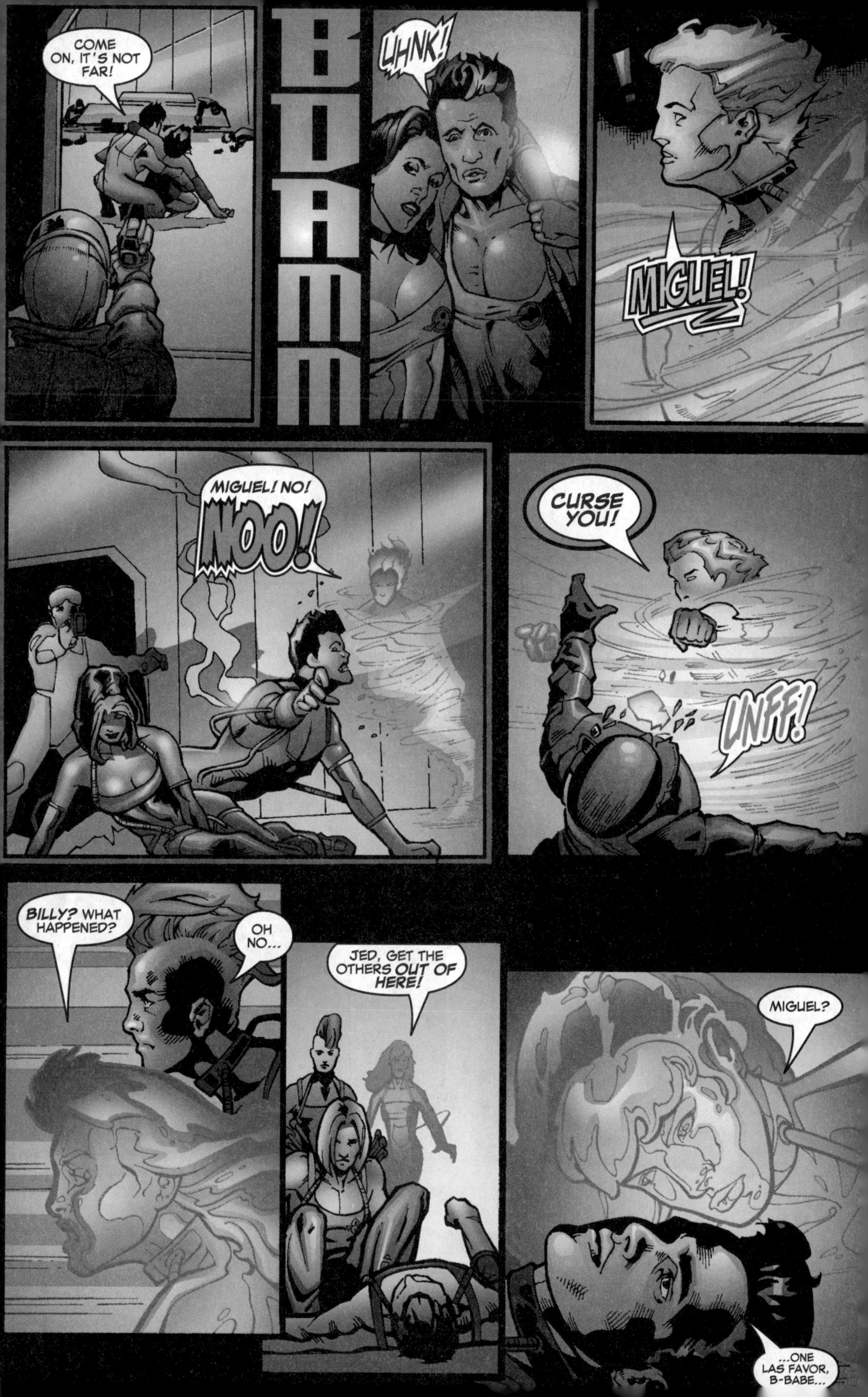
COME ON, IT'S NOT FAR!
BDAMM
UHNK!
!
MIGUEL!
MIGUEL! NO!
NOO!
CURSE YOU!
UNFF!
BILLY? WHAT HAPPENED?
OH NO...
JED, GET THE OTHERS OUT OF HERE!
MIGUEL?
...ONE LAS FAVOR, B-BABE...

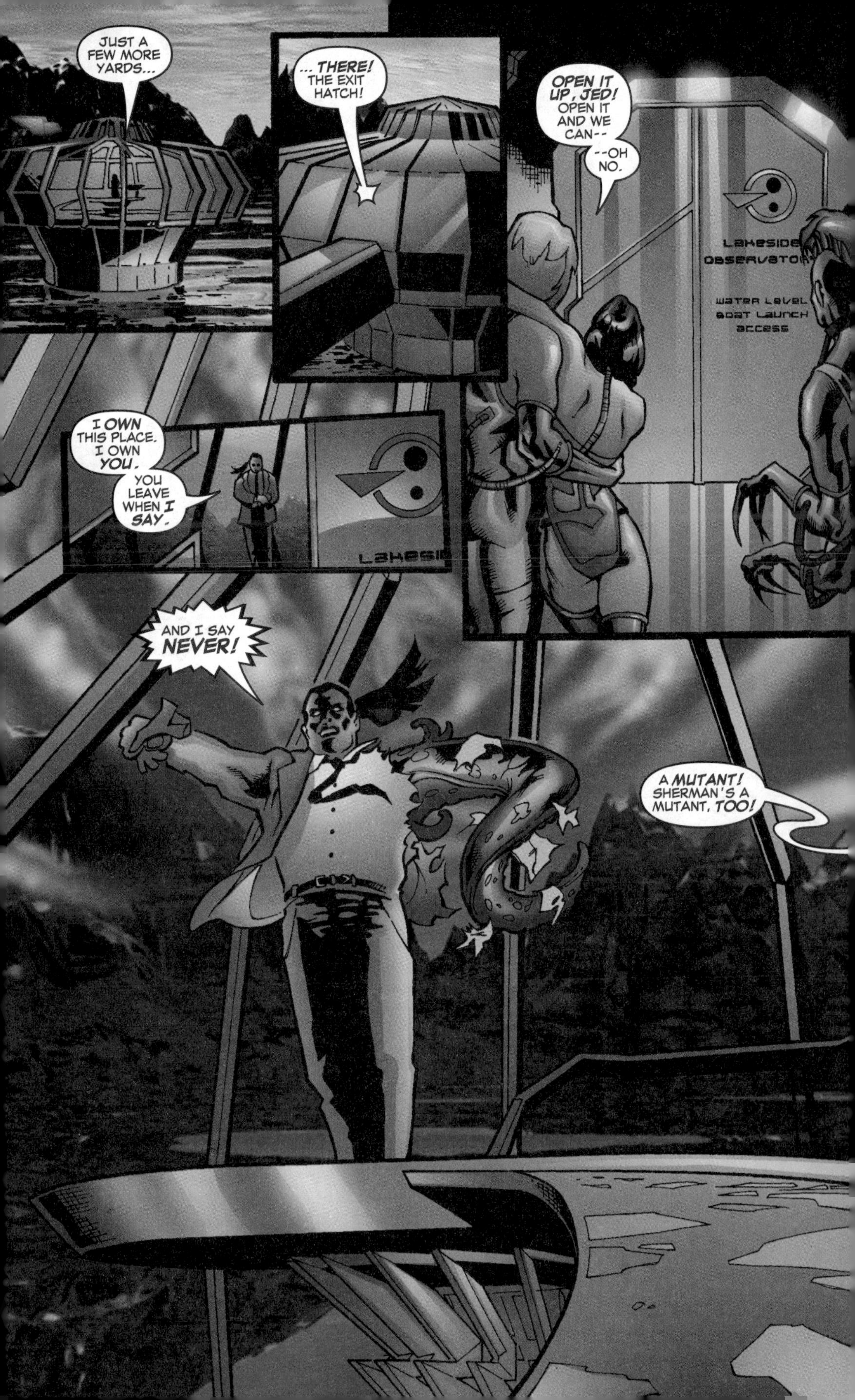
JUST A FEW MORE YARDS...
...THERE! THE EXIT HATCH!
OPEN IT UP, JED! OPEN IT AND WE CAN--
--OH NO.
LAKESIDE OBSERVATORY
WATER LEVEL BOAT LAUNCH ACCESS
I OWN THIS PLACE. I OWN YOU.
YOU LEAVE WHEN I SAY.
AND I SAY NEVER!
A MUTANT! SHERMAN'S A MUTANT, TOO!

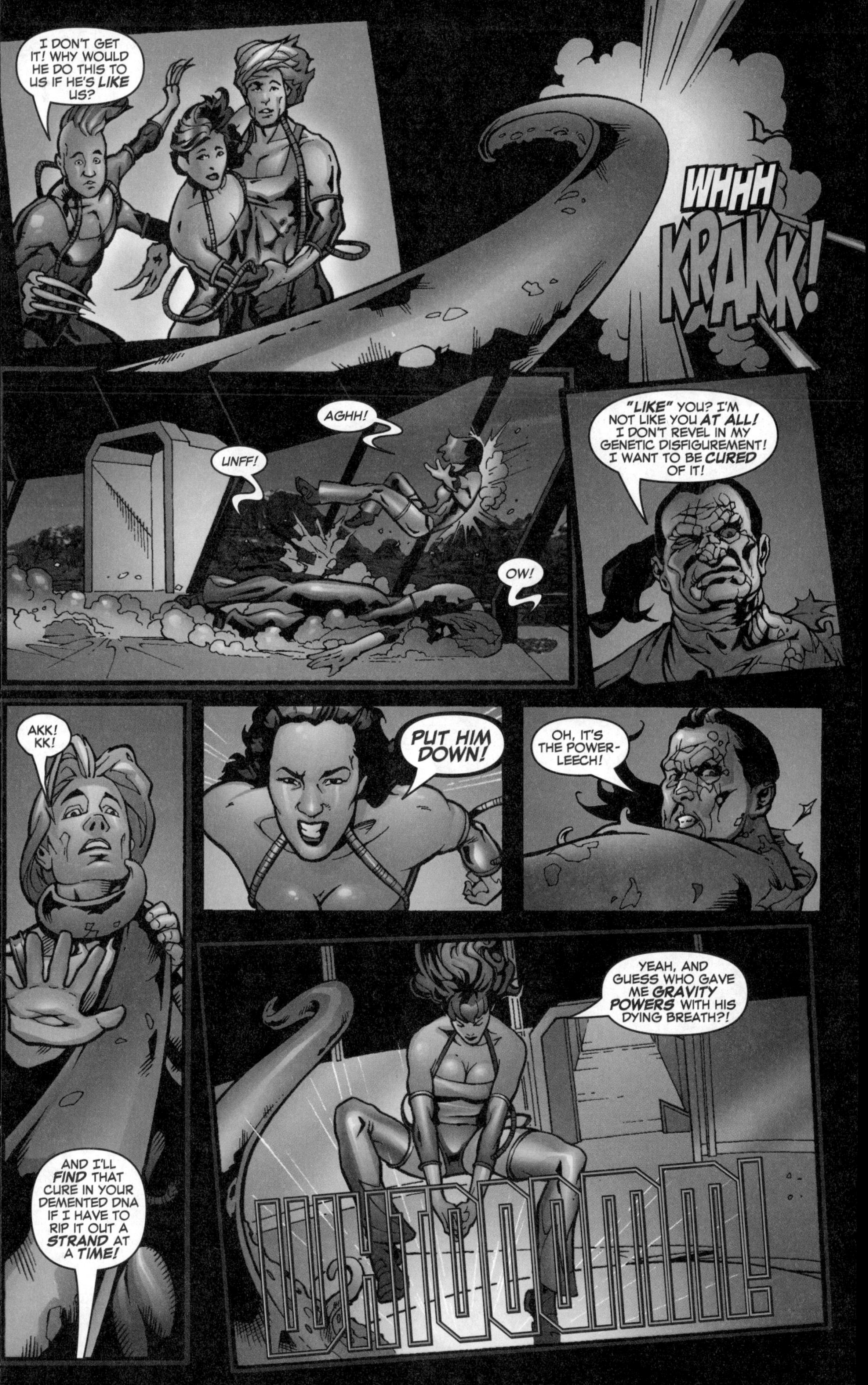
I DON'T GET IT! WHY WOULD HE DO THIS TO US IF HE'S LIKE US?
WHHH
KRAKK!
AGHH!
UNFF!
OW!
"LIKE" YOU? I'M NOT LIKE YOU AT ALL! I DON'T REVEL IN MY GENETIC DISFIGUREMENT! I WANT TO BE CURED OF IT!
AKK! KK!
PUT HIM DOWN!
OH, IT'S THE POWER-LEECH!
YEAH, AND GUESS WHO GAVE ME GRAVITY POWERS WITH HIS DYING BREATH?!
AND I'LL FIND THAT CURE IN YOUR DEMENTED DNA IF I HAVE TO RIP IT OUT A STRAND AT A TIME!

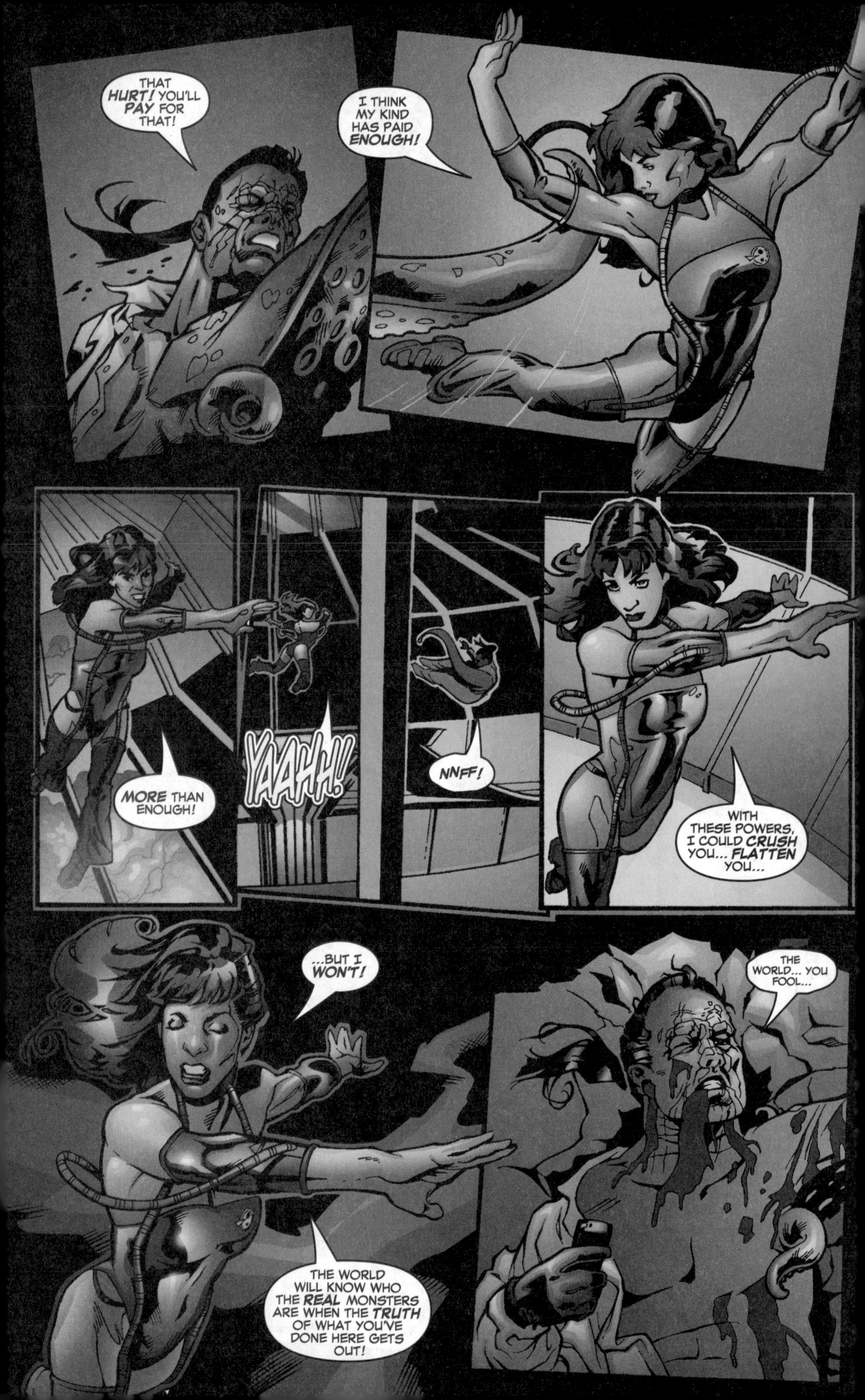
THAT HURT! YOU'LL PAY FOR THAT!
I THINK MY KIND HAS PAID ENOUGH!
MORE THAN ENOUGH!
YAAHH!
NNFF!
WITH THESE POWERS, I COULD CRUSH YOU... FLATTEN YOU...
...BUT I WON'T!
THE WORLD WILL KNOW WHO THE REAL MONSTERS ARE WHEN THE TRUTH OF WHAT YOU'VE DONE HERE GETS OUT!
THE WORLD... YOU FOOL...

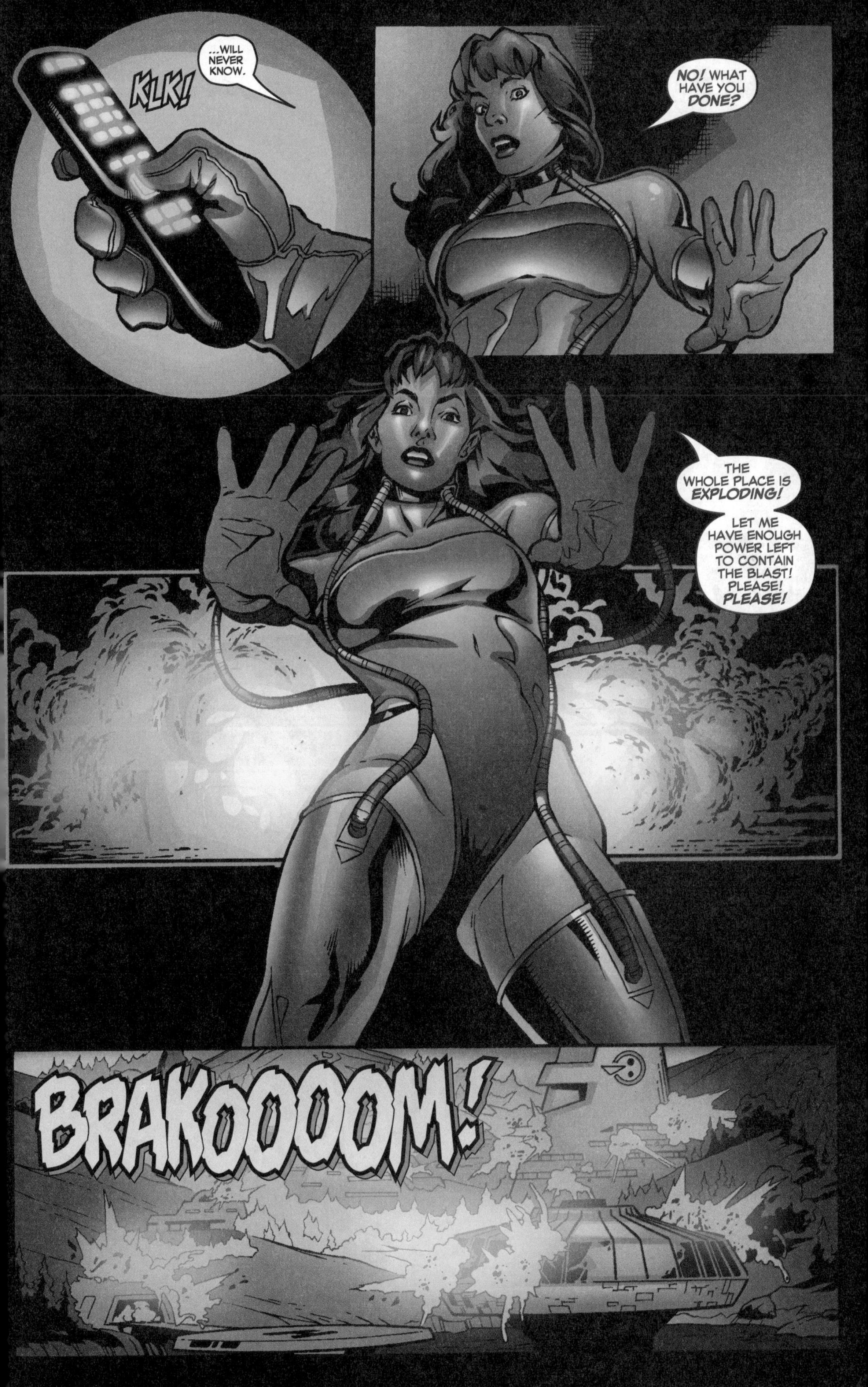
...WILL NEVER KNOW.
KLK!
NO! WHAT HAVE YOU DONE?
THE WHOLE PLACE IS EXPLODING!
LET ME HAVE ENOUGH POWER LEFT TO CONTAIN THE BLAST! PLEASE! PLEASE!
BRAKOOOOM!

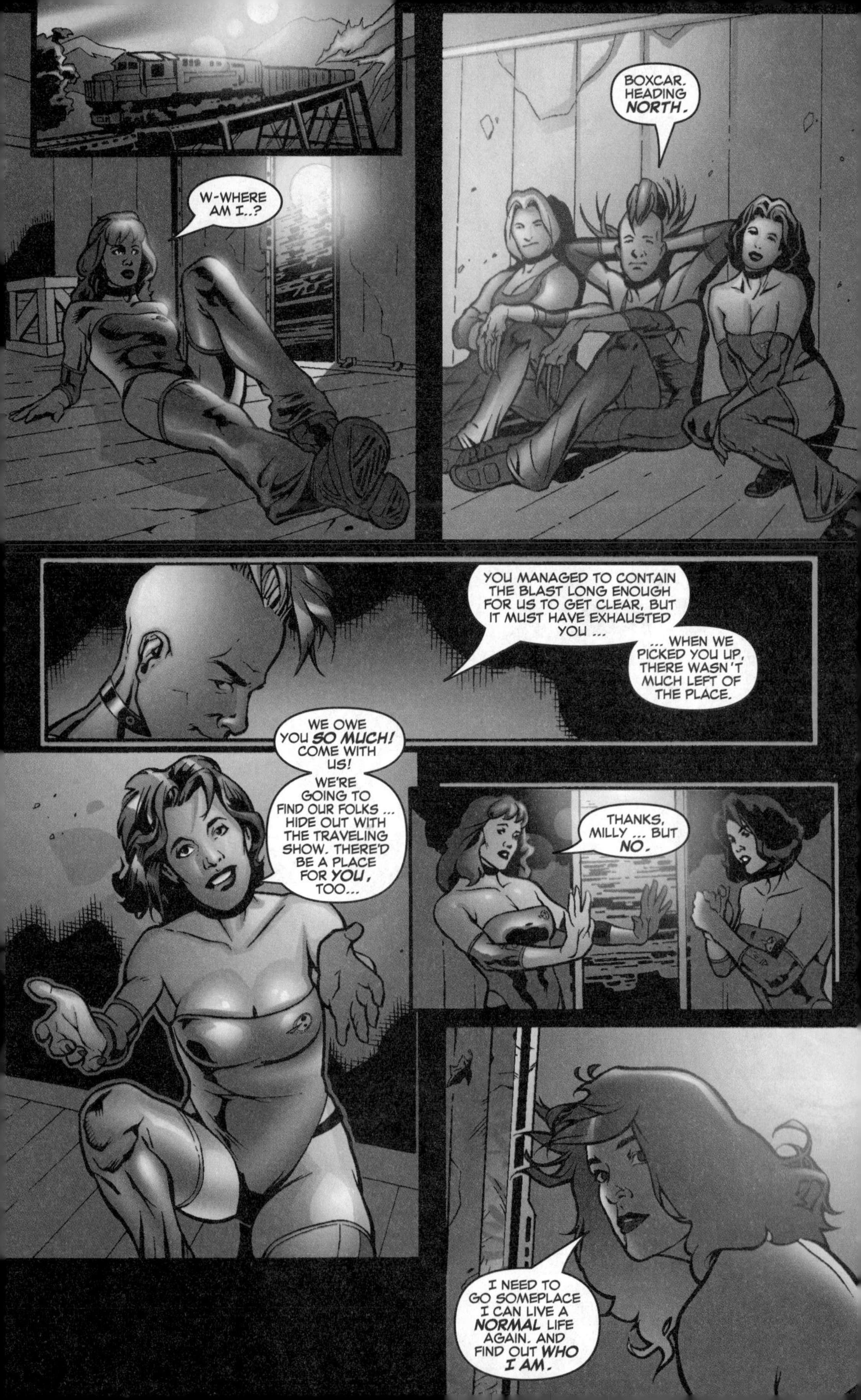
W-WHERE AM I..?
BOXCAR. HEADING NORTH.
YOU MANAGED TO CONTAIN THE BLAST LONG ENOUGH FOR US TO GET CLEAR, BUT IT MUST HAVE EXHAUSTED YOU ...
... WHEN WE PICKED YOU UP, THERE WASN'T MUCH LEFT OF THE PLACE.
WE OWE YOU SO MUCH! COME WITH US!
WE'RE GOING TO FIND OUR FOLKS ... HIDE OUT WITH THE TRAVELING SHOW. THERE'D BE A PLACE FOR YOU, TOO...
THANKS, MILLY ... BUT NO.
I NEED TO GO SOMEPLACE I CAN LIVE A NORMAL LIFE AGAIN. AND FIND OUT WHO I AM.

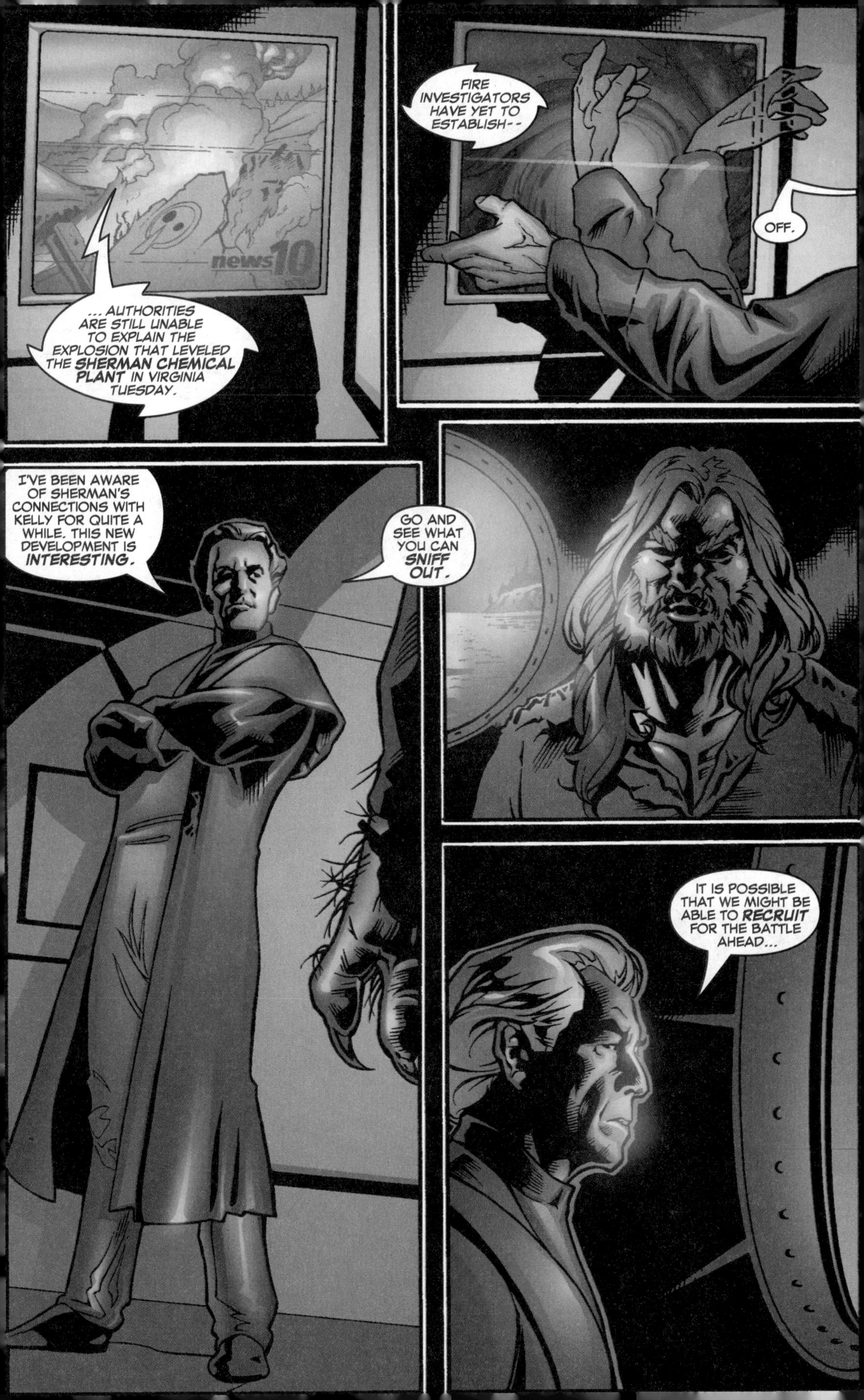
news10
... AUTHORITIES ARE STILL UNABLE TO EXPLAIN THE EXPLOSION THAT LEVELED THE SHERMAN CHEMICAL PLANT IN VIRGINIA TUESDAY.
FIRE INVESTIGATORS HAVE YET TO ESTABLISH--
OFF.
I'VE BEEN AWARE OF SHERMAN'S CONNECTIONS WITH KELLY FOR QUITE A WHILE. THIS NEW DEVELOPMENT IS INTERESTING.
GO AND SEE WHAT YOU CAN SNIFF OUT.
IT IS POSSIBLE THAT WE MIGHT BE ABLE TO RECRUIT FOR THE BATTLE AHEAD...

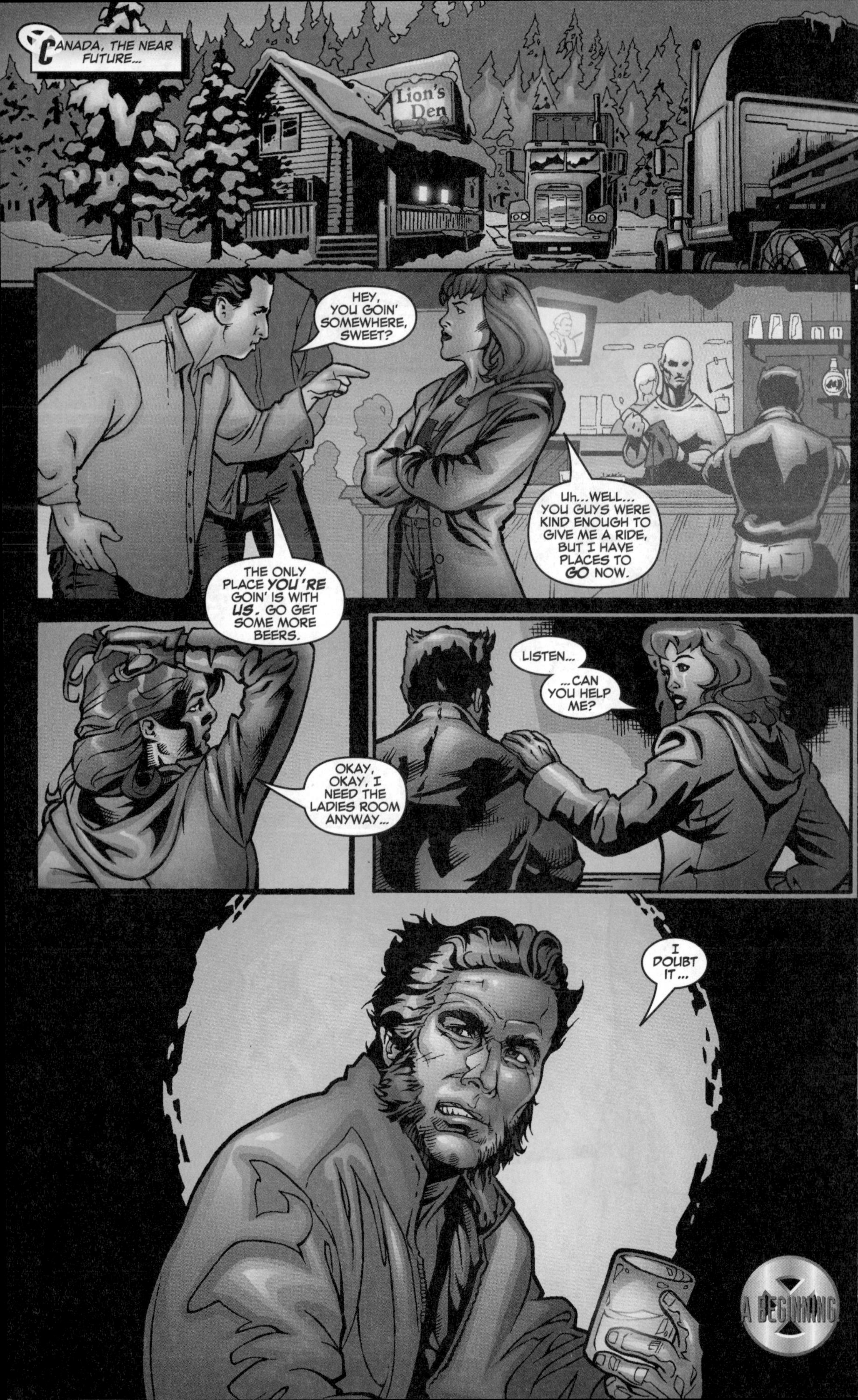
CANADA, THE NEAR FUTURE...
Lion's Den
HEY, YOU GOIN' SOMEWHERE, SWEET?
UH...WELL... YOU GUYS WERE KIND ENOUGH TO GIVE ME A RIDE, BUT I HAVE PLACES TO GO NOW.
THE ONLY PLACE YOU'RE GOIN' IS WITH US. GO GET SOME MORE BEERS.
OKAY, OKAY, I NEED THE LADIES ROOM ANYWAY...
LISTEN...
...CAN YOU HELP ME?
I DOUBT IT...
A BEGINNING

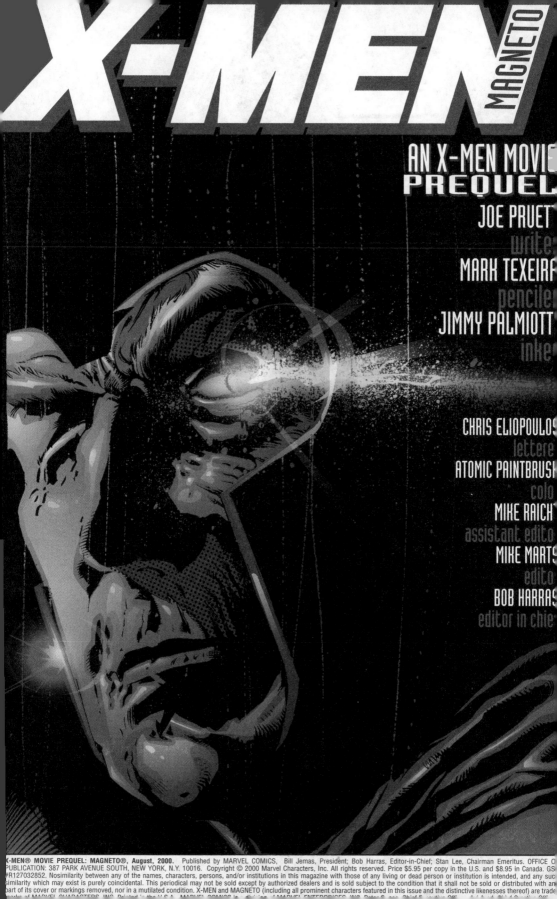

X-MEN

MAGNETO

AN X-MEN MOVIE PREQUEL

JOE PRUET
writer

MARK TEXEIRA
penciler

JIMMY PALMIOTT
inker

CHRIS ELIOPOULOS
letterer

ATOMIC PAINTBRUSH
color

MIKE RAICH
assistant editor

MIKE MARTS
editor

BOB HARRAS
editor in chief

X-MEN® MOVIE PREQUEL: MAGNETO®, August, 2000. Published by MARVEL COMICS, Bill Jemas, President; Bob Harras, Editor-in-Chief; Stan Lee, Chairman Emeritus. OFFICE O
PUBLICATION: 387 PARK AVENUE SOUTH, NEW YORK, N.Y. 10016. Copyright © 2000 Marvel Characters, Inc. All rights reserved. Price $5.95 per copy in the U.S. and $8.95 in Canada. GS
#R127032852. Nosimilarity between any of the names, characters, persons, and/or institutions in this magazine with those of any living or dead person or institution is intended, and any su
similarity which may exist is purely coincidental. This periodical may not be sold except by authorized dealers and is sold subject to the condition that it shall not be sold or distributed with an
part of its cover or markings removed, nor in a mutilated condition. X-MEN and MAGNETO (including all prominent characters featured in this issue and the distinctive likenesses thereof) are trade

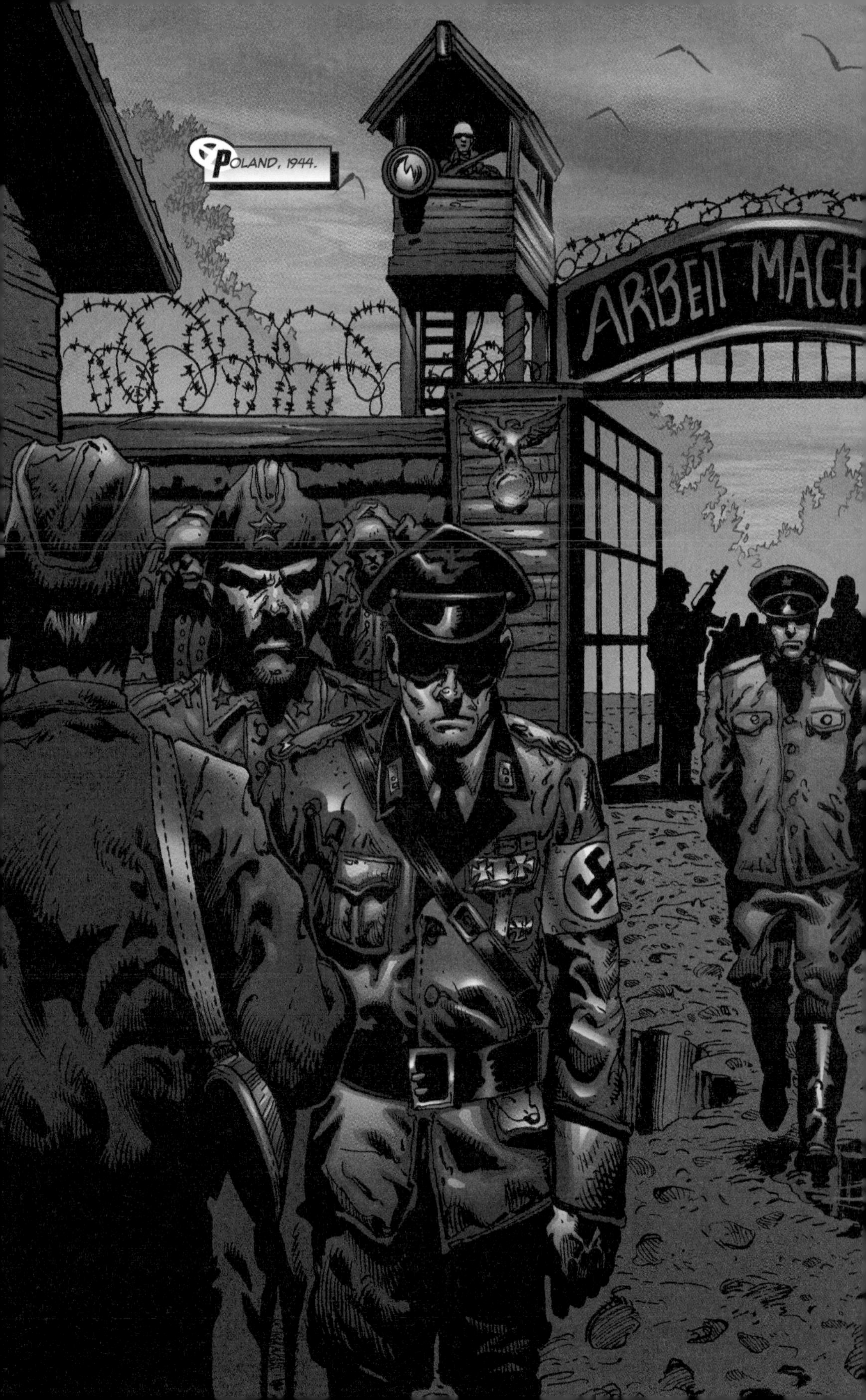
POLAND, 1944.
ARBEIT MACH

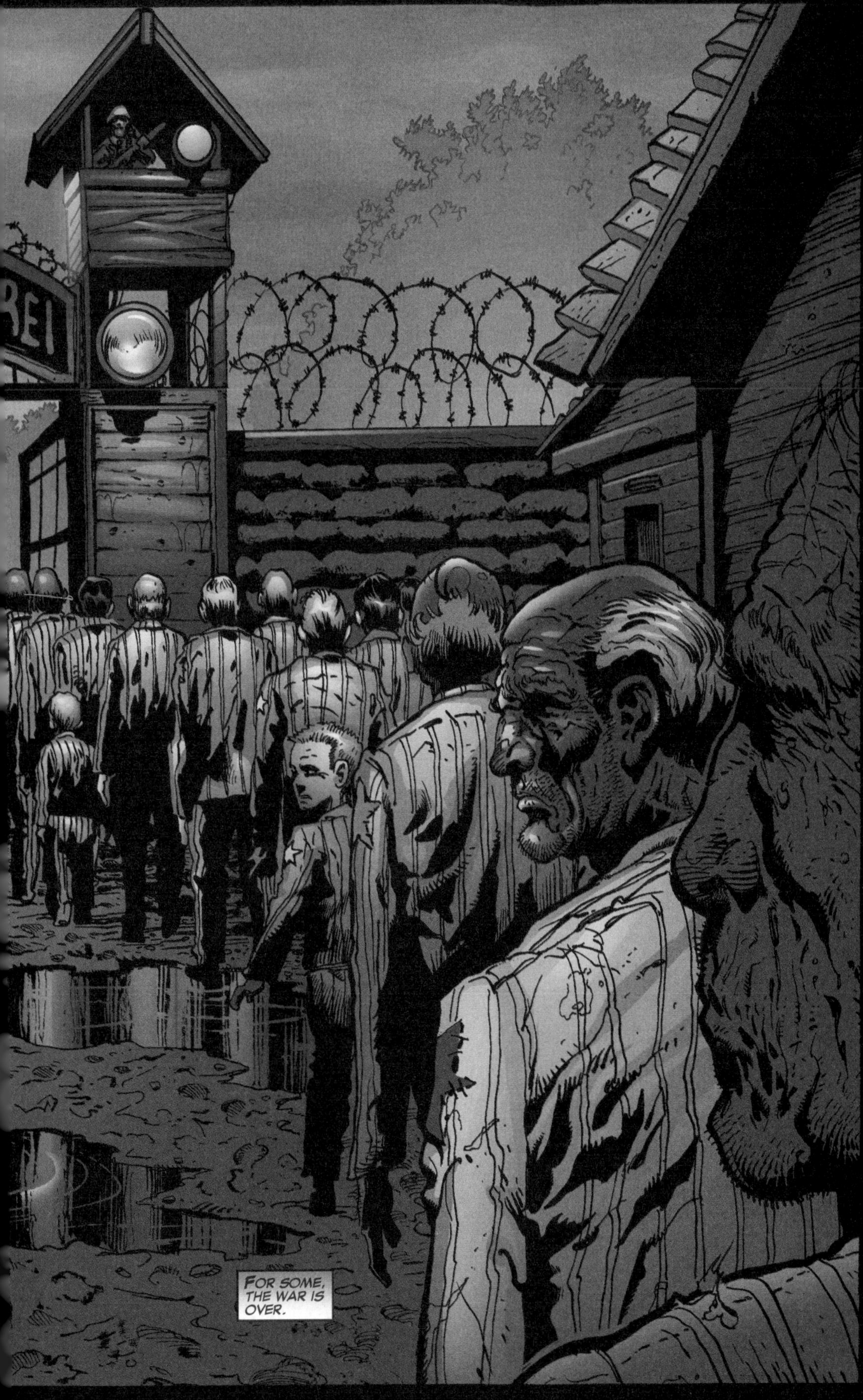
FOR SOME, THE WAR IS OVER.

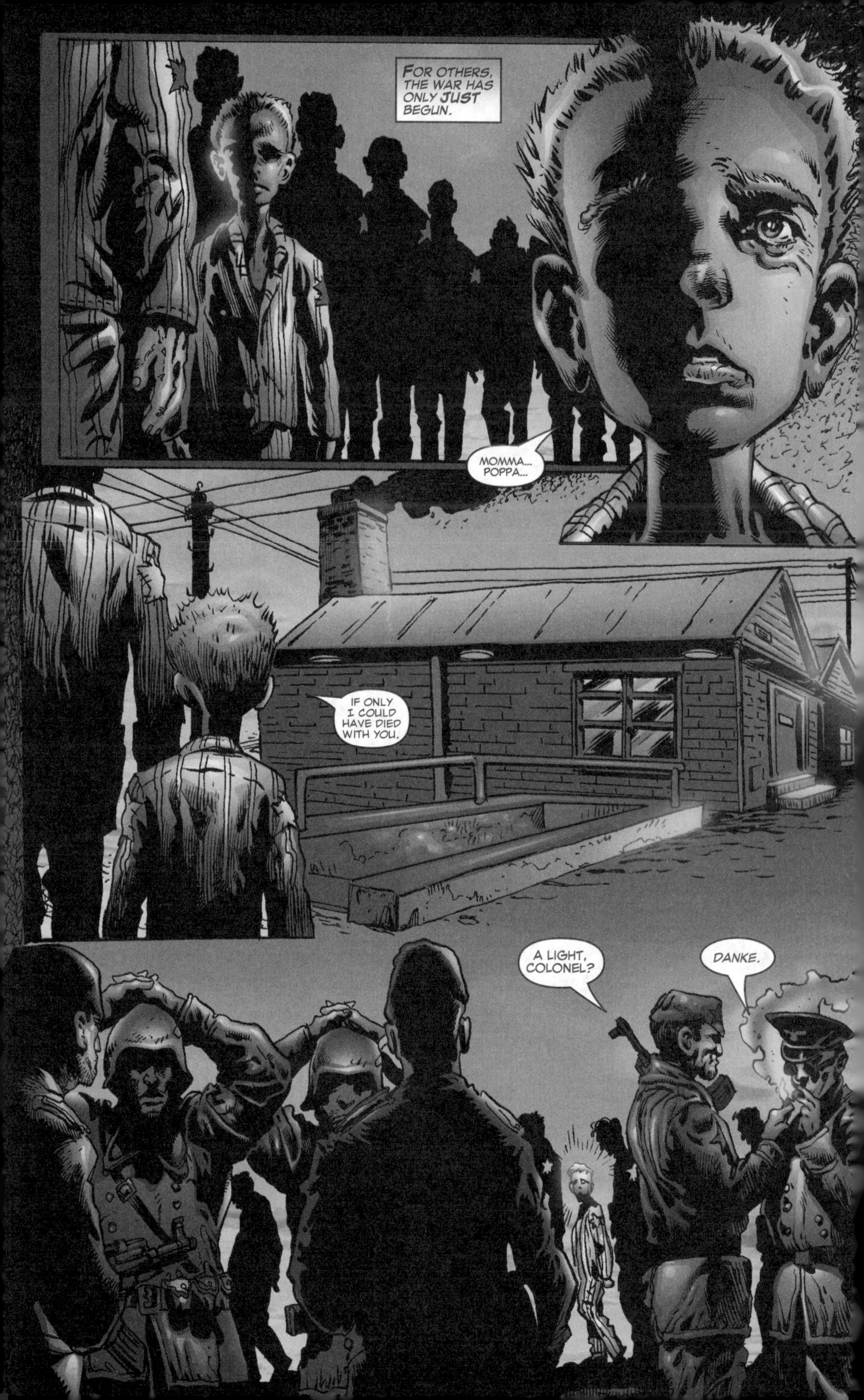
FOR OTHERS, THE WAR HAS ONLY JUST BEGUN.
MOMMA... POPPA...
IF ONLY I COULD HAVE DIED WITH YOU.
A LIGHT, COLONEL?
DANKE.

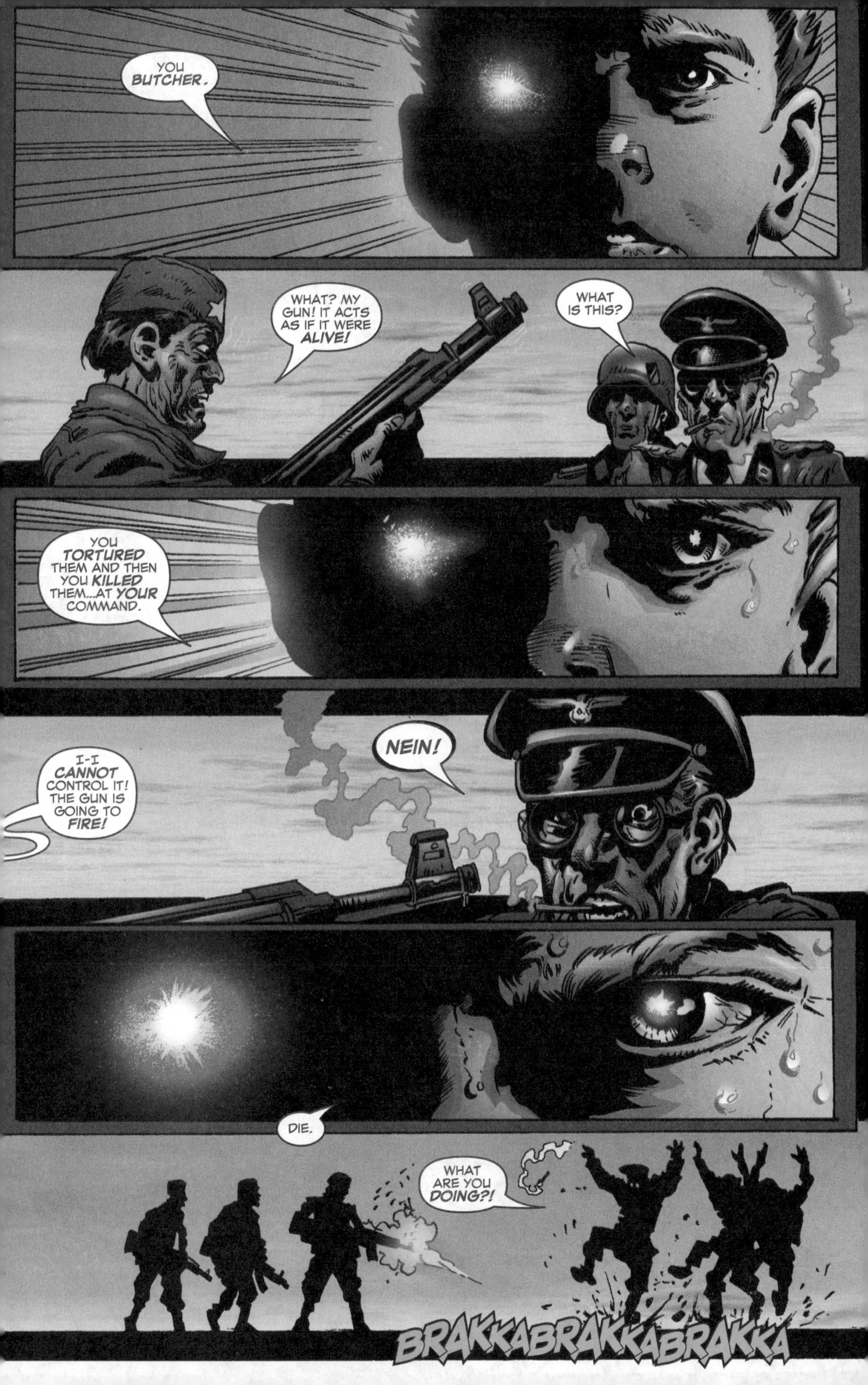
YOU BUTCHER.
WHAT? MY GUN! IT ACTS AS IF IT WERE ALIVE!
WHAT IS THIS?
YOU TORTURED THEM AND THEN YOU KILLED THEM...AT YOUR COMMAND.
NEIN!
I-I CANNOT CONTROL IT! THE GUN IS GOING TO FIRE!
DIE.
WHAT ARE YOU DOING?!
BRAKKABRAKKABRAKKA

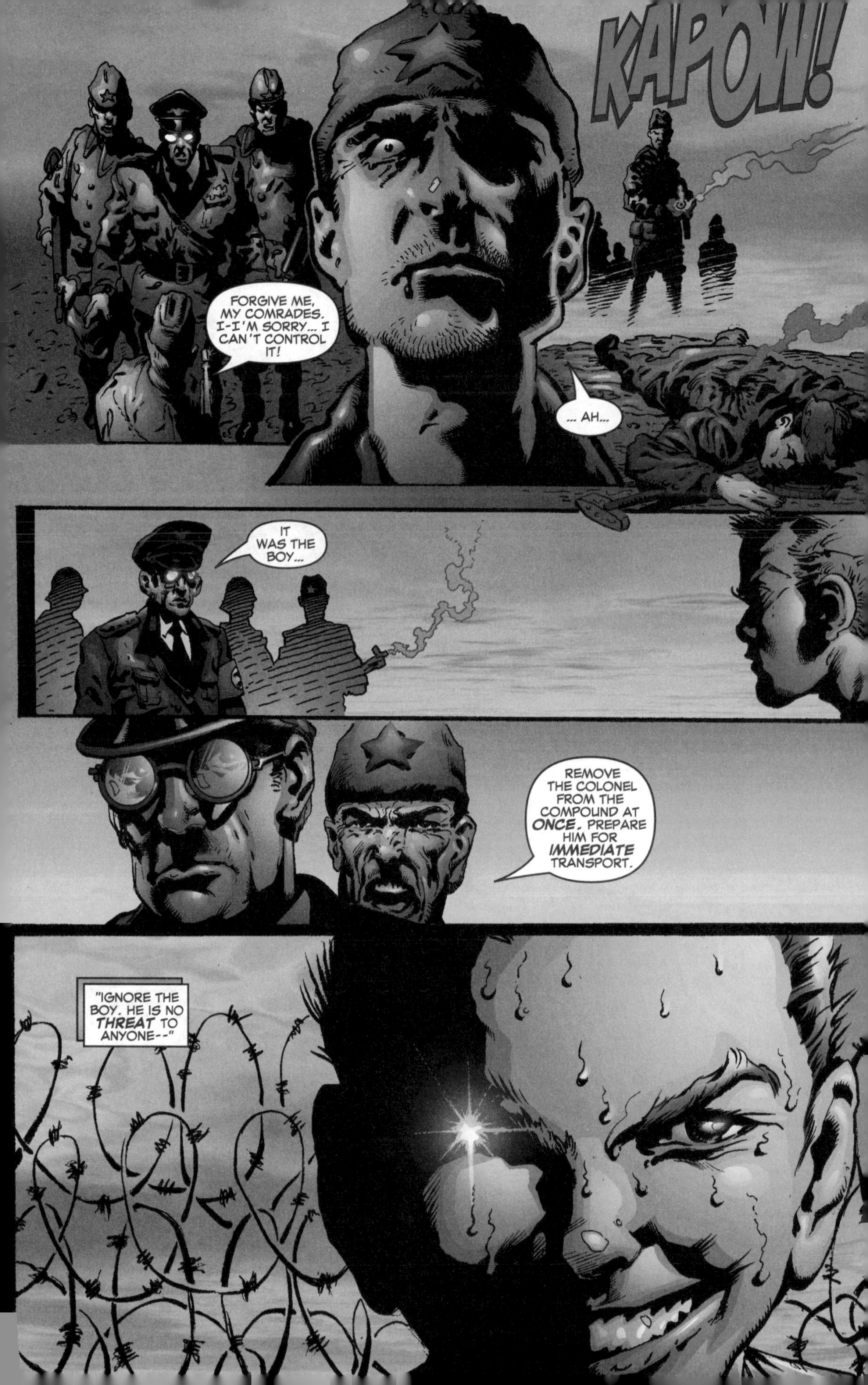
KAPOW!
FORGIVE ME, MY COMRADES. I-I'M SORRY... I CAN'T CONTROL IT!
... AH...
IT WAS THE BOY...
REMOVE THE COLONEL FROM THE COMPOUND AT ONCE. PREPARE HIM FOR IMMEDIATE TRANSPORT.
"IGNORE THE BOY. HE IS NO THREAT TO ANYONE--"

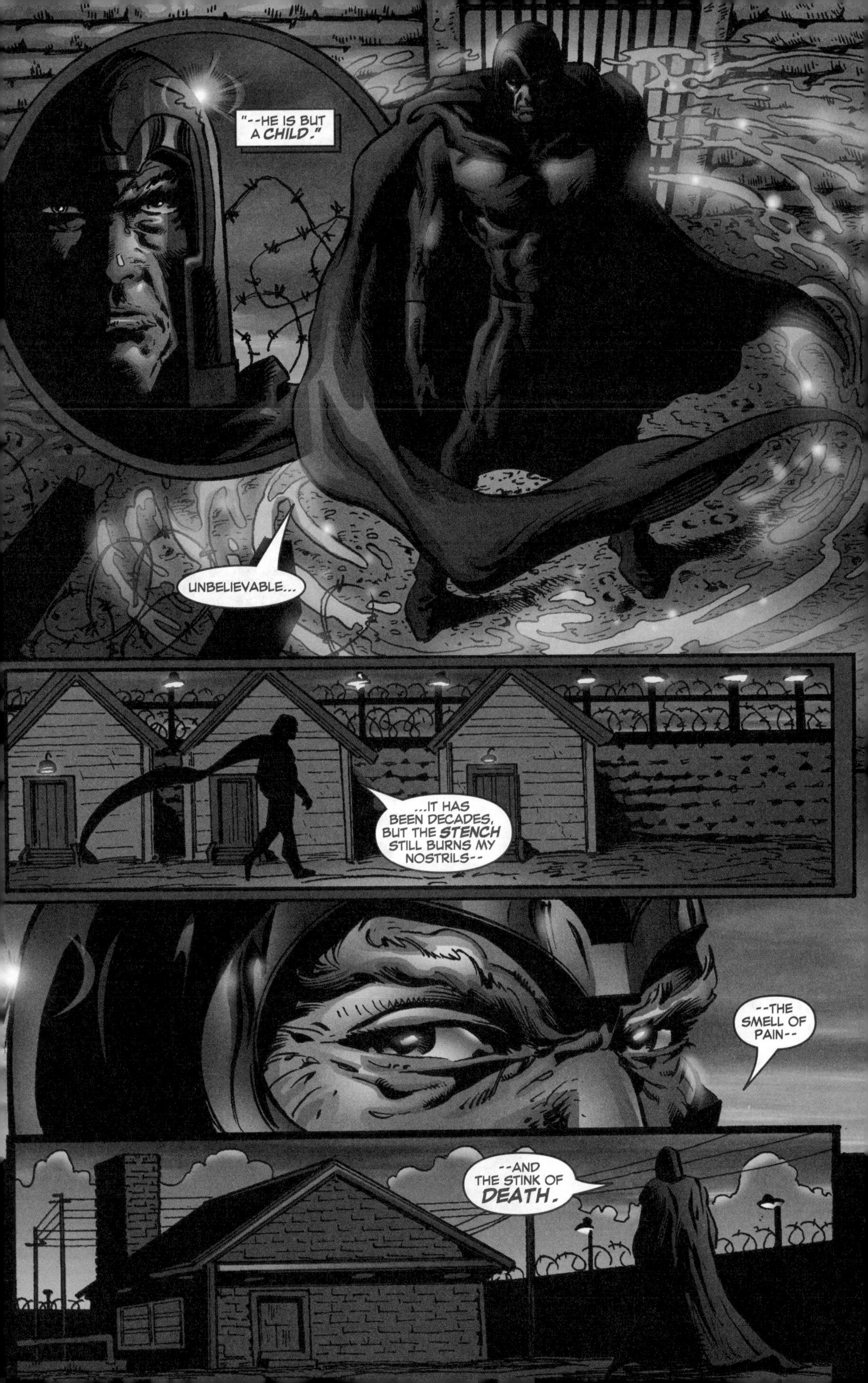
"--HE IS BUT A CHILD."
UNBELIEVABLE...
...IT HAS BEEN DECADES, BUT THE STENCH STILL BURNS MY NOSTRILS--
--THE SMELL OF PAIN--
--AND THE STINK OF DEATH.

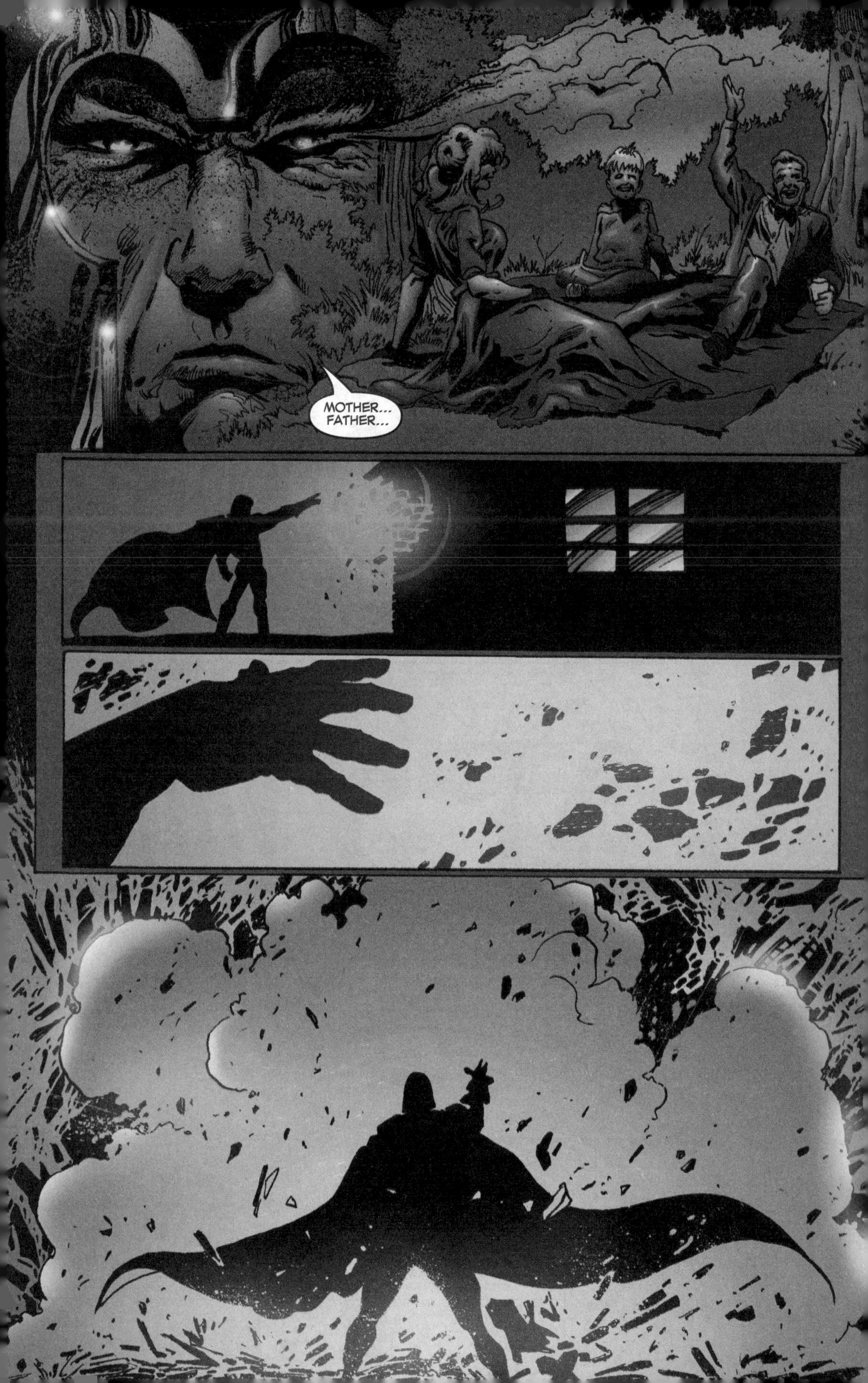
MOTHER...
FATHER...

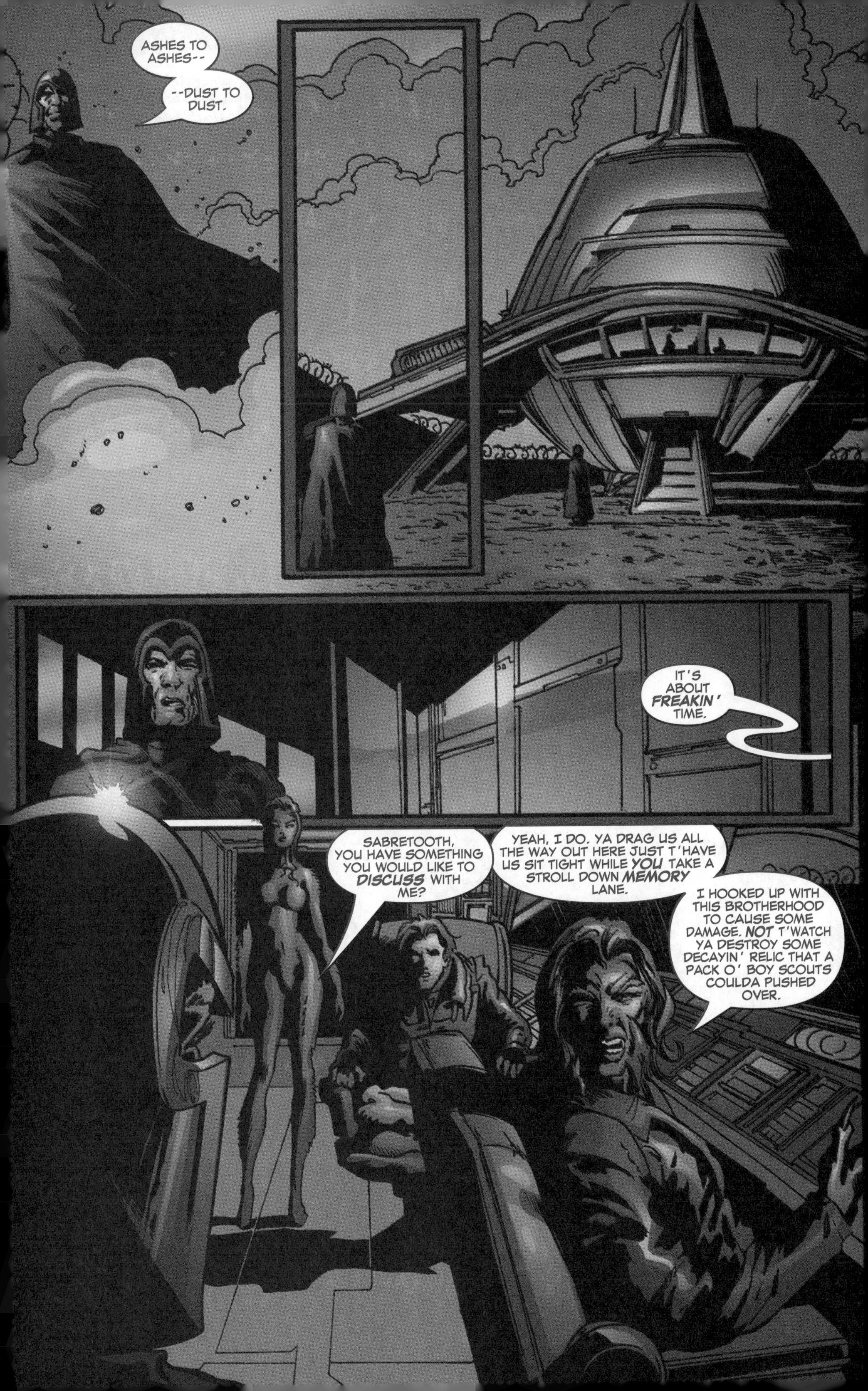
ASHES TO ASHES--
--DUST TO DUST.
IT'S ABOUT FREAKIN' TIME.
SABRETOOTH, YOU HAVE SOMETHING YOU WOULD LIKE TO DISCUSS WITH ME?
YEAH, I DO. YA DRAG US ALL THE WAY OUT HERE JUST T'HAVE US SIT TIGHT WHILE YOU TAKE A STROLL DOWN MEMORY LANE.
I HOOKED UP WITH THIS BROTHERHOOD TO CAUSE SOME DAMAGE. NOT T'WATCH YA DESTROY SOME DECAYIN' RELIC THAT A PACK O' BOY SCOUTS COULDA PUSHED OVER.

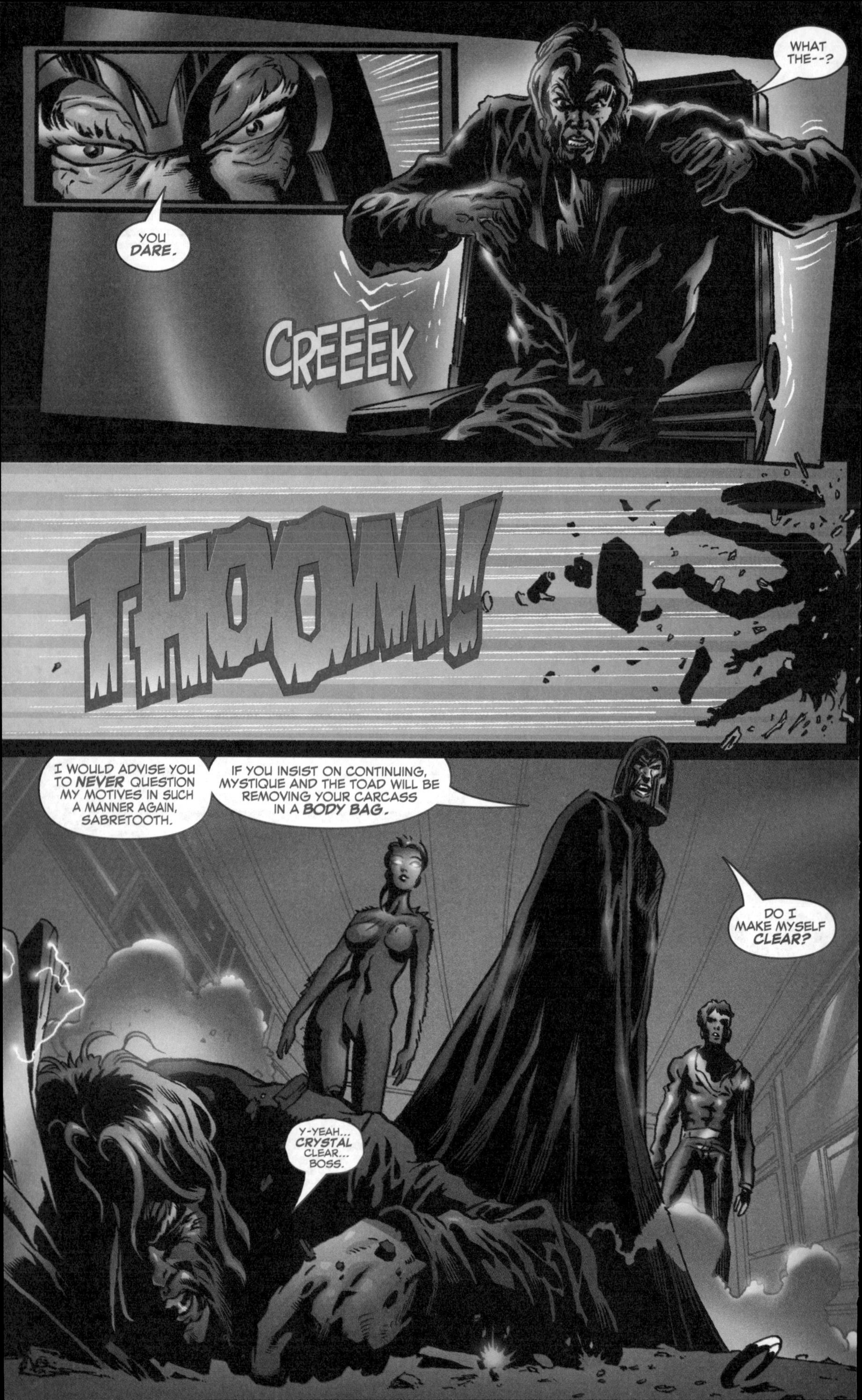
WHAT THE--?
YOU DARE.
CREEEK
THOOM!
I WOULD ADVISE YOU TO NEVER QUESTION MY MOTIVES IN SUCH A MANNER AGAIN, SABRETOOTH.
IF YOU INSIST ON CONTINUING, MYSTIQUE AND THE TOAD WILL BE REMOVING YOUR CARCASS IN A BODY BAG.
DO I MAKE MYSELF CLEAR?
Y-YEAH... CRYSTAL CLEAR... BOSS.

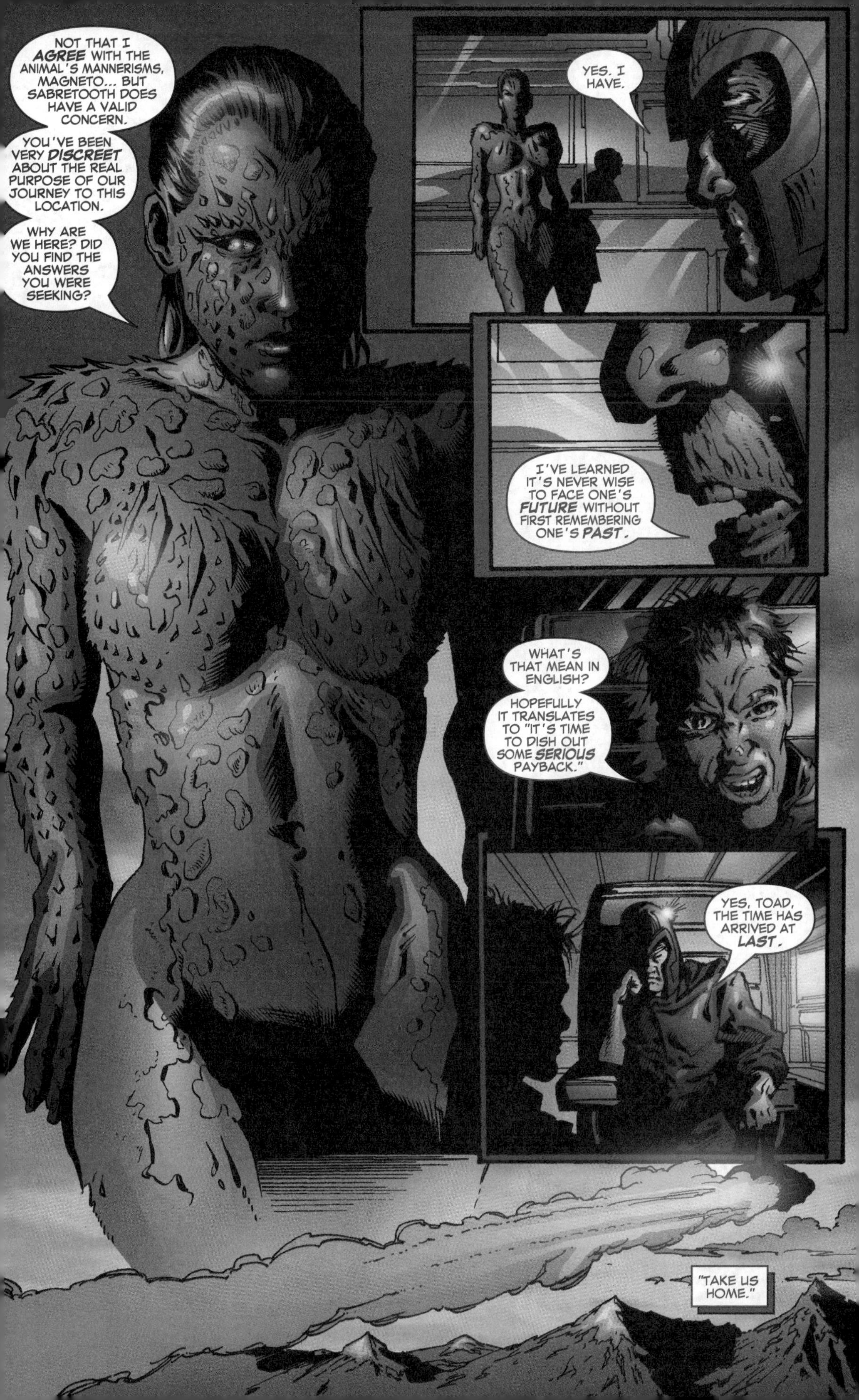
NOT THAT I AGREE WITH THE ANIMAL'S MANNERISMS, MAGNETO... BUT SABRETOOTH DOES HAVE A VALID CONCERN.
YOU'VE BEEN VERY DISCREET ABOUT THE REAL PURPOSE OF OUR JOURNEY TO THIS LOCATION.
WHY ARE WE HERE? DID YOU FIND THE ANSWERS YOU WERE SEEKING?
YES. I HAVE.
I'VE LEARNED IT'S NEVER WISE TO FACE ONE'S FUTURE WITHOUT FIRST REMEMBERING ONE'S PAST.
WHAT'S THAT MEAN IN ENGLISH?
HOPEFULLY IT TRANSLATES TO "IT'S TIME TO DISH OUT SOME SERIOUS PAYBACK."
YES, TOAD, THE TIME HAS ARRIVED AT LAST.
"TAKE US HOME."

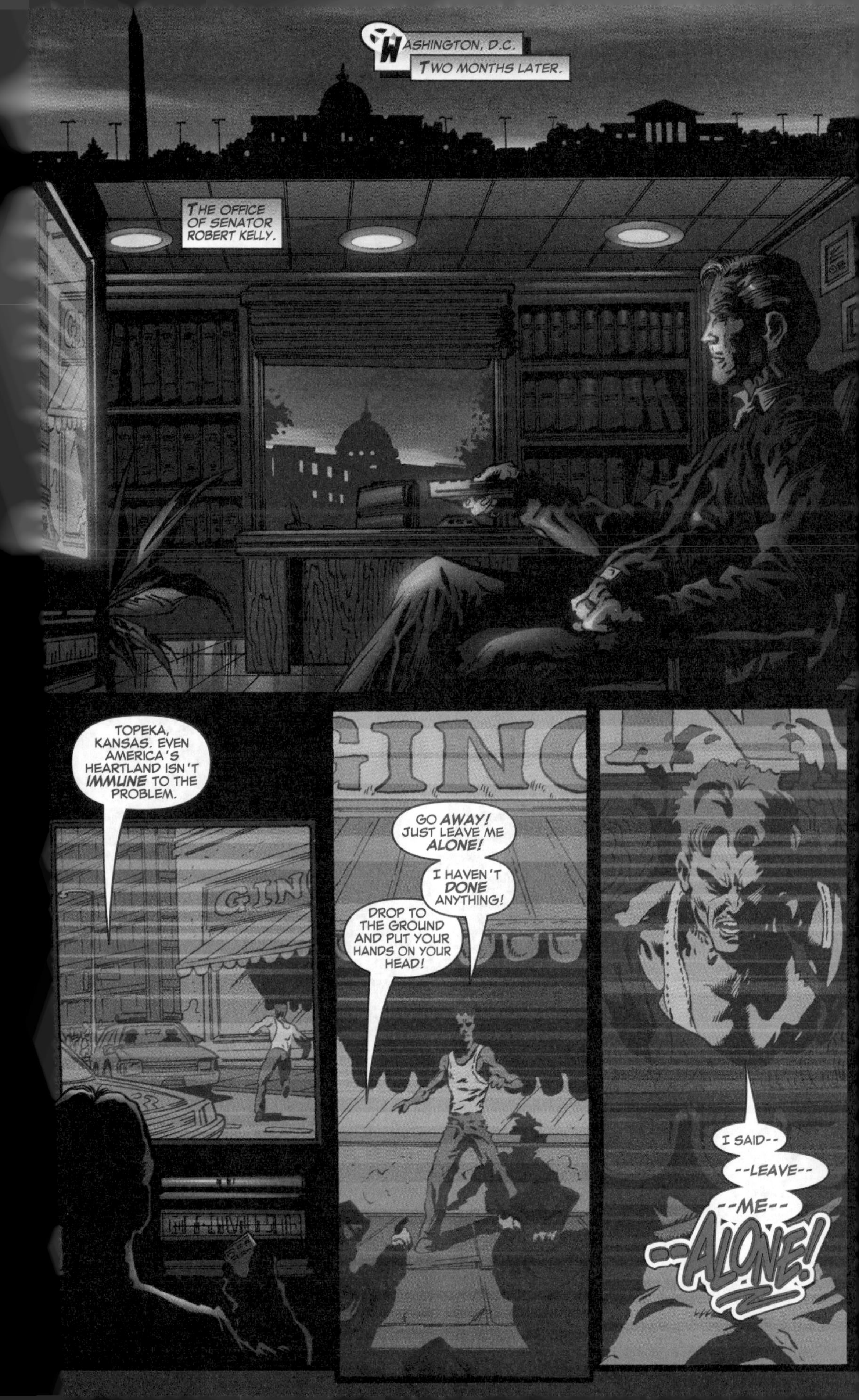
WASHINGTON, D.C.
TWO MONTHS LATER.
THE OFFICE OF SENATOR ROBERT KELLY.
TOPEKA, KANSAS. EVEN AMERICA'S HEARTLAND ISN'T IMMUNE TO THE PROBLEM.
GO AWAY! JUST LEAVE ME ALONE!
I HAVEN'T DONE ANYTHING!
DROP TO THE GROUND AND PUT YOUR HANDS ON YOUR HEAD!
I SAID--
--LEAVE--
--ME--
--ALONE!

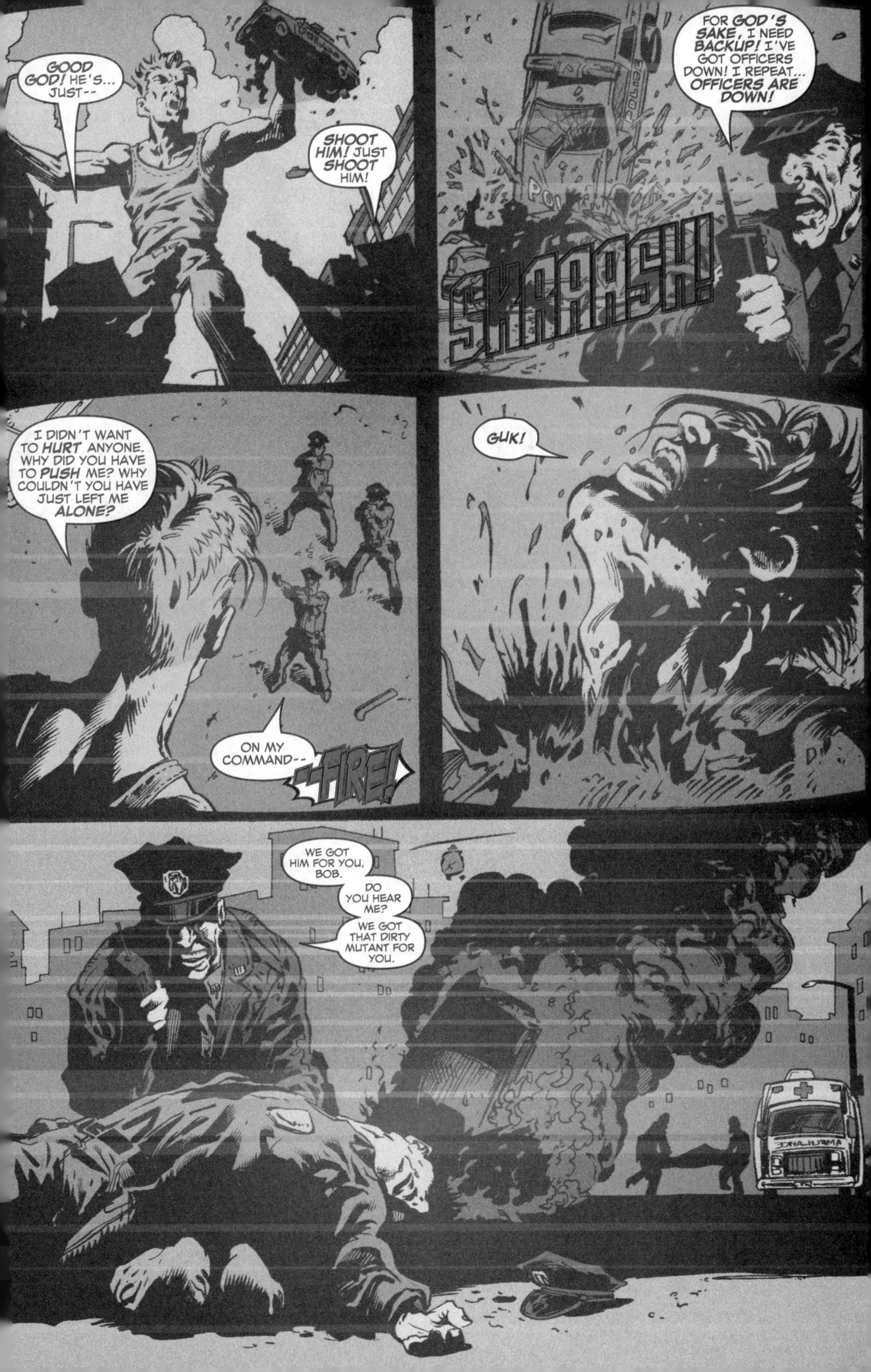
GOOD GOD! HE'S... JUST--
SHOOT HIM! JUST SHOOT HIM!
FOR GOD'S SAKE, I NEED BACKUP! I'VE GOT OFFICERS DOWN! I REPEAT... OFFICERS ARE DOWN!
SKRAASH!
I DIDN'T WANT TO HURT ANYONE. WHY DID YOU HAVE TO PUSH ME? WHY COULDN'T YOU HAVE JUST LEFT ME ALONE?
ON MY COMMAND--
--FIRE!
GUK!
WE GOT HIM FOR YOU, BOB.
DO YOU HEAR ME?
WE GOT THAT DIRTY MUTANT FOR YOU.

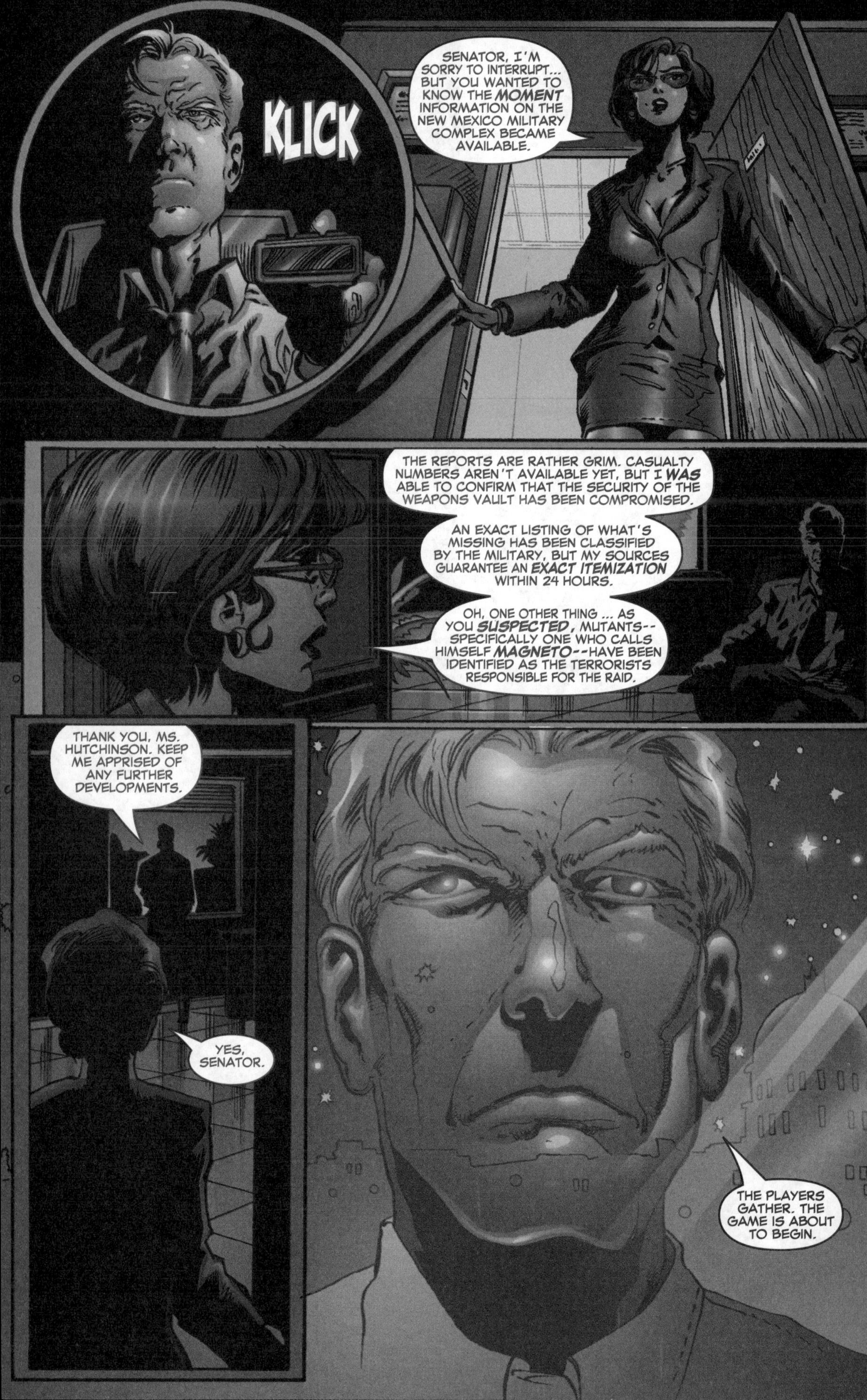
KLICK
SENATOR, I'M SORRY TO INTERRUPT... BUT YOU WANTED TO KNOW THE MOMENT INFORMATION ON THE NEW MEXICO MILITARY COMPLEX BECAME AVAILABLE.
THE REPORTS ARE RATHER GRIM. CASUALTY NUMBERS AREN'T AVAILABLE YET, BUT I WAS ABLE TO CONFIRM THAT THE SECURITY OF THE WEAPONS VAULT HAS BEEN COMPROMISED.
AN EXACT LISTING OF WHAT'S MISSING HAS BEEN CLASSIFIED BY THE MILITARY, BUT MY SOURCES GUARANTEE AN EXACT ITEMIZATION WITHIN 24 HOURS.
OH, ONE OTHER THING ... AS YOU SUSPECTED, MUTANTS--SPECIFICALLY ONE WHO CALLS HIMSELF MAGNETO--HAVE BEEN IDENTIFIED AS THE TERRORISTS RESPONSIBLE FOR THE RAID.
THANK YOU, MS. HUTCHINSON. KEEP ME APPRISED OF ANY FURTHER DEVELOPMENTS.
YES, SENATOR.
THE PLAYERS GATHER. THE GAME IS ABOUT TO BEGIN.

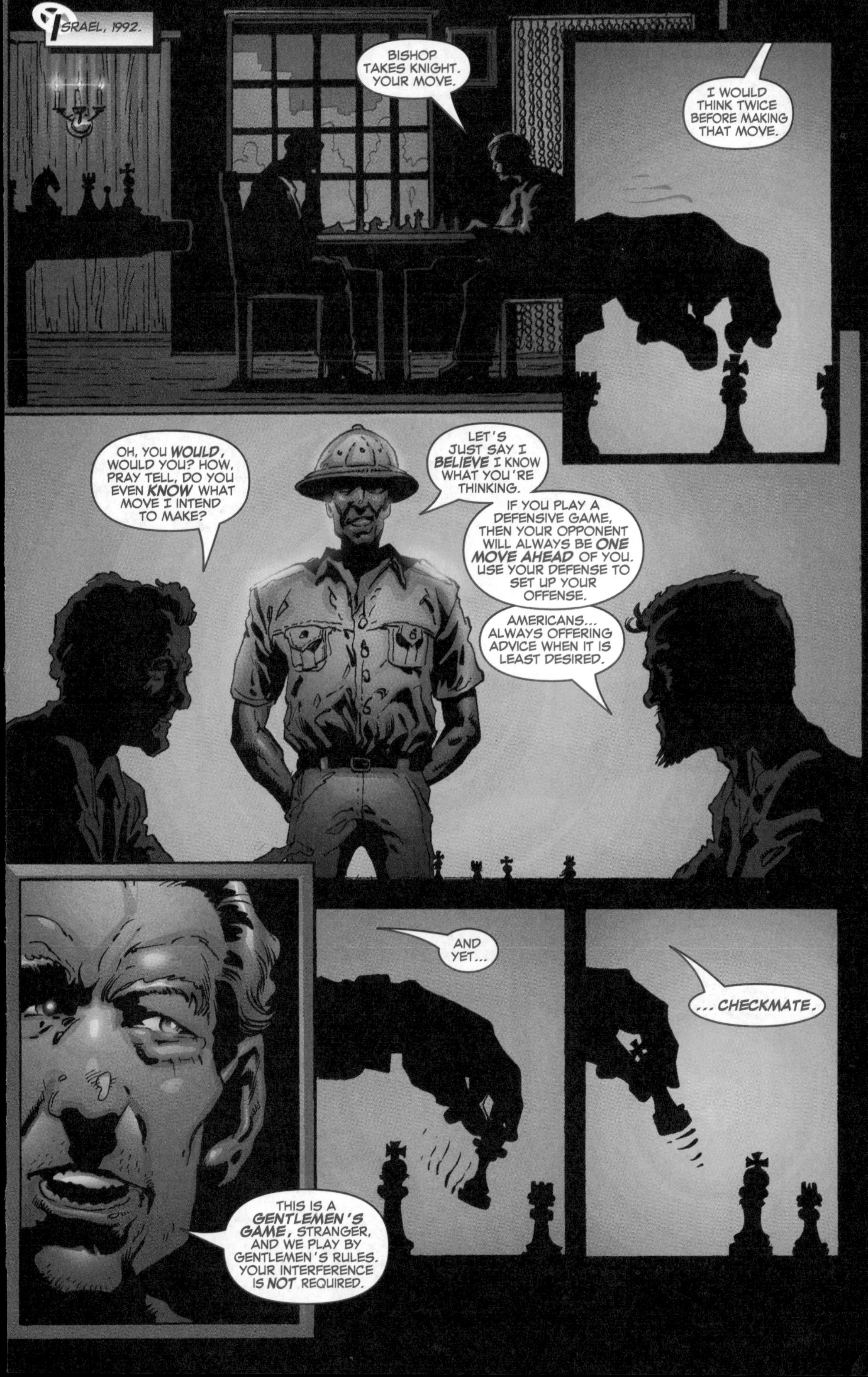
ISRAEL, 1992.
BISHOP TAKES KNIGHT. YOUR MOVE.
I WOULD THINK TWICE BEFORE MAKING THAT MOVE.
OH, YOU WOULD, WOULD YOU? HOW, PRAY TELL, DO YOU EVEN KNOW WHAT MOVE I INTEND TO MAKE?
LET'S JUST SAY I BELIEVE I KNOW WHAT YOU'RE THINKING.
IF YOU PLAY A DEFENSIVE GAME, THEN YOUR OPPONENT WILL ALWAYS BE ONE MOVE AHEAD OF YOU. USE YOUR DEFENSE TO SET UP YOUR OFFENSE.
AMERICANS... ALWAYS OFFERING ADVICE WHEN IT IS LEAST DESIRED.
THIS IS A GENTLEMEN'S GAME, STRANGER, AND WE PLAY BY GENTLEMEN'S RULES. YOUR INTERFERENCE IS NOT REQUIRED.
AND YET...
...CHECKMATE.

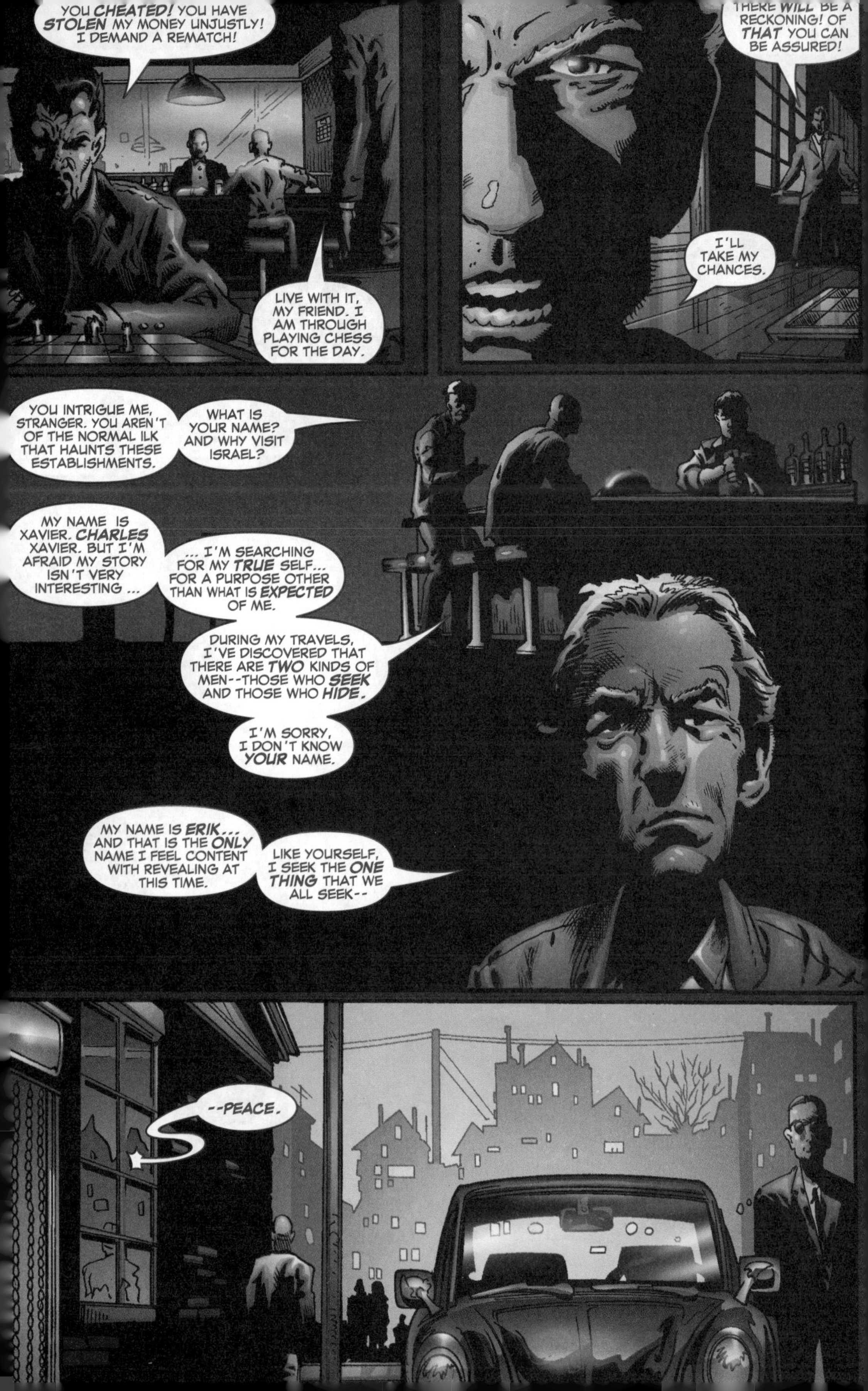

YOU CHEATED! YOU HAVE STOLEN MY MONEY UNJUSTLY! I DEMAND A REMATCH!
LIVE WITH IT, MY FRIEND. I AM THROUGH PLAYING CHESS FOR THE DAY.
THERE WILL BE A RECKONING! OF THAT YOU CAN BE ASSURED!
I'LL TAKE MY CHANCES.
YOU INTRIGUE ME, STRANGER. YOU AREN'T OF THE NORMAL ILK THAT HAUNTS THESE ESTABLISHMENTS.
WHAT IS YOUR NAME? AND WHY VISIT ISRAEL?
MY NAME IS XAVIER. CHARLES XAVIER. BUT I'M AFRAID MY STORY ISN'T VERY INTERESTING ...
... I'M SEARCHING FOR MY TRUE SELF... FOR A PURPOSE OTHER THAN WHAT IS EXPECTED OF ME.
DURING MY TRAVELS, I'VE DISCOVERED THAT THERE ARE TWO KINDS OF MEN--THOSE WHO SEEK AND THOSE WHO HIDE.
I'M SORRY, I DON'T KNOW YOUR NAME.
MY NAME IS ERIK... AND THAT IS THE ONLY NAME I FEEL CONTENT WITH REVEALING AT THIS TIME.
LIKE YOURSELF, I SEEK THE ONE THING THAT WE ALL SEEK--
--PEACE.

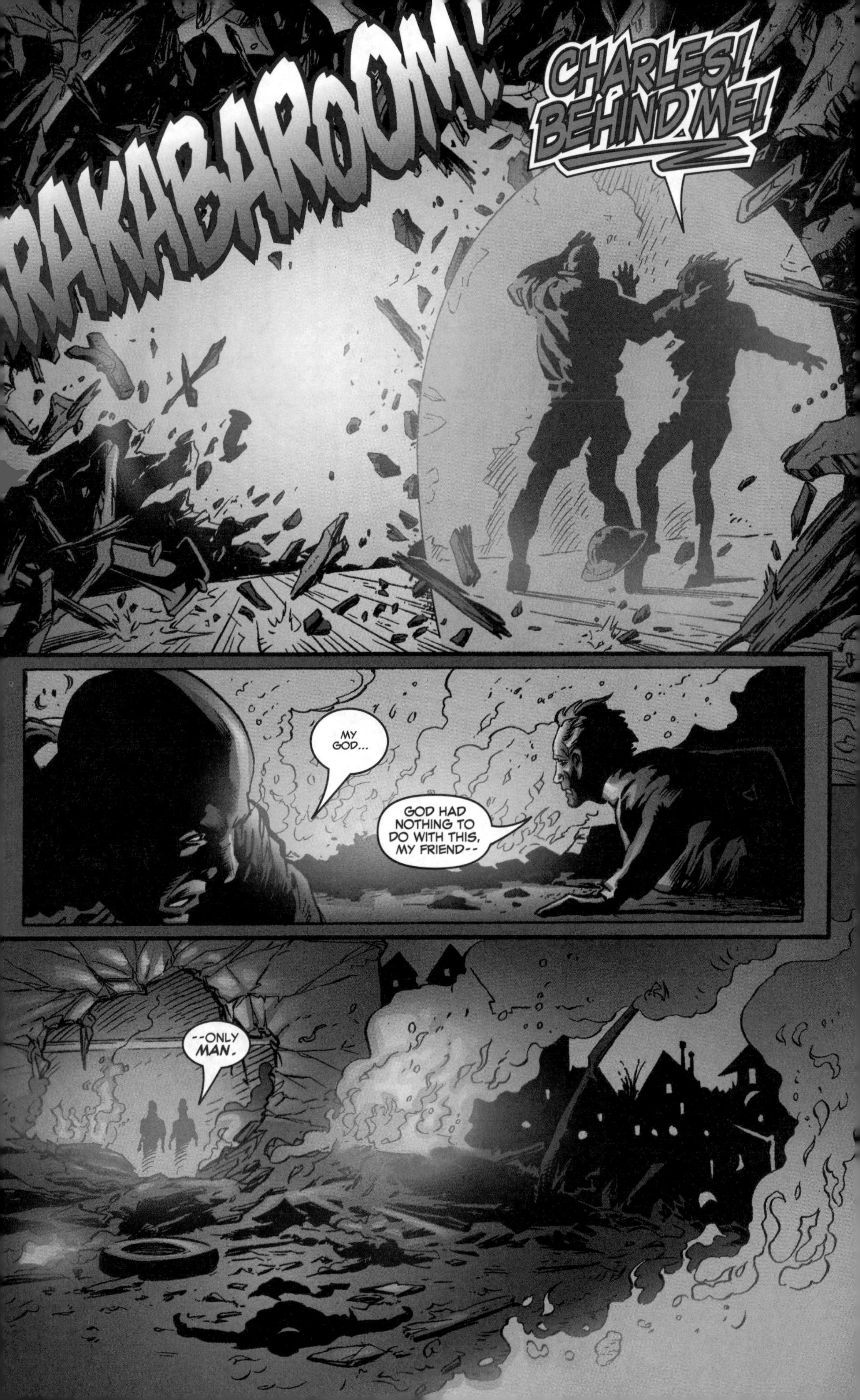
RAKABAROOM!
CHARLES! BEHIND ME!
MY GOD...
GOD HAD NOTHING TO DO WITH THIS, MY FRIEND--
--ONLY MAN.

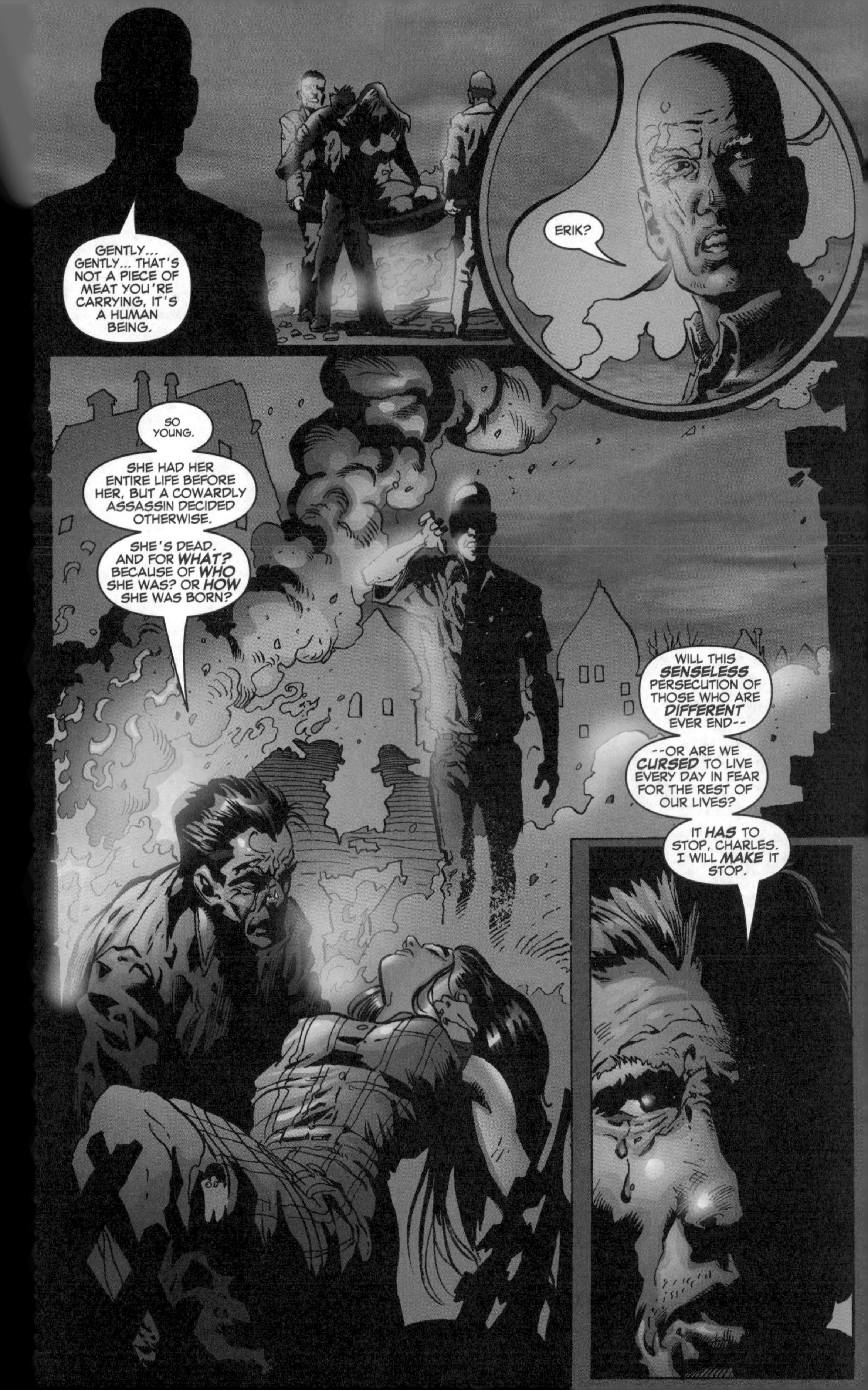
GENTLY... GENTLY... THAT'S NOT A PIECE OF MEAT YOU'RE CARRYING, IT'S A HUMAN BEING.
ERIK?
SO YOUNG.
SHE HAD HER ENTIRE LIFE BEFORE HER, BUT A COWARDLY ASSASSIN DECIDED OTHERWISE.
SHE'S DEAD. AND FOR WHAT? BECAUSE OF WHO SHE WAS? OR HOW SHE WAS BORN?
WILL THIS SENSELESS PERSECUTION OF THOSE WHO ARE DIFFERENT EVER END--
--OR ARE WE CURSED TO LIVE EVERY DAY IN FEAR FOR THE REST OF OUR LIVES?
IT HAS TO STOP, CHARLES. I WILL MAKE IT STOP.

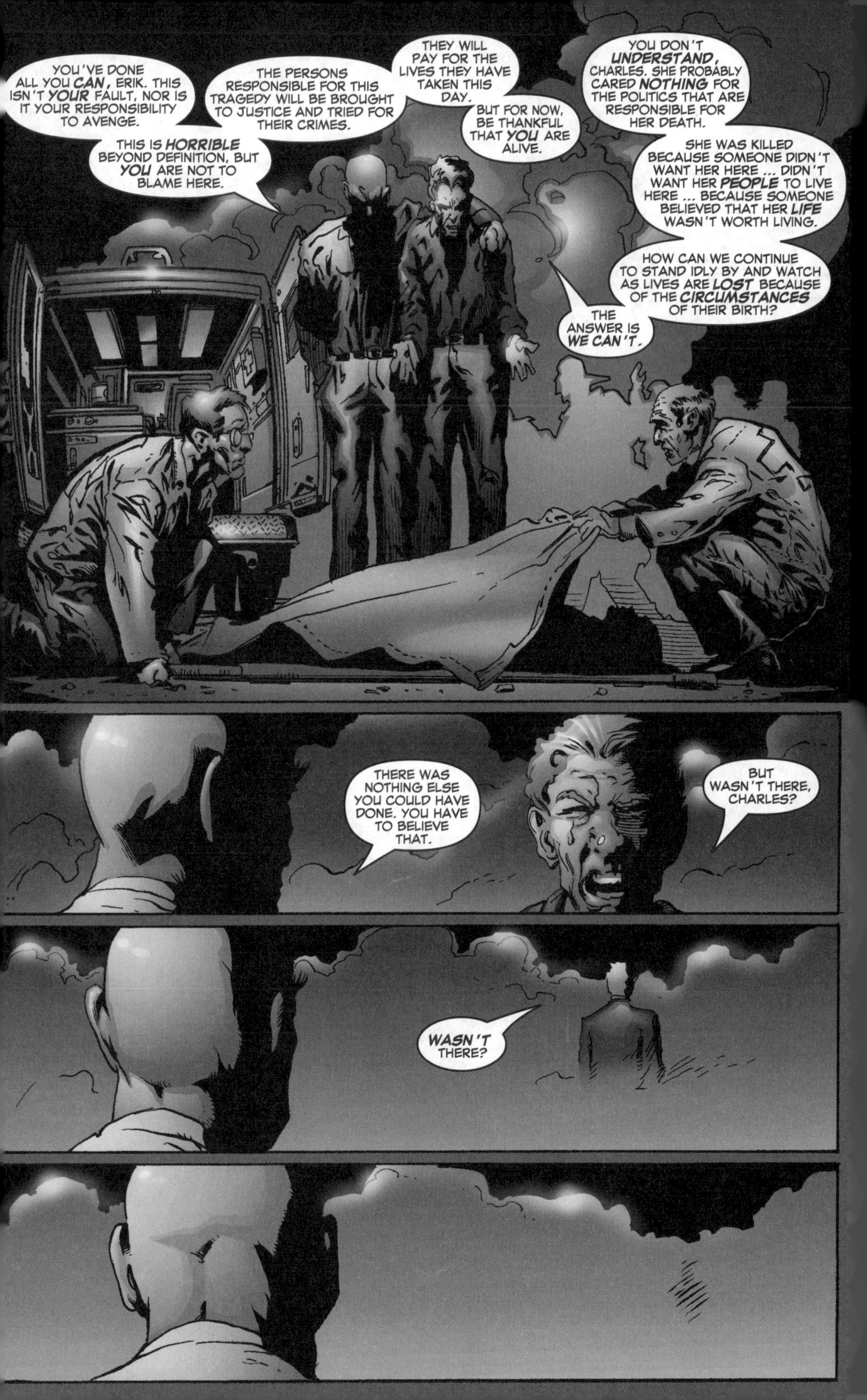
YOU'VE DONE ALL YOU CAN, ERIK. THIS ISN'T YOUR FAULT, NOR IS IT YOUR RESPONSIBILITY TO AVENGE.
THIS IS HORRIBLE BEYOND DEFINITION, BUT YOU ARE NOT TO BLAME HERE.
THE PERSONS RESPONSIBLE FOR THIS TRAGEDY WILL BE BROUGHT TO JUSTICE AND TRIED FOR THEIR CRIMES.
THEY WILL PAY FOR THE LIVES THEY HAVE TAKEN THIS DAY.
BUT FOR NOW, BE THANKFUL THAT YOU ARE ALIVE.
YOU DON'T UNDERSTAND, CHARLES. SHE PROBABLY CARED NOTHING FOR THE POLITICS THAT ARE RESPONSIBLE FOR HER DEATH.
SHE WAS KILLED BECAUSE SOMEONE DIDN'T WANT HER HERE ... DIDN'T WANT HER PEOPLE TO LIVE HERE ... BECAUSE SOMEONE BELIEVED THAT HER LIFE WASN'T WORTH LIVING.
HOW CAN WE CONTINUE TO STAND IDLY BY AND WATCH AS LIVES ARE LOST BECAUSE OF THE CIRCUMSTANCES OF THEIR BIRTH?
THE ANSWER IS WE CAN'T.
THERE WAS NOTHING ELSE YOU COULD HAVE DONE. YOU HAVE TO BELIEVE THAT.
BUT WASN'T THERE, CHARLES?
WASN'T THERE?

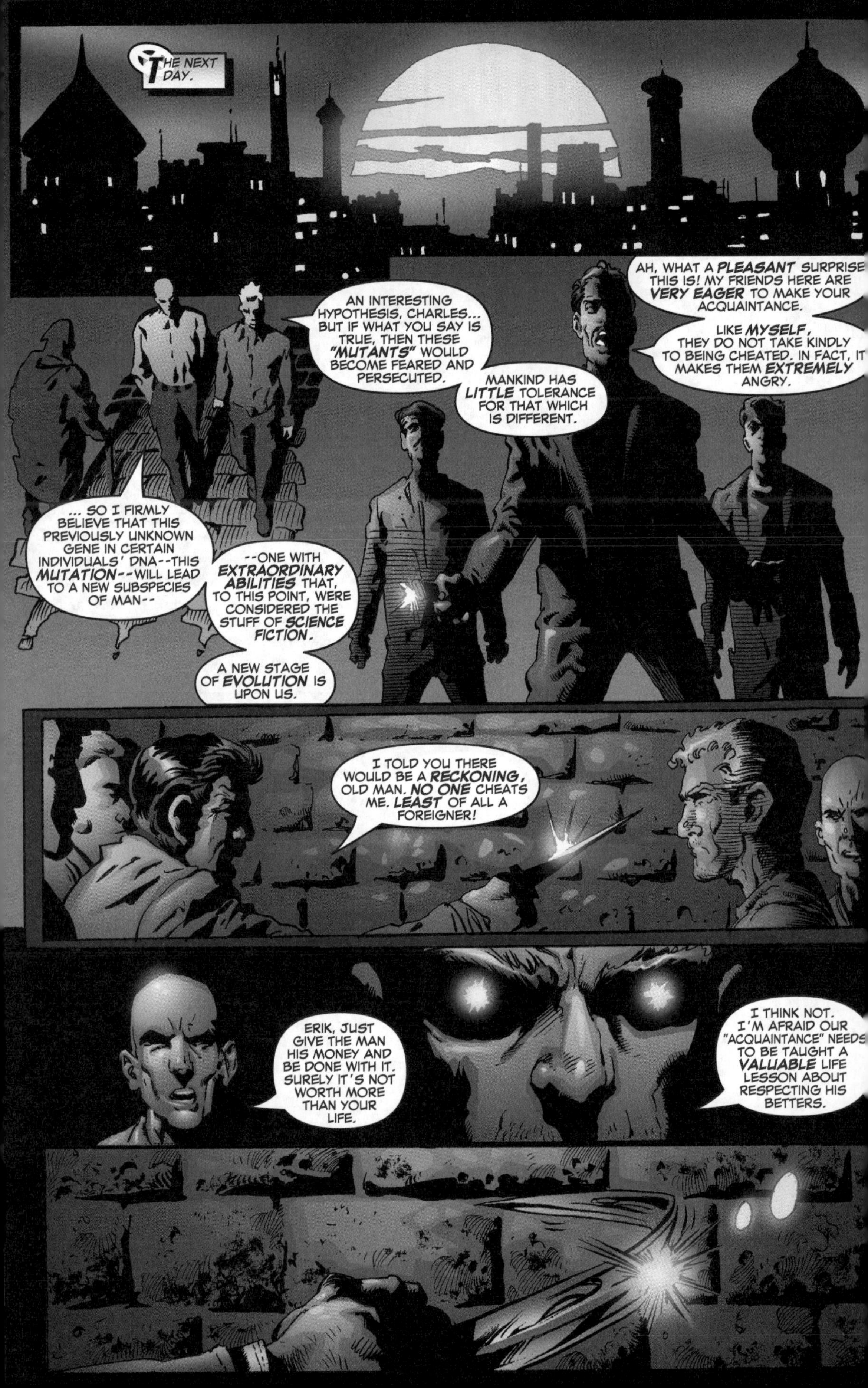
THE NEXT DAY.
... SO I FIRMLY BELIEVE THAT THIS PREVIOUSLY UNKNOWN GENE IN CERTAIN INDIVIDUALS' DNA--THIS MUTATION--WILL LEAD TO A NEW SUBSPECIES OF MAN--
--ONE WITH EXTRAORDINARY ABILITIES THAT, TO THIS POINT, WERE CONSIDERED THE STUFF OF SCIENCE FICTION.
A NEW STAGE OF EVOLUTION IS UPON US.
AN INTERESTING HYPOTHESIS, CHARLES... BUT IF WHAT YOU SAY IS TRUE, THEN THESE "MUTANTS" WOULD BECOME FEARED AND PERSECUTED.
MANKIND HAS LITTLE TOLERANCE FOR THAT WHICH IS DIFFERENT.
AH, WHAT A PLEASANT SURPRISE THIS IS! MY FRIENDS HERE ARE VERY EAGER TO MAKE YOUR ACQUAINTANCE.
LIKE MYSELF, THEY DO NOT TAKE KINDLY TO BEING CHEATED. IN FACT, IT MAKES THEM EXTREMELY ANGRY.
I TOLD YOU THERE WOULD BE A RECKONING, OLD MAN. NO ONE CHEATS ME. LEAST OF ALL A FOREIGNER!
ERIK, JUST GIVE THE MAN HIS MONEY AND BE DONE WITH IT. SURELY IT'S NOT WORTH MORE THAN YOUR LIFE.
I THINK NOT. I'M AFRAID OUR "ACQUAINTANCE" NEEDS TO BE TAUGHT A VALUABLE LIFE LESSON ABOUT RESPECTING HIS BETTERS.

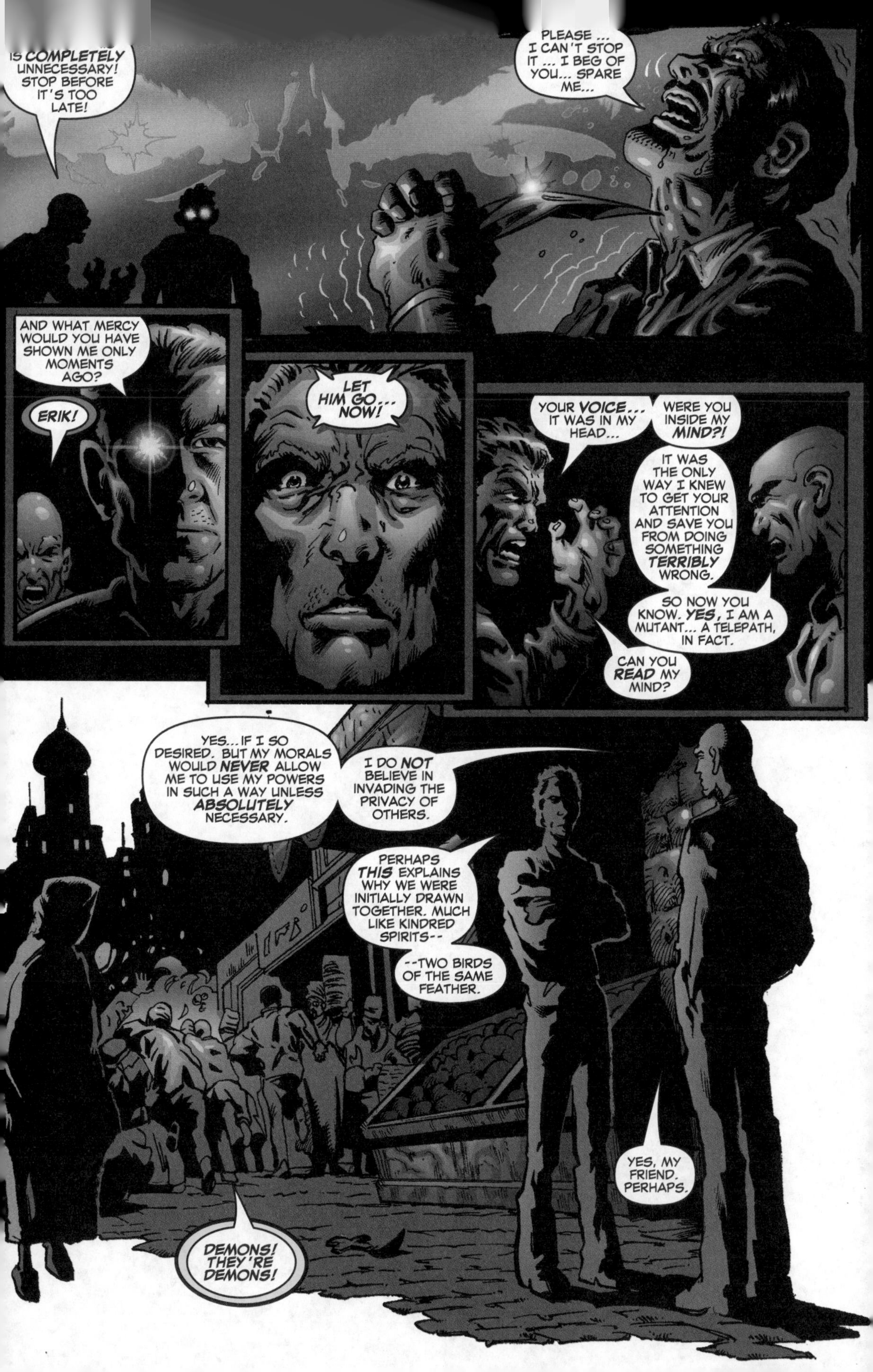

IS COMPLETELY UNNECESSARY! STOP BEFORE IT'S TOO LATE!
PLEASE ... I CAN'T STOP IT ... I BEG OF YOU... SPARE ME...
AND WHAT MERCY WOULD YOU HAVE SHOWN ME ONLY MOMENTS AGO?
ERIK!
LET HIM GO... NOW!
YOUR VOICE... IT WAS IN MY HEAD...
WERE YOU INSIDE MY MIND?!
IT WAS THE ONLY WAY I KNEW TO GET YOUR ATTENTION AND SAVE YOU FROM DOING SOMETHING TERRIBLY WRONG.
SO NOW YOU KNOW. YES, I AM A MUTANT... A TELEPATH, IN FACT.
CAN YOU READ MY MIND?
YES... IF I SO DESIRED. BUT MY MORALS WOULD NEVER ALLOW ME TO USE MY POWERS IN SUCH A WAY UNLESS ABSOLUTELY NECESSARY.
I DO NOT BELIEVE IN INVADING THE PRIVACY OF OTHERS.
PERHAPS THIS EXPLAINS WHY WE WERE INITIALLY DRAWN TOGETHER. MUCH LIKE KINDRED SPIRITS--
--TWO BIRDS OF THE SAME FEATHER.
YES, MY FRIEND. PERHAPS.
DEMONS! THEY'RE DEMONS!

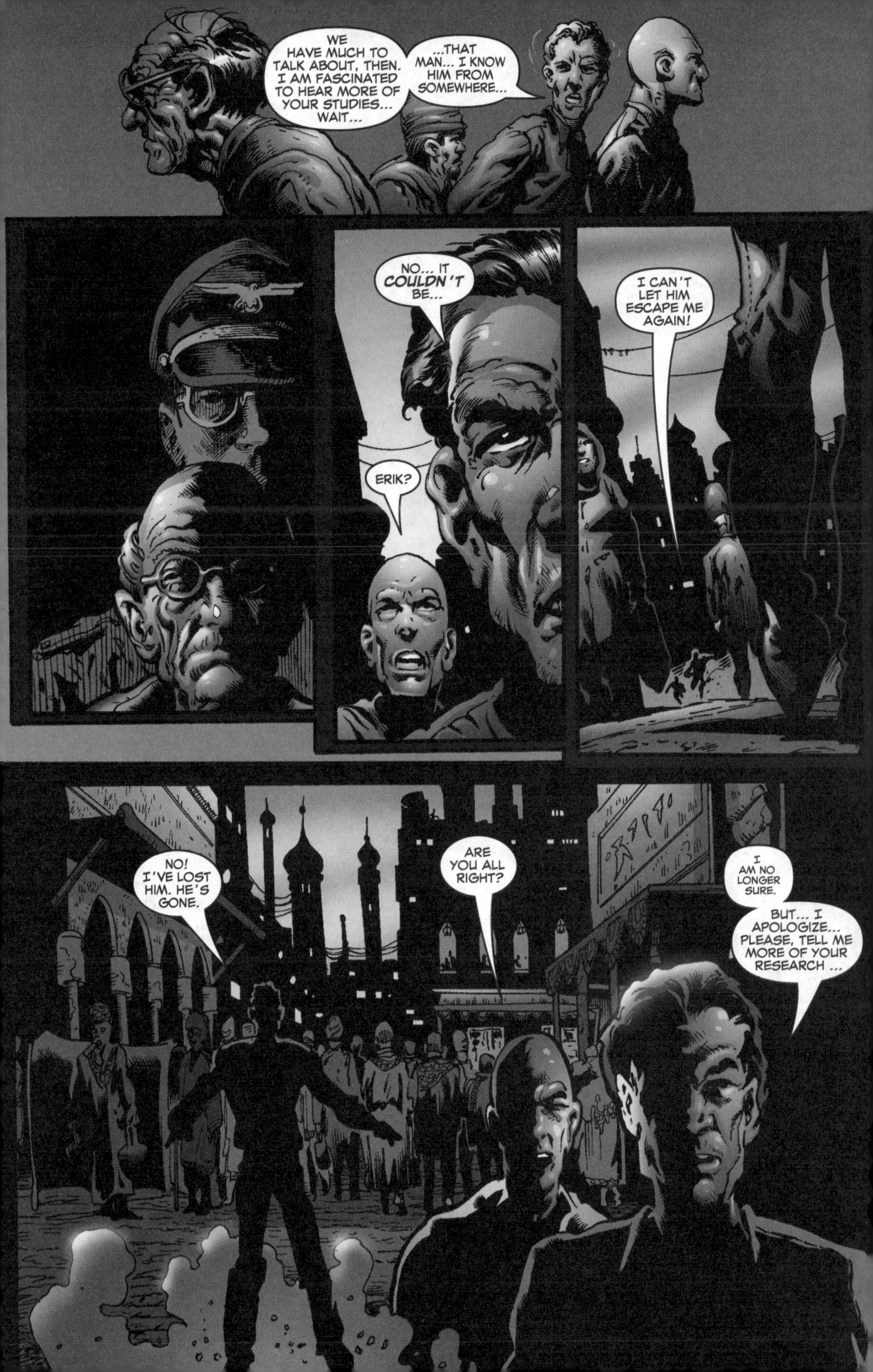
WE HAVE MUCH TO TALK ABOUT, THEN. I AM FASCINATED TO HEAR MORE OF YOUR STUDIES... WAIT...
...THAT MAN... I KNOW HIM FROM SOMEWHERE...
NO... IT COULDN'T BE...
ERIK?
I CAN'T LET HIM ESCAPE ME AGAIN!
NO! I'VE LOST HIM. HE'S GONE.
ARE YOU ALL RIGHT?
I AM NO LONGER SURE.
BUT... I APOLOGIZE... PLEASE, TELL ME MORE OF YOUR RESEARCH ...

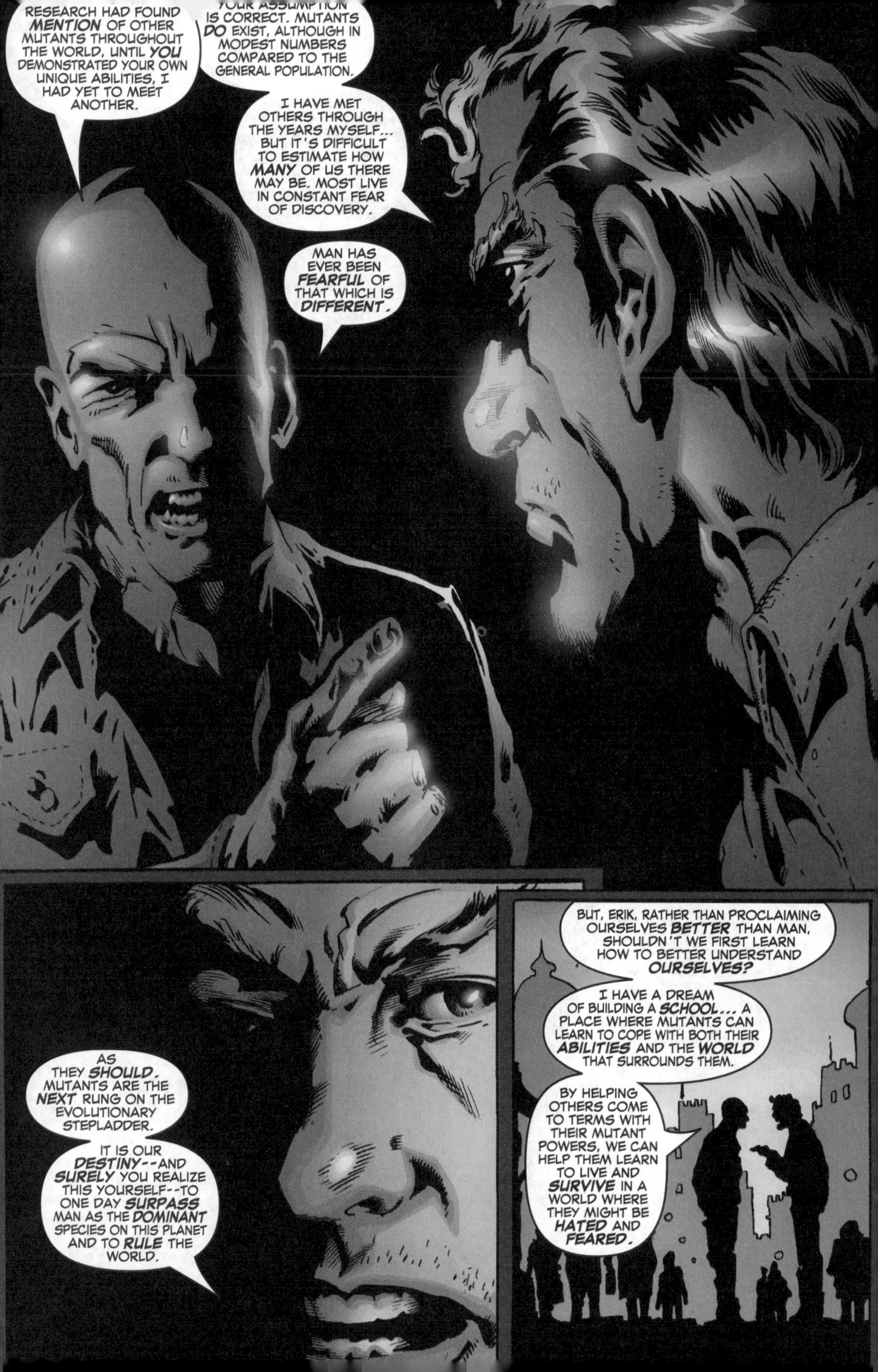
RESEARCH HAD FOUND MENTION OF OTHER MUTANTS THROUGHOUT THE WORLD, UNTIL YOU DEMONSTRATED YOUR OWN UNIQUE ABILITIES, I HAD YET TO MEET ANOTHER.
YOUR ASSUMPTION IS CORRECT. MUTANTS DO EXIST, ALTHOUGH IN MODEST NUMBERS COMPARED TO THE GENERAL POPULATION.
I HAVE MET OTHERS THROUGH THE YEARS MYSELF... BUT IT'S DIFFICULT TO ESTIMATE HOW MANY OF US THERE MAY BE. MOST LIVE IN CONSTANT FEAR OF DISCOVERY.
MAN HAS EVER BEEN FEARFUL OF THAT WHICH IS DIFFERENT.
AS THEY SHOULD. MUTANTS ARE THE NEXT RUNG ON THE EVOLUTIONARY STEPLADDER.
IT IS OUR DESTINY--AND SURELY YOU REALIZE THIS YOURSELF--TO ONE DAY SURPASS MAN AS THE DOMINANT SPECIES ON THIS PLANET AND TO RULE THE WORLD.
BUT, ERIK, RATHER THAN PROCLAIMING OURSELVES BETTER THAN MAN, SHOULDN'T WE FIRST LEARN HOW TO BETTER UNDERSTAND OURSELVES?
I HAVE A DREAM OF BUILDING A SCHOOL... A PLACE WHERE MUTANTS CAN LEARN TO COPE WITH BOTH THEIR ABILITIES AND THE WORLD THAT SURROUNDS THEM.
BY HELPING OTHERS COME TO TERMS WITH THEIR MUTANT POWERS, WE CAN HELP THEM LEARN TO LIVE AND SURVIVE IN A WORLD WHERE THEY MIGHT BE HATED AND FEARED.

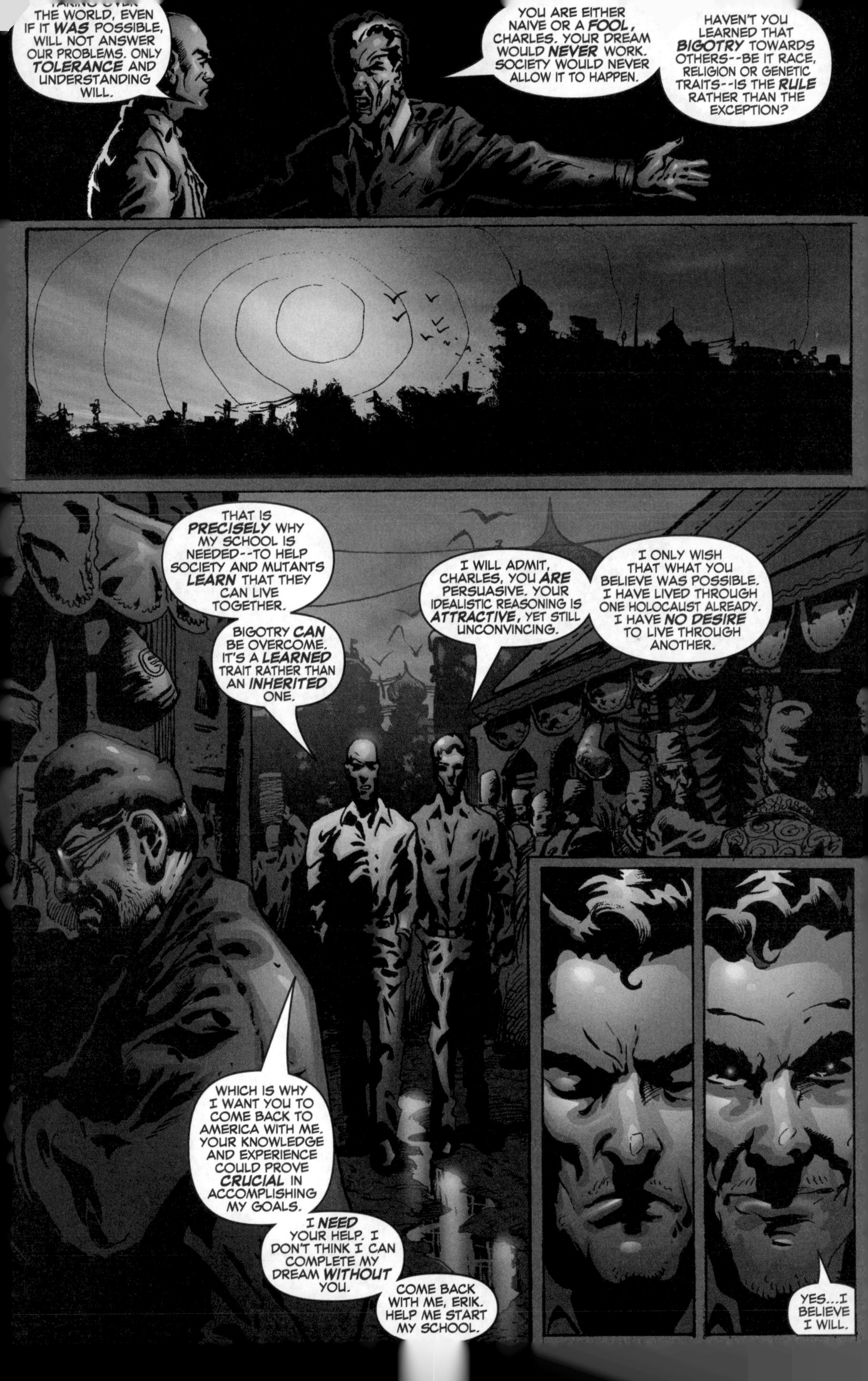
THE WORLD, EVEN IF IT WAS POSSIBLE, WILL NOT ANSWER OUR PROBLEMS. ONLY TOLERANCE AND UNDERSTANDING WILL.
YOU ARE EITHER NAIVE OR A FOOL, CHARLES. YOUR DREAM WOULD NEVER WORK. SOCIETY WOULD NEVER ALLOW IT TO HAPPEN.
HAVEN'T YOU LEARNED THAT BIGOTRY TOWARDS OTHERS--BE IT RACE, RELIGION OR GENETIC TRAITS--IS THE RULE RATHER THAN THE EXCEPTION?
THAT IS PRECISELY WHY MY SCHOOL IS NEEDED--TO HELP SOCIETY AND MUTANTS LEARN THAT THEY CAN LIVE TOGETHER.
BIGOTRY CAN BE OVERCOME. IT'S A LEARNED TRAIT RATHER THAN AN INHERITED ONE.
I WILL ADMIT, CHARLES, YOU ARE PERSUASIVE. YOUR IDEALISTIC REASONING IS ATTRACTIVE, YET STILL UNCONVINCING.
I ONLY WISH THAT WHAT YOU BELIEVE WAS POSSIBLE. I HAVE LIVED THROUGH ONE HOLOCAUST ALREADY. I HAVE NO DESIRE TO LIVE THROUGH ANOTHER.
WHICH IS WHY I WANT YOU TO COME BACK TO AMERICA WITH ME. YOUR KNOWLEDGE AND EXPERIENCE COULD PROVE CRUCIAL IN ACCOMPLISHING MY GOALS.
I NEED YOUR HELP. I DON'T THINK I CAN COMPLETE MY DREAM WITHOUT YOU.
COME BACK WITH ME, ERIK. HELP ME START MY SCHOOL.
YES...I BELIEVE I WILL.

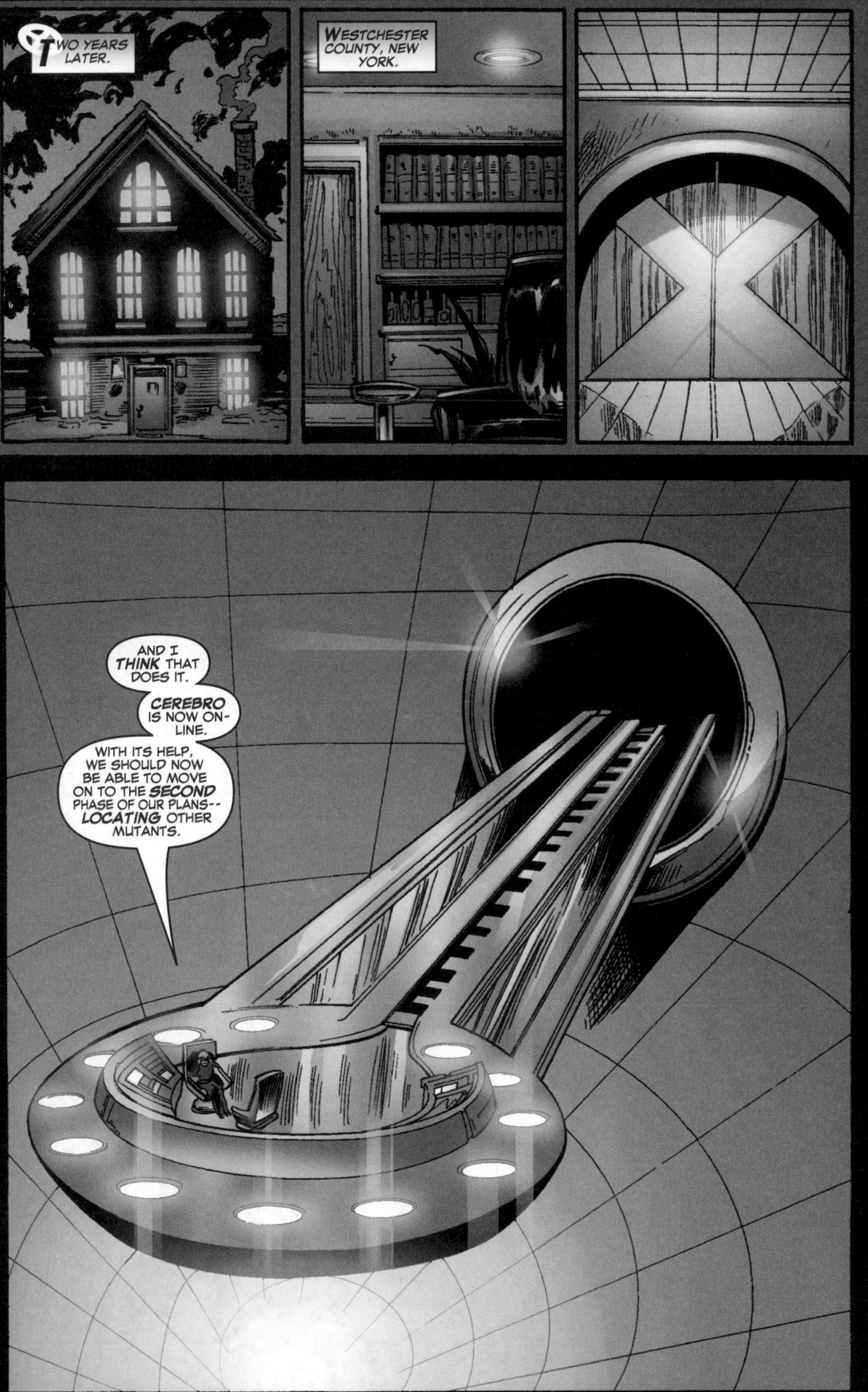
TWO YEARS LATER.
WESTCHESTER COUNTY, NEW YORK.
AND I THINK THAT DOES IT.
CEREBRO IS NOW ON-LINE.
WITH ITS HELP, WE SHOULD NOW BE ABLE TO MOVE ON TO THE SECOND PHASE OF OUR PLANS-- LOCATING OTHER MUTANTS.

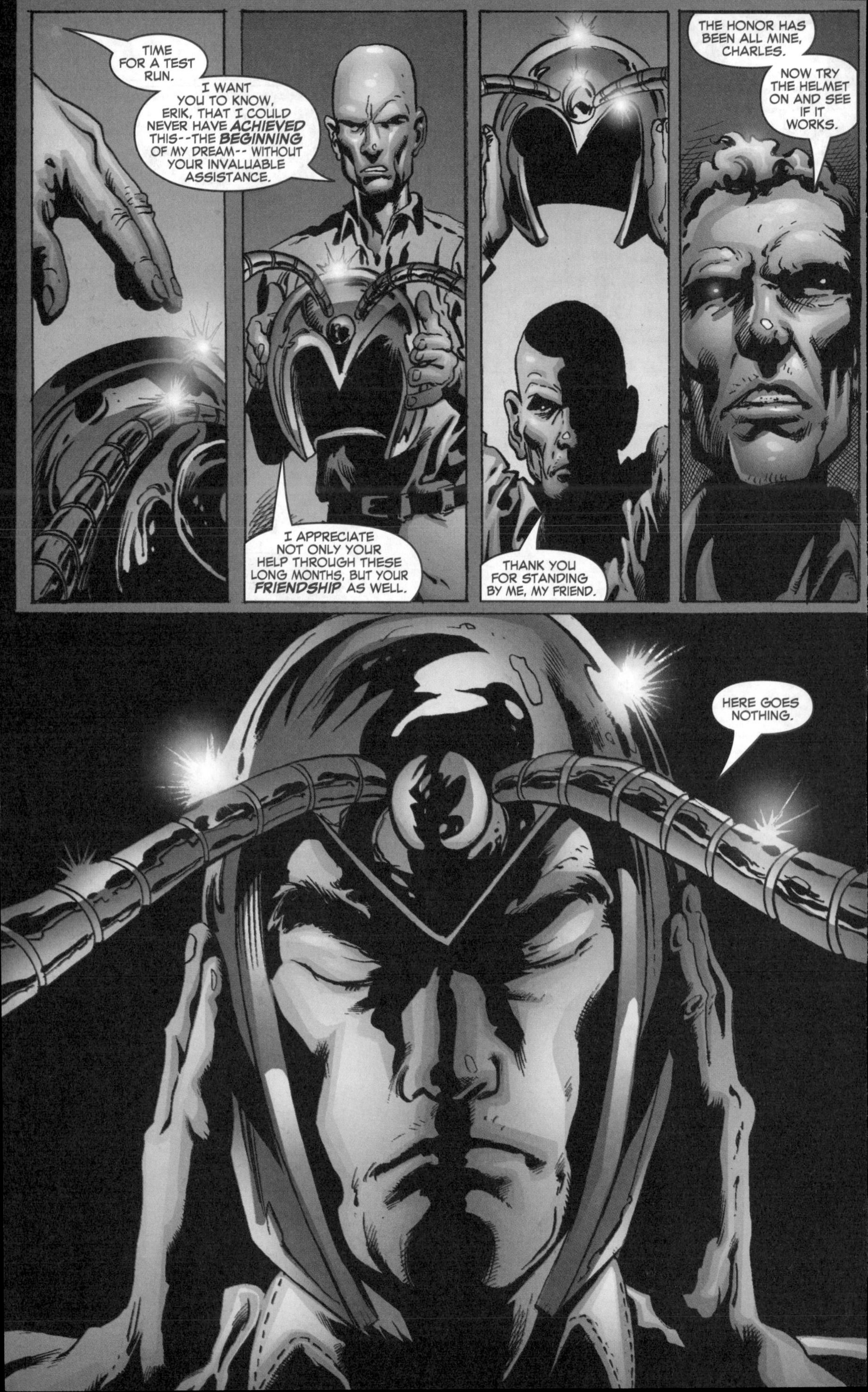

TIME FOR A TEST RUN.
I WANT YOU TO KNOW, ERIK, THAT I COULD NEVER HAVE ACHIEVED THIS--THE BEGINNING OF MY DREAM-- WITHOUT YOUR INVALUABLE ASSISTANCE.
I APPRECIATE NOT ONLY YOUR HELP THROUGH THESE LONG MONTHS, BUT YOUR FRIENDSHIP AS WELL.
THANK YOU FOR STANDING BY ME, MY FRIEND.
THE HONOR HAS BEEN ALL MINE, CHARLES.
NOW TRY THE HELMET ON AND SEE IF IT WORKS.
HERE GOES NOTHING.

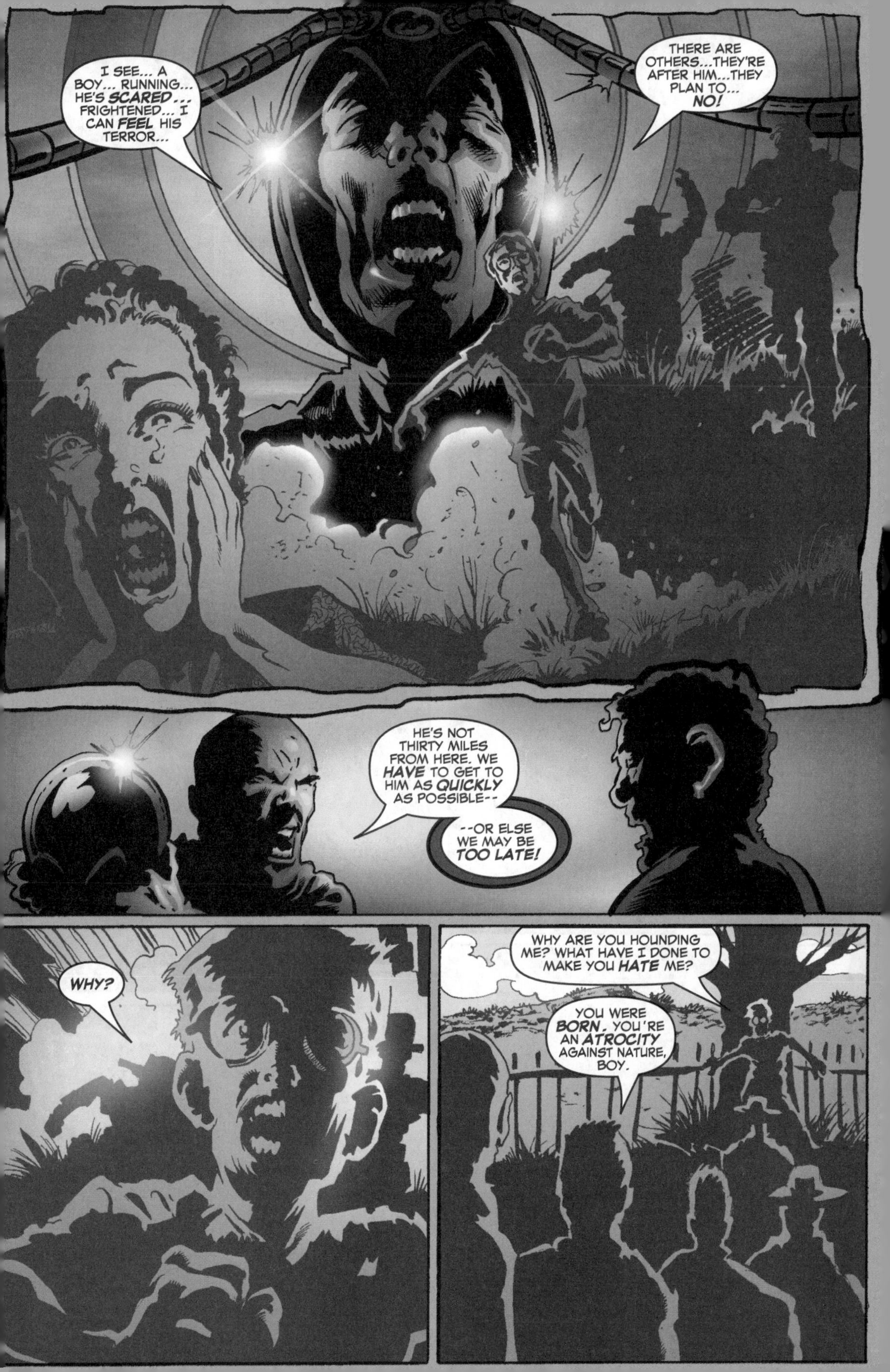
I SEE... A BOY... RUNNING... HE'S SCARED... FRIGHTENED... I CAN FEEL HIS TERROR...
THERE ARE OTHERS...THEY'RE AFTER HIM...THEY PLAN TO... NO!
HE'S NOT THIRTY MILES FROM HERE. WE HAVE TO GET TO HIM AS QUICKLY AS POSSIBLE--
--OR ELSE WE MAY BE TOO LATE!
WHY?
WHY ARE YOU HOUNDING ME? WHAT HAVE I DONE TO MAKE YOU HATE ME?
YOU WERE BORN. YOU'RE AN ATROCITY AGAINST NATURE, BOY.

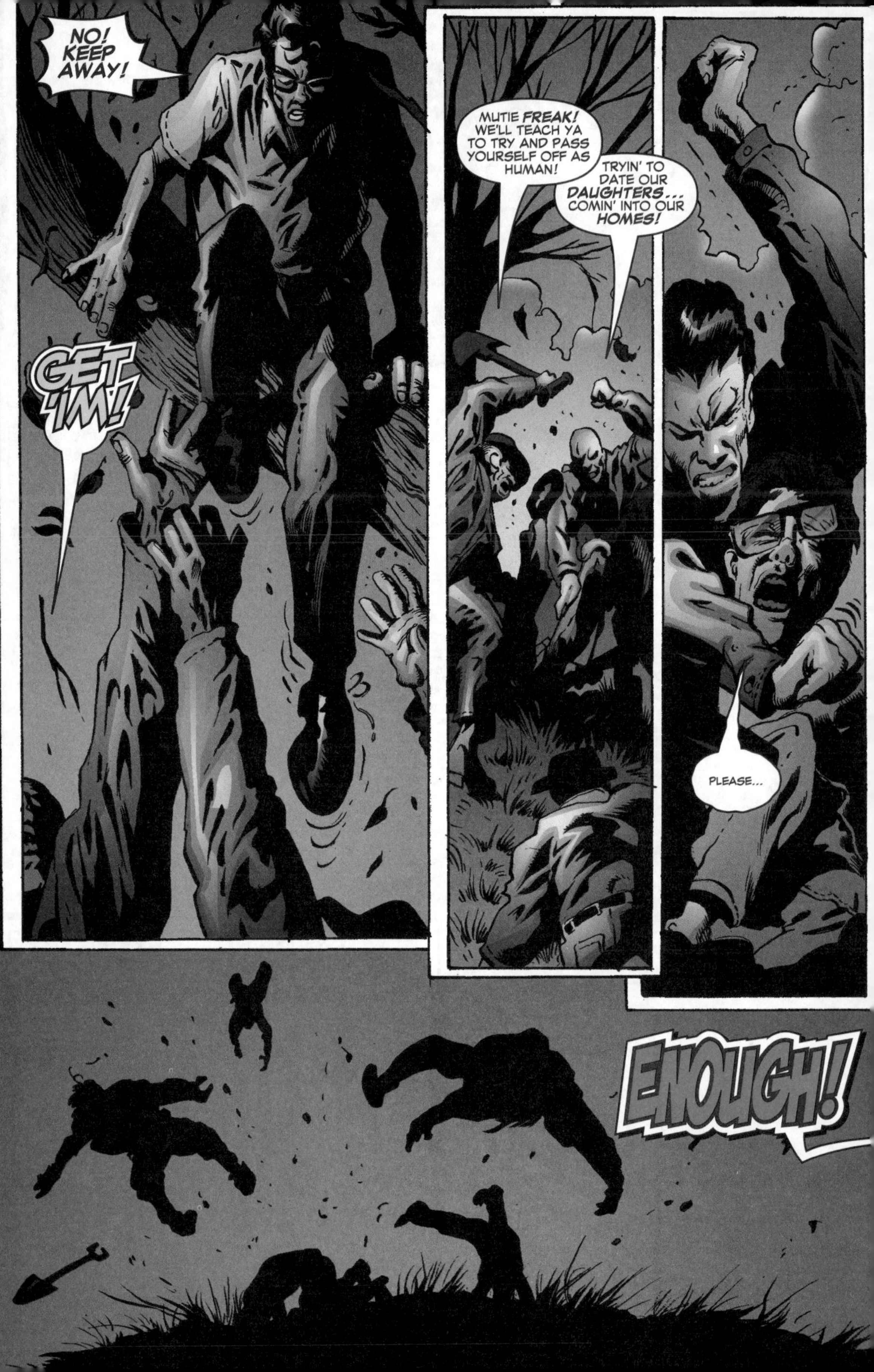
NO! KEEP AWAY!
GET 'IM!
MUTIE FREAK! WE'LL TEACH YA TO TRY AND PASS YOURSELF OFF AS HUMAN!
TRYIN' TO DATE OUR DAUGHTERS... COMIN' INTO OUR HOMES!
PLEASE...
ENOUGH!

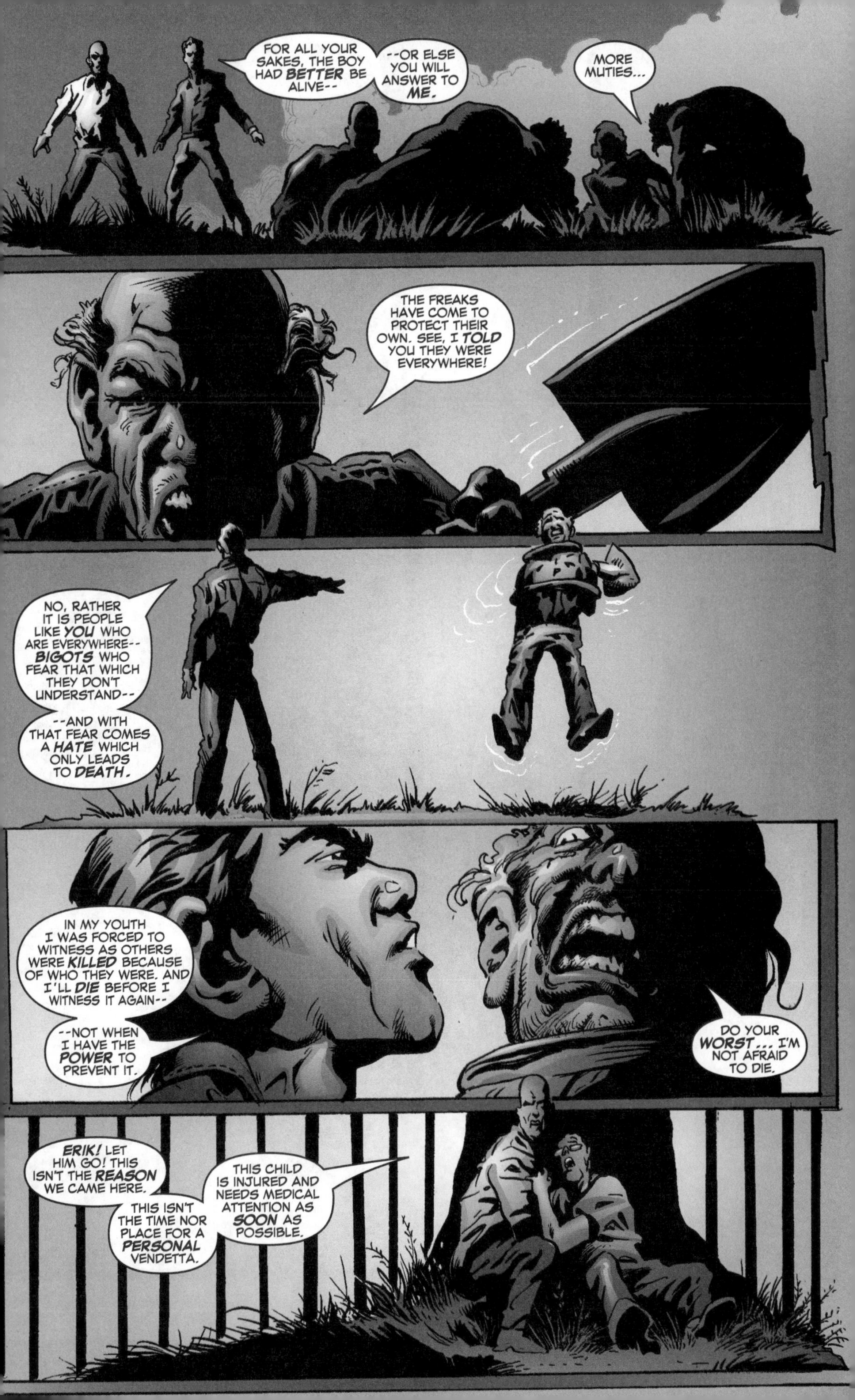
FOR ALL YOUR SAKES, THE BOY HAD BETTER BE ALIVE--
--OR ELSE YOU WILL ANSWER TO ME.
MORE MUTIES...
THE FREAKS HAVE COME TO PROTECT THEIR OWN. SEE, I TOLD YOU THEY WERE EVERYWHERE!
NO, RATHER IT IS PEOPLE LIKE YOU WHO ARE EVERYWHERE-- BIGOTS WHO FEAR THAT WHICH THEY DON'T UNDERSTAND--
--AND WITH THAT FEAR COMES A HATE WHICH ONLY LEADS TO DEATH.
IN MY YOUTH I WAS FORCED TO WITNESS AS OTHERS WERE KILLED BECAUSE OF WHO THEY WERE. AND I'LL DIE BEFORE I WITNESS IT AGAIN--
--NOT WHEN I HAVE THE POWER TO PREVENT IT.
DO YOUR WORST... I'M NOT AFRAID TO DIE.
ERIK! LET HIM GO! THIS ISN'T THE REASON WE CAME HERE.
THIS ISN'T THE TIME NOR PLACE FOR A PERSONAL VENDETTA.
THIS CHILD IS INJURED AND NEEDS MEDICAL ATTENTION AS SOON AS POSSIBLE.

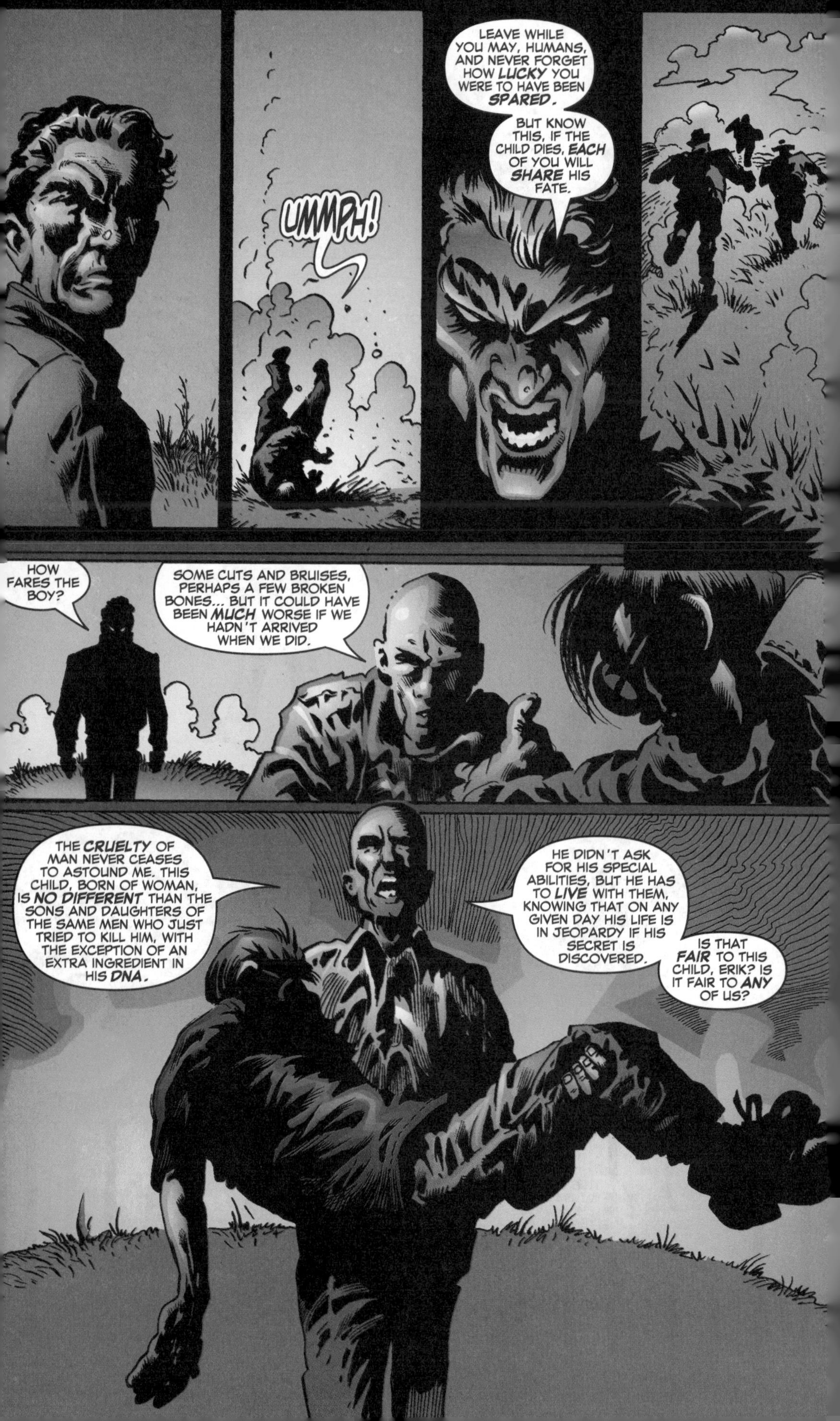
UMMPH!
LEAVE WHILE YOU MAY, HUMANS, AND NEVER FORGET HOW LUCKY YOU WERE TO HAVE BEEN SPARED.
BUT KNOW THIS, IF THE CHILD DIES, EACH OF YOU WILL SHARE HIS FATE.
HOW FARES THE BOY?
SOME CUTS AND BRUISES, PERHAPS A FEW BROKEN BONES... BUT IT COULD HAVE BEEN MUCH WORSE IF WE HADN'T ARRIVED WHEN WE DID.
THE CRUELTY OF MAN NEVER CEASES TO ASTOUND ME. THIS CHILD, BORN OF WOMAN, IS NO DIFFERENT THAN THE SONS AND DAUGHTERS OF THE SAME MEN WHO JUST TRIED TO KILL HIM, WITH THE EXCEPTION OF AN EXTRA INGREDIENT IN HIS DNA.
HE DIDN'T ASK FOR HIS SPECIAL ABILITIES, BUT HE HAS TO LIVE WITH THEM, KNOWING THAT ON ANY GIVEN DAY HIS LIFE IS IN JEOPARDY IF HIS SECRET IS DISCOVERED.
IS THAT FAIR TO THIS CHILD, ERIK? IS IT FAIR TO ANY OF US?

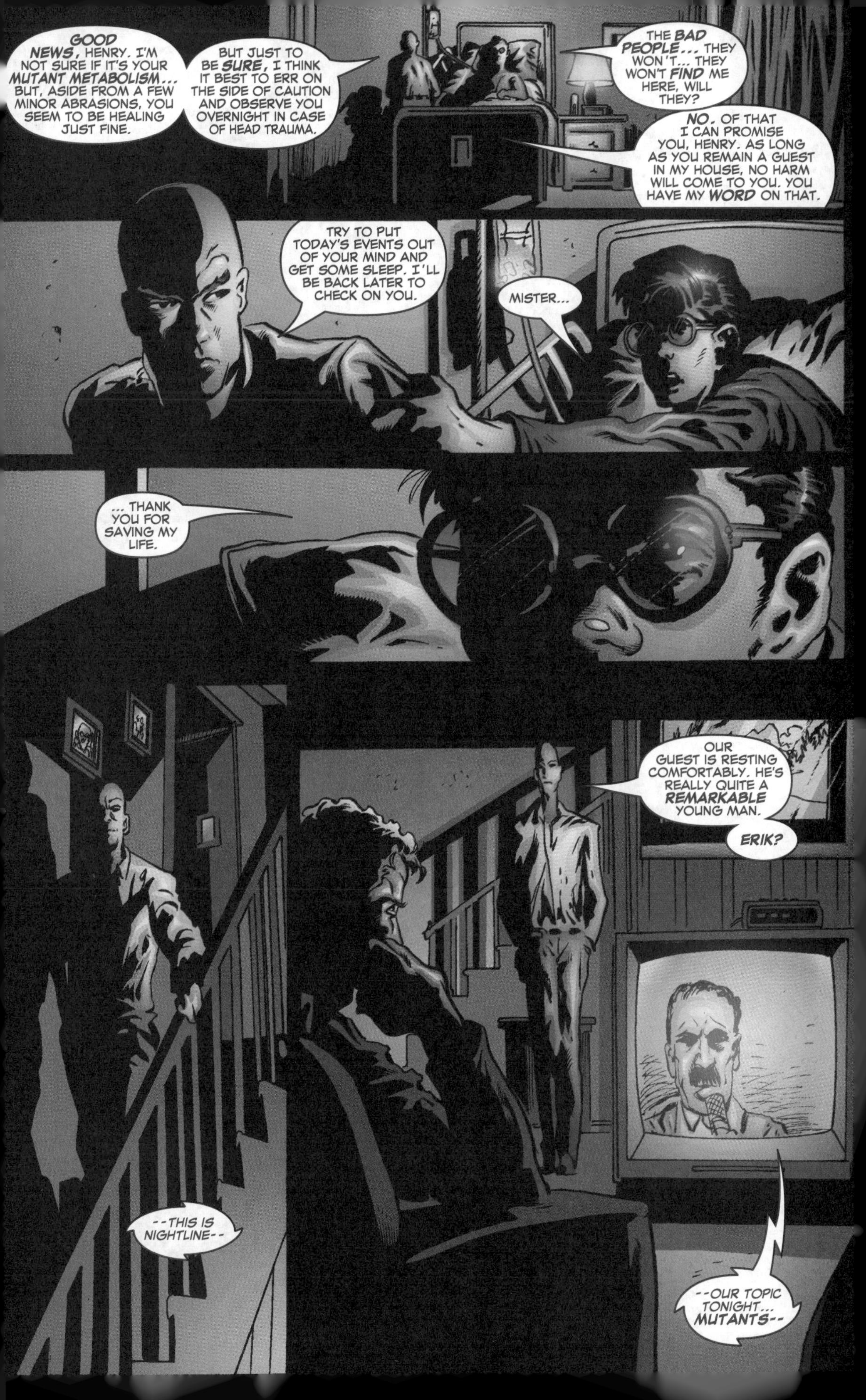
GOOD NEWS, HENRY. I'M NOT SURE IF IT'S YOUR MUTANT METABOLISM... BUT, ASIDE FROM A FEW MINOR ABRASIONS, YOU SEEM TO BE HEALING JUST FINE.
BUT JUST TO BE SURE, I THINK IT BEST TO ERR ON THE SIDE OF CAUTION AND OBSERVE YOU OVERNIGHT IN CASE OF HEAD TRAUMA.
THE BAD PEOPLE... THEY WON'T... THEY WON'T FIND ME HERE, WILL THEY?
NO. OF THAT I CAN PROMISE YOU, HENRY. AS LONG AS YOU REMAIN A GUEST IN MY HOUSE, NO HARM WILL COME TO YOU. YOU HAVE MY WORD ON THAT.
TRY TO PUT TODAY'S EVENTS OUT OF YOUR MIND AND GET SOME SLEEP. I'LL BE BACK LATER TO CHECK ON YOU.
MISTER...
... THANK YOU FOR SAVING MY LIFE.
OUR GUEST IS RESTING COMFORTABLY. HE'S REALLY QUITE A REMARKABLE YOUNG MAN.
ERIK?
--THIS IS NIGHTLINE--
--OUR TOPIC TONIGHT... MUTANTS--

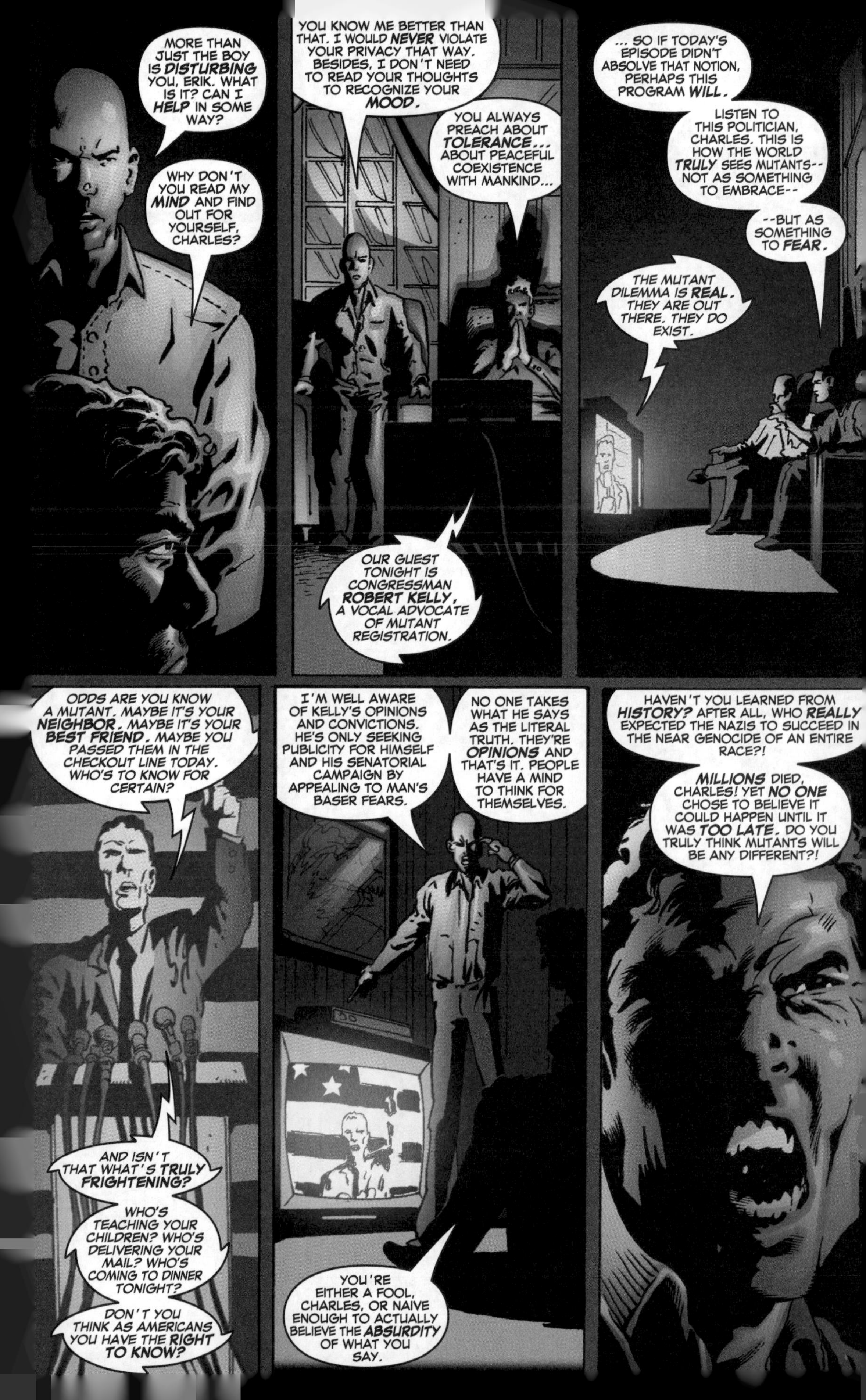
MORE THAN JUST THE BOY IS DISTURBING YOU, ERIK. WHAT IS IT? CAN I HELP IN SOME WAY?
WHY DON'T YOU READ MY MIND AND FIND OUT FOR YOURSELF, CHARLES?
YOU KNOW ME BETTER THAN THAT. I WOULD NEVER VIOLATE YOUR PRIVACY THAT WAY. BESIDES, I DON'T NEED TO READ YOUR THOUGHTS TO RECOGNIZE YOUR MOOD.
YOU ALWAYS PREACH ABOUT TOLERANCE... ABOUT PEACEFUL COEXISTENCE WITH MANKIND...
OUR GUEST TONIGHT IS CONGRESSMAN ROBERT KELLY, A VOCAL ADVOCATE OF MUTANT REGISTRATION.
... SO IF TODAY'S EPISODE DIDN'T ABSOLVE THAT NOTION, PERHAPS THIS PROGRAM WILL.
LISTEN TO THIS POLITICIAN, CHARLES. THIS IS HOW THE WORLD TRULY SEES MUTANTS-- NOT AS SOMETHING TO EMBRACE--
--BUT AS SOMETHING TO FEAR.
THE MUTANT DILEMMA IS REAL. THEY ARE OUT THERE. THEY DO EXIST.
ODDS ARE YOU KNOW A MUTANT. MAYBE IT'S YOUR NEIGHBOR. MAYBE IT'S YOUR BEST FRIEND. MAYBE YOU PASSED THEM IN THE CHECKOUT LINE TODAY. WHO'S TO KNOW FOR CERTAIN?
AND ISN'T THAT WHAT'S TRULY FRIGHTENING?
WHO'S TEACHING YOUR CHILDREN? WHO'S DELIVERING YOUR MAIL? WHO'S COMING TO DINNER TONIGHT?
DON'T YOU THINK AS AMERICANS YOU HAVE THE RIGHT TO KNOW?
I'M WELL AWARE OF KELLY'S OPINIONS AND CONVICTIONS. HE'S ONLY SEEKING PUBLICITY FOR HIMSELF AND HIS SENATORIAL CAMPAIGN BY APPEALING TO MAN'S BASER FEARS.
NO ONE TAKES WHAT HE SAYS AS THE LITERAL TRUTH. THEY'RE OPINIONS AND THAT'S IT. PEOPLE HAVE A MIND TO THINK FOR THEMSELVES.
YOU'RE EITHER A FOOL, CHARLES, OR NAIVE ENOUGH TO ACTUALLY BELIEVE THE ABSURDITY OF WHAT YOU SAY.
HAVEN'T YOU LEARNED FROM HISTORY? AFTER ALL, WHO REALLY EXPECTED THE NAZIS TO SUCCEED IN THE NEAR GENOCIDE OF AN ENTIRE RACE?!
MILLIONS DIED, CHARLES! YET NO ONE CHOSE TO BELIEVE IT COULD HAPPEN UNTIL IT WAS TOO LATE. DO YOU TRULY THINK MUTANTS WILL BE ANY DIFFERENT?!

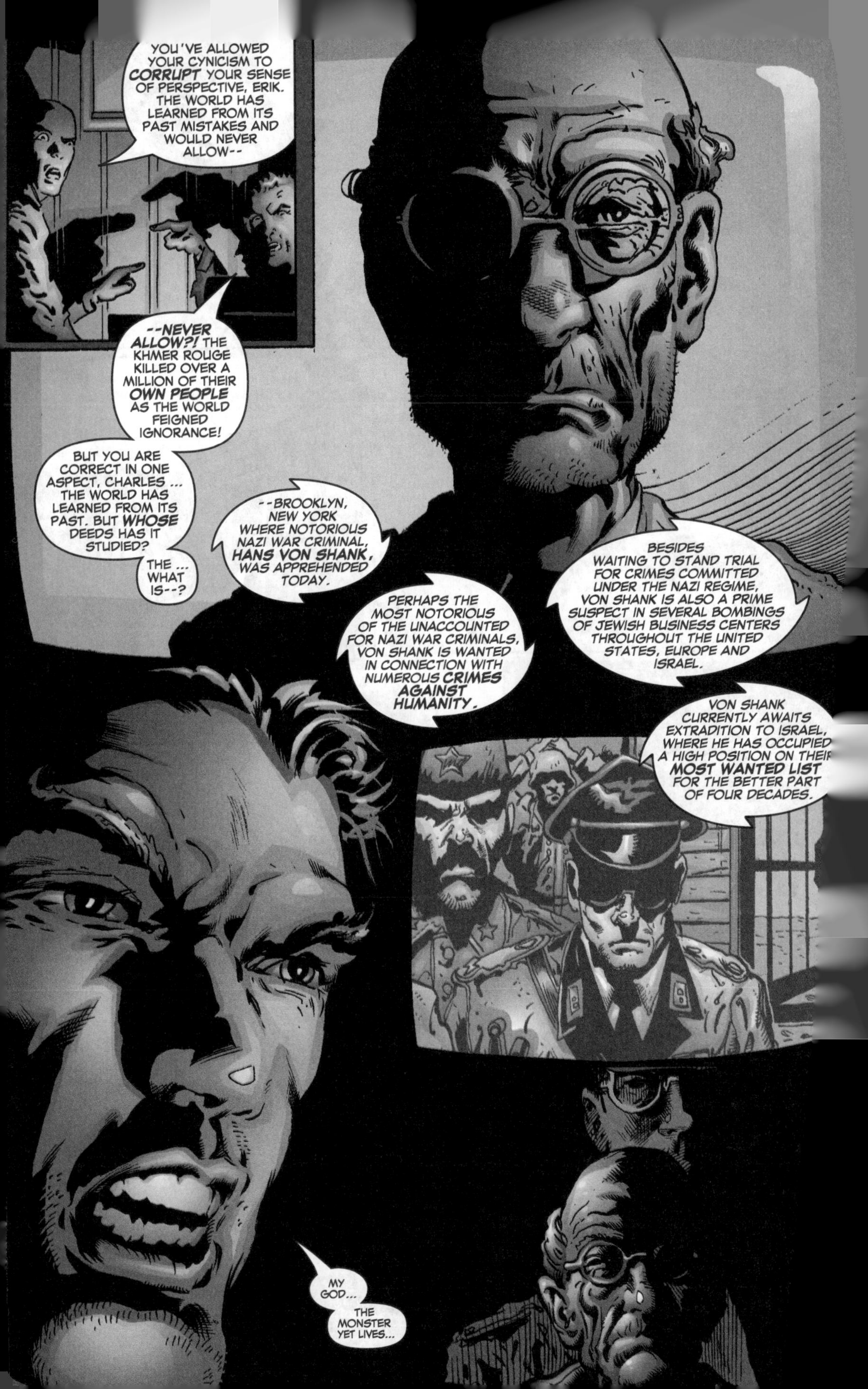
YOU'VE ALLOWED YOUR CYNICISM TO CORRUPT YOUR SENSE OF PERSPECTIVE, ERIK. THE WORLD HAS LEARNED FROM ITS PAST MISTAKES AND WOULD NEVER ALLOW--
--NEVER ALLOW?! THE KHMER ROUGE KILLED OVER A MILLION OF THEIR OWN PEOPLE AS THE WORLD FEIGNED IGNORANCE!
BUT YOU ARE CORRECT IN ONE ASPECT, CHARLES ... THE WORLD HAS LEARNED FROM ITS PAST. BUT WHOSE DEEDS HAS IT STUDIED?
THE ... WHAT IS--?
--BROOKLYN, NEW YORK WHERE NOTORIOUS NAZI WAR CRIMINAL, HANS VON SHANK, WAS APPREHENDED TODAY.
PERHAPS THE MOST NOTORIOUS OF THE UNACCOUNTED FOR NAZI WAR CRIMINALS, VON SHANK IS WANTED IN CONNECTION WITH NUMEROUS CRIMES AGAINST HUMANITY.
BESIDES WAITING TO STAND TRIAL FOR CRIMES COMMITTED UNDER THE NAZI REGIME, VON SHANK IS ALSO A PRIME SUSPECT IN SEVERAL BOMBINGS OF JEWISH BUSINESS CENTERS THROUGHOUT THE UNITED STATES, EUROPE AND ISRAEL.
VON SHANK CURRENTLY AWAITS EXTRADITION TO ISRAEL, WHERE HE HAS OCCUPIED A HIGH POSITION ON THEIR MOST WANTED LIST FOR THE BETTER PART OF FOUR DECADES.
MY GOD...
THE MONSTER YET LIVES...

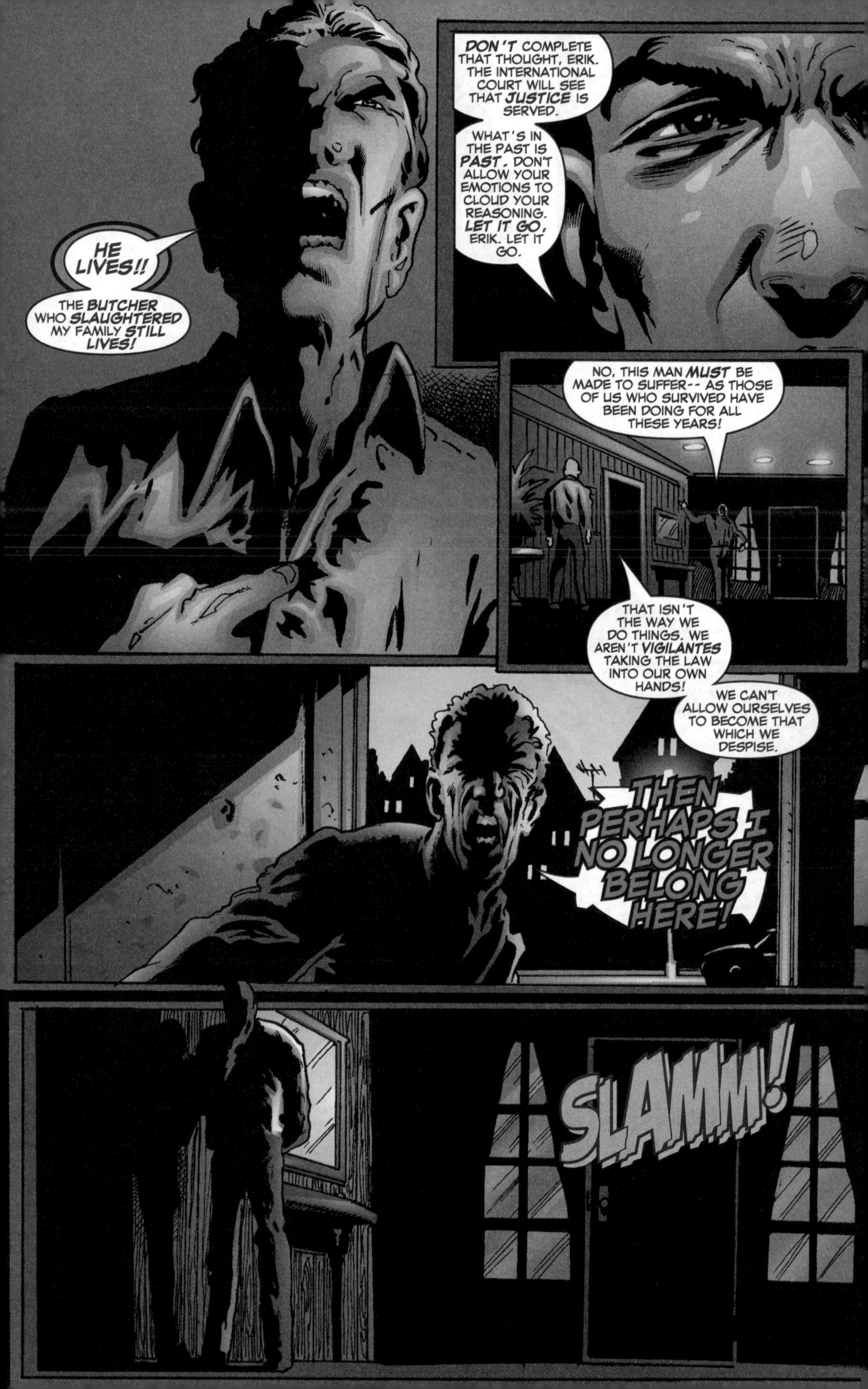
HE LIVES!!
THE BUTCHER WHO SLAUGHTERED MY FAMILY STILL LIVES!
DON'T COMPLETE THAT THOUGHT, ERIK. THE INTERNATIONAL COURT WILL SEE THAT JUSTICE IS SERVED.
WHAT'S IN THE PAST IS PAST. DON'T ALLOW YOUR EMOTIONS TO CLOUD YOUR REASONING. LET IT GO, ERIK. LET IT GO.
NO, THIS MAN MUST BE MADE TO SUFFER-- AS THOSE OF US WHO SURVIVED HAVE BEEN DOING FOR ALL THESE YEARS!
THAT ISN'T THE WAY WE DO THINGS. WE AREN'T VIGILANTES TAKING THE LAW INTO OUR OWN HANDS!
WE CAN'T ALLOW OURSELVES TO BECOME THAT WHICH WE DESPISE.
THEN PERHAPS I NO LONGER BELONG HERE!
SLAMM!

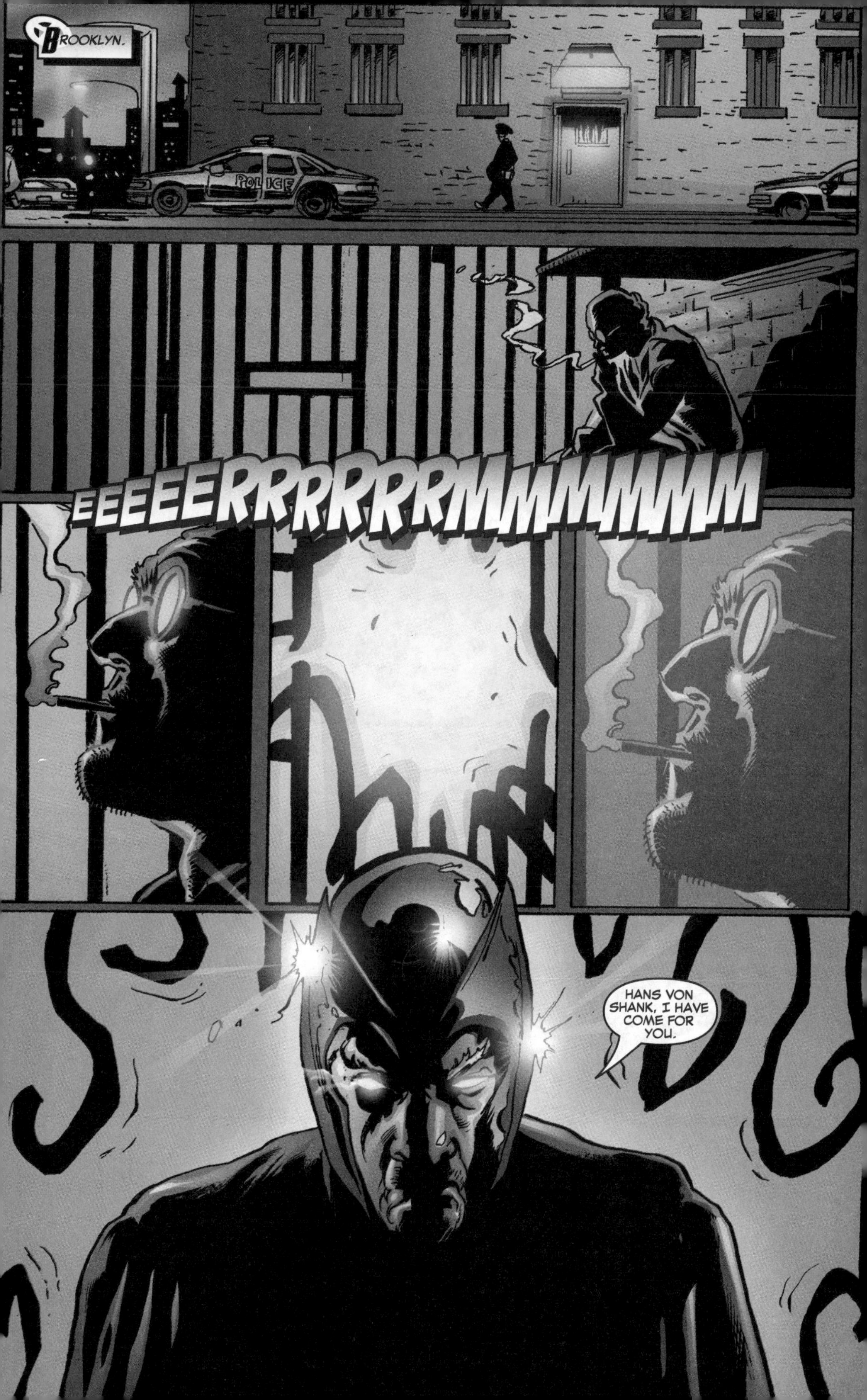
BROOKLYN.
POLICE
EEEEERRRRRRMMMMMMMM
HANS VON SHANK, I HAVE COME FOR YOU.

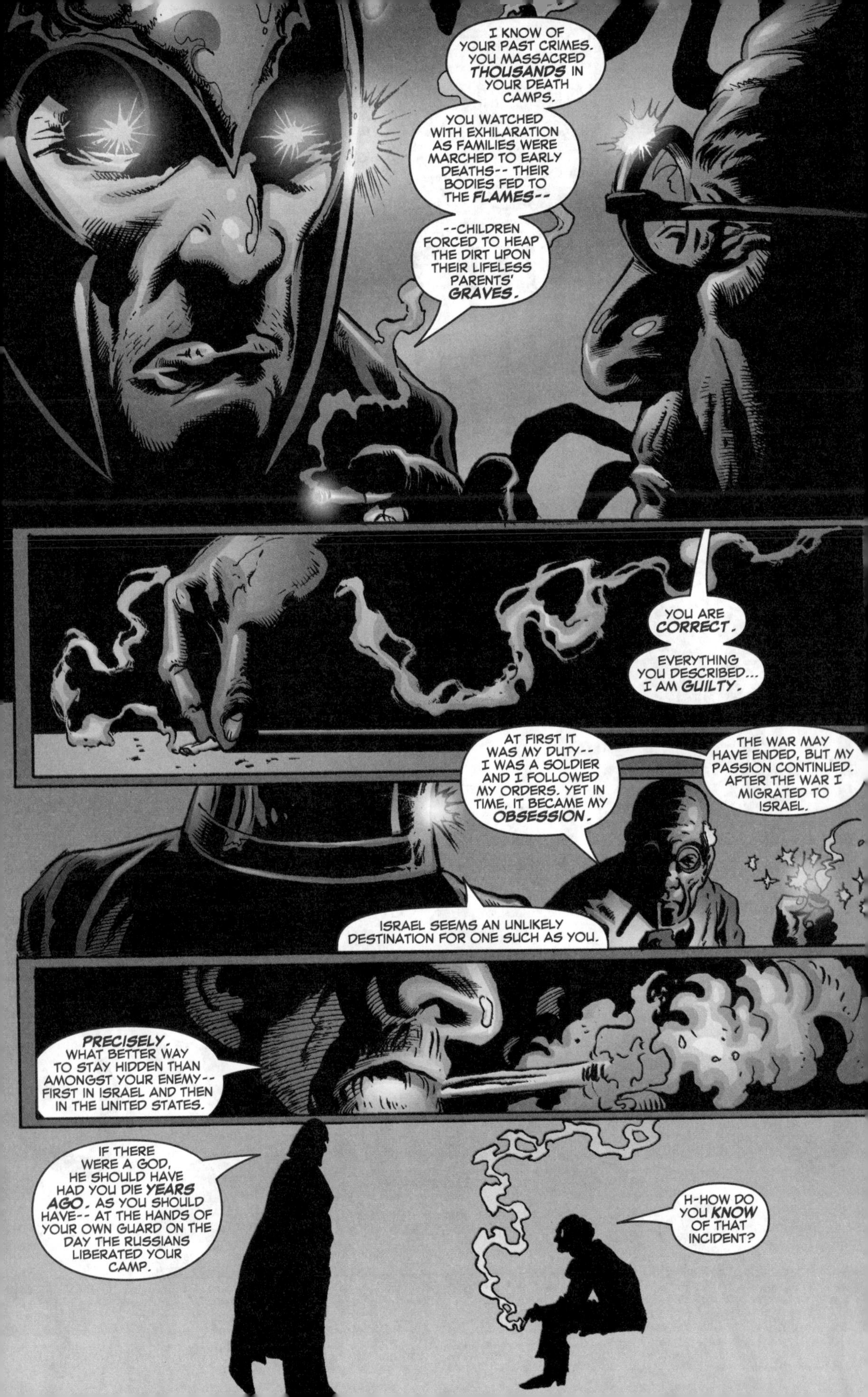
I KNOW OF YOUR PAST CRIMES. YOU MASSACRED THOUSANDS IN YOUR DEATH CAMPS.
YOU WATCHED WITH EXHILARATION AS FAMILIES WERE MARCHED TO EARLY DEATHS-- THEIR BODIES FED TO THE FLAMES--
--CHILDREN FORCED TO HEAP THE DIRT UPON THEIR LIFELESS PARENTS' GRAVES.
YOU ARE CORRECT.
EVERYTHING YOU DESCRIBED... I AM GUILTY.
AT FIRST IT WAS MY DUTY-- I WAS A SOLDIER AND I FOLLOWED MY ORDERS. YET IN TIME, IT BECAME MY OBSESSION.
THE WAR MAY HAVE ENDED, BUT MY PASSION CONTINUED. AFTER THE WAR I MIGRATED TO ISRAEL.
ISRAEL SEEMS AN UNLIKELY DESTINATION FOR ONE SUCH AS YOU.
PRECISELY. WHAT BETTER WAY TO STAY HIDDEN THAN AMONGST YOUR ENEMY-- FIRST IN ISRAEL AND THEN IN THE UNITED STATES.
IF THERE WERE A GOD, HE SHOULD HAVE HAD YOU DIE YEARS AGO. AS YOU SHOULD HAVE-- AT THE HANDS OF YOUR OWN GUARD ON THE DAY THE RUSSIANS LIBERATED YOUR CAMP.
H-HOW DO YOU KNOW OF THAT INCIDENT?

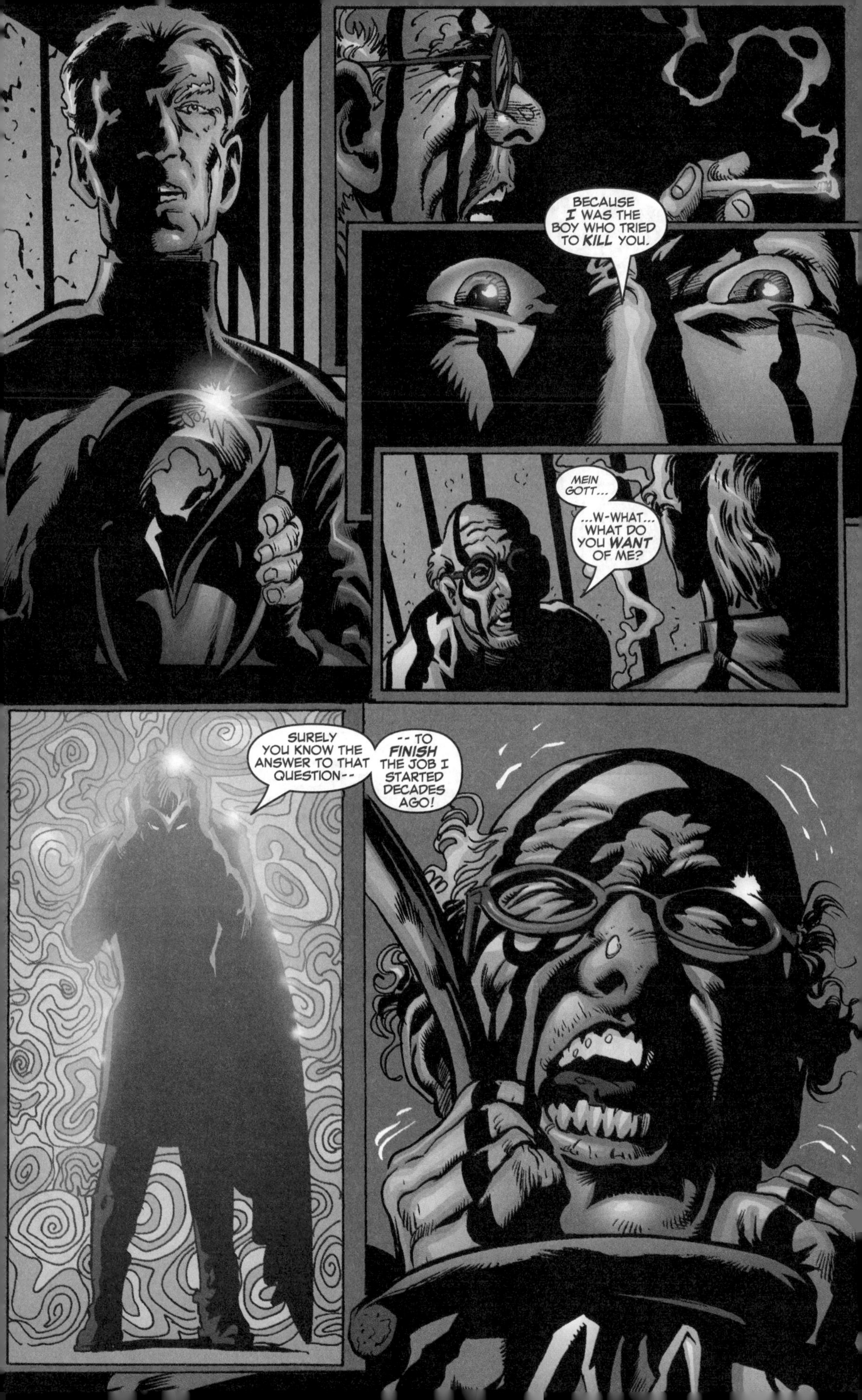
BECAUSE I WAS THE BOY WHO TRIED TO KILL YOU.
MEIN GOTT...
...W-WHAT... WHAT DO YOU WANT OF ME?
SURELY YOU KNOW THE ANSWER TO THAT QUESTION--
-- TO FINISH THE JOB I STARTED DECADES AGO!

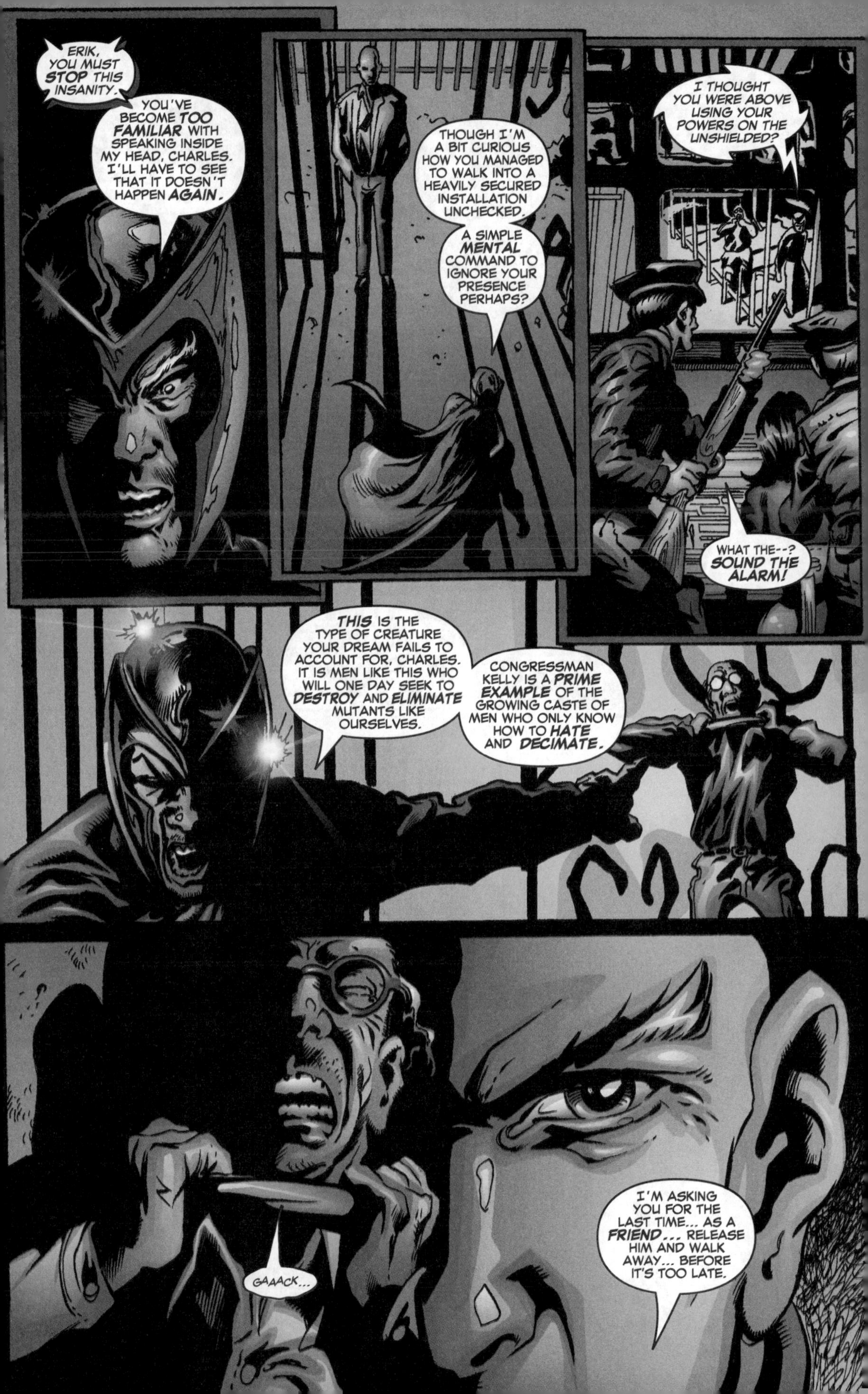
ERIK, YOU MUST STOP THIS INSANITY.
YOU'VE BECOME TOO FAMILIAR WITH SPEAKING INSIDE MY HEAD, CHARLES. I'LL HAVE TO SEE THAT IT DOESN'T HAPPEN AGAIN.
THOUGH I'M A BIT CURIOUS HOW YOU MANAGED TO WALK INTO A HEAVILY SECURED INSTALLATION UNCHECKED.
A SIMPLE MENTAL COMMAND TO IGNORE YOUR PRESENCE PERHAPS?
I THOUGHT YOU WERE ABOVE USING YOUR POWERS ON THE UNSHIELDED?
WHAT THE--? SOUND THE ALARM!
THIS IS THE TYPE OF CREATURE YOUR DREAM FAILS TO ACCOUNT FOR, CHARLES. IT IS MEN LIKE THIS WHO WILL ONE DAY SEEK TO DESTROY AND ELIMINATE MUTANTS LIKE OURSELVES.
CONGRESSMAN KELLY IS A PRIME EXAMPLE OF THE GROWING CASTE OF MEN WHO ONLY KNOW HOW TO HATE AND DECIMATE.
GAAACK...
I'M ASKING YOU FOR THE LAST TIME... AS A FRIEND... RELEASE HIM AND WALK AWAY... BEFORE IT'S TOO LATE.

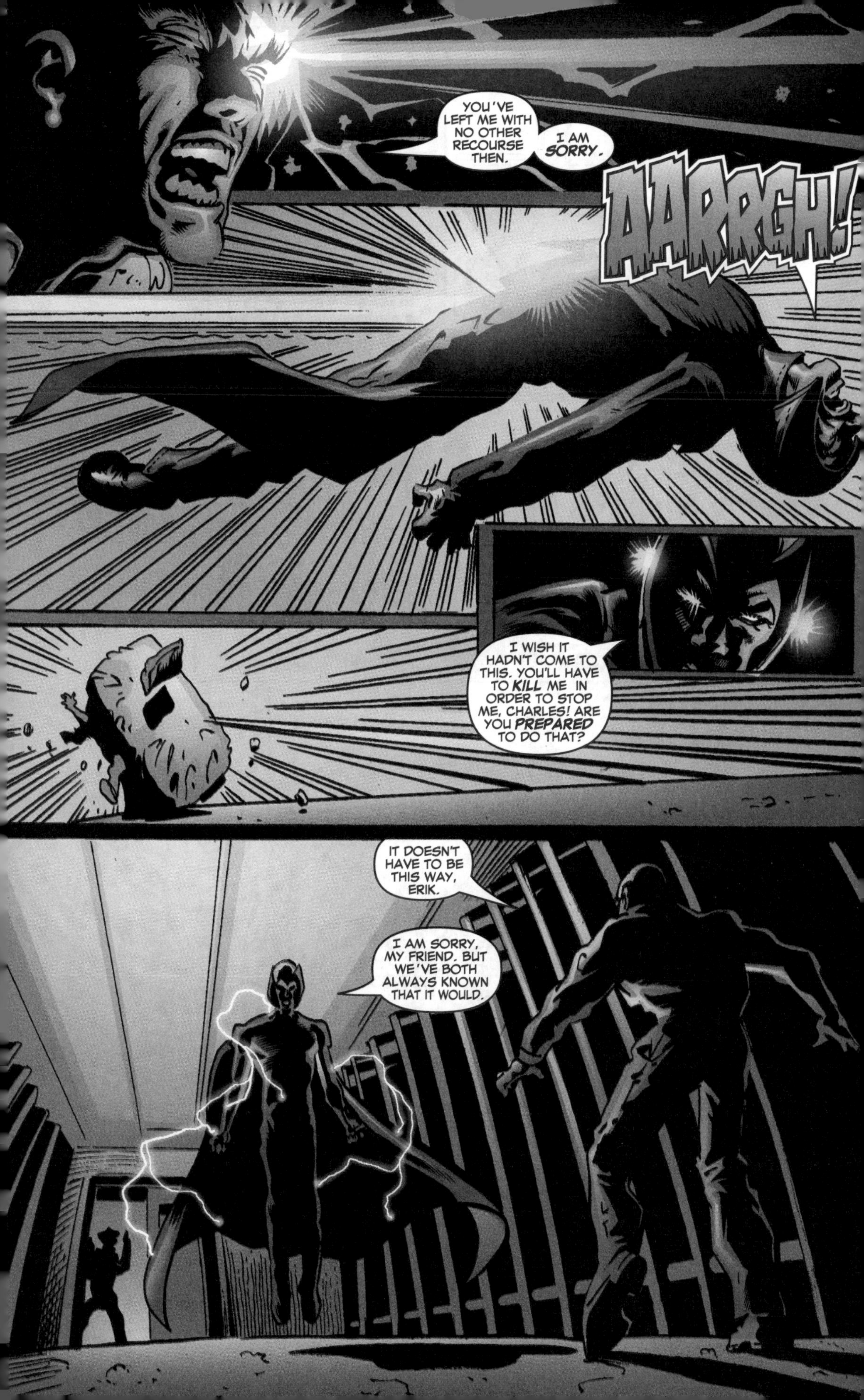

YOU'VE LEFT ME WITH NO OTHER RECOURSE THEN.
I AM SORRY.
AARRGH!
I WISH IT HADN'T COME TO THIS. YOU'LL HAVE TO KILL ME IN ORDER TO STOP ME, CHARLES! ARE YOU PREPARED TO DO THAT?
IT DOESN'T HAVE TO BE THIS WAY, ERIK.
I AM SORRY, MY FRIEND. BUT WE'VE BOTH ALWAYS KNOWN THAT IT WOULD.

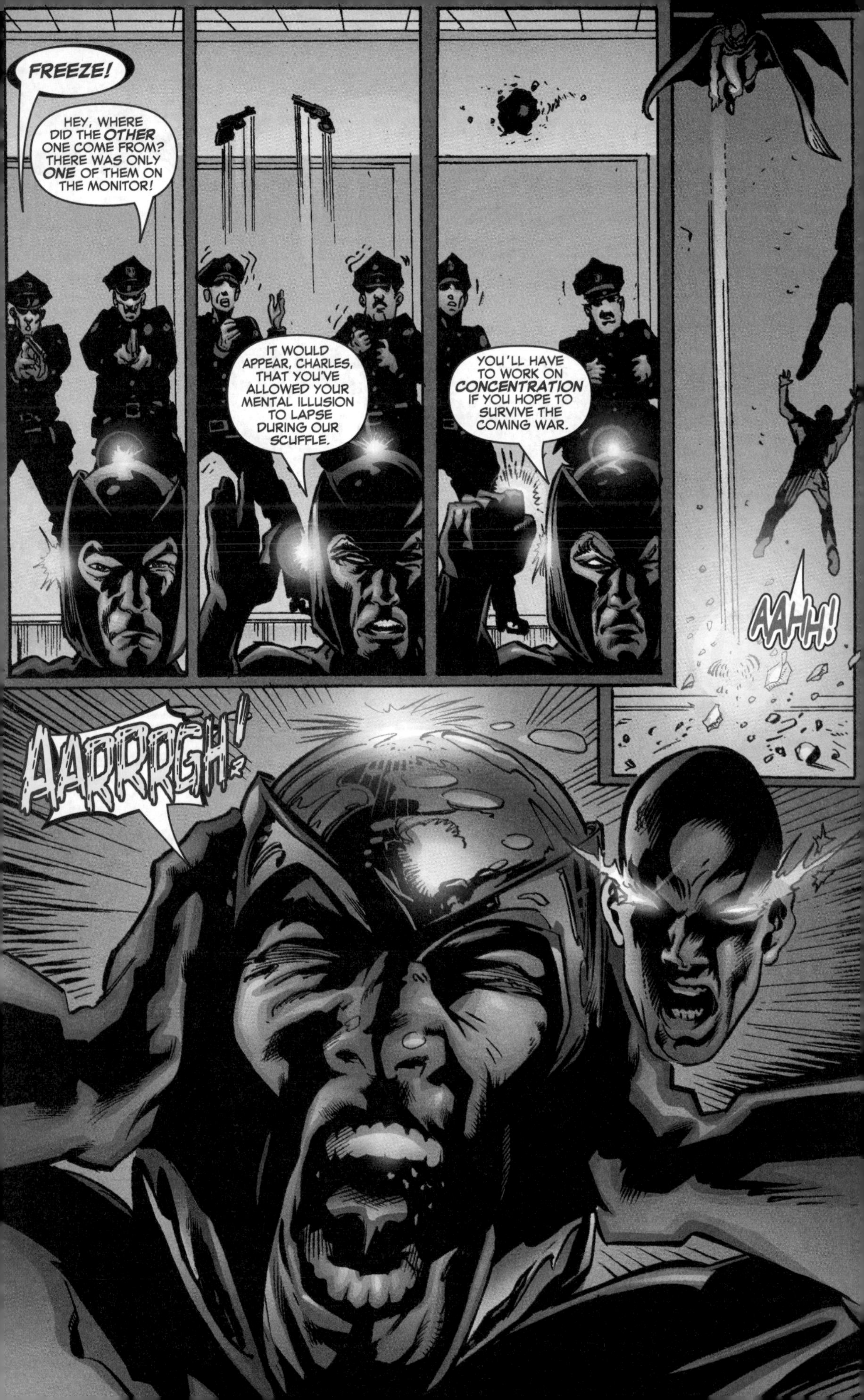
FREEZE!
HEY, WHERE DID THE OTHER ONE COME FROM? THERE WAS ONLY ONE OF THEM ON THE MONITOR!
IT WOULD APPEAR, CHARLES, THAT YOU'VE ALLOWED YOUR MENTAL ILLUSION TO LAPSE DURING OUR SCUFFLE.
YOU'LL HAVE TO WORK ON CONCENTRATION IF YOU HOPE TO SURVIVE THE COMING WAR.
AAHH!
AARRGH!

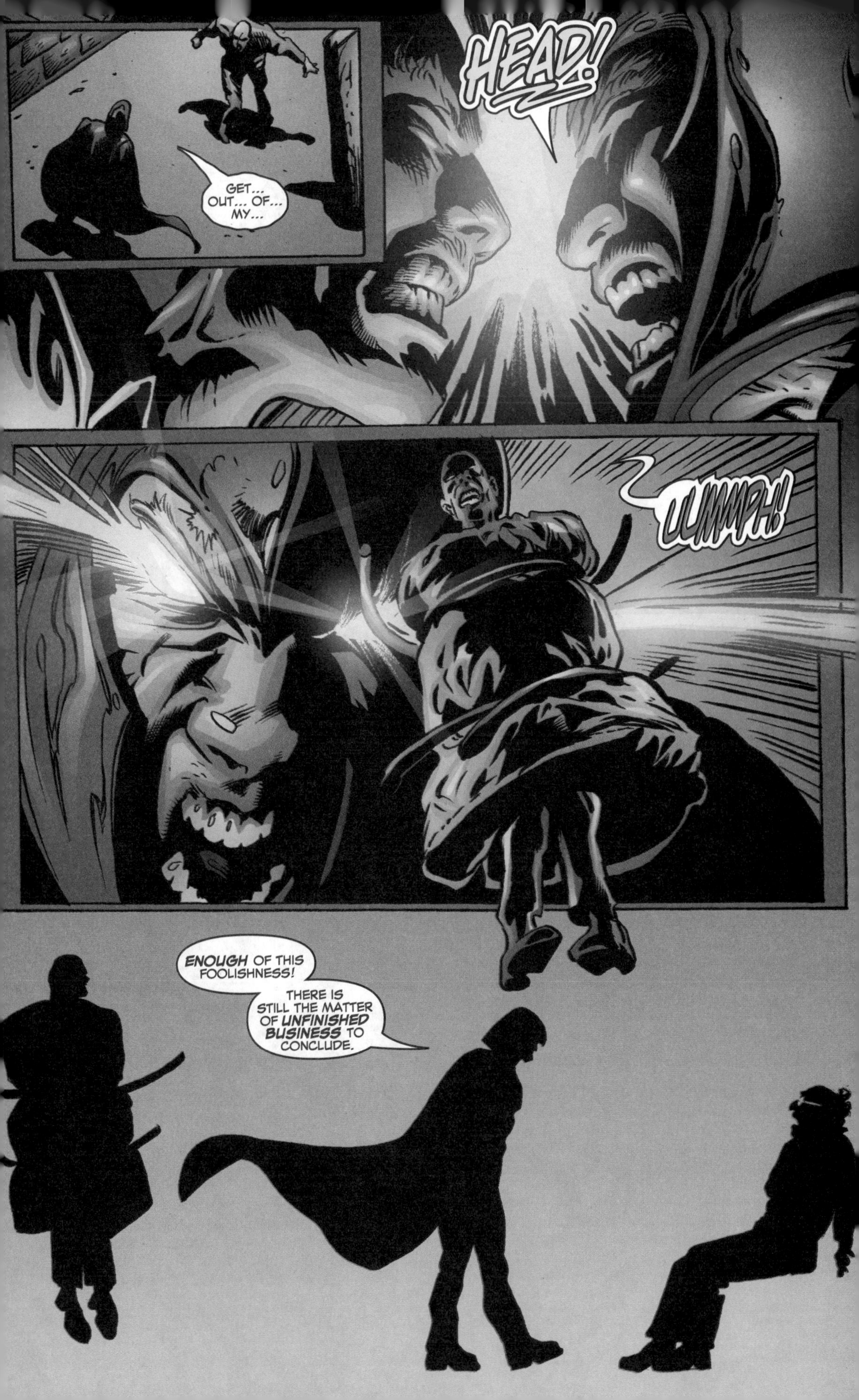
GET... OUT... OF... MY...
HEAD!
UUMMPH!
ENOUGH OF THIS FOOLISHNESS!
THERE IS STILL THE MATTER OF UNFINISHED BUSINESS TO CONCLUDE.

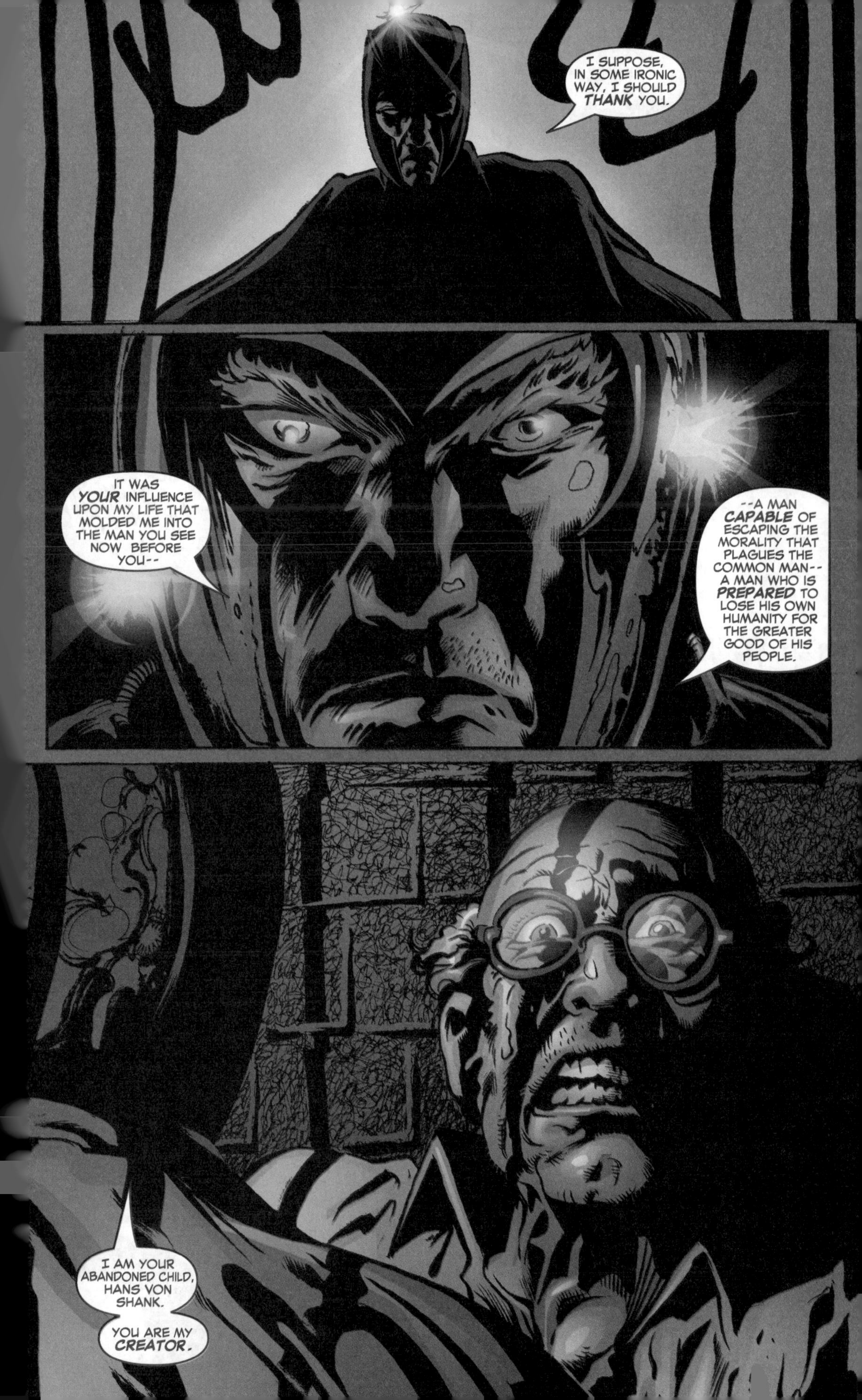

I SUPPOSE, IN SOME IRONIC WAY, I SHOULD THANK YOU.
IT WAS YOUR INFLUENCE UPON MY LIFE THAT MOLDED ME INTO THE MAN YOU SEE NOW BEFORE YOU--
--A MAN CAPABLE OF ESCAPING THE MORALITY THAT PLAGUES THE COMMON MAN--A MAN WHO IS PREPARED TO LOSE HIS OWN HUMANITY FOR THE GREATER GOOD OF HIS PEOPLE.
I AM YOUR ABANDONED CHILD, HANS VON SHANK.
YOU ARE MY CREATOR.

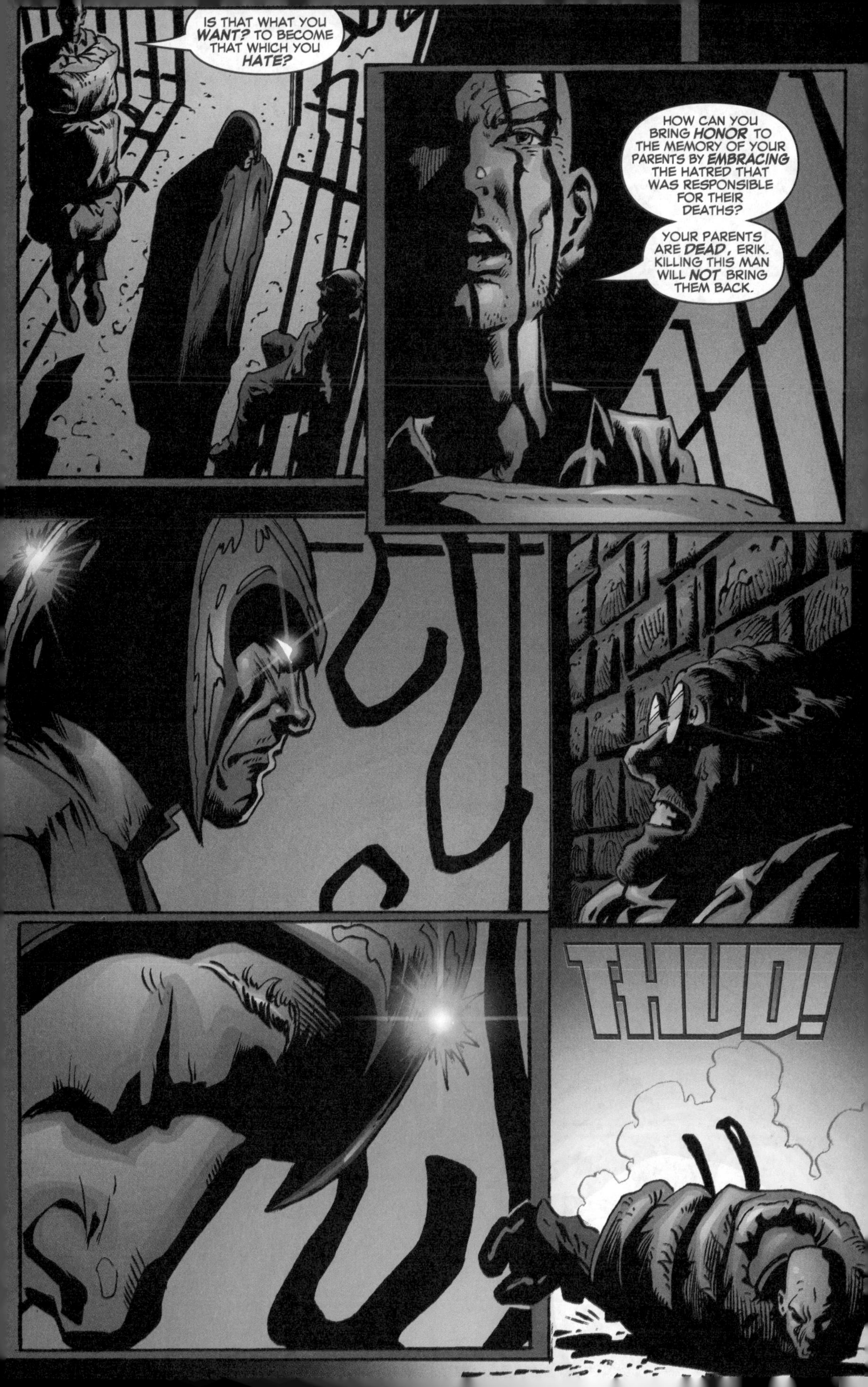
IS THAT WHAT YOU WANT? TO BECOME THAT WHICH YOU HATE?
HOW CAN YOU BRING HONOR TO THE MEMORY OF YOUR PARENTS BY EMBRACING THE HATRED THAT WAS RESPONSIBLE FOR THEIR DEATHS?
YOUR PARENTS ARE DEAD, ERIK. KILLING THIS MAN WILL NOT BRING THEM BACK.
THUD!

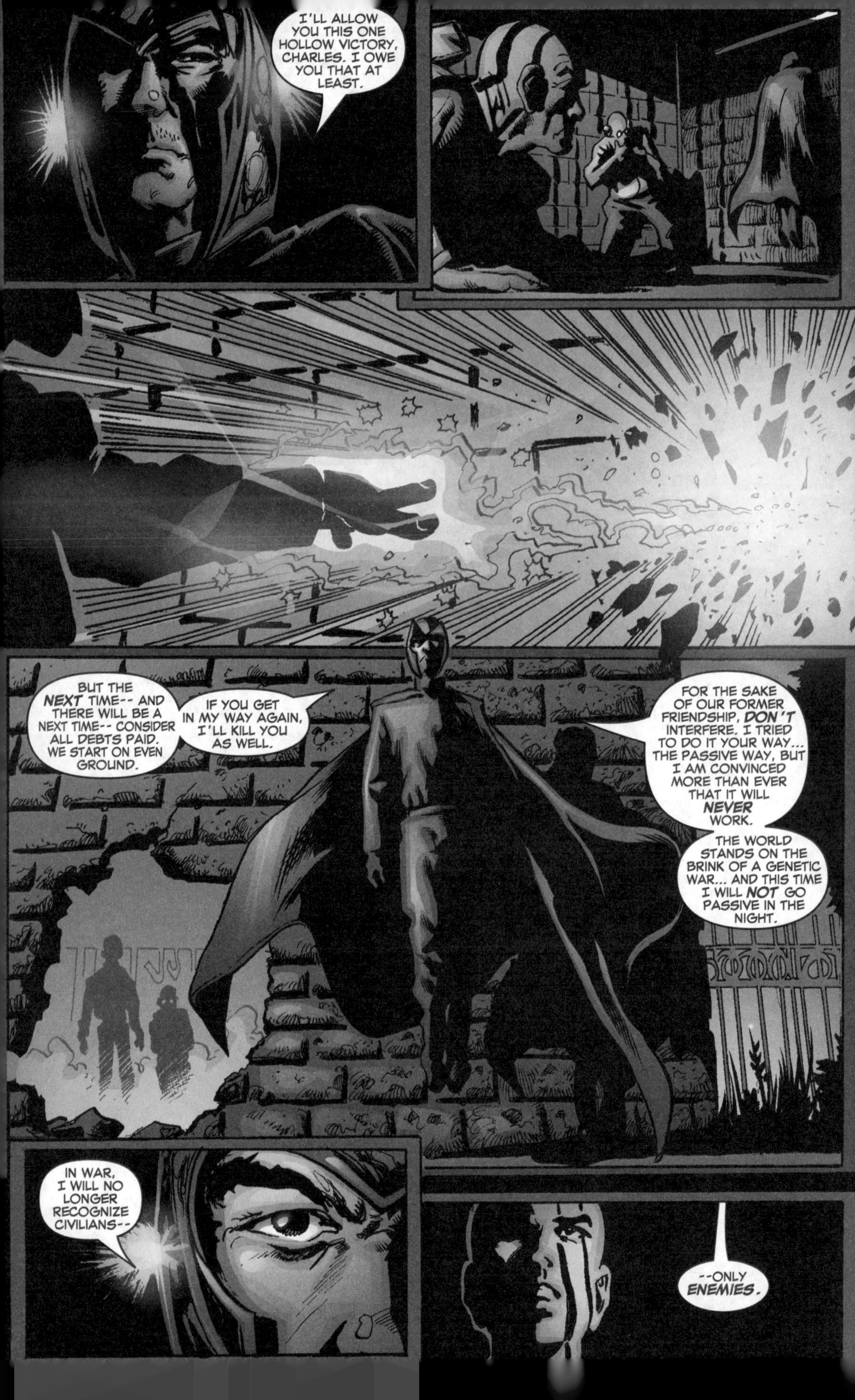
I'LL ALLOW YOU THIS ONE HOLLOW VICTORY, CHARLES. I OWE YOU THAT AT LEAST.
BUT THE NEXT TIME-- AND THERE WILL BE A NEXT TIME-- CONSIDER ALL DEBTS PAID. WE START ON EVEN GROUND.
IF YOU GET IN MY WAY AGAIN, I'LL KILL YOU AS WELL.
FOR THE SAKE OF OUR FORMER FRIENDSHIP, DON'T INTERFERE. I TRIED TO DO IT YOUR WAY... THE PASSIVE WAY, BUT I AM CONVINCED MORE THAN EVER THAT IT WILL NEVER WORK.
THE WORLD STANDS ON THE BRINK OF A GENETIC WAR... AND THIS TIME I WILL NOT GO PASSIVE IN THE NIGHT.
IN WAR, I WILL NO LONGER RECOGNIZE CIVILIANS--
--ONLY ENEMIES.

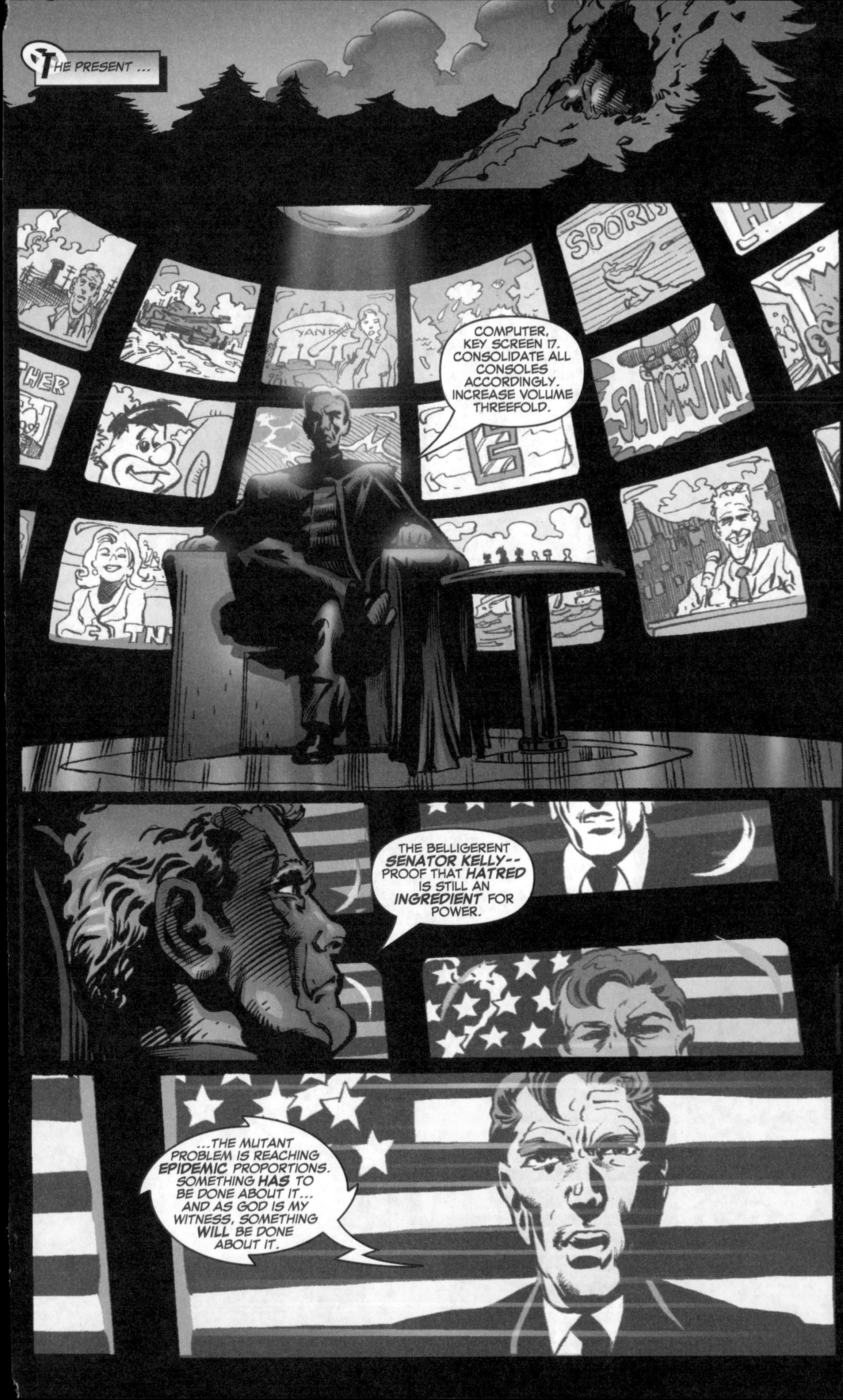
THE PRESENT ...
COMPUTER, KEY SCREEN 17. CONSOLIDATE ALL CONSOLES ACCORDINGLY. INCREASE VOLUME THREEFOLD.
THE BELLIGERENT SENATOR KELLY-- PROOF THAT HATRED IS STILL AN INGREDIENT FOR POWER.
...THE MUTANT PROBLEM IS REACHING EPIDEMIC PROPORTIONS. SOMETHING HAS TO BE DONE ABOUT IT... AND AS GOD IS MY WITNESS, SOMETHING WILL BE DONE ABOUT IT.

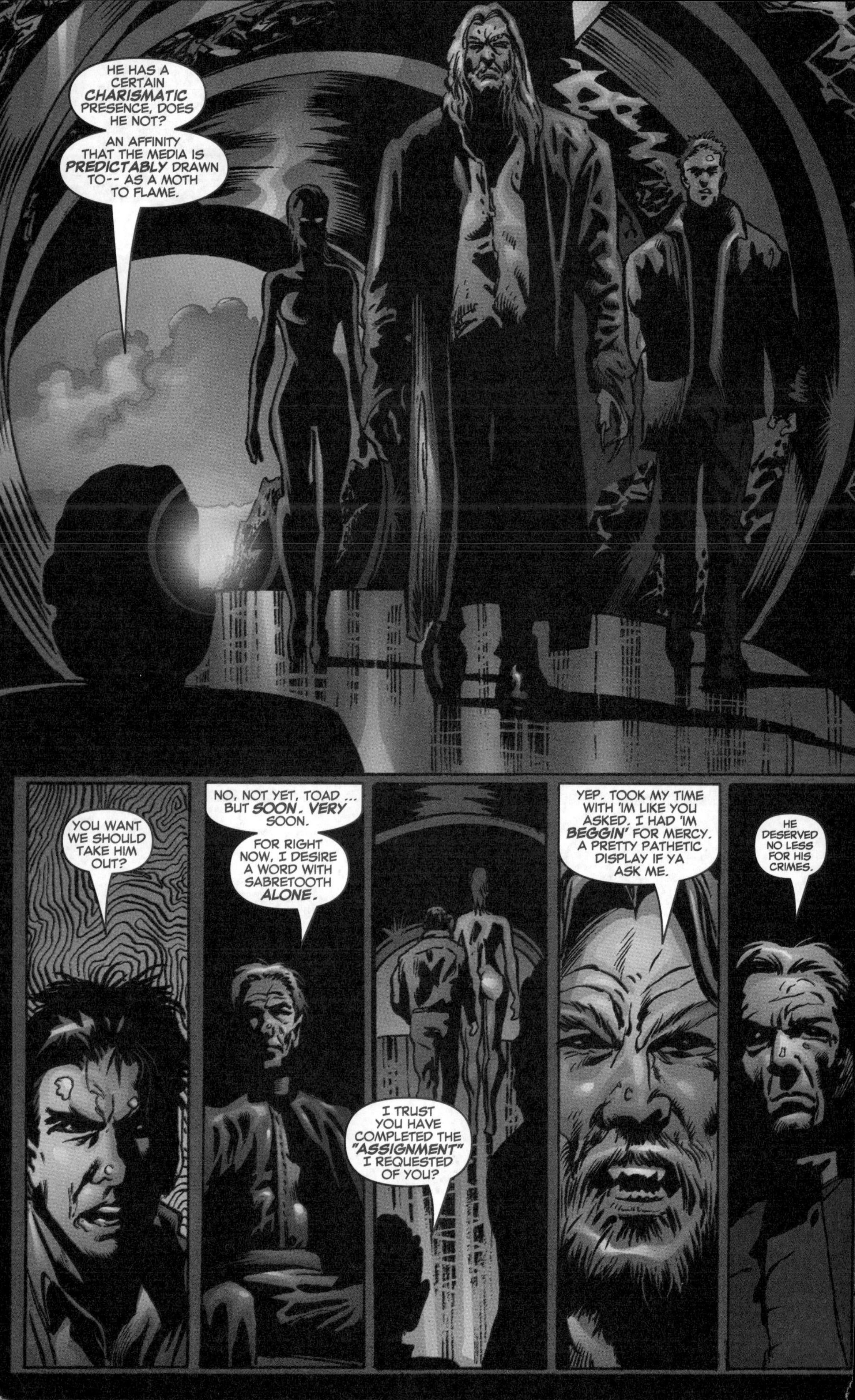
HE HAS A CERTAIN CHARISMATIC PRESENCE, DOES HE NOT?
AN AFFINITY THAT THE MEDIA IS PREDICTABLY DRAWN TO-- AS A MOTH TO FLAME.
YOU WANT WE SHOULD TAKE HIM OUT?
NO, NOT YET, TOAD ... BUT SOON. VERY SOON.
FOR RIGHT NOW, I DESIRE A WORD WITH SABRETOOTH ALONE.
I TRUST YOU HAVE COMPLETED THE "ASSIGNMENT" I REQUESTED OF YOU?
YEP. TOOK MY TIME WITH 'IM LIKE YOU ASKED. I HAD 'IM BEGGIN' FOR MERCY. A PRETTY PATHETIC DISPLAY IF YA ASK ME.
HE DESERVED NO LESS FOR HIS CRIMES.

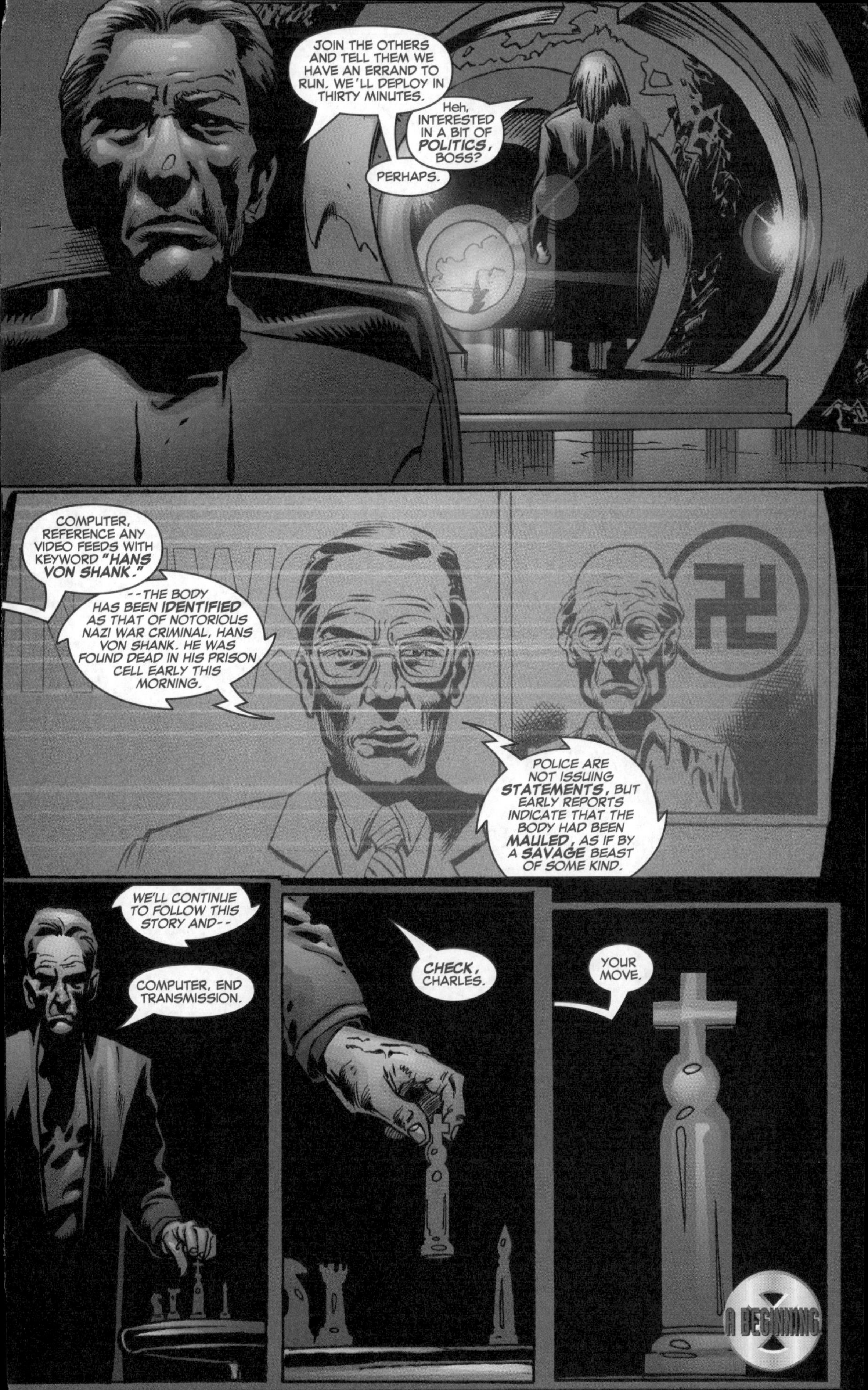

JOIN THE OTHERS AND TELL THEM WE HAVE AN ERRAND TO RUN. WE'LL DEPLOY IN THIRTY MINUTES.
Heh, INTERESTED IN A BIT OF POLITICS, BOSS?
PERHAPS.
COMPUTER, REFERENCE ANY VIDEO FEEDS WITH KEYWORD "HANS VON SHANK."
--THE BODY HAS BEEN IDENTIFIED AS THAT OF NOTORIOUS NAZI WAR CRIMINAL, HANS VON SHANK. HE WAS FOUND DEAD IN HIS PRISON CELL EARLY THIS MORNING.
POLICE ARE NOT ISSUING STATEMENTS, BUT EARLY REPORTS INDICATE THAT THE BODY HAD BEEN MAULED, AS IF BY A SAVAGE BEAST OF SOME KIND.
WE'LL CONTINUE TO FOLLOW THIS STORY AND--
COMPUTER, END TRANSMISSION.
CHECK, CHARLES.
YOUR MOVE.
A BEGINNING